REMINISCENCES OF THE CIVIL WAR

REMINISCENCES OF THE
CIVIL WAR

GENERAL JOHN B. GORDON

With a New Introduction by Ralph Lowell Eckert

LOUISIANA STATE UNIVERSITY PRESS

Baton Rouge

First published in 1903 by Charles Scribner's Sons
Louisiana Paperback Edition, 1993
02   5

Library of Congress Cataloging-in-Publication Data

Gordon, John Brown, 1832–1904.
    Reminiscences of the Civil War / John B. Gordon ; with a new
introduction by Ralph Lowell Eckert.—Louisiana pbk. ed.
      p.   cm.
    Includes index.
    Originally published: New York : Scribner, 1903.
    ISBN 0-8071-1863-X (paper : acid-free paper)
    1. Gordon, John Brown, 1832–1904.   2. United States—History—
Civil War, 1861–1865—Campaigns.   3. United States—History—Civil
War, 1861–1865—Personal narratives, Confederate.   4. Confederate
States of America.   Army—Biography.   5. Generals—Southern States—
Biography.   I. Title.
E470.G67   1993
973.7'82—dc20   93-1861
                                                                CIP

The paper in this book meets the guidelines for permanence and durability of
the Committee on Production Guidelines for Book Longevity of the Council on
Library Resources. ∞

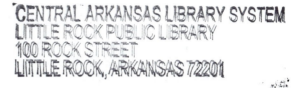
CONTENTS

ILLUSTRATIONS

ix

INTRODUCTION TO THE 1993 EDITION

IN *Reminiscences of the Civil War,* John Brown Gordon tells one of the most touching and enduring stories of the American Civil War. According to Gordon, while pressing his attack against the Union right flank north of Gettysburg on the first day of the battle, he came across a badly wounded Union general, Francis C. Barlow. Believing Barlow to be mortally wounded, Gordon stopped to comfort his fallen opponent. He had Barlow carried out of the brutal July sun into the shade, honored his request that letters from his wife be destroyed, and assured the Federal that he would tell Mrs. Barlow that her husband's final thoughts were of her. Certain Barlow would soon be dead, Gordon sadly left his prostrate foe and returned to the battle. Barlow, despite the severity of his wounds, did not die and within a year returned to duty with the Army of the Potomac. When he learned of the death of another Confederate General J. B. Gordon in May, 1864, he naturally assumed it was the Rebel who had aided him. Even though both men survived the war, each believed the other had died. Well, again according to Gordon, in the late 1870s he and Barlow met by accident at a dinner party in Washington, D.C. "Nothing short of an actual resurrection from the dead could have amazed either of us more," said Gordon. And the friendship begun at Gettysburg, now renewed, remained strong until Barlow's 1896 death did in fact part the old warriors.

Obviously a heart-warming tale, even if fictitious. Recent evidence indicates that the Gordon-Barlow encounter never actually took place and that this story recounted in *Remi-*

niscences was likely a romantic invention by John B. Gordon.[1] Before dismissing his reminiscences as a collection of baseless fabrications, however, one must consider both Gordon's purpose and the time in which he wrote. In the decades after the war, during which differences between northerners and southerners persisted although the battle-flags had been furled, Gordon labored tirelessly to heal the wounds of this conflict. In *Reminiscences,* published in 1903, Gordon preached the same message he had spread in the last third of the nineteenth century. He expounded a new sense of national identity—one supplanting the sectional antagonisms of the past with a common commitment to building a stronger, more unified nation. For Gordon, *Reminiscences* was to serve as a monument to the men of both sides who fought the Civil War and, as such, was to contribute mightily to national reconciliation.

Perhaps no story better illustrates the objective of *Reminiscences* than the Gordon-Barlow anecdote, for it acts as a metaphor for the American experience in the second half of the 1800s. Two noble warriors, sincerely committed to their respective causes, come to blows on the field of battle but are respectful of each other even in the heat of combat. Each loses and sacrifices much in the bloodletting, perhaps believing that meaningful reunion is impossible. And yet, against all odds, the two rediscover each other years after the divisive conflict and establish even stronger bonds of friendship and cooperation than had been formed initially. Gordon, I think, regarded his account of the Gordon-Barlow meeting as a symbol of what had taken place and was taking place in the United States. The North and the South, despite the differences that separated them and led them to civil war, were now reunited, forging firmer bonds of unity and building a truly bright future. *Reminiscences,* like much of Gordon's postwar career, was devoted to na-

1. See William F. Hanna, "A Gettysburg Myth Exploded," *Civil War Times Illustrated,* XXIV (May, 1985), 42–47.

tional pacification and to reconciliation of the formerly war-ring sections.

Gordon, by virtue of the reputation he earned on the bat-tlefields of the Civil War, was especially well qualified to champion this lofty cause. Indeed, no Confederate emerged from the war with a record more stunning. Hailed as "the Chevalier Bayard of the army," the "beau ideal of military leaders," the "idol of the whole army," and the hero of Appomattox, Gordon proved himself a natural soldier and leader of men. An amateur in an army overwhelmingly com-manded by professionals, Gordon rose rapidly from captain to corps commander. Despite his lack of formal military training, he displayed boldness, vigilance, aggressiveness, and a sound military sense on all of his battlefields. His cour-age, moral resolve, and audaciously offensive spirit made him a superb combat officer.[2]

Moreover, Gordon was one of the war's most picturesque and inspiring soldiers. Six feet tall, slight of build, and straight as a ramrod, Gordon with his coal black hair, high forehead, closely cropped chin beard, and penetrating gray eyes looked every inch a soldier.[3] His martial appearance led one of his men to remark: "He's most the prettiest thing you ever did see on a field of fight. It'ud put fight into a whipped chicken just to look at him." According to Ste-phen Dill Lee, Gordon's "imposing and magnificent sol-dierly bearing, coupled with his splendid ringing voice, and magnetic oratory gave him a god-given talent, not equalled or possessed by any other officer in either army—that of getting in front of his troops, and in a few ringing appeals,

2. *The War of the Rebellion: A Compilation of the Official Records of the Union and Confederate Armies* (130 vols.; Washington, D.C., 1880–1901), Ser. I, Vol. XIX, Pt. 1, p. 1027; Atlanta *Constitution*, January 13, 1904.

3. Much of this physical description is drawn from Caroline Lewis Gordon, "De Gin'ral an' Miss Fanny" (MS in Gordon Family Collection, University of Georgia, Athens). See also Morris Schaff, *The Sunset of the Confederacy* (Boston, 1912), 57, and John S. Wise, "Two Great Confederates. General John B. Gordon and Gen-eral James Longstreet: Characterizations by a Friend of Both," *American Monthly Review of Reviews*, XXIX (February, 1904), 204.

inspiring them almost to madness, and being able to lead them into the very Jaws of death." His outstanding oratorical abilities persuaded one soldier that he never again wanted to hear Gordon speak before going into action "because he makes me feel like I could storm h——ll." Another recalled Gordon as "the most gallant man I ever saw on a Battlefield. He had a way of putting things to the men that was irresistible, and he showed the men, at all times, that he shrank from nothing in battle on account of himself."[4] Idolized by the men he commanded, Gordon emerged from the war perhaps second only to Lee in distinction and belovedness.

John Brown Gordon began life amidst modest circumstances on the fringe of Georgia's frontier. Descended from Scotsmen who first migrated to America in 1724, he was born on February 6, 1832, in Upson County, Georgia, the fourth of twelve children. In 1851, Gordon entered the University of Georgia, where he distinguished himself academically and demonstrated particular skill as a public speaker. Despite his success, he failed to graduate, withdrawing for personal reasons early in his senior year. He then studied law, passed the Georgia bar examination, and practiced with the Atlanta firm of Overby & Bleckley. Although his career as a lawyer proved short-lived, his brief association with the firm led to his 1854 marriage to Fanny Rebecca Haralson, Mrs. Overby's younger sister. Their nearly fifty-year union would be one of the most solid and stabilizing influences in Gordon's life. In the years before the Civil War, Gordon and his family returned to northwestern Georgia, where he joined his father in successfully developing coal mining enterprises in the region. He became active in

4. Robert Stiles, *Four Years Under Marse Robert* (New York, 1904), 212; Atlanta *Journal*, January 14, 1904; A Distinguished Southern Journalist [E. A. Pollard], *The Early Life, Campaigns and Public Services of Robert E. Lee, with a Record of the Campaigns and Heroic Deeds of his Companions in Arms* (New York, 1871), 540; John H. Worsham, *One of Jackson's Foot Cavalry* (New York, 1912), 228.

politics and strongly supported secession as the sectional crisis deepened.[5]

Shortly after the firing on Fort Sumter, Gordon helped raise a company of volunteers for Confederate service. He was elected captain of the self-styled "Raccoon Roughs," who were assigned to the Sixth Alabama. Promotion came quickly, as the Georgian rose to colonel and command of the regiment by April, 1862. In his first actual clash of arms during the Peninsula Campaign, Gordon acquitted himself well at Seven Pines and Malvern Hill. He led his regiment conspicuously at South Mountain and at Antietam's Bloody Lane, where he received five wounds. After rejoining the Army of Northern Virginia in the spring of 1863 and being confirmed as brigadier general, Gordon ably commanded a brigade of Georgians at Chancellorsville and Gettysburg.

During the final year of the war, as he was entrusted with greater command responsibilities, Gordon met the demands of each new situation. He performed brilliantly at the Wilderness and Spotsylvania Court House in May, 1864. His conduct at the Mule Shoe salient on May 12 helped save Lee's divided army and resulted in his promotion to major general two days later. When the Second Corps moved to the Shenandoah Valley the following month, Gordon led a division under Jubal A. Early, fighting at Monocacy, Third Winchester, Fisher's Hill, and Cedar Creek. Actions in the Valley resulted in a bitter quarrel between Early and Gordon, which sowed the seeds of postwar controversies fully developed by Gordon, from his perspective, in *Reminiscences*.[6] Upon his return to Lee's army around Petersburg that winter, Gordon took command of the Second Corps and became the commanding general's confidant. He planned

5. For a full biographical treatment of Gordon, see Ralph Lowell Eckert, *John Brown Gordon: Soldier, Southerner, American* (Baton Rouge, 1989).

6. In *Reminiscences*, Gordon criticizes Early's conduct at Gettysburg, the Wilderness, Third Winchester, Fisher's Hill, and especially Cedar Creek. For an analysis of the validity of Gordon's criticisms, see Eckert, *Gordon*, 56–57, 64–69, 88–104.

and led the assault against Fort Stedman in March, 1865. On the retreat from Petersburg, his men fought primarily as the rearguard of the army and were still heavily engaged when the final truce was ordered. At Appomattox Court House, Gordon rode at the head of the Confederate surrender column—an honor bestowed upon him because of his superb service during the war's last year. In his final address to his troops, he appealed to them to return home in peace and to aid in rebuilding the South and the nation.

After the surrender at Appomattox, Gordon returned to Georgia. He considered leaving the country, but decided to remain and eventually made Atlanta his permanent residence. He engaged in a variety of business activities before assuming the presidency of the Southern Life Insurance Company in 1868. At about the same time, he also accepted the vice-presidency of a publishing company that was to provide southern schools and colleges with nonpartisan textbooks. Fearful that children of former Confederates might turn on their parents for their part in the war, Gordon early on devoted himself to preserving the South's heritage and ensuring that the motives that led southerners to war in 1861 would not be disparaged. In later years, he would become one of the leading proponents of the myth of the Old South and the cult of the Lost Cause.

Given his military reputation, Gordon naturally drifted into Reconstruction politics. Although defeated in his 1868 campaign for governor of Georgia, he emerged a leader in the state's Democratic party. He strongly supported efforts to preserve white domination when Republicans attempted to provide blacks with political, social, and economic equality. His exact involvement with the Ku Klux Klan remains undisclosed, but it is reasonably certain that he served as at least titular head of the Klan in Georgia. In 1873, Gordon won election to the United States Senate and quickly established himself as a spokeman for Georgia and the South as a whole. Time after time in the 1870s he eloquently defended the honor and integrity of southern whites as well as promoted their interests in the Senate. He also fought doggedly to restore white Democratic home rule in the South and was prominently involved in the final act of Reconstruction, the Compromise of 1877. His secret negotiations with Republicans resulted in pledges to remove the remaining federal troops from the South and to end federal support for Republican governments in South Carolina and Louisiana.

In May, 1880, only one year into his second term as senator, Gordon suddenly and unexpectedly resigned, as he explained, to pursue business opportunities. Although he steadfastly denied charges of prearrangements between himself, Joseph E. Brown (who replaced him), and Governor Alfred H. Colquitt (who appointed Brown), recently uncovered material clearly shows that extensive secret negotiations between all the parties took place before Gordon stepped down. A storm of protest and outrage greeted the resignation and appointment controversy, but the political reputations of the three figures were not badly damaged. Indeed, in the 1880s, they would be referred to as the Bourbon Triumvirate because of their apparent domination of Georgia politics. Gordon, though he concentrated on his business career between 1880 and 1886, remained very influential in the state. He and his fellow Bourbons unabashedly capitalized on southerners' reverence for the past by appealing to memories of the Confederacy while at the same time heralding the New South—a more industrial, commercially oriented South. Seeking a balanced economy, they eagerly courted eastern capital and helped bring new industries, especially the railroad, to Georgia and the rest of the South. Gordon's business career best represents the hustling entrepreneurial spirit of the emerging New South.

As a result of the complicated negotiations preceding his resignation from the Senate, Gordon secured an advantageous position from which he entered the wild world of railroading. He organized and served as president of the Georgia Pacific Railroad, an ambitious effort to link Atlanta to the Mississippi River. Soundly capitalized at $12,500,000, the Georgia Pacific proved a spectacular success and earned Gordon a great deal of money when he sold it to the sprawling Richmond and Danville syndicate soon after beginning construction. Recognized as one of the leading railroad promoters in the South, Gordon also invested in a broad range of other businesses—including manufacturing, mining, dredging, publishing, and agriculture—and widely speculated in real estate throughout the South. His grandest scheme, however, revolved around the International Railroad and Steamship Company of Florida. This grandiose vision involved both the construction of a railroad through Florida all the way to Key West and the establishment of steamship and telegraph lines across the Caribbean into Central and South America. Gordon loudly trumpeted this venture, but despite his immense exertions at home and abroad, legal and financial difficulties ultimately doomed the project and, with its demise, his dreams of a financial empire in Florida and the Caribbean.

Although Gordon obviously espoused the adventuresome spirit of a new order, he remained true to the old order as well. He played a central role in helping southerners accept their defeat in the Civil War and, in doing so, contributed significantly to the development of the myth of the Old South. In the final decades of the nineteenth century, he repeatedly painted a picture of the antebellum era as one of prosperity and social harmony. His view extolled the virtue of a peaceful, pastoral South and a way of life worth preserving. This idealized Old South helped southerners justify their actions and erase the haunting sense of inferiority lingering from the war. Gordon's glorification of the past also included the celebration of the Confederacy and of the war. When veterans in Virginia organized the Association of the Army of Northern Virginia and the Southern

Historical Society, Gordon joined his former comrades in promoting the cult of the Lost Cause. He, perhaps more than any other non-Virginian, contributed to the canonization of Robert E. Lee. In addition to his efforts to insulate, and virtually deify, his former commander, Gordon in the late 1800s knew no peer as a dedicator of monuments to Confederate officials and soldiers. In all of his public activities in the postwar period—whether as a promoter of impartial textbooks, or in government service, or as a public speaker, or in *Reminiscences*—"the General," as he was known, sought to protect southerners' self-image and self-respect by popularizing and preserving their Confederate past. Still, he looked to the future, as his commitment to the economics of the New South evinced.

Despite his almost frenetic involvement in business, Gordon by 1886 had lost most of his money in his Florida enterprise and looked to reenter the political arena. His opponent had an almost insurmountable advantage, but Gordon with the able assistance and skillful guidance of Henry W. Grady set out to capture the governorship of Georgia. Perceiving the great political benefit to be gained by tapping the wellspring of Confederate patriotism still running deep, Grady persuaded Jefferson Davis to visit Georgia. Gordon's close association with the former president of the Confederacy reawakened old memories and helped propel the General back into the political spotlight. He won the bitter, brawling gubernatorial contest of 1886 and was reelected without opposition two years later. Concentrating on economy in government and espousing the philosophy of limited government, Gordon accomplished little during his quite ordinary four-year tenure as governor. Nevertheless, in 1890, the Georgia legislature again selected him to represent the state in the United States Senate. He served a full six-year term but did not play nearly as important a role in the Senate as he had during the 1870s.

In the final decade of his life, Gordon continued vindicating the South while redoubling his efforts to heal completely the wounds still festering from the Civil War. In November, 1893, Gordon embarked on a career as public lecturer when he first presented his soon-to-be-famous "Last Days of the Confederacy." During the next ten years, he would deliver this lecture—and later a companion lecture, "First Days of the Confederacy"—hundreds of times as he traversed the country on lengthy speaking tours. His deft descriptions of the scenes of the Civil War intermingled with many of the stories later retold in *Reminiscences* warmed the hearts of even the coldest of listeners. His skillful blending of humor, pathos, and patriotism in a broad nationalistic perspective captivated audiences throughout the United States and further enhanced his reputation as the very embodiment of the Lost Cause.

When southern veterans had organized in the late 1880s, Gordon had been selected commander-in-chief of the United Confederate Veterans. His appearance at the annual reunions always set off spontaneous demonstrations, and whenever he tried to step down as the head of the UCV, he was greeted with wild, almost uncontrolled outbursts of affection; the General would lead the veterans' organization until his death in 1904. Gordon took his position as ceremonial and symbolic head of all Confederate veterans quite seriously and carefully guarded the image of the UCV. He worked to keep alive the fraternal spirit born in the trials of war and ensure that southerners and their actions were not portrayed in an uncomplimentary light, but he also used the UCV to help bridge the gap still existing between the North and the South. Gordon employed his prominence in his continuing efforts to eradicate sectional differences and widen the path leading toward national unity.

Although he devoted much of his postwar career to national pacification, Gordon's most enduring contribution to reconciliation came with the publication of *Reminiscences of the Civil War*. Gordon had long been encouraged to record his wartime experiences, but his hectic way of life and numerous commitments had made it difficult for him to devote sufficient time to such a project. In December, 1896, however, Gordon approached Charles S. Scribner's Sons about the possibility of publishing recollections of the Civil War that he had been preparing for some time. He proposed to present a side of the war—the soldiers' story—that he believed had not yet been written. His overarching purpose, though, was to contribute to the fraternal spirit that was helping reunite the formerly warring sections. He wanted to show that both sides fought for what they believed and that each could take pride in its motives and conduct.

Gordon's uplifting, nationalistic message and his desire to avoid personal and sectional prejudices made *Reminiscences* an immediate success in all parts of the country. Published in 1903, *Reminiscences* went through several printings in the first year. In 1904, following the General's death, Scribner's released a special Memorial Edition, which included an introduction by Stephen Dill Lee, Gordon's successor as commander-in-chief of the UCV, and a sketch of his final hours and funeral by his daughter, Frances Gordon Smith. In *Reminiscences*, Gordon chose not to discuss the causes of the war at length; rather, he provided a brief analysis of the controversies that precipitated the conflict. He admitted slavery was the most obvious cause of the war, but contended that it was not the most important. For him, clashing constitutional points of view regarding the powers of the national and state governments were the primary basis of conflict. Over time, he explained, these differing interpretations of the Constitution assumed sectional dimensions and inexorably led to war. Southerners, perceiving efforts to restrict slavery as infringements of their rights, exercised what they saw as their constitutional prerogative to secede when they withdrew from the Union. From Gordon's perspective, southerners were as justified in dissolving the Union as northerners were in preserving it. Rather than engage in the controversy over slavery or who was right or wrong, he simply declared that each side acted sincerely and honorably and that the northern victory finally resolved all questions concerning the nature of the Union.

As vital as it was to put such questions to rest, Gordon considered it equally, if not more, important to preserve a record of those who wore the gray and those who wore the blue. In *Reminiscences,* he extols the honor, bravery, and patriotism of the American soldier. With only a few exceptions, he praises the leaders and men of both armies. His tribute to "Billy Yank" and "Johnny Reb" is so overflowing—almost saccharinelike—that it is impossible to discern any distinction between the character of the two. Gordon, in his veneration of the American soldier, established a common ground upon which northerners and southerners alike could stand. An appreciation of the strength of character exhibited by soldiers in both armies coupled with recognition that each side fought equally hard for what it believed was right, in Gordon's mind, could only hasten and ensure complete reconciliation.

Reminiscences of the Civil War preached essentially the same sermon that Gordon had delivered so often in the years following the war. Still, it provides his most complete statement on the war and its centrality in the American experience. For him, the Civil War served as the crucible of the American nation. The war's white-hot fires of battle tested, tempered, purified, and ultimately strengthened the character of *all* Americans. He urged his fellow citizens to forget or at least forgive the unseemly aspects of the war and instead concentrate on what was good and noble about America's special war. *Reminiscences* serves as an eloquent capstone to Gordon's nearly forty-year commitment to reconciling the North and the South.

Despite its noble purpose, *Reminiscences* must be read with care. Even Douglas Southall Freeman, who admired Gordon and never questioned his intent to state the facts accurately, was "perplexed . . . to know where General Gordon's memory ended and where his imagination began." This authority on Lee and his lieutenants regarded *Reminiscences* as "altogether charming" but cautioned that it must be subjected to the same "critique that always must be applied to oft-told stories committed to print late in life."[7] Beyond the declining faculties of the aging warrior, it is impossible to determine how much Gordon's desire to insulate Lee from critics and his involvement in postwar controversies distorted his view of the past. In the main, Gordon in *Reminiscences* is uncritical and inoffensive except when criticizing James Longstreet at Gettysburg, attacking Early on numerous occasions, or commenting upon a few officers he personally disliked. Gordon provides documentation for his accounts of the battles, but he tends to embellish—though humbly—his wartime experiences; and he apparently concocted more than one story.[8] In truth, his conduct during the war did not require such creative writing, for none fought harder or better than Gordon. So why did he invent tales like the Gordon-Barlow meeting? It is likely that Gordon believed his patriotic purpose in writing *Reminiscences* justified a touch of literary license. Filled with heart-warming anecdotes that humanized the war and written in a florid, romantic style, *Reminiscences* presents the Civil War in a positive, nationalistic way so that northerners and southerners could take pride not only in their conduct but in that of their former opponents as well.

Even with its faults and shortcomings, *Reminiscences* remains an exceedingly valuable piece of literature, maybe

7. Douglas Southall Freeman, *R. E. Lee: A Biography* (4 vols.; New York, 1934–35), III, 302n; Douglas Southall Freeman, *Lee's Lieutenants: A Study in Command* (3 vols.; New York, 1942–44), III, 813.

8. Historians have long accepted Gordon's version of a May 6, 1864, afternoon conference in the Wilderness. In *Reminiscences*, he contends that he attended this conference and that he persuaded Lee to order him directly to undertake a turning movement against the Union right flank, which he had been urging all day. Gordon's private postwar correspondence with Lee, however, strongly suggests that neither occurred. See also Eckert, *Gordon*, 67–69.

less as a factual source of what happened on and behind the battlefields of the Civil War than as a statement by a citizen-soldier who fondly remembered the central event in his life—and the central event in his nation's history— some thirty years after the experience. *Reminiscences* tells us much about how southern Americans struggled to come to grips with their defeat in the War Between the States. It also tells us much about how far down the road toward national reconciliation Americans had traveled by the turn of the century. John Brown Gordon's *Reminiscences of the Civil War,* with its glorification of the American soldier and its celebration of our nation's trial by fire, continues to speak to us today.

RALPH LOWELL ECKERT
Penn State Erie, The Behrend College

INTRODUCTION

FOR many years I have been urged to place on record my reminiscences of the war between the States. In undertaking the task now, it is not my purpose to attempt a comprehensive description of that great struggle, nor an elaborate analysis of the momentous interests and issues involved. The time may not have arrived for a full and fair history of that most interesting period in the Republic's life. The man capable of writing it with entire justice to both sides is perhaps yet unborn. He may appear, however, at a future day, fully equipped for the great work. If endowed with the requisite breadth and clearness of view, with inflexible mental integrity and absolute freedom from all bias, he will produce the most instructive and thrilling record in the world's deathless annals, and cannot fail to make a contribution of measureless value to the American people and to the cause of free government throughout the world.

Conscious of my own inability to meet the demands of so great an undertaking, I have not attempted it, but with an earnest desire to contribute something toward such future history these reminiscences have been written. I have endeavored to make my review of that most heroic era so condensed as to claim the attention of busy people, and so impartial as to command the confidence of the fair-minded in all sections. It has been my fixed purpose to make a brief but dispassionate and judicially fair analysis of the divergent opinions and ceaseless controversies which for half a century produced an ever-widening alienation between the sections, and which finally plunged into the fiercest and bloodiest of fratricidal wars a great and enlightened people who were of the same race, supporters of the same Constitution, and joint heirs of the same freedom. I have endeavored to demonstrate that the courage displayed and the ratio of losses sustained were unprecedented in modern warfare. I have also recorded in this volume a large number of those characteristic and thrilling incidents which illustrate a unique and hitherto unwritten phase of the war, the story of which should not be lost, because it is luminous with the noblest lessons. Many of these incidents came under my own observation. They marked every step of the war's progress, were often witnessed by both armies, and were of almost daily occurrence in the camps, on the marches, and between the lines; increasing in frequency and pathos as the war progressed, and illustrating the distinguishing magnanimity and lofty manhood of the American soldier.

It will be found, I trust, that no injustice has been done to either section, to any army, or to any of the great leaders, but that the substance and spirit of the following pages will tend rather to lift to a higher plane the estimate placed by victors and vanquished upon their countrymen of the opposing section, and thus strengthen the sentiment of intersectional fraternity which is essential to complete national unity.

J. B. GORDON.

REMINISCENCES OF THE CIVIL WAR

CHAPTER I

MY FIRST COMMAND AND THE OUTBREAK OF THE WAR

A company of mountaineers—Joe Brown's pikes—The Raccoon Roughs
—The first Rebel yell—A flag presented to the company—Arrival at
Montgomery, Alabama—Analysis of the causes of the war—Slavery's
part in it—Liberty in the Union of the States, and liberty in the independence of the States.

THE outbreak of war found me in the mountains of
Georgia, Tennessee, and Alabama, engaged in the
development of coal-mines. This does not mean that I
was a citizen of three States; but it does mean that I
lived so near the lines that my mines were in Georgia,
my house in Alabama, and my post-office in Tennessee.
The first company of soldiers, therefore, with which I
entered the service was composed of stalwart mountaineers from the three States. I had been educated
for the bar and for a time practised law in Atlanta. In
September, 1854, I had married Miss Fanny Haralson,
third daughter of General Hugh A. Haralson, of La
Grange, Georgia. The wedding occurred on her seven-
teenth birthday and when I was but twenty-two. We
had two children, both boys. The struggle between devotion to my family on the one hand and duty to my
country on the other was most trying to my sensibilities. My spirit had been caught up by the flaming enthusiasm that swept like a prairie-fire through the land,
and I hastened to unite with the brave men of the mountains in organizing a company of volunteers. But what

3

was I to do with the girl-wife and the two little boys? The wife and mother was no less taxed in her effort to settle this momentous question. But finally yielding to the promptings of her own heart and to her unerring sense of duty, she ended doubt as to what disposition was to be made of her by announcing that she intended to accompany me to the war, leaving her children with my mother and faithful "Mammy Mary." I rejoiced at her decision then, and had still greater reasons for rejoicing at it afterward, when I felt through every fiery ordeal the inspiration of her near presence, and had, at need, the infinite comfort of her tender nursing.

The mountaineers did me the honor to elect me their captain. It was the first office I had ever held, and I verily believed it would be the last; for I expected to fight with these men till the war ended or until I should be killed. Our first decision was to mount and go as cavalry. We had not then learned, as we did later, the full meaning of that war-song, "If you want to have a good time, jine the cavalry"; but like most Southerners we were inured to horseback, and all preferred that great arm of the service.

This company of mounted men was organized as soon as a conflict seemed probable and prior to any call for volunteers. They were doomed to a disappointment, "No cavalry now needed" was the laconic and stunning reply to the offer of our services. What was to be done, was the perplexing question. The proposition to wait until mounted men were needed was promptly negatived by the suggestion that we were so far from any point where a battle was likely to occur, and so hidden from view by the surrounding mountains, that we might be forgotten and the war might end before we had a chance.

"Let us dismount and go at once as infantry." This proposition was carried with a shout and by an almost unanimous vote. My own vote and whatever influence

I possessed were given in favor of the suggestion, although my desire for cavalry service had grown to a passion. Accustomed to horseback on my father's plantation from my early childhood, and with an untutored imagination picturing the wild sweep of my chargers upon belching batteries and broken lines of infantry, it was to me, as well as to my men, a sad descent from dashing cavalry to a commonplace company of slow, plodding foot-soldiers. Reluctantly, therefore, we abandoned our horses, and in order certainly to reach the point of action before the war was over, we resolved to go at once to the front as infantry, without waiting for orders, arms, or uniforms. Not a man in the company had the slightest military training, and the captain himself knew very little of military tactics.

The new government that was to be formed had no standing army as a nucleus around which the volunteers could be brought into compact order, with a centre of disciplined and thoroughly drilled soldiery; and the States which were to form it had but few arms, and no artisans or factories to supply them. The old-fashioned squirrel rifles and double-barrelled shot-guns were called into requisition. Governor Joseph E. Brown, of Georgia, put shops in the State to work, making what were called "Joe Brown's pikes." They were a sort of rude bayonet, or steel lance, fastened, not to guns, but to long poles or handles, and were to be given to men who had no other arms. Of course, few if any of these pikemen ever had occasion to use these warlike implements, which were worthy of the Middle Ages, but those who bore them were as gallant knights as ever levelled a lance in close quarters. I may say that very few bayonets of any kind were actually used in battle, so far as my observation extended. The one line or the other usually gave way under the galling fire of small arms, grape, and canister, before the bayonet could be brought into requisition. The bristling points and the glitter of the bayonets were fearful to look upon as they were levelled in front of a charging line; but they were rarely reddened with blood. The day of the bayonet is passed except for use in hollow squares, or in resisting cavalry charges, or as an implement in constructing light and temporary fortifications. It may still serve a purpose in such emergencies or to impress the soldier's imagination, as the loud-sounding and ludicrous gongs are supposed to stiffen the backs and steady the nerves of the grotesque soldiers of China. Of course, Georgia's able war governor did not contemplate any very serious execution with these pikes; but the volunteers came in such numbers and were so eager for the fray that something had to be done; and this device served its purpose. It at least shows the desperate straits in securing arms to which the South was driven, even after seizing the United States arsenals within the Confederate territory.

The irrepressible humor and ready rustic wit which afterward relieved the tedium of the march and broke the monotony of the camp, and which, like a star in the darkness, seemed to grow more brilliant as the gloom of war grew denser, had already begun to sparkle in the intercourse of the volunteers. A woodsman who was noted as a " crack shot" among his hunting companions felt sure that he was going to win fame as a select rifleman in the army; for he said that in killing a squirrel he always put the bullet through the head, though the squirrel might be perched at the time on the topmost limb of the tallest tree. An Irishman who had seen service in the Mexican War, and was attentively listening to this young hunter's boast, fixed his twinkling eye upon the aspiring rifleman and said to him: " Yes; but Dan, me boy, ye must ricollict that the squirrel had no gon in his hand to shoot back at ye." The young huntsman had not thought about that; but he doubtless found later on, as the marksmen of both armies did, that it made a vast difference in the accuracy of aim when those in front not only had "gons" in their hands, but were firing them with distracting rapidity. This rude Irish philosopher had explained in a sentence one cause of the wild and aimless firing which wasted more tons of lead in a battle than all its dead victims would weigh.

There was at the outbreak of the war and just preceding it a class of men both North and South over whose inconsistencies the thoughtful, self-poised, and determined men who did the fighting made many jokes, as the situation grew more serious. It was that class of men in both sections who were most resolute in words and most prudent in acts; who urged the sections to the conflict and then did little to help them out of it; who, like the impatient war-horse, snuffed the battle from afar—very far: but who, when real war began to roll its crimson tide nearer and nearer to them, came to the conclusion that it was better for the country, as well as for themselves, to labor in other spheres; and that it was their duty, as America's great humorist put it, to sacrifice not themselves but their wives' relations on patriotism's altar. One of these furious leaders at the South declared that if we would secede from the Union there would be no war, and if there should be a war, we could "whip the Yankees with children's pop-guns." When, after the war, this same gentleman was addressing an audience, he was asked by an old maimed soldier: " Say, Judge, ain't you the same man that told us before the war that we could whip the Yankees with pop-guns?"

"Yes," replied the witty speaker, "and we could, but, confound 'em, they would n't fight us that way."

My company, dismounted and ready for infantry service, did not wait for orders to move, but hastily bidding adieu to home and kindred, were off for Milledgeville, then capital of Georgia. At Atlanta a telegram from the governor met us, telling us to go back home, and stay there until our services were needed. Our discomfiture can be better imagined than described. In fact, there broke out at once in my ranks a new rebellion. These rugged mountaineers resolved that they would not go home; that they had a right to go to the war, had started to the war, and were not going to be trifled with by the governor or any one else. Finally, after much persuasion, and by the cautious exercise of the authority vested in me by my office of captain, I prevailed on them to get on board the home-bound train. As the engine-bell rang and the whistle blew for the train to start, the rebellion broke loose again with double fury. The men rushed to the front of the train, uncoupled the cars from the engine, and gravely informed me that they had reconsidered and were not going back; that they intended to go to the war, and that if Governor Brown would not accept them, some other governor would. Prophetic of future dash as this wild impetuosity might be, it did not give much promise of soldierly discipline; but I knew my men and did not despair. I was satisfied that the metal in them was the best of steel and only needed careful tempering.

They disembarked and left the empty cars on the track, with the trainmen looking on in utter amazement. There was no course left me but to march them through the streets of Atlanta to a camp on the outskirts. The march, or rather straggle, through that city was a sight marvellous to behold and never to be forgotten. Totally undisciplined and undrilled, no two of these men marched abreast; no two kept the same step; no two wore the same colored coats or trousers. The only pretence at uniformity was the rough fur caps made of raccoon skins, with long, bushy, streaked raccoon tails hanging from behind them. The streets were packed with men, women, and children, eager to catch a glimpse of this grotesque company. Naturally we were the observed of all observers. Curiosity was on tip-toe, and from the crowded sidewalks there came to me the inquiry, "Are you the captain of that company, sir?" With a pride which I trust was pardonable, I indicated that I was. In a moment there came to me the second inquiry, "What company is that, sir?" Up to this time no name had been chosen—at least, none had been announced to the men. I had myself, however, selected a name which I considered both poetic and appropriate, and I replied to the question, "This company is the Mountain Rifles." Instantly a tall mountaineer said in a tone not intended for his captain, but easily overheard by his companions and the bystanders: "Mountain hell! we are no Mountain Rifles; we are the Raccoon Roughs." It is scarcely necessary to say that my selected name was never heard of again. This towering Ajax had killed it by a single blow. The name he gave us clung to the company during all of its long and faithful service.

Once in camp, we kept the wires hot with telegrams to governors of other States, imploring them to give us a chance. Governor Moore, of Alabama, finally responded, graciously consenting to incorporate the captain of the "Raccoon Roughs" and his coon-capped company into one of the regiments soon to be organized. The reading of this telegram evoked from my men the first wild Rebel yell it was my fortune to hear. Even then it was weird and thrilling. Through all the stages of my subsequent promotions, in all the battles in which I was engaged, this same exhilarating shout from these same trumpet-like throats rang in my ears, growing fainter and fainter as these heroic men became fewer and fewer at the end of each bloody day's work; and when the last hour of the war came, in the last desperate charge at Appomattox, the few and broken remnants of the Raccoon Roughs were still near their first captain's side, cheering him with the dying echoes of that first yell in the Atlanta camp.

Alabama's governor had given us the coveted "chance," and with bounding hearts we joined the host of volunteers then rushing to Montgomery. The line of our travel was one unbroken scene of enthusiasm. Bonfires blazed from the hills at night, and torch-light processions, with drums and fifes, paraded the streets of the towns. In the absence of real cannon, blacksmiths' anvils were made to thunder our welcome. Vast throngs gathered at the depots, filling the air with their shoutings, and bearing banners with all conceivable devices, proclaiming Southern independence, and pledging the last dollar and man for the success of the cause. Staid matrons and gayly bedecked maidens rushed upon the cars, pinned upon our lapels the blue cockades, and cheered us by chanting in thrilling chorus:

> In Dixie-land I take my stand
> To live and die in Dixie.

At other points they sang "The Bonnie Blue Flag," and the Raccoon Roughs, as they were thenceforward known, joined in the transporting chorus:

> Hurrah, hurrah, for Southern rights hurrah!
> Hurrah for the Bonnie Blue Flag that bears a single star!

The Hon. R. M. T. Hunter, of Virginia, who had been Speaker of the National House of Representatives, and United States senator, and who afterward became the Confederate Secretary of State and one of the Hampton Roads commissioners to meet President Lincoln and the Federal representatives, was travelling upon the same train that carried my company to Montgomery. This famous and venerable statesman, on his way to Alabama's capital to aid in organizing the new Government, made, in answer to the popular demand, a number of speeches at the different stations. His remarks on these occasions were usually explanatory of the South's attitude in the threatened conflict. They were concise, clear, and forcible. The people did not need argument; but they applauded his every utterance, as he carefully described the South's position as one not of aggression but purely of defence; discussed the doctrine promulgated in the Declaration of the Fathers, that all governments derive their just powers from the consent of the governed; asserted the sovereignty of the States, and their right to peaceably assume that sovereignty, as evidenced by the declaration of New York, Rhode Island, and Virginia when they entered the Union; explained the protection given the South's peculiar property by the plain provisions of the Constitution and the laws; urged the necessity of separation both for Southern security and the permanent peace of the sections; and closed with the declaration that, while there was no trace of authority in the Constitution for the invasion and coercion of a sovereign State, yet it was the part of prudence and of patriotism to prepare for defence in case of necessity.

Although I was a young man, yet, as the only captain on board, it fell to my lot also to respond to frequent calls. In the midst of this wild excitement and boundless enthusiasm, I was induced to make some promises which I afterward found inconvenient and even impossible to fulfil. A flag was presented bearing a most embarrassing motto. That motto consisted of two words: "No Retreat." I was compelled to accept it. There was, indeed, no retreat for me then; and in my speech accepting the flag I assured the fair donors that those coon-capped boys would make that motto ring with their cracking rifles on every battle-field; and in the ardor and inexperience of my young manhood, I related to these ladies and to the crowds at the depot the story of the little drummer-boy of Switzerland who, when captured and ordered to beat upon his drum a retreat, proudly replied, "Switzerland knows no such music!" Gathering additional inspiration from the shouts and applause which the story evoked, I exclaimed, "And these brave mountaineers and the young Confederacy, like glorious little Switzerland, will never know a retreat!" My men applauded and sanctioned this outburst of inconsiderate enthusiasm, but we learned better after a while. A little sober experience vastly modified and assuaged our youthful impetuosity. War is a wonderful developer, as well as destroyer, of men; and our four years of tuition in it equalled in both these particulars at least forty years of ordinary schooling. The first battle carried us through the rudimentary course of a military education; and several months before the four years' course was ended, the thoughtful ones began to realize that though the expense account had been great, it had at least reasonably well prepared us for final graduation, and for receiving the brief little diploma handed to us at Appomattox.

If any apology be needed for my pledge to the patriotic women who presented the little flag with the big motto, "No Retreat," it must be found in the depth of the conviction that our cause was just. From great leaders and constitutional expounders, from schools and colleges, from debates in Congress, in the convention that adopted the Constitution, and from discussions on the hustings, we had learned the lesson of the sovereignty of the States. We had imbibed these political principles from our childhood. We were, therefore, prepared to defend them, ready to die for them, and it was impossible at the beginning for us to believe that they would be seriously and forcibly assailed.

But I must return to our trip to Montgomery. We reached that city at night to find it in a hubbub over

the arrival of enthusiastic, shouting volunteers. The
hotels and homes were crowded with visiting statesmen
and private citizens, gathered by a common impulse
around the cradle of the new-born Confederacy. There
was a determined look on every face, a fervid prayer on
every lip, and a bounding hope in every heart. There
was the rumbling of wagons distributing arms and ammunition at every camp, and the tramping of freshly enlisted
men on every street. There was a roar of cannon on
the hills and around the Capitol booming welcome to
the incoming patriots; and all nature seemed palpitating
in sympathy with the intensity of popular excitement.
It fell to the lot of the Raccoon Roughs to be assigned
to the Sixth Alabama Regiment, and, contrary to my
wishes and most unexpectedly to me, I was unanimously
elected major.

When my company of mountaineers reached Montgomery, the Provisional Government of the "Confederate States of America" had been organized. At first
it was composed only of six States: South Carolina,
Georgia, Alabama, Florida, Mississippi, and Louisiana.
The States of Texas, Virginia, Arkansas, Tennessee, and
North Carolina were admitted into the Southern Union
in the order, I believe, in which I have named them.
Thus was launched the New Republic, with only eleven
stars on its banner; but it took as its chart the same
old American Constitution, or one so nearly like it that
it contained the same limitations upon Federal power,
the same guarantees of the rights of the States, the
same muniments of public and personal liberty.

The historian of the future, who attempts to chronicle
the events of this period and analyze the thoughts and
purposes of the people, will find far greater unanimity
at the South than at the North. This division at the
North did not last long; but it existed in a marked degree for some time after the secession movement began

and after twenty or more United States forts, arsenals, and barracks had been seized by State authorities, and even after the steamer *Star of the West* had been fired upon by State troops and driven back from the entrance of Charleston Harbor.

At the South, the action of each State in withdrawing from the Union was the end, practically, of all division within the borders of such State; and the roar of the opening battle at Fort Sumter in South Carolina was the signal for practical unanimity at the North.

Prior to actual secession there was even at the South more or less division of sentiment—not as to principle, but as to policy. Scarcely a man could be found in all the Southern States who doubted the constitutional *right* of a State to withdraw from the Union; but many of its foremost men thought that such movement was ill-advised or should be delayed. Among these were Robert E. Lee, who became the commander-in-chief of all the Confederate armies; Alexander Hamilton Stephens, who became the Confederate Vice-President; Benjamin H. Hill, who was a Confederate senator and one of the Confederate administration's most ardent and perhaps its most eloquent supporter; and even Jefferson Davis himself is said to have shed tears when, at his seat in the United States Senate, he received the telegram announcing that Mississippi had actually passed the ordinance of secession. The speech of Mr. Davis on taking leave of the Senate shows his loyal devotion to the Republic's flag, for which he had shed his blood in Mexico. In profoundly sincere and pathetic words he thus alludes to his unfeigned sorrow at the thought of parting with the Stars and Stripes. He said: "I shall be pardoned if I here express the deep sorrow which always overwhelms me when I think of taking a last leave of that object of early affection and proud association, feeling that henceforth it is not to be the banner which by day and by night I am ready to follow, to hail with the rising and bless with the setting sun."

He agreed, however, with an overwhelming majority of the Southern people, in the opinion that both honor and security, as well as permanent peace, demanded separation. Referring to the denial of the right of Southerners to carry their property in slaves into the common Territories, he said: "Your votes refuse to recognize our domestic institutions, which preëxisted the formation of the Union—our property, which was guarded by the Constitution. You refuse us that equality without which we should be degraded if we remained in the Union. . . . Is there a senator on the other side who, to-day, will agree that we shall have equal enjoyment of the Territories of the United States? Is there one who will deny that we have equally paid in their purchases and equally bled in their acquisition in war? . . . Whose is the fault, then, if the Union be dissolved? . . . If you desire, at this last moment, to avert civil war, so be it; it is better so. If you will but allow us to separate from you peaceably, since we cannot live peaceably together, to leave with the rights we had before we were united, since we cannot enjoy them in the Union, then there are many relations, drawn from the associations of our (common) struggles from the Revolutionary period to the present day, which may be beneficial to you as well as to us."

Abraham Lincoln, on the other hand, the newly elected President, was deeply imbued with the conviction that the future welfare of the Republic demanded that slavery should be prohibited forever in all the Territories. Indeed, upon such platform he had been nominated and elected. He, therefore, urged his friends not to yield on this point. His language was: " On the territorial question—that is, the question of extending slavery under national auspices—I am inflexible. I am for no compromise which assists or permits the extension of the institution on soil owned by the Nation." *

Thus these two great leaders of antagonistic sectional thought were pitted against each other before they had actually taken in hand the reins of hostile governments. The South in her marvellous fecundity had given birth to both these illustrious Americans. Both were of Southern lineage and born under Southern skies. Indeed, they were born within a few months and miles of each other, and nurtured by Kentucky as their common mother. But they were destined in God's mysterious providence to find homes in different sections, to grow up under different institutions, to imbibe in youth and early manhood opposing theories of constitutional construction, to become the most conspicuous representatives of conflicting civilizations, and the respective Presidents of contending republics.

After long, arduous, and distinguished services to their country and to liberty, both of these great sons of the South were doomed to end their brilliant careers in a manner shocking to the sentiment of enlightened Christendom. The one was to die disfranchised by the Government he had long and faithfully served and for the triumph of whose flag he had repeatedly pledged his life. The other was to meet his death by an assassin's bullet, at a period when his life, more than that of any other man, seemed essential to the speedy pacification of his country.

As stated, there was less division of sentiment in the South at this period than at the North. It is a great mistake to suppose, as was believed by Northern people, that Southern politicians were "dragooning the masses," or beguiling them into secession. The literal truth is that the people were leading the leaders. The rush of volunteers was so great when we reached Mont-

* Letter to Seward, February 1.

gomery that my company, the Raccoon Roughs, felt
that they were the favorites of fortune when they found
the company enrolled among the "accepted." Hon. L.
P. Walker, of Alabama, the first Secretary of War, was
literally overwhelmed by the vast numbers wishing to
enlist. The applicants in companies and regiments
fatigued and bewildered him. The pressure was so great
during his office hours that comparatively few of those
who sought places in the fighting line could reach him.
With a military ardor and patriotic enthusiasm rarely
equalled in any age, the volunteers actually waylaid the
War Secretary on the streets to urge him to accept at
once their services. He stated that he found it necessary, when leaving his office for his hotel, to go by some
unfrequented way, to avoid the persistent appeals of
those who had commands ready to take the field. Before the Confederate Government left Montgomery for
Richmond, about 360,000 men and boys, representing the
best of Southern manhood, had offered their services,
and were ready to pledge their fortunes and their lives to
the cause of Southern independence. What was the
meaning of this unparalleled spontaneity that pervaded
all classes of the Southern people? The only answer is
that it was the impulse of self-defence. One case will
illustrate this unsolicited outburst of martial enthusiasm;
this excess of patriotism above the supposed exigencies
of the hour; this vast surplus of volunteers, beyond the
power of the new Government to arm. Mr. W. C. Heyward, of South Carolina, was a gentleman of fortune and
a West Pointer, graduating in the same class with President Davis. As soon as the Confederate Government
was organized, Mr. Heyward went to Montgomery in
person to tender his services with an entire regiment.
He was unable for some time to obtain even an interview
on the subject, and utterly failed to secure an acceptance
of himself or his regiment. Returning to his home dis-

appointed, this wealthy, thoroughly educated, and trained military man joined the Home Guards, and died doing duty as a private in the ranks.

I know of nothing in all history that more brilliantly illustrates the lofty spirit, the high and holy impulse that sways a people aroused by the sentiment of self-defence, than this spontaneous uprising of Southern youth and manhood; than this readiness to stand for inherited convictions and constitutional rights, as they understood them; than the marvellous unanimity with which they rushed to the front with old flint and steel muskets, long-barrelled squirrel rifles, and double-barrelled shot-guns, in defence of their soil, their States, their homes, and, as they verily believed, in defence of imperilled liberty.

There is no book in existence, I believe, in which the ordinary reader can find an analysis of the issues between the two sections, which fairly represents both the North and the South. Although it would require volumes to contain the great arguments, I shall attempt here to give a brief summary of the causes of our sectional controversy, and it will be my purpose to state the cases of the two sections so impartially that just-minded people on both sides will admit the statement to be judicially fair.

The causes of the war will be found at the foundation of our political fabric, in our complex organism, in the fundamental law, in the Constitution itself, in the conflicting constructions which it invited, and in the institution of slavery which it recognized and was intended to protect. If asked what was the real issue involved in our unparalleled conflict, the average American citizen will reply, " The negro"; and it is fair to say that had there been no slavery there would have been no war. But there would have been no slavery if the South's protests could have availed when it was first introduced; and now that it is gone, although its sudden and violent

abolition entailed upon the South directly and incidentally a series of woes which no pen can describe, yet it is
true that in no section would its reëstablishment be
more strongly and universally resisted.   The South
steadfastly maintains that responsibility for the presence
of this political Pandora's box in this Western world
cannot be laid at her door.   When the Constitution was
adopted and the Union formed, slavery existed in practically all the States; and it is claimed by the Southern
people that its disappearance from the Northern and its
development in the Southern States is due to climatic
conditions and industrial exigencies rather than to the
existence or absence of great moral ideas.

Slavery was undoubtedly the immediate fomenting
cause of the woful American conflict.   It was the great
political factor around which the passions of the sections
had long been gathered—the tallest pine in the political
forest around whose top the fiercest lightnings were to
blaze and whose trunk was destined to be shivered in
the earthquake shocks of war.   But slavery was far from
being the sole cause of the prolonged conflict.   Neither
its destruction on the one hand, nor its defence on the
other, was the energizing force that held the contending
armies to four years of bloody work.   I apprehend that
if all living Union soldiers were summoned to the wit-
ness-stand, every one of them would testify that it was
the preservation of the American Union and not the destruction of Southern slavery that induced him to volunteer at the call of his country.   As for the South, it is
enough to say that perhaps eighty per cent. of her armies
were neither slave-holders, nor had the remotest interest
in the institution.   No other proof, however, is needed
than the undeniable fact that at any period of the war
from its beginning to near its close the South could have
saved slavery by simply laying down its arms and returning to the Union.

We must, therefore, look beyond the institution of slavery for the fundamental issues which dominated and inspired all classes of the contending sections. It is not difficult to find them. The "Old Man Eloquent," William E. Gladstone, who was perhaps England's foremost statesman of the century, believed that the Government formed by our fathers was the noblest political fabric ever devised by the brain of man. This undoubtedly is true; and yet before these inspired builders were dead, controversy arose as to the nature and powers of their free constitutional government. Indeed, in the very convention that framed the Constitution the clashing theories and bristling arguments of 1787 presaged the glistening bayonets of 1861. In the cabinet of the first President, the contests between Hamilton and Jefferson, representatives of conflicting constitutional constructions, were so persistent and fierce as to disturb the harmony of executive councils and tax the patience of Washington. The disciples of each of these political prophets numbered in their respective ranks the greatest statesmen and purest patriots. The followers of each continuously battled for these conflicting theories with a power and earnestness worthy of the founders of the Republic. Generation after generation, in Congress, on the hustings, and through the press, these irreconcilable doctrines were urged by constitutional expounders, until their arguments became ingrained into the very fibre of the brain and conscience of the sections. The long war of words between the leaders waxed at last into a war of guns between their followers.

During the entire life of the Republic the respective rights and powers of the States and general government had furnished a question for endless controversy. In process of time this controversy assumed a somewhat sectional phase. The dominating thought of the North and of the South may be summarized in a few sentences.

The South maintained with the depth of religious conviction that the Union formed under the Constitution was a Union of consent and not of force; that the original States were not the creatures but the creators of the Union; that these States had gained their independence, their freedom, and their sovereignty from the mother country, and had not surrendered these on entering the Union; that by the express terms of the Constitution all rights and powers not delegated were reserved to the States; and the South challenged the North to find one trace of authority in that Constitution for invading and coercing a sovereign State.

The North, on the other hand, maintained with the utmost confidence in the correctness of her position that the Union formed under the Constitution was intended to be perpetual; that sovereignty was a unit and could not be divided; that whether or not there was any express power granted in the Constitution for invading a State, the right of self-preservation was inherent in all governments; that the life of the Union was essential to the life of liberty; or, in the words of Webster, "liberty and union are one and inseparable."

To the charge of the North that secession was rebellion and treason, the South replied that the epithets of rebel and traitor did not deter her from the assertion of her independence, since these same epithets had been familiar to the ears of Washington and Hancock and Adams and Light Horse Harry Lee. In vindication of her right to secede, she appealed to the essential doctrine, "the right to govern rests on the consent of the governed," and to the right of independent action as among those reserved by the States. The South appealed to the acts and opinions of the Fathers and to the report of the Hartford Convention of New England States asserting the power of each State to decide as to the remedy for infraction of its rights; to the petitions presented and positions assumed by ex-President John Quincy Adams; to the contemporaneous declaration of the 8th of January assemblage in Ohio indicating that 200,000 Democrats in that State alone were ready to stand guard on the banks of the border river and resist invasion of Southern territory; and to the repeated declarations of Horace Greeley and the admission of President Lincoln himself that there was difficulty on the question of force, since ours ought to be a fraternal Government.

In answer to all these points, the North also cited the acts and opinions of the same Fathers, and urged that the purpose of those Fathers was to make a more perfect Union and a stronger government. The North offset the opinions of Greeley and others by the emphatic declaration of Stephen A. Douglas, the foremost of Western Democrats, and by the official opinion as to the power of the Government to collect revenues and enforce laws, given to President Buchanan by Jere Black, the able Democratic Attorney-General.

Thus the opposing arguments drawn from current opinions and from the actions and opinions of the Fathers were piled mountain high on both sides. Thus the mighty athletes of debate wrestled in the political arena, each profoundly convinced of the righteousness of his position; hurling at each other their ponderous arguments, which reverberated like angry thunderbolts through legislative halls, until the whole political atmosphere resounded with the tumult. Long before a single gun was fired public sentiment North and South had been lashed into a foaming sea of passion; and every timber in the framework of the Government was bending and ready to break from "the heaving ground-swell of the tremendous agitation." Gradually and naturally in this furnace of sectional debate, sectional ballots were crystallized into sectional bullets; and both sides came at last to the position formerly held by the great Troup of Georgia: "The argument is exhausted; we stand to our guns."

I submit that this brief and incomplete summary is sufficient to satisfy those who live after us that these great leaders of conflicting thought, and their followers who continued the debate in battle and blood, while in some sense partisans, were in a far juster sense patriots.

The opinions of Lee and Grant, from each of whom I briefly quote, will illustrate in a measure the convictions of their armies. Every Confederate appreciates the magnanimity exhibited by General Grant at Appomattox; and it has been my pleasure for nearly forty years to speak in public and private of his great qualities. In his personal memoirs, General Grant has left on record his estimate of the Southern cause. This estimate represents a strong phase of Northern sentiment, but it is a sentiment which it is extremely difficult for a Southern man to comprehend. In speaking of his feelings as "sad and depressed," as he rode to meet General Lee and receive the surrender of the Southern armies at Appomattox, General Grant says: "I felt like anything rather than rejoicing at the downfall of a foe who had fought so long and valiantly, and who had suffered so much for a cause, though that cause was, I believe, *one of the worst for which a people ever fought, and one for which there was the least excuse.*" He adds: "I do not question, however, the sincerity of the great mass of those who were opposed to us."

The words above quoted, showing General Grant's opinion of the Southern cause, are italicized by me and not by him. My object in emphasizing them is to invite special attention to their marked contrast with the opinions of General Robert E. Lee as to that same Southern cause. This peerless Confederate soldier and representative American, than whom no age or country ever produced a loftier spirit or more clear-sighted, conscientious Christian gentleman, in referring, two days before the surrender, to the apparent hopelessness of our cause, used these immortal words: " *We had, I was satisfied, sacred principles to maintain and rights to defend for which we were in duty bound to do our best, even if we perished in the endeavor.*"

There were those, a few years ago, who were especially devoted to the somewhat stereotyped phrase that in our Civil War one side (meaning the North) "was wholly and eternally right," while the other side (meaning the South) "was wholly and eternally wrong." I might cite those on the Southern side of the great controversy, equally sincere and fully as able, who would have been glad to persuade posterity that the North was "wholly and eternally wrong"; that her people waged war upon sister States who sought peacefully to set up a homogeneous government, and meditated no wrong or warfare upon the remaining sister States. These Southern leaders steadfastly maintained that the Southern people, in the exercise of the freedom and sovereign rights purchased by Revolutionary blood, were asserting a second independence according to the teachings and example of their fathers.

But what good is to come to the country from partisan utterances on either side? My own well-considered and long-entertained opinion, my settled and profound conviction, the correctness of which the future will vindicate, is this: that the one thing which is "wholly and eternally wrong" is the effort of so-called statesmen to inject one-sided and jaundiced sentiments into the youth of the country in either section. Such sentiments are neither consistent with the truth of history, nor conducive to the future welfare and unity of the Republic. The assumption on either side of all the righteousness and all the truth would produce a belittling arrogance, and an offensive intolerance of the opposing section; or, if either section could be persuaded that it was "wholly and eternally wrong," it would inevitably destroy the self-respect and manhood of its people. A far broader, more truthful, and statesmanlike view was presented by the Hon. A. E. Stevenson, of Illinois, then Vice-President of the United States, in his opening remarks as presiding officer at the dedication of the National Park at Chickamauga. In perfect accord with the sentiment of the occasion and the spirit which led to the establishment of this park as a bond of national brotherhood, Mr. Stevenson said: "Here, in the dread tribunal of last resort, valor contended against valor. Here brave men struggled and died for the right as God gave them to see the right."

Mr. Stevenson was right — "wholly and eternally right." Truth, justice, and patriotism unite in proclaiming that both sides fought and suffered for liberty as bequeathed by the Fathers—the one for liberty in the union of the States, the other for liberty in the independence of the States.

While the object of these papers is to record my personal reminiscences and to perpetuate incidents illustrative of the character of the American soldier, whether he fought on the one side or the other, I am also moved to write by what I conceive to be a still higher aim; and that is to point out, if I can, the common ground on which all may stand; where justification of one section does not require or imply condemnation of the other— the broad, high, sunlit middle ground where fact meets fact, argument confronts argument, and truth is balanced against truth.

CHAPTER II

THE TRIP FROM CORINTH

The Raccoon Roughs made a part of the Sixth Alabama—The journey
to Virginia—Families divided in Tennessee, Kentucky, and Missouri
—A father captured by a son in battle—The military spirit in Virginia—Andrew Johnson and Parson Brownlow Union leaders in
Tennessee—Johnson's narrowness afterward exhibited as President.

THE Raccoon Roughs made an imposing twelfth
part of the Sixth Alabama, which was one of the
largest regiments in the Confederate army. Governor
Moore, in order to comply with his promise to incorporate my company into one of the first regiments to be
organized, consented that the Sixth should contain twelve
instead of the regulation number of ten companies. A
movement had been started in Atlanta to uniform my
mountaineers: but when the message was received
from Governor Moore, inviting us to come to Montgomery, all thought of uniformity in dress was lost in
the enthusiasm evoked by the knowledge that our services were accepted; and even after the hastily prepared
uniforms were issued by the new Government my company clung tenaciously to "coonskin" head-dress, which
made a striking contrast to the gray caps worn by the
other companies.

No regulation uniform had at this time been adopted
for field officers, and in deference to the wishes and the
somewhat quaint taste of Colonel Seibles, the regimental
commander, the mounted officers of the Sixth wore double-

breasted frock-coats made of green broadcloth, with
the brass buttons of the United States army. These
green coats—more suited to Irishmen than to Americans
—were not discarded during the entire term of our first
enlistment for twelve months, nor until we were enrolled
as a part of the army that was to serve until Southern
independence was won or lost. I do not know what
became of my bottle-green coat, with the bullet-holes
through it, which would now be an object of interest to
my children. It is remarkable that during the war no
care was taken of any of these battle-marked articles.
All minds and hearts were absorbed in the one thought
of defence. It was a long time before even the flags
borne in battle became objects of special veneration, or
gathered about them the sentiment which grew into a
passion as the war neared its close. After one of the
early battles one of my color-bearers had secured and
fastened to the staff a beautiful new flag. When I asked
him what he had done with the old one, he replied:

"I threw it away, sir. It was so badly shot that it
was not worth keeping."

Our departure from Montgomery for Corinth, Mississippi, where we were to go into camp of instruction for
an indefinite period, was amid the roar of cannon, the
shouts of the multitude, the waving of flags and hand-
kerchiefs, and the prayers and tears of mothers, wives,
and sisters. The encampment at Corinth was brief and
uneventful; but our trip thence to Virginia was intensely
interesting, because of the danger and threat of conflict
between my troops and the citizens in certain localities.
The line of our travel was through East Tennessee,
where, even at that early period, there were evidences of
the radical conflict of opinion between neighbors which
was destined to eventuate in many bloody feuds. At
the depots crowds of men were gathered, some cheering,
some jeering, my troops as they passed. From the tops

of houses on one side of the street floated the Stars and Stripes; from those on the other were ensigns showing sympathy with the new-born Confederacy. The responsibility on my shoulders was not a light one, for it was my duty on every account to restrain the ardor of my own men and prevent the slightest imprudence of speech or action. No other locality approached East Tennessee in the extent of suffering from this peculiarly harassing sort of strife, unless possibly it was the State of Kentucky. In both public sentiment was divided. There was intense loyalty to the Union on the one hand, and to the Confederate cause on the other.

War's visage is grim enough at best; and to the people of those localities which were constantly subjected to raids, first by one side and then by the other, its frowning face was rarely relieved by one gleam of alleviating tenderness. These divided communities were the fated grist which the demon of border war seemed determined to grind to dust between his upper and nether millstones.

In East Tennessee, Kentucky, and Missouri, neighbors who had been lifelong friends became extremely embittered. Families were divided, brother against brother, and father against son. In Kentucky, it will be remembered, many of the most prominent families of the State, among them the Breckinridges, the Clays, and the Crittendens, were represented in both the Confederate and Union armies. John C. Breckinridge, who had just left the seat of Vice-President of the United States, and who had been the candidate of one wing of the Democratic party for President, cast his fortunes with the South, and made a brilliant record as a soldier and as the last Confederate Secretary of War. Other members of this distinguished family filled honorable positions in the opposing armies, and the distinguished and somewhat eccentric divine, the Rev. Robert J. Breckinridge, was one of the most eloquent and fervid—not to say bitter—advocates of the Union cause. His trenchant pen and lashing tongue spared neither blood relatives nor ministers nor members of the church, not even those of the same faith with himself, provided he regarded them as untrue to the Union. The intensity of Dr. Breckinridge's antagonism showed itself even on his death-bed. He and the Rev. Dr. Stuart Robinson, of Kentucky, were both eminent ministers of the same church, Dr. Robinson being as intense a sympathizer with the South as Dr. Breckinridge was with the North. From devoted friends they became fierce antagonists and uncompromising foes. When Dr. Breckinridge lay on his death-bed, his family and some of his church-members were gathered around him. They were most anxious that he should be reconciled to all men, and especially to Dr. Robinson, before he died, and they asked him, "Brother Breckinridge, have you forgiven all your enemies?"

"Oh, yes; certainly, certainly I have."

"Well, Brother Breckinridge, have you forgiven our brother Dr. Stuart Robinson?"

"Certainly I have. Did n't I just tell you that I had forgiven all my enemies?"

"But, Brother Breckinridge, when you meet Brother Stuart Robinson in heaven, do you feel that you can greet him as all the redeemed ought to greet one another?"

"Don't bother me with such questions. Stuart Robinson will never get there!"

During the year 1895 I was honored with an invitation to address an audience in Maysville, Kentucky. I was deeply impressed by the fact conveyed to me that a large number of those who sat before me had the harmony and happiness of their homes destroyed for the four years of war by the inexpressibly horrid thought that sons of the same parents were pitted against each other in battle. I was personally presented to a number of these formerly divided brothers who had bravely fought from the beginning to the end in opposing lines, but were now reunited under the old family roof and in the common Republic. It was a Kentucky father, I believe, both of whose sons had been killed in battle, the one in the Confederate, the other in the Union army, who erected to the memory of both over their common grave the monument on which he had inscribed these five monosyllables: "God knows which was right."

So much has been said and written of the peculiar trials and horrors experienced by the divided communities in Missouri, East Tennessee, and Kentucky that it is a privilege to record one of the incidents which at rare intervals sent rays of light through those unhappy localities. Major Edwards, of the Confederate army, who afterward became an editor of distinction in Missouri, had, at the beginning of the war, a neighbor and friend who was as intense a Unionist as the major was an enthusiastic Confederate. Each felt it his duty to go into the service, and when the war came they parted to take their places in opposing battle lines. Later on, Major Edwards captured this former neighbor and friend behind the Southern lines, and near their Missouri home. In reply to the question as to why he had taken such risk of being captured and sent to a Southern prison, the Union soldier explained that his wife was behind those lines and extremely ill—probably dying; that he had taken the risk of slipping at night between the Confederate picket posts in order to receive her last blessing and embrace. This statement was enough for the knightly man in gray. The Union soldier was at once made a prisoner, but only in the bonds of brotherly tenderness. His house was carefully guarded by Major Edwards himself until the sad parting with his wife was over, and then he was safely conducted through the Confederate lines and sent with a Confederate's sympathy to his post of duty in the Union camps.

At a recent reunion of the United Confederate Veterans, I was told of a thrilling incident which still further and more strikingly illustrates the tragedy of war in these divided States. At the beginning of the war Major M. H. Clift, of Tennessee, was a mere lad, and was attending school in another State. His father was an East Tennesseean and was devoted to the cause of the Union. Young Clift, however, was carried away by the storm of Southern enthusiasm and joined the Confederate army. The father soon yielded to his own sense of patriotic duty, and enlisted in one of the Union regiments formed in the neighborhood. In the fortunes of war, the two, father and son, were soon called to confront each other under hostile banners and in battle array. Neither had the remotest thought that the other stood in his front. In a furious charge by the Southern lines this young Confederate forced a Union soldier to surrender to him. Looking into the captured soldier's face, the young man recognized his own father. No pen could adequately depict his consternation when he realized that he had been on the point of killing his father, nor the joy which filled his heart that this dire calamity had been averted. Steps were at once taken to render it certain that no such contingency should again occur.

But the horrors of family division were not confined to these States. There were conspicuous instances elsewhere of the disruption of the most sacred ties. The Virginia kindred of that able soldier General George H. Thomas, and of ex-President Harrison, were in the Confederate service, while those of Generals Lovell and Pemberton, who fought for the Southern cause, and of Mrs. General Longstreet, supported the flag of the Union.

In my own State the wife of a Confederate officer saw

her husband retreat from Savannah under the Confederate commander, while her own dearly loved kindred marched into the town under General W. T. Sherman. This wife was Nellie Kinsey, said to be the first white child born in Chicago. She grew to accomplished womanhood, and married William W. Gordon of Savannah, who made a brilliant record as a Confederate officer, and during our recent war with Spain was commissioned brigadier-general by President McKinley. Mrs. Gordon was intensely loyal to her husband and to the cause he loved, but her kindred—her only kindred—were in the Union army and conspicuous for their gallantry in almost every arm of the service. As she stood with her children watching the Federal troops march in triumphant array under the windows of her Southern home, a splendid brass band at the head of one of the divisions began playing that familiar old air, "When this Cruel War is Over." As soon as the notes struck the ears of her little daughter, this enthusiastic young Confederate exclaimed, "Mamma, just listen to the Yankees playing 'When this Cruel War is Over,' and they just doing it themselves!"

When we reached Virginia the military spirit was in full flood-tide. The State had just passed the ordinance of secession, and almost every young and middle-aged man was volunteering for service. Even the servants were becoming interested in the military positions to which the aspiring young men of the household might be assigned. I recall an incident so strikingly characteristic that it seems due to a proper appreciation of these old-time loyal and faithful slaves that I give it in this connection.

Old Simon was the trusted and devoted butler of a leading Virginia family, and was very proud of his young master, who had just enlisted as a private in the cavalry, and, dressed in his new uniform and mounted upon his blooded horse, was drilling every day with his company. He was, in old Simon's estimation, the equal, if not the superior, of any soldier that was ever booted and spurred. The time came for the company to start to the front, and one of them rode up and asked old Simon:

"Is Bob here, Simon, or has he gone to camp?"

"Is you talking about my young marster, *Colonel Robert?*"

"Yes; of course I am, Simon," replied the trooper. "But I should like to know how in the —— Bob got to be a colonel?"

"Lawd, sir, he's des born a colonel!" said Simon; and his genuine and unaffected pride in this belief flashed in his old eyes and rang in his tones.

No account of East Tennessee's condition and experiences at this period would be complete without a few words in reference to those impetuous East Tennessee Union leaders, Andrew Johnson, who afterward became President, and the redoubtable Parson Brownlow, whose fiery denunciations of the Southern cause filled the columns of his paper, "Brownlow's Whig." Lifelong political antagonists, the one a Democrat, the other a Whig, and both aggressive and unrelenting, they nevertheless, when civil war approached, buried the partisan tomahawk and wielded the Union battle-axe side by side. They became coadjutors and the most powerful civil supporters of the Union cause in the State, if not in the South. Andrew Johnson, as is well known, was a tailor when a young man, and, it is said, was taught to read by his faithful wife. He deserved and received immense credit for the laborious study and untiring perseverance which converted the scissors of his shop into the sceptre of Chief Executive of the world's greatest Republic; but he did not broaden in sentiment in proportion to the elevation he attained and the gravity of the responsibilities imposed. He was strong but narrow. He could not be a statesman in the highest sense of that term, because he was swayed by prejudice more than by lofty convictions. That he was impelled by motives intensely patriotic in adhering to the Union there can be no reasonable doubt; but his utter failure to rise to a full conception of the situation in which he found himself after President Lincoln's unfortunate death was painfully apparent to every thoughtful observer. His intolerant bigotry, and his failure to appreciate the obligations imposed upon him by General Grant's magnanimous and solemn compact with the Southern army at Appomattox, were manifested by his desire to arrest General Lee and other prominent prisoners of war who had protecting paroles. His blind prejudice against our best people was shown in his selection of classes for amnesty; and the low plane on which he planted his administration was evidenced by his inconsistencies, his vacillations, and his reversal of the wise, generous, and statesmanly policy of his great predecessor. But the narrowness of the man and the amazing absurdity of his prejudice are sufficiently exhibited in a circumstance trivial in itself, but which, perhaps on that account, more clearly indicates his calibre. A few months after the war was over, I was passing through Washington, and called to pay my respects to General Grant, who had shown me personally, at the close of hostilities, marked consideration and kindness, of which I shall make mention in another chapter. General Grant offered to introduce me to President Johnson, whom I had never met. We walked across to the Executive Mansion, and General Grant gave the usher a card on which was written, "General Grant, with General Gordon of Georgia," with instructions to the usher to hand it to the President. We were at once admitted to his presence, and I was introduced by General Grant as "General Gordon," with some complimentary reference to my rank and service in General Lee's army. The President met this introduction by these words, pronounced with peculiar emphasis, "How are you, Mr. Gordon?" especially accentuating the word Mister. I was neither angry nor indignant, but my contempt was sincere for the ineffable littleness of the man whose untimely ascendancy to power at that critical period I can but regard as the veriest mockery of fate.

Contrast this foolish and abortive effort at insult with the conduct of President Grant, who succeeded him, or of General Grant as soldier, or with that of any other prominent soldier or high-minded citizen of the country. The conduct of General Hancock at General Grant's funeral in New York is perhaps in still greater contrast with that of President Johnson. Although the incident I am about to relate is chronologically out of place here, it is emphatically in place as illustrating the point I am making in reference to President Johnson.

It will be remembered that General Hancock was commander of the Department of the East (United States army) at the time of General Grant's death, and was, by reason of his military rank, the chief marshal of that stupendous and most impressive pageant witnessed in New York at General Grant's obsequies. I was included among those ex-Confederate officers who had been specially invited to participate in the honors to be paid to the dead soldier and former President. General Hancock had requested that I should ride with him at the head of the mighty procession, and he had playfully said to the staff that each of us should take his place according to rank. Of course I had no thought of claiming any rank, and I took my place in the rear of the regular staff. General Hancock sent one after another of his immediate staff to request me to ride up to the front, with the message that I must obey orders and report to him at once at the head of the column. When I reached the head of the column, General Hancock directed the staff to compare dates and ascertain the ranking officer who should ride on his right. My rank as a Confederate general was higher than that of any other member of his staff, and he ordered that I should take the place of honor. As I could not gracefully resist this assignment any longer, I accepted it, saying to the Union generals, who also served on General Hancock's staff, that they had overwhelmed me some twenty-odd years before, but that I had them down now. General Fitzhugh Lee was similarly honored.

In closing this chapter, it is not necessary, I trust, for me to say that I would do no injustice to the memory of President Johnson, but it seems to me that the future manhood of our country can be ennobled by the contemplation of the marked and notable contrasts here presented, and by a realization of the truth that no station in life, however conspicuous, can conceal from view the weakness of its possessor. Certainly it can inflict no damage upon the character of our youth to let them understand that the gulf is both broad and deep which separates the highest type of courage from petty and ignoble spite, and that the line which divides true nobility of soul from narrowness of spirit was drawn by God's hand, and will become clearer to human apprehension as we approach nearer to Him in thought and action.

CHAPTER III

The first great battle of the war—A series of surprises—Mishaps and mistakes of the Confederates—Beauregard's lost order—General Ewell's rage—The most eccentric officer in the Confederate army—Anecdotes of his career—The wild panic of the Union troops—Senseless frights that cannot be explained—Illustrated at Cedar Creek.

THE battle of Bull Run or Manassas was the first, and in many respects the most remarkable, battle of our Civil War. It was a series of surprises—the unexpected happening at almost every moment of its progress. Planned by the Union chieftain with consummate skill, executed for the most part with unquestioned ability, and fought by the Union troops for a time with magnificent courage, it ended at last in their disastrous rout and the official decapitation of their able commander. On the Confederate side it was a chapter of mishaps, miscarriages, and of some mistakes. It was also a chapter of superb fighting by the Southern army, and of final complete and overwhelming victory. The breaking down of the train bearing General Joseph E. Johnston's troops was an accident which almost defeated the consummation of that splendid piece of strategy by which he had eluded General Patterson in the Valley, and which had enabled him to hurry almost his entire force to the support of General Beauregard at Manassas. The mistakes are represented by the fact that the feint of General McDowell on the Confederate front was believed to be the real attack, until the Union general was hurling his army on Beauregard's flank. Finally, the most serious miscarriage was that the order from Beauregard to Ewell directing an assault on the Union left failed to reach that officer. This strange miscarriage prevented General Ewell from making a movement which it then seemed probable and now appears certain would have added materially to McDowell's disaster. I had already been instructed by him to make a reconnaissance in the direction of the anticipated assault, but I had been suddenly recalled just as my skirmishers were opening fire. I was recalled because General Ewell had not received the promised order. For me it was perhaps a most fortunate recall, for in my isolated position I should probably have been surrounded and my little command cut to pieces. On my return I found General Ewell in an agony of suspense. He was chafing like a caged lion, infuriated by the scent of blood. He would mount his horse one moment and dismount the next. He would walk rapidly to and fro, muttering to himself, "No orders, no orders." General Ewell, who afterward became a corps commander, had in many respects the most unique personality I have ever known. He was a compound of anomalies, the oddest, most eccentric genius in the Confederate army. He was my friend, and I was sincerely and deeply attached to him. No man had a better heart nor a worse manner of showing it. He was in truth as tender and sympathetic as a woman, but, even under slight provocation, he became externally as rough as a polar bear, and the needles with which he pricked sensibilities were more numerous and keener than porcupines' quills. His written orders were full, accurate, and lucid; but his verbal orders or directions, especially when under intense excitement, no man could comprehend. At such times his eyes would flash with a peculiar brilliancy, and his brain far outran his tongue.

His thoughts would leap across great gaps which his words never touched, but which he expected his listener to fill up by intuition, and woe to the dull subordinate who failed to understand him!

When he was first assigned to command at the beginning of the war, he had recently returned from fighting Indians on the Western frontier. He had been dealing only with the enlisted men of the standing army. His experience in that wild border life, away from churches, civilization, and the refining influences of woman's society, were not particularly conducive to the development of the softer and better side of his nature. He became a very pious man in his later years, but at this time he was not choice in the manner of expressing himself. He asked me to take a hasty breakfast with him just before he expected the order from Beauregard to ford Bull Run and rush upon McDowell's left. His verbal invitation was in these words: "Come and eat a cracker with me; we will breakfast together here and dine together in hell." To a young officer like myself, who had never been under fire except at long range, on scouting excursions, or on the skirmish-line, such an invitation was not inspiring or appetizing; but Ewell's spirits seemed to be in a flutter of exultation.

An hour later, after I had been recalled from my perilous movement to "feel of the enemy," I found General Ewell, as I have said, almost frenzied with anxiety over the non-arrival of the anticipated order to move to the attack. He directed me to send to him at once a mounted man "with sense enough to go and find out what was the matter." I ordered a member of the governor's Horse Guard to report immediately to General Ewell. This troop represented some of the best blood of Virginia. Its privates were refined and accomplished gentlemen, many of them University graduates, who, at the first tocsin of war, had sprung into their saddles as volunteers. The intelligent young trooper who was selected to ride upon this most important mission under the verbal direction of General Ewell himself, mounted his high-spirited horse, and, with high-top boots, polished spurs, and clanking sabre, galloped away to where the general was impatiently waiting at his temporary headquarters on the hill. Before this inexperienced but promising young soldier had time to lift his hat in respectful salutation, the general was slashing away with tongue and finger, delivering his directions with such rapidity and incompleteness that the young man's thoughts were dancing through his brain in inextricable confusion. The general, having thus delivered himself, quickly asked, "Do you understand, sir?" Of course the young man did not understand, and he began timidly to ask for a little more explicit information. The fiery old soldier cut short the interview with "Go away from here and send me a man who has some sense!"

Later in the war, when I was commanding a division in Stonewall Jackson's old corps, then commanded by General Ewell, I had a very similar experience with this eccentric officer. It was in the midst of one of the battles between Lee and Grant in the Wilderness. As already explained, General Ewell's spirits, like the eagle's wings gathering additional power in the storm, seemed to mount higher and higher as the fury of the battle increased. My division of his corps was advancing under a galling fire. General Ewell rode at full speed to the point where I was intensely engaged directing the charge, and asked me to lend him one of my staff, his own all having been despatched with orders to different portions of the field. I indicated a staff-officer whom he might command, and he began, in his characteristic style under excitement, to tell this officer what to do. My staff-officer had learned to interpret the general fairly well, but to catch his meaning at one point stopped him and said: "Let me see if I understand you, sir?" General Ewell was so incensed at this insinuation of lack of perspicuity that he turned away abruptly, without a word of explanation, simply throwing up his hand and blowing away the young officer with a sort of "whoo-oo-oot." There is no way to spell out this indignant and resounding puff; but even in the fierce battle that was raging there was a roar of laughter from the other members of my staff as the droll and doughty warrior rushed away to another part of the field.

I cannot conclude this imperfect portrayal of the peculiarities of this splendid soldier and eccentric genius without placing upon record one more incident connected with the first battle of Bull Run. While he waited for the order from Beauregard (which never came), I sat on my horse near him as he was directing the location of a battery to cover the ford, and fire upon a Union battery and its supports on the opposite hills. As our guns were unlimbered, a young lady, who had been caught between the lines of the two armies, galloped up to where the general and I were sitting on our horses, and began to tell the story of what she had seen. She had mounted her horse just in front of General McDowell's troops, who it was expected would attempt to force a crossing at this point. This Virginia girl, who appeared to be seventeen or eighteen years of age, was in a flutter of martial excitement. She was profoundly impressed with the belief that she really had something of importance to tell. The information which she was trying to convey to General Ewell she was sure would be of vast import to the Confederate cause, and she was bound to deliver it. General Ewell listened to her for a few minutes, and then called her attention to the Union batteries that were rushing into position and getting ready to open fire upon the Confederate lines. He said to her, in his quick, quaint manner: "Look there, look there, miss! Don't you see those men with blue clothes on, in the edge of the woods? Look at those men loading those big guns. They are going to fire, and fire quick, and fire right here. You'll get killed. You'll be a *dead damsel* in less than a minute. *Get away from here! Get away!*" The young woman looked over at the blue coats and the big guns, but paid not the slightest attention to either. Nor did she make any reply to his urgent injunction, "Get away from here!" but continued the story of what she had seen. General Ewell, who was a crusty old bachelor at that time, and knew far less about women than he did about wild Indians, was astounded at this exhibition of feminine courage. He gazed at her in mute wonder for a few minutes, and then turned to me suddenly, and, with a sort of jerk in his words, said: "Women—I tell you, sir, women would make a grand brigade—if it was not for snakes and spiders!" He then added much more thoughtfully: "They don't mind bullets—women are not afraid of bullets; but one big black-snake would put a whole army to flight." And he had not fired very wide of the mark. It requires the direst dangers, especially where those dangers threaten some cause or object around which their affections are entwined, to call out the marvellous courage of women. Under such conditions they will brave death itself without a quiver. I have seen one of them tested. I saw Mrs. Gordon on the streets of Winchester, under fire, her soul aflame with patriotic ardor, appealing to retreating Confederates to halt and form a new line to resist the Union advance. She was so transported by her patriotic passion that she took no notice of the whizzing shot and shell, and seemed wholly unconscious of her great peril. And yet she will precipitately fly from a bat, and a big black bug would fill her with panic.

Those who are inclined to investigate the mysteries of that strange compound which makes up our mental, moral, and physical natures will find abundant material in the wild panic which seized and shook to pieces the Union army at Bull Run, scattering it in disorganized fragments through woods and fields and by-ways, and filling the roads with broken wagons and knapsacks, and small arms—an astounding experience which was the prototype of similar scenes to be enacted in both armies in the later stages of the war. No better troops were ever marshalled than those who filled the Union and Confederate ranks. Indeed, taking them all in all, I doubt whether they have been equalled. How courage of the noblest type, such as these American soldiers possessed, could be converted in an instant into apparent — even apparent — cowardice is one of the secrets, unsolvable perhaps, of our being. What was the special, sufficient, and justifiable ground for such uncontrollable apprehensions in men who enlisted to meet death, and did meet it, or were ready to meet it, bravely and grandly on a hundred fields? The panic at Bull Run seized McDowell's whole army; and yet a large portion of it at the moment the panic occurred was perhaps not under fire—certainly in no danger of annihilation or of serious harm. Yet they fled, all or practically all—fled with uncontrollable terror. Of course there were times when it was necessary to retreat. Occasions came, I presume, to every command that did much fighting during those four years, when the most sensible thing to do was to go, and without much thought as to the order of the going—the faster the better. It is not that class of retreats that I am considering. These were not panics; nor did they bear any special resemblance to panics, except that in both cases it was flight—even disorganized flight. There was, however, this radical difference between the two: in one case the men were ready to halt, reform their lines, and fight again; in the other case these same men were as heedless of an officer's orders (supposing the officer to have retained his senses) as a herd of wild buffaloes.

The soldiers on both sides who may read this book will recall many instances of both kinds of flight. One of the good-natured gibes with which the infantry poked the ribs of the cavalry was that they had too many feet and legs under them to stand and be shot at; but what old soldier of either arm of the service will refuse to bear testimony to the fact that the Confederate cavalry on many occasions charged batteries and solid lines, and, after being repulsed, would retreat, reform, and charge again and again—a constant alternation of charges and rapid retreats without the slightest indication of panic? I saw Sheridan's cavalry in the Valley of Virginia form in my front, charge across the open fields and almost over my lines, which were posted behind stone fences. They rode at a furious rate, driving spurs into their horses' sides as they rushed like a mountain torrent against the rock wall. Some of them went over it, only to be captured or shot. They discharged carbines in our faces, and then retreated in fairly good order, under a furious fire, with apparently no more of panic than if they had been fighting a sham battle.

But those sudden and sometimes senseless frights which deprived brave men of all self-control for the time, were so unexpected, so strange and terrible, so inconsistent with the conduct of the same men at other times and under circumstances equally and perhaps even more trying, that they justify a few additional illustrations.

The battle of Cedar Creek in the Shenandoah Valley, on October 19, 1864, about which I shall have more to say in its chronological order, furnishes cases in point by both armies and on the same day. Neither the panic which struck with such resistless terror, Sheridan's two corps as they were assaulted at dawn, and which sent them, as the sun rose over the adjacent mountains, flying in wildest rout from the fields and for miles to the rear, with no enemy in pursuit; nor the panic which seized and sent General Early's army, as that same sun was setting behind the opposite mountains, rushing across the bridges, or into the chilly waters, and through the dense cedars of the limestone cliffs—neither of these was the necessary, logical, or even natural sequence of the conditions which preceded them. There is no logic in a panic. It is true that in both cases the armies had been assailed in front and flank; and the cry, "We are flanked!" not infrequently produced upon the steadiest battalions an effect similar to that caused among passengers at sea by the alarm of fire. But the point is that while it might not have been possible to prevent the opposing forces from achieving a victory after the flank movement was under full headway, yet the retreat in each case could have been accomplished with far lighter losses in killed, wounded, and prisoners. If the armies had not allowed the unnecessary panic to deprive them of their reason and thus of all control of will power, they would have had a better chance for life in a somewhat orderly retreat, distracting and confusing the aim of the advancing lines by returning fire for fire, than by permitting the pursuers deliberately to shoot them in the back.

The strangest fact of all is that many of these men in both armies had often exhibited before, as they did on many succeeding fields and under just as trying conditions, a heroism rarely equalled and never excelled in military annals—a heroism that defied danger and was impervious to panic. Sheridan's men, who threw away everything that could impede their flight in the morning at Cedar Creek, fought with splendid courage before and afterward. Indeed, they returned that same afternoon and made most honorable amends for the mistakes of the morning. Some of these same Confederates had been flanked and almost surrounded by McDowell's army in the early hours at Bull Run and yet felt no symptoms of panic. Some of them had been with me at South Mountain in '62, detached for the moment from the main army, at times nearly surrounded, attacked first in front, then upon the right, and then upon the left flank, changing front under fire, retreating now slowly, now rapidly, but in every case halting at the command and forming a new line to repeat the manœuvres, and without a semblance of panic. I verily believe they would have died, almost to a man, on the rocks of that rugged mountain-side, but for the gracious dropping of night's curtain on the scene. They did die, nearly or quite half of them, the next day at Antietam or Sharpsburg. Still more striking the contrast—large numbers of these Confederates who were overwhelmed with panic at Cedar Creek fought upon the last dreadful retreat from Petersburg with marvellous intrepidity, while flanked and forced to move rapidly from one position to another. And on that last morning at Appomattox these same Confederates were fighting in almost every direction, surrounded on all sides except one, with a column plainly in view and advancing to complete the circle of fire around them; and they continued to fight bravely and grandly until the flag of truce heralded the announcement that the war was over.

CHAPTER IV

THE SPRING OF 1862—BATTLE OF SEVEN PINES OR FAIR OAKS

Indomitable Americanism, North and South—Rally of the North after Bull Run—Severity of winter quarters in Virginia—McClellan's army landed at Yorktown—Retreat of the Confederates—On the Chicka-hominy—Terrible slaughter at Seven Pines—A brigade commander.

THE North had lost, the South had won, in the first bloody battle of the war, and all chances for compromise were obliterated, if indeed they had ever existed. The Northern army had been defeated and driven back beyond the Potomac, but the defeat simply served to arouse the patriotic people of that section to more determined effort. Party passion was buried, party lines were almost entirely erased, and party organizations were merged into the one compact body of a united people, led by the all-pervading purpose to crush out the Southern movement and save the Union. With that tenacity of will, that unyielding Anglo-Saxon perseve-rance—or, I prefer to say, that indomitable American-ism—for which the people of the United States are so justly famed, the North rose superior to the disaster, and resolved, as did old Andrew Jackson, that "the Union should be preserved."

The South, on the other hand, greatly encouraged by the victory, bowed at its altars and thanked Heaven for this indication of ultimate triumph. Her whole people, with an equally tenacious Americanism, and fully persuaded that the independent States, now united under another and similar Constitution, had a right to set up their own homogeneous government, resolved that, if sacrifices and fighting could secure it, the South should become an independent republic. With a deeper consecration than ever, if possible, they pledged anew to that cause their honor, their wealth, their faith, their prayers, their lofty manhood and glorious womanhood, resolving never to yield as long as hope or life endured. And they did not yield until their whole section, "with its resources all exhausted, lay prostrate and powerless, bleeding at every pore."

The North soon rallied after the defeat at Bull Run. Her armies were placed under the immediate command of that brilliant young chieftain, George B. McClellan, whose genius as organizer, ability as disciplinarian, and magnetism in contact with his men, rapidly advanced his heavily reënforced army to a high plane of efficiency. The pride felt in him was manifested by the title "Young Napoleon," bestowed upon him by his admiring countrymen. No advance, however, was made by his army until the following spring. The Confederate army, under General Joseph E. Johnston, was occupied during the remaining months of summer and fall, mainly in drilling, recruiting its ranks, doing picket duty, and, as winter approached, in gathering supplies and preparing, as far as possible, for protection against Virginia freezes and snows.

My men were winter-quartered in the dense pine thickets on the rough hills that border the Occoquan. Christmas came, and was to be made as joyous as our surroundings would permit, by a genuine Southern eggnog with our friends. The country was scoured far and near for eggs, which were exceedingly scarce. Of sugar we still had at that time a reasonable supply, but our small store of eggs and the other ingredients could not be increased in all the country round about. Mrs. Gordon superintended the preparation of this favorite Christmas beverage, and at last the delicious potion was ready. All stood anxiously waiting with camp cups in hand. The servant started toward the company with full and foaming bowl, holding it out before him with almost painful care. He had taken but a few steps when he struck his toe against the uneven floor of the rude quarters and stumbled. The scattered fragments of crockery and the aroma of the wasted nectar marked the melancholy wreck of our Christmas cheer.

The winter was a severe one and the men suffered greatly—not only for want of sufficient preparation, but because those from farther South were unaccustomed to so cold a climate. There was much sickness in camp. It was amazing to see the large number of country boys who had never had the measles. Indeed, it seemed to me that they ran through the whole catalogue of complaints to which boyhood and even babyhood are subjected. They had everything almost except teething, nettle-rash, and whooping-cough. I rather think some of them were afflicted with this latter disease. Those who are disposed to wonder that Southern troops should suffer so much from a Virginia winter will better appreciate the occasional severity of that climate when told of the incident which I now relate. General R. A. Alger, of the Union army, ex-Governor of Michigan and ex-Secretary of War, states that he was himself on picket duty in winter and at night in this same section of Virginia. It was his duty as officer in charge to visit during the night the different picket posts and see that the men were on the alert, so as to avoid surprises. It was an intensely cold night, and on one of his rounds, a few hours before daylight, he approached a post where a solitary picket stood on guard. As he neared the post he was greatly surprised to find that the soldier did not halt him and force him to give the countersign. He could plainly see the soldier standing on his post, leaning against a tree, and was indignant because he supposed he had found one of his men asleep on duty, when to remain awake and watchful was essential to the army's safety. Walking up to his man, he took him by the arm to arouse him from sleep and place him under immediate arrest. He was horrified to find that the sentinel was dead. Frozen, literally frozen, was this faithful picket, but still standing at the post of duty where his commander had placed him, his form erect and rigid—dead on his post!

Even at that early period the Southern men were scantily clad, though we had not then reached the straits to which we came as the war progressed, and of which a simple-hearted countrywoman gave an approximate conception when she naïvely explained that her son's only pair of socks did not wear out, because " when the feet of the socks got full of holes I just knitted new feet to the tops, and when the tops wore out I just knitted new tops to the feet."

This remarkable deficiency in heavy clothing among the Southern troops even at the beginning of the war is easily explained. We were an agricultural people. Farming or planting was fairly remunerative and brought comfort, with not only financial but personal independence, which induced a large majority of our population to cling to rural life and its delightful occupations. Little attention, comparatively, was paid to mining or manufacturing. The railroads were constructed through cotton belts rather than through coal- and iron-fields. There were some factories for the manufacture of cloth, but these were mainly engaged upon cotton fabrics, and those which produced woollens or heavy goods were few and of limited capacity. It will be seen that in this situation, with small milling facilities, with great armies on our hands, and our ports closed against foreign importations, we were reduced to the dangerous extremity of blockade-running, and to the still more hazardous contingency of capturing now and then overcoats and trousers from the Union forces.

Perhaps the utter lack of preparation for the war on the part of the South is proof that its wisest statesmen anticipated no such stupendous struggle as ensued. After the inauguration of the government at Montgomery, the Confederacy could have purchased the entire cotton crop—practically every bale left in the Southern States at that season—with Confederate bonds or with Confederate currency.   The people, as a rule, had absolute faith in the success and stability of the government. Thoughtful business men took the bonds as an investment.   Careful and conscientious guardians sold the property of minors and invested the proceeds in Confederate bonds.   If, therefore, Southern statesmen had believed that the Northern people would with practical unanimity back the United States Government in a vigorous and determined war to prevent the withdrawal of the Southern States, those able men who led the South would undoubtedly have sought to place the Confederacy in control of the cotton then on hand, and of succeeding crops.   It will be readily seen what an enormous financial strength would have been thus acquired, and what a basis for negotiations abroad would have been furnished.   When the price of cotton rose to twenty-five, forty, fifty cents per pound (it was worth, I think, over ninety cents per pound at one time), a navy for the Confederate Government could have been purchased strong enough to have broken, by concentrated effort, the blockade of almost any port on the Southern coast, thus admitting arms, ammunition, clothing, tents, and medicine, which would have largely increased the efficiency of the Confederate armies.

At last after the winter months, each one of which seemed to us almost a year, the snows on the Occoquan melted. The buds began to swell, the dogwood to blossom, and the wild onions, which the men gathered by the bushel and ate, began to shed their pungent odor on the soft warm air. With the spring came also the marching and the fighting. General McClellan landed his splendid army at Yorktown, and threatened Richmond from the Virginia peninsula. The rush then came to relieve from capture the small force of General Magruder and to confront General McClellan's army at his new base of operations. Striking camp and moving to the nearest depot, we were soon on the way to Yorktown. The long trains packed with their living Confederate freight were hurried along with the utmost possible speed. As the crowded train upon which I sat rushed under full head of steam down grade on this single track, it was met by another train of empty cars flying with great speed in the opposite direction. The crash of the fearful collision and its harrowing results are indescribable. Nearly every car on the densely packed train was telescoped and torn in pieces; and men, knapsacks, arms, and shivered seats were hurled to the front and piled in horrid mass against the crushed timbers and ironwork. Many were killed, many maimed for life, and the marvel is that any escaped unhurt. Mrs. Gordon, who was with me on this ill-fated train, was saved, by a merciful Providence, without the slightest injury. Her hands were busied with the wounded, while I superintended the cutting away of débris to rescue the maimed and remove the dead.

From Yorktown it was the Confederates' time to retreat, and it was a retreat to the very gates of Richmond. General Johnston, however, like a lion pursued to his den, turned upon McClellan, when there, with a tremendous bound.

On that memorable retreat it was my fortune for a time to bring up the rear. The roads were in horrible condition. In the mud and slush and deep ruts cut by the wagon-trains and artillery of the retreating army, a number of heavy guns became bogged and the horses were unable to drag them. My men, weary with the march and belonging to a different arm of the service, of course felt that it was a trying position to be compelled to halt and attempt to move this artillery, with the Union advance pressing so closely upon them. But they were tugging with good grace when I rode up from the extreme rear. An extraordinary effort, however, was required to save the guns. As I dismounted from my horse and waded into the deep mud and called on them to save the artillery, they raised a shout and crowded around the wheels. Not a gun or caisson was lost, and there was never again among those brave men a moment's hesitation about leaping into the mud and water whenever it became necessary on any account.

At another time on this march I found one of my youngest soldiers—he was a mere lad—lying on the roadside, weeping bitterly. I asked him what was the matter. He explained that his feet were so sore that he could not walk any farther and that he knew he would be captured. His feet were in a dreadful condition. I said to him, "You shall not be captured," and ordered him to mount my horse and ride forward until he could get into an ambulance or wagon, and to tell the quartermaster to send my horse back to me as soon as possible. He wiped his eyes, got into my saddle, and rode a few rods to where the company of which he was a member had halted to rest. He stopped his horse in front of his comrades, who were sitting for the moment on the roadside, and straightening himself up, he lifted his old slouch-hat with all the dignity of a commander-in-chief and called out: "Attention, men! I'm about to bid you farewell, and I want to tell you before I go that I am very sorry for you. I was poor once myself!" Having thus delivered himself, he galloped away, bowing and waving his hat to his comrades in acknowledgment of the cheers with which they greeted him.

After a few hours' pause and a brief but sharp engagement at Williamsburg, General Johnston continued his retreat to his new lines near the city of Richmond. On the banks of the Chickahominy, if the Chickahominy can be said to have banks, both armies prepared for the desperate struggles which were soon to follow and decide the fate of the Confederate capital. " On the Chickahominy ! " Whatever emotions these words may awaken in others, they bring to me some of the saddest memories of those four years, in which were crowded the experiences of an ordinary lifetime. Standing on picket posts in the dreary darkness and sickening dampness of its miasmatic swamps, hurrying to the front through the slush and bogs that bordered it, fighting hip-deep in its turbid waters, I can see now the faces of those brave men who never faltered at a command, whatever fate obedience to it might involve.

During the weary days and nights preceding these battles, the Southern troops, as they returned from outpost duty, kept the camp in roars of laughter with soldier "yarns" about their experiences at night at the front: how one man, relieved temporarily from guard duty by his comrade of the next relief, lay down on a log to catch a brief nap, and dreaming that he was at home in his little bed, turned himself over and fell off the log into the water at its side; how another, whose imagination had been impressed by his surroundings, made the outpost hideous with his frog-like croaking or snoring; and so on in almost endless variety. I recall one private who had a genius for drawing, and whose imaginative, clever caricatures afforded much amusement in camp. He would represent this or that comrade with a frog-like face and the body and legs of a frog, standing in the deep water, with knapsack high up on his back, his gun in one hand and a "johnny-cake" in the other—the title below it being Bill or Bob or Jake "on picket in the Chickahominy." A characteristic story is told of a mess that was formed, with the most remarkable regulations or by-laws. The men were to draw straws to ascertain who should be the cook. The by-laws further provided that the party thus designated should continue to cook for the mess until some one complained of his cooking, whereupon the man who made the first complaint should at once be initiated into the office and the former incumbent relieved. Of course, with this chance of escape before him, a cook had no great incentive to perfect himself in the culinary art. The first cook was not long in forcing a complaint. Calling his mess to supper spread on an oil-cloth in the little tent, he confidently awaited the result. One after another tasted and quickly withdrew from the repast. One member, who was very hungry and outraged at the character of the food, asked: "Joe, what do you call this stuff, anyhow?"

"That? Why, that's pie," said Joe. "Well," replied the hungry member, "if you call that pie, all I've got to say is, it's the ―― est pie that I ever tasted."

Then, suddenly remembering that the penalty for complaining was to take Joe's place, he quickly added, "But it's all right, Joe; I like it, but I am not hungry to-night." This after-thought came too late, however. The by-laws were inflexible, and Joe's supper had won his freedom. The poor complainant whose indignant stomach had slaughtered his prudence was quietly but promptly inducted into the position of chef for the mess.

Whatever rank may be assigned in history to the battle of Seven Pines, or Fair Oaks, as the Union men call it, it was to my regiment one of the bloodiest of my war experience. Hurled, in the early morning, against the breastworks which protected that portion of McClellan's lines, my troops swept over and captured them, but at heavy cost. As I spurred my horse over the works with my men, my adjutant, who rode at my side, fell heavily with his horse down the embankment, and both were killed. Reforming my men under a galling fire, and ordering them forward in another charge upon the supporting lines, which fought with the most stubborn resistance, disputing every foot of ground, I soon found that Lieutenant-Colonel Willingham, as gallant a soldier as ever rode through fire and who was my helper on the right, had also been killed and his horse with him. Major Nesmith, whose towering form I could still see on the left, was riding abreast of the men and shouting in trumpet tones: "Forward, men, forward!" but a ball soon silenced his voice forever. Lieutenant-colonel, major, adjutant, with their horses, were all dead, and I was left alone on horseback, with my men dropping rapidly around me. My soldiers declared that they distinctly heard the command from the Union lines, "Shoot that man on horseback." In both armies it was thought that the surest way to demoralize troops was to shoot down the officers. Nearly or quite half the line officers of the twelve companies had by this time fallen, dead or wounded. General Rodes, the superb brigade-commander, had been disabled. Still I had marvellously escaped, with only my clothing pierced. As I rode up and down my line, encouraging the men forward, I passed my young brother, only nineteen years old, but captain of one of the companies. He was lying with a number of dead companions near him. He had been shot through the lungs and was bleeding profusely. I did not stop; I could not stop, nor would he permit me to stop. There was no time for that—no time for anything except to move on and fire on. At this time my own horse, the only one left, was killed. He could, however, have been of little service to me any longer, for in the edge of this flooded swamp heavy timber had been felled, making an abatis quite impassable on horseback, and I should have been compelled to dismount. McClellan's men were slowly being pressed back into and through the Chickahominy swamp, which was filled with water; but at almost every step they were pouring terrific vollies into my lines. My regiment had been in some way separated from the brigade, and at this juncture seemed to reach the climax of extremities. My field officers and adjutant were all dead. Every horse ridden into the fight, my own among them, was dead. Fully one half of my line officers and half my men were dead or wounded. A furious fire still poured from the front, and reënforcements were nowhere in sight. The brigade-commander was disabled, and there was no horse or means at hand of communication with his headquarters or any other headquarters, except by one of my soldiers on foot, and the chances ten to one against his living to bear my message. In water from knee- to hip- deep, the men were fighting and falling, while a detail propped up the wounded against stumps or trees to prevent their drowning. Fresh troops in blue were moving to my right flank and pouring a raking fire down my line, and compelling me to change front with my companies there. In ordering Captain Bell, whom I had placed in command of that portion of my line, I directed that he should beat back that flanking force at any cost. This faithful officer took in at a glance the whole situation, and, with a courage that never was and never will be surpassed, he and his Spartan band fought until he and nearly all his men were killed; and the small remnant, less than one fifth of the number carried into the battle, were fighting still when the order came at last for me to withdraw. Even in the withdrawal there was no confusion, no precipitancy. Slowly moving back, carrying their wounded comrades with them, and firing as they moved, these shattered remnants of probably the largest regiment in the army took their place in line with the brigade.

The losses were appalling. All the field officers except myself had been killed. Of forty-four officers of the line, but thirteen were left for duty. Nearly two thirds of the entire command were killed or wounded. My young brother, Captain Augustus Gordon, who had been shot through the lungs, was carried back with the wounded. He recovered, and won rapid promotion by his high soldierly qualities, but fell at the head of his regiment in the Wilderness with his face to the front, a grape-shot having penetrated his breast at almost the same spot where he had been formerly struck.

The disabling of General Rodes left the brigade temporarily without a commander; but movement was succeeding movement and battle following battle so rapidly that some one had to be placed in command at once. This position fell to my lot. It was not only unexpected, but unwelcome and extremely embarrassing; for, of all the regimental commanders in the brigade, I was the junior in commission and far the youngest in years. My hesitation became known to my brother officers. With entire unanimity and a generosity rarely witnessed in any sphere of life, they did everything in their power to lessen my embarrassment and uphold my hands. No young man with grave responsibilities suddenly placed upon him ever had more constant or more efficient support than was given to me by these noble men.

I close this chapter by quoting a few sentences penned after the battle by Major John Sutherland Lewis in reference to the terrific strain upon Mrs. Gordon's sensibilities as she sat in sound of that battle's roar. Major Lewis was Mrs. Gordon's uncle, an elderly gentleman of rare accomplishments. As he was without a family of his own, and was devoted to his niece, he naturally watched over her with the tender solicitude of a father, when it was possible for him to be near her during the war. He died in very old age some years after the close of hostilities, but he left behind him touching tributes to his cherished niece, with whose remarkable adventures he was familiar, and whose fortitude had amazed and thrilled him. I quote only a few sentences from his pen in this connection:

The battle in which Mrs. Gordon's husband was then engaged was raging near the city with great fury. The cannonade was rolling around the horizon like some vast earthquake on huge crashing wheels. Whether the threads of wedded sympathy were twisted more closely as the tremendous perils gathered around him, it was evident that her anxiety became more and more intense with each passing moment. She asked me to accompany her to a hill a short distance away. There she listened in silence. Pale and quiet, with clasped hands, she sat statue-like, with her face toward the field of battle. Her self-control was wonderful; only the quick-drawn sigh from the bottom of the heart revealed the depth of emotion that was struggling there. The news of her husband's safety afterward and the joy of meeting him later produced the inevitable reaction. The intensity of mental strain to which she had been subjected had overtasked her strength, and when the excessive tension was relaxed she was well-nigh prostrated; but a brief repose enabled her to bear up with a sublime fortitude through the protracted and trying experiences which followed the seven days' battles around Richmond.

CHAPTER V

PRESENTIMENTS AND FATALISM AMONG SOLDIERS

Wonderful instances of prophetic foresight—Colonel Lomax predicts his death—The vision of a son dying two days before it happened—General Ramseur's furlough—Colonel Augustus Gordon's calm announcement of his death—Instances of misplaced fatalism—General D. H. Hill's indifference to danger.

AT the time of this battle I had brought to my immediate knowledge, for the first time, one of those strange presentiments or revelations, whatever they may be called, which so often came to soldiers of both armies. Colonel Tennant Lomax, of Alabama, was one of the leading citizens of that State. He was a man of recognized ability and the most exalted character. With a classic face and superb form, tall, erect, and commanding, he would have been selected among a thousand men as the ideal soldier. His very presence commanded respect and inspired confidence. None who knew him doubted his certain promotion to high command if his life were spared. The very embodiment of chivalry, he was among the first to respond to the call to arms, and, alas! he was among the earliest martyrs to the cause he so promptly espoused. As he rode into the storm of lead, he turned to me and said: "Give me your hand, Gordon, and let me bid you good-by. I am going to be killed in this battle. I shall be dead in half an hour." I endeavored to remove this impression from his mind, but nothing I could say changed or appeared to modify it in any degree. I was grieved to have him go into the fight with such a burden upon him, but there was no tremor in his voice, no hesitation in his words, no doubt on his mind. The genial smile that made his face so attractive was still upon it, but he insisted that he would be dead in half an hour, and that it was "all right." The half-hour had scarcely passed when the fatal bullet had numbered him with the dead.

Doubtless there were many of these presentiments which were misleading, but I am inclined to believe that those which were never realized were not such clear perceptions of coming fate as in this case. They were probably the natural and strong apprehensions which any man is liable to feel, indeed must feel if he is a reasonable being, as he goes into a consuming fire. There were many cases, however, which seemed veritable visions into futurity.

General J. Warren Keifer, of Springfield, Ohio, a prominent Union officer in the war between the States and Major-General of Volunteers in the recent war with Spain, gave me in a letter of January 18, 1898, an account of the accurate predictions made by two of his officers as to approaching death. The first case was that of Colonel Aaron W. Ebright, of the One Hundred and Twenty-sixth Ohio Regiment, who was killed at Opequan, Virginia, September 19, 1864. General Keifer encloses me this memorandum, written at some previous date:

Colonel Ebright had a premonition of his death. A few moments before 12 M. he sought me, and coolly told me he would be killed before the battle ended. He insisted upon telling me that he wanted his remains and effects sent to his home in Lancaster, Ohio, and I was asked to write his wife as to some property in the West which he feared she did not know about. He was impatient when I tried to remove the thought of imminent death from his mind. A few moments later the time for another advance came and the interview with Colonel Ebright closed.

In less than ten minutes, while he was riding near me, he fell dead from his horse, pierced in the breast by a rifle-ball. His apprehension of death was not prompted by fear. He had been through the slaughters of the Wilderness and Cold Harbor, had fought his regiment in the *dead-angle* of Spottsylvania, and led it at Monocacy. It is needless to say I complied with his request.

Another remarkable presentiment to which General Keifer has called my attention was that of Captain William A. Hathaway, who served on General Keifer's staff as assistant adjutant-general. At Monocacy, Maryland, July 9, 1864, where my division did the bulk of the fighting for the Confederates, Captain Hathaway assured his brother officers of the certainty of his early death. Turning a deaf ear to their efforts to drive the presentiment from his mind, he rode bravely into the storm, and fell at almost the first deadly volley.

Colonel Warren Akin was one of Georgia's leading lawyers before the war. He was a Whig and a Union man and opposed to secession, but followed his State when she left the Union. Although he was neither by profession nor practice a politician, his recognized ability, and the universal confidence of the people in his integrity as well as in his fidelity to every trust, caused his power to be felt in the State, and led a great political party to nominate him before the war as candidate for governor. Few men of his day were better known or more loved and respected. He was a Christian without cant, and his courage, while conspicuous, had in it none of the elements of wanton recklessness. He was a thoughtful, brave, and balanced man. In 1861 and 1863 he was Speaker of the Georgia House of Representatives. During the remainder of the war he was a member from Georgia of the Confederate House of Representatives, where he was an ardent and faithful champion of President Davis and his administration.

A revelation or soul-sight so strange and true came to him shortly before Lee's surrender that it seems necessary to accompany its insertion here by this hasty analysis of his exalted mental and moral characteristics. Just before day on the morning of February 8, 1865, while in Richmond, he had a vision—whether an actual dream or some inexplicable manifestation akin thereto he never knew. In this vision he saw his eldest son lying on his back at the foot of a chinaberry-tree on the sidewalk in front of the home he then occupied in Elberton, Georgia, his head in a pool of blood. He ran to him, found him not dead but speechless and unconscious, raised him up by his left hand, and the blood ran out of his right ear. With a start, Colonel Akin came to full consciousness, inexpressibly disturbed. He immediately decided to leave for home, telegraphic communication being cut off. But in a few minutes he received a cheerful letter from his wife, stating that all were well, and this reassured him. On the afternoon of the second day after, this son was thrown from a horse against this same chinaberry-tree, at the foot of which he lay, unconscious and speechless; and a neighbor, seeing him fall, ran up to him, grasped him by his left hand, and lifted him from the pool of blood which ran from his right ear. On the third day after the boy died, unconscious to the end. Colonel Akin knew nothing of his death until about three weeks later, no intelligence of the sad event reaching him sooner because of interrupted mails. Thus happened, two days after he foresaw it, a tragedy which from its nature was wholly unexpected, and which occurred in minutest detail exactly as Colonel Akin had seen it in his vision of the night.

Major-General Ramseur, of North Carolina, was an officer whose record was equalled by few in the Confederate army. He had won his major-general's stars and wreath by his notable efficiency on the march and in the camp, as well as in battle. Of the men of high rank in the army with whom I was intimately associated, none were further removed from superstition or vain and unreal fancies. He had been married since the war began, and there had been born to him, at his home in North Carolina, a son whom he had never seen. On the night preceding the great battle of Cedar Creek, the corps which I commanded, and in which he commanded a division, was filing slowly and cautiously in the darkness along the dim and almost impassable trail around the point, and just over the dangerous precipices of Massanutten Mountain. General Ramseur and I sat on the bluff overlooking the field on which he was soon to lay down his life. He talked most tenderly and beautifully of his wife and baby boy, whom he so longed to see. Finally, a little before dawn, the last soldier of the last division had passed the narrow defile, and the hour for the advance upon the Union forces had arrived. As General Ramseur was ready to ride into battle at the head of his splendid division, he said to me, "Well, general, I shall get my furlough to-day." I did not know what he meant. I did not ask what he meant. It was not a time for questions. But speedily the message came, and his furlough was granted. It came not by mail or wire from the War Department at Richmond, but from the blue lines in his front, flying on the bullet's wing. The chivalric soldier, the noble-hearted gentleman, the loving husband, had been furloughed—forever furloughed from earth's battles and cares.

My younger brother, Augustus Gordon, captain and later lieutenant-colonel, furnished another illustration of this remarkable foresight of approaching death. Brave and lovable, a modest though brilliant young soldier, he was rapidly winning his way to distinction. A youth of scarcely twenty-one years, he was in command of the Sixth Regiment of Alabama. Before going into the fight in the Wilderness, he quietly said: "My hour has come." I joked and chided him. I told him that he must not permit such impressions to affect or take hold upon his imagination. He quickly and firmly replied: "You need not doubt me. I will be at my post. But this is our last meeting." Riding at the head of his regiment, with his sword above him, the fire of battle in his eye and words of cheer for his men on his lips, the fatal grape-shot plunged through his manly heart, and the noble youth slept his last sleep in that woful Wilderness.

It would require a volume simply to record without comment the hundreds of such presentiments in both the Union and Confederate armies during the war. The few here noted will suffice, however, to raise the inquiry as to what they meant. Who shall furnish a satisfactory solution? What were these wonderful presentiments? They were not the outpourings of a disordered brain. They came from minds thoroughly balanced, clear and strong—minds which worked with the precision of perfect machinery, even amid the excitement and fury of battle. They were not the promptings of an unmanly fear of danger or apprehension of death; for no men ever faced both danger and death with more absolute self-poise, sublimer courage, or profounder consecration. Nor were these presentiments mere speculations as to chances. They were perceptions. There was about them no element of speculation. Their conspicuous characteristic was certainty. The knowledge seemed so firmly fixed that no argument as to possible mistake, no persuasion, could shake it. Where did that knowledge come from? It seems to me there can be but one answer, and that answer is another argument for immortality. It was the whispering of the Infinite beyond us to the Infinite within us—a whispering inaudible to the natural ear, but louder than the roar of battle to the spirit that heard it.

There was another class of soldiers who had a sort of blind faith in their own invulnerability; but it differed wholly, radically, from the presentiments which I am considering. Several of these cases came also under my immediate observation. In one case, this blind faith, as I term it, was the result of long army experience of the man whose remarkable escape from wounds in several wars had left upon his mind its natural effect. In another case it was a highly developed belief in the doctrine of predestination, which gave great comfort to its possessor, adding to the courage that was inherent in him another element which rendered him indifferent, apparently, to exposure to fire or protection from it.

The first illustration was that of a soldier under my command—Vickers of the Sixth Alabama Regiment. There was no better soldier in either army than Vickers. He had passed unscathed through two previous wars, in Mexico, I believe, and in Nicaragua. He was in every battle with his regiment in our Civil War until his death, and always at the front. The greater the danger, the higher his spirits seemed to soar. The time came, however, when his luck, or fate, in whose fickle favor he so implicitly trusted, deserted him. At Antietam—Sharpsburg—I called for some one who was willing to take the desperate chances of carrying a message from me to the commander on my right. Vickers promptly volunteered, with some characteristic remark which indicated his conviction that he was not born to be killed in battle. There was a cross-fire from two directions through which he had to pass and of which he had been advised; but he bounded away with the message almost joyously. He had not gone many steps from my side when a ball through his head, the first and last that ever struck him, had placed this brave soldier beyond the possibility of realizing, in this world at least, the treachery of that fate on which he depended.

The other case was that of Lieutenant-General D. H. Hill, and the particular occasion which I select, and which aptly illustrates his remarkable faith, was the battle of Malvern Hill. At that time he was major-general of the division in which I commanded Rodes's brigade. He was my friend. The personal and official relations between us, considering the disparity in our ages, were most cordial and even intimate. He was closely allied to Stonewall Jackson, and in many respects his counterpart. His brilliant career as a soldier is so well known that any historical account of it, in such a book as I am writing, would be wholly unnecessary. I introduce him here as a most conspicuous illustration of a faith in Providence which, in its steadiness and strength and in its sustaining influence under great peril, certainly touched the margin of the sublime. At Malvern Hill, where General McClellan made his superb and last stand against General Lee's forces, General Hill took his seat at the root of a large tree and began to write his orders. At this point McClellan's batteries from the crest of a high ridge, and his gunboats from the James River, were ploughing up the ground in every direction around us. The long shells from the gunboats, which our men called "McClellan's gate-posts," and the solid shot from his heavy guns on land, were knocking the Confederate batteries to pieces almost as fast as they could be placed in position. The Confederate artillerists fell so rapidly that I was compelled to detail untrained infantry to take their places. And yet there sat that intrepid officer, General D. H. Hill, in the midst of it all, coolly writing his orders. He did not place the large tree between himself and the destructive batteries, but sat facing them. I urged him to get on the other side of the tree and avoid such needless and reckless exposure. He replied, "Don't worry about me; look after the men. I am not going to be killed until my time comes." He had scarcely uttered these words when a shell exploded in our immediate presence, severely shocking me for the moment, a portion of it tearing through the breast of his coat and rolling him over in the newly ploughed ground. This seemed to convert him to a more rational faith; for he rose from the ground, and, shaking the dirt from his uniform, quietly took his seat on the other side of the tree.

As for myself, I was never in a battle without realizing that every moment might be my last; but I never had a presentiment of certain death at a given time or in a particular battle. There did come to me, on one occasion, a feeling that was akin to a presentiment. It was, however, the result of no supposed perception of certain coming fate, but an unbidden, unwelcome calculation of chances—suggested by the peculiar circumstances in which I found myself at the time. It was at Winchester, in the Valley of Virginia. My command was lying almost in the shadow of a frowning fortress in front, in which General Milroy, of the Union army, was strongly intrenched with forces which we had been fighting during the afternoon. In the dim twilight, with the glimmer of his bayonets and brass howitzers still discernible, I received an order to storm the fortress at daylight the next morning. To say that I was astounded at the order would feebly express the sensation which its reading produced; for on either side of the fort was an open country, miles in width, through which Confederate troops could easily pass around and to the rear of the fort, cutting off General Milroy from the base of his supplies, and thus forcing him to retire and meet us in the open field. There was nothing for me to do, however, but to obey the order. As in the night I planned the assault and thought of the dreadful slaughter that awaited my men, there came to me, as I have stated, a calculation as to chances, which resulted in the conclusion that I had not one chance in a thousand to live through it. The weary hours of the night had nearly passed, and by the dim light of my bivouac fire I wrote, with pencil, what I supposed was my last letter to Mrs. Gordon, who, as usual, was near me. I summoned my quartermaster, whose duties did not call him into the fight, and gave him the letter, with directions to deliver it to Mrs. Gordon after I was dead. Mounting my horse, my men now ready, I spoke to them briefly and encouraged them to go with me into the fort. Before the dawn we were moving, and soon ascending the long slope. At every moment I expected the storm of shell and ball that would end many a life, my own among them; but on we swept, and into the fort, to find not a soldier there! It had been evacuated during the night.

CHAPTER VI

BATTLE OF MALVERN HILL

Continuous fighting between McClellan's and Lee's armies—Hurried
burial of the dead—How "Stonewall" Jackson got his name—The
secret of his wonderful power—The predicament of my command at
Malvern Hill—A fruitless wait for reënforcements—Character the
basis of true courage—Anecdote of General Polk.

AFTER the bloody encounter at Seven Pines, or Fair
Oaks, the dead of both armies were gathered, under
a flag of truce, for burial. An inspection of the field
revealed a scene sickening and shocking to those whose
sensibilities were not yet blunted by almost constant
contact with such sights. It would not require a very
vivid imagination to write of Chickahominy's flooded
swamps as "incarnadined waters," in which floated side
by side the dead bodies clad in blue and in gray. All
over the field near the swamp were scattered in indis-
criminate confusion the motionless forms and ghastly
faces of fellow-countrymen who had fallen bravely fighting each other in a battle for principles—enemies the
day before, but brothers then in the cold embrace of an
honorable death. Dying at each other's hands in support of profoundly cherished convictions, their released
spirits had ascended together on the battle's flame to
receive the reward of the unerring tribunal of last appeal.

The fighting between the armies of McClellan and Lee
was so nearly continuous, and engagement succeeded
engagement so rapidly, that at some points the killed

were hurriedly and imperfectly buried. I myself had a most disagreeable reminder of this fact. The losses in Rodes's brigade, which I was then commanding, had been so heavy that it was held with other troops as a reserved corps. Our experiences, however, on the particular day of which I now speak had been most trying, and after nightfall I was directed to move to a portion of the field where the fighting had been desperate on the preceding day, and to halt for the night in a woodland. Overcome with excessive fatigue, as soon as the designated point was reached I delivered my horse to a courier and dropped down on the ground for a much-needed rest. In a few moments I was sound asleep. A slightly elevated mound of earth served for a pillow. Frequently during the night I attempted to brush away from my head what I thought in my slumber was a twig or limb of the underbrush in which I was lying. My horror can be imagined when I discovered, the next morning, that it was the hand of a dead soldier sticking out above the shallow grave which had been my pillow and in which he had been only partly covered.

Up to this period my association with General Jackson (Stonewall) had not been sufficiently close for me clearly to comprehend the secret of his wonderful success, but I learned it a few days later at Malvern Hill. The sobriquet " Stonewall " was applied to him during the first great engagement of the war at Manassas, or Bull Run. His brigade was making a superb stand against General McDowell's column, which had been thrown with such momentum upon the Southern flank as to threaten the destruction of the whole army. General Bee, of South Carolina, whose blood was almost the earliest sprinkled on the Southern altar, determined to lead his own brigade to another charge, and looking across the field, he saw Jackson's men firmly, stubbornly resisting the Federal advance. General Bee, in order to kindle in the breasts of his men the ardor that glowed in his own, pointed to Jackson's line and exclaimed: "See, there stands Jackson like a stone wall!" Bee himself fell in the charge, but he had christened Jackson and his brigade by attaching to them a peculiar and distinctive name which will live while the history of our Civil War lives.

I have said that at Malvern Hill I learned the secret of Jackson's wonderful power and success as a soldier. It was due not only to his keen and quick perception of the situation in which he found himself at each moment in the rapidly changing scenes as the battle progressed or before it began, but notably to an implicit faith in his own judgment when once made up. He would formulate that judgment, risk his last man upon its correctness, and deliver the stunning blow, while others less gifted were hesitating and debating as to its wisdom and safety. Whatever this peculiar power may be called, this mental or moral gift, whether inspiration or intuition, it was in him a profound conviction that he was not mistaken, that the result would demonstrate that the means he employed must necessarily attain the end which he thought to accomplish. The incident to which I refer was trivial in itself, but it threw a flood of light upon his marvellous endowment. I sat on my horse, facing him and receiving instructions from him, when Major-General Whiting, himself an officer of high capacity, rode up in great haste and interrupted Jackson as he was giving to me a message to General Hill. With some agitation, Whiting said: "General Jackson, I find, sir, that I cannot accomplish what you have directed unless you send me some additional infantry and another battery"; and he then proceeded to give the reasons why the order could not be executed with the forces at his disposal. All this time, while Whiting explained and argued, Jackson sat on his horse like a stone statue. He looked neither to the right nor the left. He made no comment and asked no questions; but when Whiting had finished, Jackson turned his flashing eyes upon him and used these words, and only these: "I have told you what I wanted done, General Whiting"; and planting his spurs in his horse's sides, he dashed away at a furious speed to another part of the field. Whiting gazed at Jackson's disappearing figure in amazement, if not in anger, and then rode back to his command. The result indicated the accuracy of Jackson's judgment and the infallibility of his genius, for Whiting did accomplish precisely what Jackson intended, and he did it with the force which Jackson had placed in his hands.

Returning, after my interview with Jackson, to my position on the extreme right, I found General Hill in a fever of impatience for the advance upon McClellan's troops, who were massed, with their batteries, on the heights in our front. The hour for the general assault which was to be made in the afternoon by the whole Confederate army had come and passed. There had been, however, the delays usual in all such concerted movements. Some of the divisions had not arrived upon the field; others, from presumably unavoidable causes, had not taken their places in line: and the few remaining hours of daylight were passing. Finally a characteristic Confederate yell was heard far down the line. It was supposed to be the beginning of the proposed general assault. General Hill ordered me to lead the movement on the right, stating that he would hurry in the supports to take their places on both my flanks and in rear of my brigade. I made the advance, but the supports did not come. Indeed, with the exception of one other brigade, which was knocked to pieces in a few minutes, no troops came in view. Isolated from the rest of the army and alone, my brigade moved across this shell-ploughed plain toward the heights, which were per-

haps more than half a mile away. Within fifteen or
twenty minutes the centre regiment (Third Alabama),
with which I moved, had left more than half of its number
dead and wounded along its track, and the other regiments had suffered almost as severely. One shell had
killed six or seven men in my immediate presence. My
pistol, on one side, had the handle torn off; my canteen,
on the other, was pierced, emptying its contents—water
merely—on my trousers; and my coat was ruined by
having a portion of the front torn away: but, with the
exception of this damage, I was still unhurt. At the foot
of the last steep ascent, near the batteries, I found that
McClellan's guns were firing over us, and as any further
advance by this unsupported brigade would have been
not only futile but foolhardy, I halted my men and
ordered them to lie down and fire upon McClellan's
standing lines of infantry. I stood upon slightly elevated ground in order to watch for the reënforcements,
or for any advance from the heights upon my command.
In vain I looked behind us for the promised support.
Anxiously I looked forward, fearing an assault upon my
exposed position. No reënforcements came until it was
too late. As a retreat in daylight promised to be almost
or quite as deadly as had been the charge, my desire for
the relief which nothing but darkness could now bring
can well be imagined. In this state of extreme anxiety
a darkness which was unexpected and terrible came to
me alone. A great shell fell, buried itself in the ground,
and exploded near where I stood. It heaved the dirt over
me, filling my face and ears and eyes with sand. I was literally blinded. Not an inch before my face could I see;
but I could think, and thoughts never ran more swiftly
through a perplexed mortal brain. Blind! Blind in
battle! Was this to be permanent? Suppose reënforcements now came, what was I to do? Suppose there
should be an assault upon my command from the front?

Such were the unspoken but agonizing questions which throbbed in my brain with terrible swiftness and intensity. The blindness, however, was of short duration. The delicate and perfect machinery of the eye soon did its work. At last came, also, the darkness for which I longed, and under its thick veil this splendid brigade was safely withdrawn.

Large bodies of troops had been sent forward, or rather led forward, by that intrepid commander, General Hill; but the unavoidable delay in reaching the locality, and other intervening difficulties, prevented them from ever reaching the advanced position from which my men withdrew. In the hurry and bustle of trying to get them forward, coming as they did from different directions, there was necessarily much confusion, and they were subjected to the same destructive fire through which my troops had previously passed. In the darkness, even after the firing had ceased, there occurred, in the confusion, among these mixed up bodies of men, many amusing mistakes as to identity, and some altercations between officers which were not so amusing and not altogether complimentary. One of my men ran to me and asked, "Did you hear —— say to —— that he and his men," etc.—I forbear to quote the remaining part of the question. I replied that I had not heard it, but if it had occurred as reported to me we would probably hear of it again—and we did. Early the next morning a challenge was sent, but the officer who had given the offence was in a playful mood when the challenge reached him; so, instead of accepting it, or answering it in the formal style required by the duelling code, he replied in about these words:

MY DEAR ——: I did not volunteer to fight you or any other Confederate, but if you and your men will do better in the next battle I will take back all I said to you last night. In the meantime, I am,   Very truly yours,   ——.

These officers are both dead now, and I give this incomplete account of the incident to show how easy it was to get up a fight along in the sixties, if one were so disposed, either in a general mêlée with the blue-coated lines, or single-handed with a gray-clad comrade.

I believe it was in this battle that was first perpetrated that rustic witticism which afterward became so famous in the army. Through one of the wide gaps made in the Confederate lines by McClellan's big guns as they sent their death-dealing missiles from hill and river, there ran a panic-stricken rabbit, flying in terror to the rear. A stalwart mountaineer noticed the speed and the direction which the rabbit took to escape from his disagreeable surroundings. He was impressed by the rabbit's prudence, and shouted, so that his voice was heard above the din of the battle: "Go it, Molly Cottontail! I wish I could go with you!" One of his comrades near by caught up the refrain, and answered: "Yes, and, 'y golly, Jim, I'd go with Molly, too, if it wasn't for my character."

"Character." What a centre shot this rough soldier had fired in that short sentence! He had analyzed unconsciously but completely the loftiest type of courage. He felt like flying to the rear, as "Molly" was flying, but his character carried him forward. His sense of the awful dangers, the ominous hissing of the deadly Minié balls, and the whizzing of the whirling shells tearing through the ranks and scattering the severed limbs of his falling comrades around him, all conspired to bid him fly to the rear; but his character, that noblest of human endowments, commanded, "Forward!" and forward he went.

In this connection I am reminded of the commonplace but important truth that the aggregate character of a people of any country depends upon the personal character of its individual citizens; and that the stability of popular government depends far more upon the character, the individual personal character of its people, than it does upon any constitution that could be adopted or statutes that could be enacted. What would safeguards be worth if the character of the people did not sustain and enforce them? The constitution would be broken, the laws defied; riot and anarchy would destroy both, and with them the government itself. I am not assuming or suggesting that this country is in any present danger of such an experience; but of all the countries on earth this one, with its universal suffrage, its divergent and conflicting interests, its immense expanse of territory, and its large population, made up from every class and clime, and still to be increased in the coming years, is far more dependent than any other upon the character of its people. It is a great support to our hope for the future and to our confidence in the stability of this government to recall now and then some illustration of the combination of virtues which make up character, as they gleam with peculiar lustre through the darkest hours of our Civil War period. That war not only gave the occasion for its exhibition, but furnished the food upon which character fed and grew strong. There were many thousands of men in both armies who did not say in words, but said by deeds, that "character" would not let them consult their fears or obey the impulse of their heels. I could fill this book with such cases, and yet confine myself to either one of the armies.

I received the particulars of another incident illustrating this truth from a Union officer who was present when the desperate and successful effort was made to hold the little fort at Altoona, Georgia, against the assault by the Confederates. They had surrounded it and demanded its surrender. The demand was refused, whereupon an awful and consuming fire was opened upon the small force locked up in the little fortress.

Steadily and rapidly the men fell in the fort. No place could be found within its dirt walls where even the wounded could be laid, so as to protect them from the galling Confederate fire; but still they fought and refused to surrender. Finally, in utter despair, some one proposed to raise the white flag. Instantly there rang around the fort a chorus of indignant protest: "Who says surrender? Shoot the man who proposes it!" In the face of the fact that at every moment the men were dying, and that apparently certain destruction awaited all, what was it that inspired that protest against surrender? There is but one answer. It was character. Those men had been ordered there to hold that fort. A grave responsibility had been imposed; a trust of most serious nature had been committed to them; and although their commander had been shot down, all the officers killed or wounded, and the ammunition nearly exhausted, yet their manhood, their fidelity, their character bade them fight on. They had no "Molly," with its white cotton-tail, bidding them fly to the rear, but they did have the suggestion of the white flag. Around them, as around the high-spirited Confederate at Malvern Hill, the storm of death in wildest fury was raging; and in both cases, as in ten thousand other cases, they turned a deaf ear to all suggestions of personal danger. The answer to such suggestions, though differing in phraseology, was the same in both cases—character.

While the heroic men at Altoona were rapidly falling but still fighting, with chances of successful resistance diminishing as each dreadful moment passed, the signal-flag from a spur of Kennesaw Mountain sent them that famous message from General Sherman: "Hold the fort. I am coming."

During a visit to northern Pennsylvania, in recent years, an officer of that signal corps stated incidentally that they had succeeded in interpreting the Confederate signals, and that while General Johnston's army was at Kennesaw this Union corps caught the signal message announcing that Lieutenant-General Polk had just been killed, and that the fact was announced in the Northern papers as soon, or perhaps before, it was announced to the Southern troops. It is probable that the signal corps of the Southern armies were at times able to interpret the signals of the other side. In one way or another, the high secrets of the two sides generally leaked out and became the property of the opponents by right of capture.

The reference to General's Polk's death recalls an anecdote told of him in the army, which aptly illustrates the great enthusiasm with which he fought, and which he never failed to impart to his splendid corps. General Leonidas Polk was a prince among men and an officer of marked ability. He was a bishop of the Episcopal Church. His character was beautiful in its simplicity and its strength. He was an ardent admirer of General Cheatham, who was one of the most furious fighters of Johnston's army. Cheatham, when the furor of battle was on him, was in the habit of using four monosyllables which were more expressive than polished, but in his case they expressed with tremendous emphasis the "gloria certaminis." These four monosyllables, which became notable in the army as "Cheatham's expression," were: "Give 'em hell, boys!" General Polk, as I have said, was an ardent admirer of General Cheatham as a soldier, and on one occasion, as the bishop-general rode along his lines, when they were charging the works in front, and as the rebel yell rang out his natural enthusiasm carried him, for the moment, off his balance. In the exhilaration of the charge the bishop was lost in the soldier, and he shouted: "Give it to 'em, boys! Give 'em what General Cheatham says!"

CHAPTER VII

ANTIETAM

Restoration of McClellan to command of the Federals—My command
at General Lee's centre—Remarkable series of bayonet charges by
the Union troops—How the centre was held—Bravery of the Union
commander—A long struggle for life.

THE war had now assumed proportions altogether
vaster than had been anticipated by either the
North or the South. No man at the North, perhaps no
man on either side, had at its beginning a clearer perception of the probable magnitude of the struggle than
General W. T. Sherman. Although he was regarded
even then by his people as an officer of unusual promise,
and a typical representative of the courage and constancy of the stalwart sons of the great West, yet he
called upon himself and his prophecy the criticism of
those whose views did not accord with his predictions.
However uncomfortable these criticisms may have been
to his friends, they did not seem to disturb his equa-
nimity or force him to modify his opinion that it would
require a vastly larger army than was generally supposed
necessary to penetrate the heart of the South. He seemed
to have, at that early period, a well-defined idea of the
desperate resistance to be made by the Southern people.
Possibly this ability to look into the future may have
been in some measure due to a superior knowledge of
the characteristics of the Southern people acquired during his former residence among them; but whatever the

source of his information, General Sherman lived to see the correctness of his opinions abundantly verified. Some years after the war, when General Sherman visited Atlanta, the brilliant and witty Henry W. Grady, in a speech made to him on his arrival, playfully referred to the former visit of the general, and to the condition in which that visit had left the city. Grady said: " And they do say, general, that you are a little careless about fire." General Sherman must have felt compensated for any allusions to the marks he had left when "marching through Georgia" by the courtesies shown him while in Atlanta, as well as by the people's appreciation of the remarkably generous terms offered by him to General Johnston's army at the surrender in North Carolina. Those terms were rejected in Washington because of their liberality.

Like two mighty giants preparing for a test of strength, the Union and Confederate armies now arrayed themselves for still bloodier encounters. In this encounter the one went down, and in that the other; but each rose from its fall, if not with renewed strength, at least with increased resolve. In the Southwest, as well as in Virginia, the blows between the mighty contestants came fast and hard. Both were in the field for two and a half years more of the most herculean struggle the world has ever witnessed.

At Antietam, or Sharpsburg, as the Confederates call it, on the soil of Maryland, occurred one of the most desperate though indecisive battles of modern times. The Union forces numbered about 60,000, the Confederates about 35,000. This battle left its lasting impress upon my body as well as upon my memory.

General George B. McClellan, after his displacement, had been again assigned to the command of the Union forces. The restoration of this brilliant soldier seemed to have imparted new life to that army. Vigorously following up the success achieved at South Mountain, McClellan, on the 16th day of September, 1862, marshalled his veteran legions on the eastern hills bordering the Antietam. On the opposite slopes, near the picturesque village of Sharpsburg, stood the embattled lines of Lee. As these vast American armies, the one clad in blue and the other in gray, stood contemplating each other from the adjacent hills, flaunting their defiant banners, they presented an array of martial splendor that was not equalled, perhaps, on any other field. It was in marked contrast with other battle-grounds. On the open plain, where stood these hostile hosts in long lines, listening in silence for the signal summoning them to battle, there were no breastworks, no abatis, no intervening woodlands, nor abrupt hills, nor hiding-places, nor impassable streams. The space over which the assaulting columns were to march, and on which was soon to occur the tremendous struggle, consisted of smooth and gentle undulations and a narrow valley covered with green grass and growing corn. From the position assigned me near the centre of Lee's lines, both armies and the entire field were in view. The scene was not only magnificent to look upon, but the realization of what it meant was deeply impressive. Even in times of peace our sensibilities are stirred by the sight of a great army passing in review. How infinitely more thrilling in the dread moments before the battle to look upon two mighty armies upon the same plain, "beneath spread ensigns and bristling bayonets," waiting for the impending crash and sickening carnage!

Behind McClellan's army the country was open and traversed by broad macadamized roads leading to Washington and Baltimore. The defeat, therefore, or even the total rout of Union forces, meant not necessarily the destruction of that army, but, more probably, its temporary disorganization and rapid retreat through a country abounding in supplies, and toward cities rich in men and means. Behind Lee's Confederates, on the other hand, was the Potomac River, too deep to be forded by his infantry, except at certain points. Defeat and total rout of his army meant, therefore, not only its temporary disorganization, but its possible destruction. And yet that bold leader did not hesitate to give battle. Such was his confidence in the steadfast courage and oft-tested prowess of his troops that he threw his lines across McClellan's front with their backs against the river. Doubtless General Lee would have preferred, as all prudent commanders would, to have the river in his front instead of his rear; but he wisely, as the sequel proved, elected to order Jackson from Harper's Ferry, and, with his entire army, to meet McClellan on the eastern shore rather than risk the chances of having the Union commander assail him while engaged in crossing the Potomac.

On the elevated points beyond the narrow valley the Union batteries were rolled into position, and the Confederate heavy guns unlimbered to answer them. For one or more seconds, and before the first sounds reached us, we saw the great volumes of white smoke rolling from the mouths of McClellan's artillery. The next second brought the roar of the heavy discharges and the loud explosions of hostile shells in the midst of our lines, inaugurating the great battle. The Confederate batteries promptly responded; and while the artillery of both armies thundered, McClellan's compact columns of infantry fell upon the left of Lee's lines with the crushing weight of a land-slide. The Confederate battle line was too weak to withstand the momentum of such a charge. Pressed back, but neither hopelessly broken nor dismayed, the Southern troops, enthused by Lee's presence, reformed their lines, and, with a shout as piercing as the blast of a thousand bugles, rushed in counter-charge upon the exulting Federals, hurled them back in confusion, and recovered all the ground that had been lost. Again and again, hour after hour, by charges and counter-charges, this portion of the field was lost and recovered, until the green corn that grew upon it looked as if it had been struck by a storm of bloody hail.

Up to this hour not a shot had been fired in my front. There was an ominous lull on the left. From sheer exhaustion, both sides, like battered and bleeding athletes, seemed willing to rest. General Lee took advantage of the respite and rode along his lines on the right and centre. He was accompanied by Division Commander General D. H. Hill. With that wonderful power which he possessed of divining the plans and purposes of his antagonist, General Lee had decided that the Union commander's next heavy blow would fall upon our centre, and those of us who held that important position were notified of this conclusion. We were cautioned to be prepared for a determined assault and urged to hold that centre at any sacrifice, as a break at that point would endanger his entire army. My troops held the most advanced position on this part of the field, and there was no supporting line behind us. It was evident, therefore, that my small force was to receive the first impact of the expected charge and to be subjected to the deadliest fire. To comfort General Lee and General Hill, and especially to make, if possible, my men still more resolute of purpose, I called aloud to these officers as they rode away: "These men are going to stay here, General, till the sun goes down or victory is won." Alas! many of the brave fellows are there now.

General Lee had scarcely reached his left before the predicted assault came. The day was clear and beautiful, with scarcely a cloud in the sky. The men in blue filed down the opposite slope, crossed the little stream (Antietam), and formed in my front, an assaulting column four lines deep. The front line came to a "charge

bayonets," the other lines to a "right shoulder shift."
The brave Union commander, superbly mounted, placed
himself in front, while his band in rear cheered them
with martial music. It was a thrilling spectacle. The
entire force, I concluded, was composed of fresh troops
from Washington or some camp of instruction. So far
as I could see, every soldier wore white gaiters around
his ankles. The banners above them had apparently
never been discolored by the smoke and dust of battle.
Their gleaming bayonets flashed like burnished silver in
the sunlight. With the precision of step and perfect
alignment of a holiday parade, this magnificent array
moved to the charge, every step keeping time to the tap
of the deep-sounding drum. As we stood looking upon
that brilliant pageant, I thought, if I did not say, " What
a pity to spoil with bullets such a scene of martial
beauty!" But there was nothing else to do. Mars is
not an æsthetic god; and he was directing every part
of this game in which giants were the contestants. On
every preceding field where I had been engaged it had
been my fortune to lead or direct charges, and not to receive them; or else to move as the tides of battle swayed
in the one direction or the other. Now my duty was to
move neither to the front nor to the rear, but to stand
fast, holding that centre under whatever pressure and
against any odds.

Every act and movement of the Union commander in
my front clearly indicated his purpose to discard bullets and depend upon bayonets. He essayed to break
through Lee's centre by the crushing weight and momentum of his solid column. It was my business to
prevent this; and how to do it with my single line was
the tremendous problem which had to be solved, and
solved quickly; for the column was coming. As I saw
this solid mass of men moving upon me with determined
step and front of steel, every conceivable plan of meet-

ing and repelling it was rapidly considered. To oppose
man against man and strength against strength was
impossible; for there were four lines of blue to my one
of gray. My first impulse was to open fire upon the
compact mass as soon as it came within reach of my
rifles, and to pour into its front an incessant hail-storm
of bullets during its entire advance across the broad,
open plain; but after a moment's reflection that plan
was also discarded. It was rejected because, during the
few minutes required for the column to reach my line, I
could not hope to kill and disable a sufficient number of
the enemy to reduce his strength to an equality with
mine. The only remaining plan was one which I had
never tried but in the efficacy of which I had the utmost
faith. It was to hold my fire until the advancing Federals were almost upon my lines, and then turn loose a
sheet of flame and lead into their faces. I did not believe that any troops on earth, with empty guns in their
hands, could withstand so sudden a shock and withering
a fire. The programme was fixed in my own mind, all
horses were sent to the rear, and my men were at once
directed to lie down upon the grass and clover. They
were quickly made to understand, through my aides and
line officers, that the Federals were coming upon them
with unloaded guns; that not a shot would be fired at
them, and that not one of our rifles was to be discharged
until my voice should be heard from the centre commanding "Fire!" They were carefully instructed in the
details. They were notified that I would stand at the
centre, watching the advance, while they were lying
upon their breasts with rifles pressed to their shoulders,
and that they were not to expect my order to fire until
the Federals were so close upon us that every Confederate bullet would take effect.

There was no artillery at this point upon either side,
and not a rifle was discharged. The stillness was liter-

ally oppressive, as in close order, with the commander
still riding in front, this column of Union infantry moved
majestically in the charge. In a few minutes they were
within easy range of our rifles, and some of my impatient men asked permission to fire. "Not yet," I replied.
"Wait for the order." Soon they were so close that we
might have seen the eagles on their buttons; but my
brave and eager boys still waited for the order. Now
the front rank was within a few rods of where I stood.
It would not do to wait another second, and with all my
lung power I shouted "Fire!"

My rifles flamed and roared in the Federals' faces like
a blinding blaze of lightning accompanied by the quick
and deadly thunderbolt. The effect was appalling. The
entire front line, with few exceptions, went down in the
consuming blast. The gallant commander and his horse
fell in a heap near where I stood—the horse dead, the
rider unhurt. Before his rear lines could recover from
the terrific shock, my exultant men were on their feet,
devouring them with successive volleys. Even then
these stubborn blue lines retreated in fairly good order.
My front had been cleared; Lee's centre had been saved;
and yet not a drop of blood had been lost by my men.
The result, however, of this first effort to penetrate the
Confederate centre did not satisfy the intrepid Union
commander. Beyond the range of my rifles he reformed
his men into three lines, and on foot led them to the
second charge, still with unloaded guns. This advance
was also repulsed; but again and again did he advance
in four successive charges in the fruitless effort to break
through my lines with the bayonets. Finally his troops
were ordered to load. He drew up in close rank and
easy range, and opened a galling fire upon my line.

I must turn aside from my story at this point to express my regret that I have never been able to ascertain
the name of this lion-hearted Union officer. His indom-

itable will and great courage have been equalled on other fields and in both armies; but I do not believe they have ever been surpassed. Just before I fell and was borne unconscious from the field, I saw this undaunted commander attempting to lead his men in another charge.

The fire from these hostile American lines at close quarters now became furious and deadly. The list of the slain was lengthened with each passing moment. I was not at the front when, near nightfall, the awful carnage ceased; but one of my officers long afterward assured me that he could have walked on the dead bodies of my men from one end of the line to the other. This, perhaps, was not literally true; but the statement did not greatly exaggerate the shocking slaughter. Before I was wholly disabled and carried to the rear, I walked along my line and found an old man and his son lying side by side. The son was dead, the father mortally wounded. The gray-haired hero called me and said: "Here we are. My boy is dead, and I shall go soon; but it is all right." Of such were the early volunteers.

My extraordinary escapes from wounds in all the previous battles had made a deep impression upon my comrades as well as upon my own mind. So many had fallen at my side, so often had balls and shells pierced and torn my clothing, grazing my body without drawing a drop of blood, that a sort of blind faith possessed my men that I was not to be killed in battle. This belief was evidenced by their constantly repeated expressions: "They can't hurt him." "He's as safe one place as another." "He's got a charmed life."

If I had allowed these expressions of my men to have any effect upon my mind the impression was quickly dissipated when the Sharpsburg storm came and the whizzing Miniés, one after another, began to pierce my body.

The first volley from the Union lines in my front sent a ball through the brain of the chivalric Colonel Tew, of North Carolina, to whom I was talking, and another ball through the calf of my right leg. On the right and the left my men were falling under the death-dealing cross-fire like trees in a hurricane. The persistent Federals, who had lost so heavily from repeated repulses, seemed now determined to kill enough Confederates to make the debits and credits of the battle's balance-sheet more nearly even. Both sides stood in the open at short range and without the semblance of breastworks, and the firing was doing a deadly work. Higher up in the same leg I was again shot; but still no bone was broken. I was able to walk along the line and give encouragement to my resolute riflemen, who were firing with the coolness and steadiness of peace soldiers in target practice. When later in the day the third ball pierced my left arm, tearing asunder the tendons and mangling the flesh, they caught sight of the blood running down my fingers, and these devoted and big-hearted men, while still loading their guns, pleaded with me to leave them and go to the rear, pledging me that they would stay there and fight to the last. I could not consent to leave them in such a crisis. The surgeons were all busy at the field-hospitals in the rear, and there was no way, therefore, of stanching the blood, but I had a vigorous constitution, and this was doing me good service.

A fourth ball ripped through my shoulder, leaving its base and a wad of clothing in its track. I could still stand and walk, although the shocks and loss of blood had left but little of my normal strength. I remembered the pledge to the commander that we would stay there till the battle ended or night came. I looked at the sun. It moved very slowly; in fact, it seemed to stand still. I thought I saw some wavering in my line, near the extreme right, and Private Vickers, of Alabama, volunteered to carry any orders I might wish to send. I directed him to go quickly and remind the men of the pledge to General Lee, and to say to them that I was still on the field and intended to stay there. He bounded away like an Olympic racer; but he had gone less than fifty yards when he fell, instantly killed by a ball through his head. I then attempted to go myself, although I was bloody and faint, and my legs did not bear me steadily. I had gone but a short distance when I was shot down by a fifth ball, which struck me squarely in the face, and passed out, barely missing the jugular vein. I fell forward and lay unconscious with my face in my cap; and it would seem that I might have been smothered by the blood running into my cap from this last wound but for the act of some Yankee, who, as if to save my life, had at a previous hour during the battle, shot a hole through the cap, which let the blood out.

I was borne on a litter to the rear, and recall nothing more till revived by stimulants at a late hour of the night. I found myself lying on a pile of straw at an old barn, where our badly wounded were gathered. My faithful surgeon, Dr. Weatherly, who was my devoted friend, was at my side, with his fingers on my pulse. As I revived, his face was so expressive of distress that I asked him: " What do you think of my case, Weatherly?" He made a manly effort to say that he was hopeful. I knew better, and said: " You are not honest with me. You think I am going to die; but I am going to get well." Long afterward, when the danger was past, he admitted that this assurance was his first and only basis of hope.

General George B. Anderson, of North Carolina, whose troops were on my right, was wounded in the foot, but, it was thought, not severely. That superb man and soldier was dead in a few weeks, though his wound was supposed to be slight, while I was mercifully sustained

through a long battle with wounds the combined effect
of which was supposed to be fatal. Such are the mysterious concomitants of cruel war.

Mrs. Gordon was soon with me. When it was known
that the battle was on, she had at once started toward
the front. The doctors were doubtful about the propriety of admitting her to my room; but I told them to
let her come. I was more apprehensive of the effect of
the meeting upon her nerves than upon mine. My face
was black and shapeless—so swollen that one eye was
entirely hidden and the other nearly so. My right leg
and left arm and shoulder were bandaged and propped
with pillows. I knew she would be greatly shocked.
As she reached the door and looked, I saw at once that
I must reassure her. Summoning all my strength, I
said: "Here's your handsome (?) husband; been to an
Irish wedding." Her answer was a suppressed scream,
whether of anguish or relief at finding me able to speak,
I do not know. Thenceforward, for the period in which
my life hung in the balance, she sat at my bedside, trying to supply concentrated nourishment to sustain me
against the constant drainage. With my jaw immov-
ably set, this was exceedingly difficult and discouraging. My own confidence in ultimate recovery, however, was never shaken until erysipelas, that deadly foe
of the wounded, attacked my left arm. The doctors told
Mrs. Gordon to paint my arm above the wound three or
four times a day with iodine. She obeyed the doctors
by painting it, I think, three or four hundred times a
day. Under God's providence, I owe my life to her incessant watchfulness night and day, and to her tender
nursing through weary weeks and anxious months.

CHAPTER VIII

A long convalescence—Enlivened by the author of "Georgia Scenes" —The movement upon Hooker's army at Chancellorsville—Remarkable interview between Lee and Stonewall Jackson—The secret of Jackson's character—The storming of Marye's Heights—Some famous war-horses.

IT was nearly seven months after the battle of Antietam, or Sharpsburg, before I was able to return to my duties at the front. Even then the wound through my face had not healed; but Nature, at last, did her perfect work, and thus deprived the army surgeons of a proposed operation. Although my enforced absence from the army was prolonged and tedious, it was not without its incidents and interest. Some of the simple-hearted people who lived in remote districts had quaint conceptions of the size of an army. One of these, a matron about fifty years of age, came a considerable distance to see me and to inquire about her son. She opened the conversation by asking: "Do you know William?"

"What William, madam?"

"My son William."

I replied: "Really, I do not know whether I have ever met your son William or not. Can you tell me what regiment or brigade or division or corps he belongs to?"

She answered: "No, I can't, but I know he belongs to Gin'al Lee's company."

I think the dear old soul left with the impression that

I was something of a fraud because I did not know every man in " Gin'al Lee's company "—especially William.

After I had begun to convalesce, it was my privilege to be thrown with the author of " Georgia Scenes," Judge Augustus Baldwin Longstreet, who was widely known in the Southern States as an able jurist, a distinguished educator, and an eminent Methodist divine, as well as a great humorist and wit. His book, " Georgia Scenes," is now rarely seen, and it may be interesting to those who have never known of Judge Longstreet or his famous stories to give an instance here of the inimitable fun of this many-sided genius, who aided me in whiling away the time of my enforced absence from the army. Judge Longstreet was at that time an old man, but still full of the fire of earlier years, and of that irresistible humor with which his conversation sparkled. On one occasion, when a number of gentlemen were present, I asked the judge to give us the facts which led him to write that remarkable story called "The Debating Society." He said that Mr. McDuffie, who afterward became one of the South's great statesmen, was his classmate and roommate at school. Both were disposed to stir into the monotony of school days a little seasoning of innocent fun. During one of the school terms, they were appointed a committee to select and propose to the society a suitable subject for debate. As they left the hall, Longstreet said to his friend, " Now, McDuffie, is our chance. If we could induce the society to adopt for debate some subject which sounds well, but in which there is no sense at all, would n't it be a great joke?" McDuffie's reply was a roar of laughter. They hastened to their room to begin the selection of the great subject for debate. They agreed that each should write all the high-sounding phrases he could think of, and then by comparing notes, and combining the best of both, they could make up their report. They sat up late, conferring and laughing at the suggestions, and at last concocted the question, "Whether at public elections should the votes of faction predominate by internal suggestions, or the bias of jurisprudence?" With boyish glee they pronounced their work well done, and laughed themselves to sleep. On the next morning their report was to be submitted, and the society was to vote as to its adoption. They arose early, full of confidence in their ability to palm off this wonderful subject on the society; for they reasoned thus: no boy will be willing to admit that he is less intelligent or less able to comprehend great public questions or metaphysical subjects than the committee, and therefore each one of them will at once pretend to be delighted at the selection, and depend upon reading and investigation to prepare himself for the following week's debate upon it. They had not miscalculated the chances of success, nor underestimated the boyish pride of their schoolmates. The question was unanimously adopted.

It is impossible to give any conception of Judge Longstreet's description of the debate upon the question; of how he and McDuffie led off with thoroughly prepared speeches full of resounding rhetoric and rounded periods, but as devoid of sense as the subject itself, the one arguing the affirmative, the other the negative of the proposition. Nor shall I attempt any description of Judge Longstreet's wonderful mimicry of the boys, many of whom became men of distinction in after years; of how they stammered and struggled and agonized in the effort to rise to the height of the great argument; and finally, of the effort of the president of the society, who was, of course, one of the schoolboys, to sum up the points made and determine on which side were the weightiest and most cogent arguments. Suffice it to say that I recall with grateful pleasure the hours spent during my convalescence in the presence of this remarkable man. His inimitable and delicate humor. was the sunshine of his useful and laborious life, and will remain a bright spot in my recollections of the sixties.

On my return to the army, I was assigned to the command of perhaps the largest brigade in the Confederate army, composed of six regiments from my own State, Georgia. No more superb material ever filled the ranks of any command in any army. It was, of course, a most trying moment to my sensibilities when the time came for my parting from the old command with which I had passed through so many scenes of bitter trial; but these men were destined to come back to me again. It is trite, but worth the repetition, to say that there are few ties stronger and more sacred than those which bind together in immortal fellowship men who with unfaltering faith in each other have passed through such scenes of terror and blood.

Years afterward, my daughter met a small son of one of these brave comrades, and asked him his name.

"Gordon Wright," was his prompt reply.

"And for whom are you named, Gordon?"

"I don't know, miss," he answered, "but I believe my mamma said I was named for General Lee."

I had been with my new command but a short time when the great battle of Chancellorsville occurred. It was just before this bloody engagement that my young brother had so accurately and firmly predicted his own death, and it was here the immortal Jackson fell. I never write or pronounce this name without an impulse to pause in veneration for that American phenomenon. The young men of this country cannot study the character of General Jackson without benefit to their manhood, and for those who are not familiar with his characteristics I make this descriptive allusion to him.

As to whether he fell by the fire of his own men, or

from that of the Union men in his front, will perhaps
never be definitely determined. The general, the almost
universal, belief at the South is that he was killed by a
volley from the Confederate lines; but I have had grave
doubts of this raised in my own mind by conversations
with thoughtful Union officers who were at the time in
his front and near the point where he was killed. It
seems to me quite possible that the fatal ball might have
come from either army. This much-mooted question as
to the manner of his death is, however, of less consequence than the manner of his life. Any life of such
nobility and strength must always be a matter of vital
import and interest.

At the inception of the movement upon General
Hooker's army at Chancellorsville, a remarkable interview occurred between General Lee and General Jackson, which is of peculiar interest because it illustrates,
in a measure, the characteristics of both these great
soldiers.

It was repeated to me soon after its occurrence, by the
Rev. Dr. Lacey, who was with them at the time Jackson
rode up to the Commander-in-Chief, and said to him:
"General Lee, this is not the best way to move on
Hooker."

"Well, General Jackson, you must remember that I
am compelled to depend to some extent upon information furnished me by others, especially by the engineers,
as to the topography, the obstructions, etc., and these
engineers are of the opinion that this is a very good way
of approach."

"Your engineers are mistaken, sir."

"What do you know about it, General Jackson? You
have not had time to examine the situation."

"But I have, sir; I have ridden over the whole field."

And he had. Riding with the swiftness of the wind
and looking with the eye of an eagle, he had caught the

strong and weak points of the entire situation, and was back on his panting steed at the great commander's side to assure him that there was a better route.

"Then what is to be done, General Jackson?"

"Take the route you yourself at first suggested. Move on the flank—move on the flank."

"Then you will at once make the movement, sir."

Immediately and swiftly, Jackson's "foot cavalry," as they were called, were rushing along a byway through the dense woodland. Soon the wild shout of his charge was heard on the flank and his red cross of battle was floating over General Hooker's breastworks.

General Hooker, "Fighting Joe," as he was proudly called by his devoted followers, and whom it was my pleasure to meet and to know well after the war, was one of the brilliant soldiers of the Union army. He was afterward hailed as the hero of the "Battle of the Clouds" at Lookout Mountain, and whatever may be said of the small force which he met in the fight upon that mountain's sides and top, the conception was a bold one. It is most improbable that General Hooker was informed as to the number of Confederates he was to meet in the effort to capture the high and rugged Point Lookout, which commanded a perfect view of the city of Chattanooga and the entire field of operations around it. His movement through the dense underbrush, up the rocky steeps, and over the limestone cliffs was executed with a celerity and dash which reflected high credit upon both the commander and his men. Among these men, by the way, was one of those merrymakers—those dispensers of good cheer—found in both the Confederate and Union armies, who were veritable fountains of good-humor, whose spirits glowed and sparkled in all situations, whether in the camp, on the march, or under fire. The special rôle of this one was to entertain his comrades with song, and as Hooker's men were struggling up the sides of Lookout Mountain, climbing over the huge rocks, and being picked off them by the Confederate sharpshooters, this frolicsome soldier amused and amazed his comrades by singing, in stentorian tones, his droll camp-song, the refrain of which was "Big pig, little pig, root hog or die." The singer was H. S. Cooper, now a prominent physician of Colorado.

But to return to the consideration of General Jackson's character. Every right-minded citizen, as well as every knightly soldier, whatever the color of his uniform, will appreciate the beauty of the tribute paid by General Lee to General Jackson, when he received the latter's message announcing the loss of his left arm. "Go tell General Jackson," said Lee, "that his loss is small compared to mine; for while he loses his left arm, I lose the right arm of my army." No prouder or juster tribute was ever paid by a great commander to a soldier under him.

But a truth of more importance than anything I have yet said of Jackson may be compassed, I think, in the observation that he added to a marvellous genius for war a character as man and Christian which was absolutely without blemish. His childlike trust and faith, the simplicity, sincerity, and constancy of his unostentatious piety, did not come with the war, nor was it changed by the trials and dangers of war. If the war affected him at all in this particular, it only intensified his religious devotion, because of the tremendous responsibilities which it imposed; but long before, his religious thought and word and example were leading to the higher life young men intrusted to his care, at the Virginia Military Institute. In the army nothing deterred or diverted him from the discharge of his religious duties, nor deprived him of the solace resulting from his unaffected trust. A deep-rooted belief in God, in His word and His providence, was under him and over him and through him, permeating every fibre of his being, dominating his every thought, controlling his every action. Wherever he went and whatever he did, whether he was dispensing light and joy in the family circle; imparting lessons of lofty thought to his pupils in the schoolroom at Lexington; planning masterful strategy in his tent; praying in the woods for Heaven's guidance; or riding like the incarnate spirit of war through the storm of battle, as his resistless legions swept the field of carnage with the fury of a tornado—Stonewall Jackson was the faithful disciple of his Divine Master. He died as he had lived, with his ever-active and then fevered brain working out the problems to which his duty called him, and, even with the chill of death upon him, his loving heart prompted the message to his weary soldiers, "Let us cross over the river and rest in the shade of the trees." That his own spirit will eternally rest in the shade of the Tree of Life, none who knew him can for one moment doubt.

An incident during this battle illustrates the bounding spirits of that great cavalry leader, General "Jeb" Stuart. After Jackson's fall, Stuart was designated to lead Jackson's troops in the final charge. The soul of this brilliant cavalry commander was as full of sentiment as it was of the spirit of self-sacrifice. He was as musical as he was brave. He sang as he fought. Placing himself at the head of Jackson's advancing lines and shouting to them "Forward," he at once led off in that song, "Won't you come out of the wilderness?" He changed the words to suit the occasion. Through the dense woodland, blending in strange harmony with the rattle of rifles, could be distinctly heard that song and words, "Now, Joe Hooker, won't you come out of the wilderness?" This dashing Confederate lost his life later in battle near Richmond.

While the battle was progressing at Chancellorsville, near which point Lee's left rested, his right extended to or near Fredericksburg. Early's division held this position, and my brigade the right of that division; and it was determined that General Early should attempt, near sunrise, to retake the fort on Marye's Heights, from which the Confederates had been driven the day before. I was ordered to move with this new brigade, with which I had never been in battle, and to lead in that assault; at least, such was my interpretation of the order as it reached me. Whether it was my fault or the fault of the wording of the order itself, I am not able to say; but there was a serious misunderstanding about it. My brigade was intended, as it afterward appeared, to be only a portion of the attacking force, whereas I had understood the order to direct me to proceed at once to the assault upon the fort; and I proceeded. As I was officially a comparative stranger to the men of this brigade, I said in a few sentences to them that we should know each other better when the battle of the day was over; that I trusted we should go together into that fort, and that if there were a man in the brigade who did not wish to go with us, I would excuse him if he would step to the front and make himself known. Of course, there was no man found who desired to be excused, and I then announced that every man in that splendid brigade of Georgians had thus declared his purpose to go into the fortress. They answered this announcement by a prolonged and thrilling shout, and moved briskly to the attack. When we were under full headway and under fire from the heights, I received an order to halt, with the explanation that the other troops were to unite in the assault; but the order had come too late. My men were already under heavy fire and were nearing the fort. They were rushing upon it with tremendous impetuosity. I replied to the order that it was too late to halt then, and that a few minutes more would decide the result of the charge. General Early playfully but earnestly re-

marked, after the fort was taken, that success had saved
me from being court-martialed for disobedience to orders.

During this charge I came into possession of a most
remarkable horse, whose fine spirit convinced me that
horses now and then, in the furor of fight, were almost
as sentient as their riders. This was especially true of
the high-strung thoroughbreds. At least, such was my
experience with a number of the noble animals I rode,
some of which it was my painful fortune to leave on the
field as silent witnesses of the storm which had passed
over it. At Marye's Heights, the horse which I had ridden into the fight was exhausted in my effort to personally watch every portion of my line as it swept
forward, and he had been in some way partially disabled, so that his movements became most unsatisfactory. At this juncture the beautiful animal to which I
have referred, and from which a Union officer had just
been shot, galloped into our lines. I was quickly upon
her back, and she proved to be the most superb battle-
horse that it was my fortune to mount during the war.
For ordinary uses she was by no means remarkable—
merely a good saddle animal, which Mrs. Gordon often
rode in camp, and which I called "Marye," from the
name of the hill where she was captured. Indeed, she
was ordinarily rather sluggish, and required free use of
the spur. But when the battle opened she was absolutely transformed. She seemed at once to catch the
ardor and enthusiasm of the men around her. The bones
of her legs were converted into steel springs and her
sinews into india-rubber. With head up and nostrils
distended, her whole frame seemed to thrill with a de-
light akin to that of foxhounds when the hunter's horn
summons them to the chase. With the ease of an ante-
lope, she would bound across ditches and over fences
which no amount of coaxing or spurring could induce
her to undertake when not under the excitement of

battle. Her courage was equal to her other high qualities. She was afraid of nothing. Neither the shouting
of troops, nor the rattle of rifles, nor the roar of artillery,
nor their bursting shells, intimidated her in the slightest degree. In addition to all this, she seemed to have
a charmed life, for she bore me through the hottest fires
and was never wounded.

I recall another animal of different temperament,
turned over to me by the quartermaster, after capture,
in exchange, as usual, for one of my own horses. In the
Valley of Virginia, during the retreat of the Union General, Milroy, my men captured a horse of magnificent
appearance and handsomely caparisoned. He was solid
black in color and dangerously treacherous in disposition. He was brought to me by his captors with the
statement that he was General Milroy's horse, and he
was at once christened "Milroy" by my men. I have
no idea that he belonged to the general, for that officer
was too true a soldier to have ridden such a beast in
battle—certainly not after one test of his cowardice.
His fear of Minié balls was absolutely uncontrollable.
He came near disgracing me in the first and only fight
in which I attempted to ride him. Indeed, if it had
chanced to be my first appearance under fire with my
men, they would probably have followed my example as
they saw me flying to the rear on this elephantine brute.
He was an immense horse of unusually fine proportions,
and had behaved very well under the cannonading; but
as we drew nearer the blue lines in front, and their musketry sent the bullets whistling around his ears, he
wheeled and fled at such a rate of speed that I was
powerless to check him until he had carried me more
than a hundred yards to the rear. Fortunately, some of
the artillerymen aided me in dismounting, and promptly
gave me a more reliable steed, on whose back I rapidly
returned in time to redeem my reputation. My obliga-

tions to General Milroy were very great for having evacuated at night the fort at Winchester (near which this horse was captured), and for permitting us to move over its deserted and silent ramparts in perfect security; but if this huge black horse were really his, General Milroy, in leaving him for me, had cancelled all the obligations under which he had placed me.

This Georgia brigade, with its six splendid regiments, whose war acquaintance I had made at Marye's Heights, contributed afterward from their pittance of monthly pay, and bought, without my knowledge, at a fabulous price, a magnificent horse, and presented him to me. These brave and self-denying men realized that such a horse would cost more than I could pay. He gave me great comfort, and I hoped that, like "Marye," he might go unscathed through successive battles; but at Monocacy, in Maryland, he paid the forfeit of his life by coming in collision with a whizzing missile, as he was proudly galloping along my lines, then advancing upon General Lew Wallace's forces. I deeply regretted this splendid animal's death, not only because of his great value at the time, but far more because he was the gift of my gallant men.

In one of the battles in the Wilderness, in 1864, and during a flank movement, a thoroughbred bay stallion was captured—a magnificent creature, said to have been the favorite war-horse of General Shaler, whom we also captured. As was customary, the horse was named for his former master, and was known by no other title than "General Shaler." My obligations to this horse are twofold and memorable: he saved me from capture, when I had ridden, by mistake, into Sedgwick's corps by night; and at Appomattox he brought me enough greenbacks to save me from walking back to Georgia. He was so handsome that a Union officer, who was a judge of horses, asked me if I wished to sell him. I at once assured this officer that I would be delighted to sell the horse or anything else I possessed, as I had not a dollar except Confederate money, which, at that period of its history, was somewhat below par. The officer, General Curtin, of Pennsylvania, generously paid me in greenbacks more than I asked for the horse. I met this gentleman in 1894, nearly thirty years afterward, at Williamsport, Pennsylvania. He gratified me again by informing me that he had sold "General Shaler" for a much higher price than he paid me for him.[1]

If there is a hereafter for horses, as there is a heaven for the redeemed among men, I fear that the old black traitor that ran away with me from the fight will never reach it, but the brave and trusty steeds that so gallantly bore their riders through our American Civil War will not fail of admittance.

Job wrote of the war-horse that "smelleth the battle from afar off." Alexander the Great had his "Bucephalus," that dashed away as if on wings as his daring master mounted him. Zachary Taylor had his "Old Whity," from whose mane and tail the American patriots pulled for souvenirs nearly all the hairs, as he grazed on the green at the White House. Lee had his "Traveller," whose memory is perpetuated in enduring bronze. Stonewall Jackson had his high-mettled "Old Sorrel," whose life was nursed with tenderest care long after the death of his immortal rider; but if I were a poet I would ignore them all and embalm in song my own glorious "Marye," whose spirit I would know was that of Joan of Arc, if the transmigration of souls were true.

[1] Since writing this chapter, I have learned that this horse was a noted animal in the Union army, and had been named "Abe," for President Lincoln.

CHAPTER IX

WAR BY THE BRAVE AGAINST THE BRAVE

The spirit of good-fellowship between Union and Confederate soldiers—Disappearance of personal hatred as the war progressed—The Union officer who attended a Confederate dance—American chivalry at Vicksburg—Trading between pickets on the Rappahannock—Incidents of the bravery of color-bearers on both sides—General Curtis's kindness—A dash for life cheered by the enemy.

THAT inimitable story-teller, Governor Robert Taylor, of Tennessee, delights his hearers by telling in charming style of a faithful colored man, Allen, a slave of his father's. Both Allen and his owner were preachers, and Allen was in the habit each Saturday afternoon of going to his master and learning from him what his text for the following day's sermon would be. On this occasion the Rev. Dr. Taylor informed the Rev. Allen that his text for the morrow would be the words, "And he healed them of divers diseases." "Yes, sir," said Allen; dat's a mighty good tex', and hit will be mine for my Sunday sarmon." Sunday came and Allen was ready. He announced his "tex'" in these words: "And he healed 'em of all sorts of diseases, and even of dat wust of complaints called de divers." Proceeding to an elucidation of his text, he described with much particularity the different kinds of diseases that earthly doctors could cure, and then, with deepest unction, said: "But, my congregation, if de divers ever gits one of you, jest make up your mind you's a gone nigger, 'cep'in' de Lord save you."

In 1861 a disorder had taken possession of the minds of the people in every section of the country. Internecine war, contagious, infectious, confluent, was spreading, and destined to continue spreading until nearly every home in the land was affected and hurt by it. This dreadful disease had about it some wonderful compensations. No one went through it from a high sense of duty without coming out of it a braver, a better, and a more consecrated man. It is.a great mistake to suppose that war necessarily demoralizes and makes obdurate those who wage it. Doubtless wars of conquest, for the sake of conquest, for the purpose of despoiling the vanquished and enriching the victors, and all wars inaugurated from unhallowed motives, do demoralize every man engaged in them, from the commanding general to the privates. But such was not the character of our Civil War. On the contrary, it became a training-school for the development of an unselfish and exalted manhood, which increased in efficiency from its opening to its close. At the beginning there was personal antagonism and even bitterness felt by individual soldiers of the two armies toward each other. The very sight of the uniform of an opponent aroused some trace of anger. But this was all gone long before the conflict had ceased. It was supplanted by a brotherly sympathy. The spirit of Christianity swayed the hearts of many, and its benign influence was perhaps felt by the great majority of both armies. The Rev. Charles Lane, recently a member of the faculty of the Georgia Technological Institute, told me of a soldier who could easily have captured or shot his antagonist at night; but the religious devotion in which that foe at the moment was engaged shielded him from molestation, and he was left alone in communion with his God. That knightly soldier of the Confederacy, whose heart so promptly sympathized with his devout antagonist, was also a "soldier of the cross."

The same spirit was shown in the case of a Pennsylvania soldier who was attracted by the songs in a Confederate prayer-meeting, and, without the slightest fear of being detained or held as prisoner, attempted in broad daylight to cross over and join the Confederates in their worship. He was ordered back by his own pickets; but his officers appreciated his impulse and he was not subjected to the slightest punishment. In a European army he most likely would have been shot for attempted desertion, although he had made no effort whatever to conceal his movements or his purposes.

The broadening of this Christian fellowship was plainly seen as the war progressed. The best illustration of this fact which I now recall is the contrast between the impulses which moved the two soldiers just mentioned, and that which inspired the quaint prayer of a devout Confederate at the beginning of the war and at the grave of his dead comrade. He concluded his prayer in about these words: " And now, Lord, we commit the body of our comrade to the grave, with the hope of meeting him again, with all the redeemed, in that great day and in the home prepared for thy children. For we are taught to believe that thy true followers shall come from the East and West as well as from the South; and we cannot help hoping, Lord, that a few will come even from the *North*."

It was not alone in the religious life of the army that these evidences of expanding brotherhood were exhibited. I should, perhaps, not exaggerate the number or importance of these evidences if I said that there were thousands of them which are perhaps the brightest illustrations and truest indices of the American soldier's character.

In 1896 an officer of the Union army told me the following story, which is but a counterpart of many which came under my own observation. A lieutenant of a Delaware regiment was officer of the picket-line on the banks of the Rappahannock. The pickets of the two armies were, as was usual at that time, very near each other and in almost constant communication. It was in midwinter and no movements of the armies were expected. The Confederate officer of pickets who was on duty on the opposite bank of the narrow stream asked the Union lieutenant if he would not come over after dark and go with him to a farm-house near the lines, where certain Confederates had invited the country girls to a dance. The Union officer hesitated, but the Confederate insisted, and promised to call for him in a boat after dark, and to lend him a suit of citizen's clothes, and pledged his honor as a soldier to see him safely back to his own side before daylight the next morning. The invitation was accepted, and at the appointed hour the Confederate's boat glided silently to the place of meeting on the opposite bank. The citizen's suit was a ludicrous fit, but it served its purpose. The Union soldier was introduced to the country girls as a new recruit just arrived in camp. He enjoyed the dance, and, returning with his Confederate escort, was safely landed in his own lines before daylight. Had the long roll of the kettledrum summoned the armies to battle on that same morning, both these officers would have been found in the lines under hostile ensigns, fighting each other in deadly conflict.

In Kansas City recently an ex-Confederate recorded his name upon the hotel register. Mr. James Locke, of Company E, One Hundredth Pennsylvania Volunteers, was in the same hotel, and observed the name on the register. Locke had lost a leg at the second Manassas, and a Confederate had carried him out of the railroad cut in which he lay suffering, and had ministered to his wants as best he could. Locke had asked this soldier in gray before leaving him to write his name in his (Locke's) war diary. The Confederate did so, and was then compelled to hurry forward with his command. He had, however, in the spirit of a true soldier, provided the suffering Pennsylvanian with a canteen of water before he left him. There was nothing unmanly in the moistened eyes of these brave men when they so unexpectedly and after so many years met in Kansas City for the first time since they parted at the railroad cut on a Virginia battle-field.

This spirit of American chivalry was exhibited almost everywhere on the wonderful retreat of Joseph E. Johnston before General Sherman from Dalton to Atlanta. At Resaca, at Kennesaw, along the banks of Peachtree Creek, and around Atlanta, between the lines that encircled the doomed city, the same friendly greetings were heard between the pickets, and the same evidences of comradeship shown before the battles began and after they had ended. In the trenches around Vicksburg, and during its long and terrible bombardment, the men in the outer lines would call to each other to stop firing for a while, that they "wanted to get out into fresh air!" The call was always heeded, and both sides poured out of their bomb-proofs like rats from their holes when the cats are away. And whenever an order came to open fire, or the time had expired, they would call: "Hello, there, Johnnie," or "Hello, there, Yank," as the case might be. "Get into your holes now; we are going to shoot."

What could have been more touchingly beautiful than that scene on the Rapidan when, in the April twilight, a great band in the Union army suddenly broke the stillness with the loved strains of "Hail Columbia, Happy Land," calling from the Union camps huzzas that rolled like reverberating thunders on the evening air. Then from the opposite hills and from Confederate bands the answer came in the thrilling strains of "Dixie." As it always does and perhaps always will, "Dixie" brought from Southern throats an impassioned response. Then, as if inspired from above, came the union of both in that immortal anthem, "Home, Sweet Home." The solemn and swelling cadence of these old familiar notes was caught by both armies, and their joint and loud acclamations made the climax of one of the most inspiring scenes ever witnessed in war.

The talking and joking, the trading and "swapping," between the pickets and between the lines became so prevalent before the war closed as to cause no comment and attract no special attention, except when the intercourse led the commanding officers to apprehend that important information might be unwittingly imparted to the foe. On the Rapidan and Rappahannock, into which the former emptied, this rollicking sort of intercourse would have been alarming in its intimacy but for the perfect confidence which the officers of both sides had in their men. Even officers on the opposite banks of this narrow stream would now and then declare a truce among themselves, in order that they might bathe in the little river. Where the water was shallow they would wade in and meet each other in the center and shake hands, and "swap" newspapers and barter Southern tobacco for Yankee coffee. Where the water was deep, so that they could not wade in and "swap," they sent the articles of traffic across in miniature boats, laden on the Southern shore with tobacco and sailed across to the Union side. These little boats were unloaded by the Union soldiers, reloaded, and sent back with Yankee coffee for the Confederates. This extraordinary international commerce was carried on to such an extent that the commanders of both armies concluded it was best to stop it. General Lee sent for me on one occasion and instructed me to break up the traffic. Riding along the lines, as I came suddenly and unexpectedly around the point of a hill upon one of the Confederate posts, I discovered an unusual commotion and confusion. I asked: "What's the matter here? What is all this confusion about?"

"Nothing at all, sir. It's all right here, general."

I expressed some doubt about its being all right, when the spokesman for the squad attempted to concoct some absurd explanation as to their effort to get ready to "present arms" to me as I came up. Of course I was satisfied that this was not true; but I could see no evidence of serious irregularity. As I started, however, I looked back and discovered the high weeds on the bank shaking, and wheeling my horse, I asked:

"What's the matter with those weeds?"

"Nothing at all, sir," he declared; but I ordered him to break the weeds down. There I found a soldier almost naked. I asked:

"Where do you belong?"

"Over yonder," he replied, pointing to the Union army on the other side.

"And what are you doing here, sir?"

"Well, general," he said, "I did n't think it was any harm to come over and see the boys just a little while."

"What boys?" I asked.

"These Johnnies," he said.

"Don't you know, sir, that there is war going on in this country?" I asked.

"Yes, general," he replied; "but we are not fighting now."

The fact that a battle was not then in progress given as an excuse for social visiting between opposing lines was so absurd that it overturned my equilibrium for the moment. If my men could have known my thoughts they would have been as much amused at my discomfiture as I was at the Union visitor's reasoning. An almost irresistible impulse to laugh outright was overcome, however, by the necessity for maintaining my official dignity. My instructions from General Lee had been to break up that traffic and intercourse; and the slightest lowering of my official crest would have been fatal to my mission. I therefore assumed the sternest aspect possible under the circumstances, and ordered the Union soldier to stand up; and I said to him: "I am going to teach you, sir, that we are at war. You have no rights here except as prisoner of war, and I am going to have you marched to Richmond, and put you in prison."

This terrible threat brought my own men quickly and vigorously to his defense, and they exclaimed: "Wait a minute, general. Don't send this man to prison. We invited him over here, and we promised to protect him, and if you send him away it will just ruin our honor."

The object of my threat had been accomplished. I had badly frightened the Northern guest and his Southern hosts. Turning to the scantily clad visitor, I said:

"Now, sir, if I permit you to go back to your own side, will you solemnly promise me, on the honor of a soldier, that—" But without waiting for me to finish my sentence, and with an emphatic "Yes, sir," he leaped like a bullfrog into the river and swam back.

I recall several incidents which do not illustrate precisely the same elements of character, but which show the heroism found on both sides, of which I know few, if any, parallels in history. After the battle of Sharpsburg, there was sent to me as an aide on my staff a very young soldier, a mere stripling. He was at that awkward, gawky age through which all boys seem to pass. He bore a letter, however, from the Hon. Thomas Watts, of Alabama, who was the Attorney-General of the Confederate States, and who assured me that this lad had in him all the essentials of a true soldier. It was not long before I found that Mr. Watts had not mistaken the mettle of his young friend, Thomas G. Jones. Late one evening, near sunset, I directed Jones to carry a message from me to General Lee or to my immediate superior. The route was through pine thickets and along dim roads or paths not easily followed. The Union pickets were posted at certain points in these dense woods; but Jones felt sure that he could go through safely. Alone on horseback he started on his hazardous ride. Darkness overtook him before he had emerged from the pine thicket, and he rode into a body of Union pickets, supposing them to be Confederates. There were six men on that post. They seized the bridle of Jones's horse, levelled their rifles at him, and ordered him to dismount. As there was no alternative, one can imagine that Jones was not slow in obeying the order. His captors were evidently new recruits, for they neglected to deprive him of the six-shooter at his belt. Jones even then had in him the oratorical power which afterward won for him distinction at the bar and helped to make him governor of the great State of Alabama. He soon engaged his captors in the liveliest conversation, telling them anecdotes and deeply enlisting their interest in his stories. The night was cold, and before daylight Jones adroitly proposed to the "boys" that they should make a fire, as there was no reason for shivering in the cold with plenty of pine sticks around them. The suggestion was at once accepted, and Jones began to gather sticks. The men, unwilling for him to do all the work, laid down their guns and began to share in this labor. Jones saw his opportunity, and burning with mortification at his failure to carry through my message, he leaped to the pile of guns, drew his revolver, and said to the men: "I can kill every one of you before you can get to me. Fall into line. I will put a bullet through the first man who moves toward me!" He delivered those six prisoners at my headquarters.

I do not now recall the name of the Confederate who was selected, on account of his conspicuous courage, as the color-bearer of his regiment, and who vowed as he received the flag that he would never surrender it. At Gaines's Mill he fell in the forefront of the fight with a mortal wound through his body. Raising himself on his elbow, he quietly tore his battle-flag from the staff, folded it under him, and died upon it.

At Big Falls, North Carolina, there lived in 1897 a one-armed soldier whose heroism will be cited by orators and poets as long as heroism is cherished by men. He was a color-bearer of his regiment, the Thirteenth North Carolina. In a charge during the first day's battle at Gettysburg, his right arm, with which he bore the colors, was shivered and almost torn from its socket. Without halting or hesitating, he seized the falling flag in his left hand, and, with his blood spouting from the severed arteries and his right arm dangling in shreds at his side, he still rushed to the front, shouting to his comrades: "Forward, forward!" The name of that modest and gallant soldier is W. F. Faucette.

At Gettysburg a Union color-bearer of one of General Barlow's regiments, which were guarding the right flank of General Meade's army, exhibited a similar dauntless devotion in defence of his colors. As my command charged across the ravine and up its steep declivity, along which were posted the Union troops, the fight became on portions of the line a hand-to-hand struggle. This lion-hearted color-bearer of a Union regiment stood firmly in his place, refusing to fly, to yield his ground, or to surrender his flag. As the Confederates crowded around him and around the stalwart men who still stood firmly by him, he became engaged in personal combat with the color-bearer of one of my Georgia regiments. What his fate was I do not now recall, but I trust and believe that his life was spared.

I sincerely pity the man who calls himself an American and who does not find in these exhibitions of American manhood on either side, a stimulant to his pride as an

American citizen and a support to his confidence in the American Republic. The true patriot must necessarily feel a glow of sincere pride in the record of the Republic's great and heroic sons from every section. There is no inconsistency, however, between a special affection for one's birthplace and a general love for one's entire country. There is nothing truer than that the love of the home is the unit, and that the sum of these units is aggregated patriotism. What would be thought of the patriotism of a son of New England or of the Old Dominion whose heart did not warm at the mention of Plymouth Rock or of Jamestown?

An incident in the war experience of General Newton M. Curtis, a leading and influential Republican member of Congress from New York, is worthy of record. A finer specimen of physical manhood it would be difficult to find. Six feet six inches in height, erect as the typical Indian, he weighs two hundred and thirty-two pounds; but if he were six feet twelve and weighed twice as much his body would not be big enough to contain the great soul which inhabits it. He had one eye shot out by a Confederate bullet, but if he had lost both his lofty spirit would have seen as clearly as now that the war was fought in defence of inherited belief, and that when it ended the Union was more closely cemented than ever.

Near Fairfax Court-House, during the war in that portion of Virginia which had been devastated by both armies, biting want necessarily came to many families near the border, particularly to those whose circumstances made it impossible for them to remove to a distant part of the State. From within the Union lines there came into the Union camps, one chilly day, a Virginia lady. She was weak and pale and thinly clad, and rode an inferior horse, with a faithful old negro as her only escort. She had come to solicit from the commissary department of the Union army supplies with which to feed her household. The orders to the commissary department in the field were necessarily stringent. The supplies did not belong to the officer in charge, but were the property of the government. That officer, therefore, had no right to donate anything even to the most deserving case of charity, except according to the orders; and the orders required all applicants for supplies to take the oath of allegiance to the United States before such supplies could be furnished. This hungry and wan woman was informed that she could have the necessaries for which she asked upon subscribing to that oath. What was she to do? Her kindred, her husband and son, were soldiers in the Confederate army. If she refused to take the oath, what would become of her and those dependent upon her? If she took the oath, what was to become of her own convictions and her loyalty to the cause of those she loved? It is not necessary to say that her sense of duty and her fidelity to the Southern cause triumphed. Sad and hungry, she turned away, resolved to suffer on. But General Curtis was in that camp. He had no power to change the orders, and no disposition to change them, and he would have scorned to violate a trust; for there was no braver or more loyal officer in the Union army. He had, however, in his private purse some of the money which he had earned as a soldier, and he illustrated in his character that native knighthood which ennobles its possessor while protecting, befriending, and blessing the weak or unfortunate. It is enough to add that this brave and suffering Virginia woman did not leave the Union camp emptyhanded. I venture the opinion that General Curtis would not exchange the pleasure which that act gave him at the time, and has given him for the thirty years since, for the amount of money expended multiplied many times over.

In 1863, when General Longstreet's forces were investing the city of Knoxville, Tennessee, there occurred an incident equally honorable to the sentiment and spirit of Confederate and Federal. During a recent visit to that city, a party representing both sides in that engagement accompanied me to the great fort which General Longstreet's forces assailed but were unable to capture. These representatives of both armies united in giving me the details of the incident. The Southern troops had made a bold assault upon the fort. They succeeded in reaching it through a galling fire, and attempted to rush up its sides, but were beaten back by the Union men, who held it. Then in the deep ditch surrounding the fortress and at its immediate base, the Confederates took their position. They were, in a measure, protected from the Union fire; but they could neither climb into the fort nor retreat, except at great sacrifice of life. The sun poured its withering rays upon them and they were famishing with thirst. A bold and self-sacrificing young soldier offered to take his life in his hands and canteens on his back and attempt to bring water to his fainting comrades. He made the dash for life and for water, and was unhurt; but the return—how was that to be accomplished? Laden with the filled and heavy canteens, he approached within range of the rifles in the fort and looked anxiously across the intervening space. He was fully alive to the fact that the chances were all against him; but, determined to relieve his suffering comrades or die in the effort, he started on his perilous run for the ditch at the fort. The brave Union soldiers stood upon the parapet with their rifles in hand. As they saw this daring American youth coming, with his life easily at their disposal, they stood silently contemplating him for a moment. Then, realizing the situation, they fired at him a tremendous volley—not of deadly bullets from their guns, but of enthusiastic shouts from their throats.

If the annals of war record any incident between hostile armies which embodies a more beautiful and touching tribute by the brave to the brave, I have never seen it.

And now what is to be said of these incidents? How much are the few recorded in this chapter worth? To the generations that are to follow, what is their value and the value of the tens of thousands which ought to be chronicled? Do they truly indicate that the war did lift the spirit of the people to better things? Was it really fought in defense of cherished convictions, and did it bury in its progress the causes of sectional dissensions? Did it develop a higher manhood in the men, and did it reveal in glorious light the latent but ever-living heroism of our women? The heroines of Sparta who gave their hair for bow-strings have been immortalized by the muse of history; but what tongue can speak or pen indite a tribute worthy of that Mississippi woman who with her own hands applied the torch to more than half a million dollars' worth of cotton, reducing herself to poverty, rather than have that cotton utilized against her people? The day will come, and I hope and believe it is rapidly approaching, when in all the sections will be seen evidences of appreciation of these inspiring incidents; when all lips will unite in expressing gratitude to God that they belong to such a race of men and women; when no man who loves his country will be found grovelling among the embers and ignoble passions of the past, but will aid in developing a still nobler national life, by inviting the youth of our country to a contemplation of the true glories of this memorable war.

In my boyhood I witnessed a scene in nature which it now seems to me fitly symbolizes that mighty struggle and the view of it which I seek to present. Standing on a mountain-top, I saw two storm-clouds lowering in the opposite horizon. They were heavily charged with electric fires. As they rose and approached each other they extended their length and gathered additional blackness and fury. Higher and higher they rose, their puffing wind-caps rolling like hostile banners above them; and when nearing each other the flashing lightning blazed along their front and their red bolts were hurled into each other's bosoms. Finally in mid-heavens they met, and the blinding flashes and fearful shocks filled my boyish spirit with awe and terror. But God's hand was in that storm, and from the furious conflict copious showers were poured upon the parched and thirsty earth, which refreshed and enriched it.

CHAPTER X

Confederate victories up to the winter of 1863—Southern confidence in
ultimate independence—Progress of Union armies in the West—Fight
for the control of the Mississippi—General Butler in possession of
New Orleans—The new era in naval construction—Significance of the
battle of the *Monitor* and *Merrimac*—Great leaders who had come into
prominence in both armies—The death of Albert Sidney Johnston—
General Lee the most unassuming of great commanders.

THE next promontories on the war's highway which
come into view are Gettysburg, Vicksburg, and
Chickamauga; and these suggest a retrospective view
of the entire field over which the armies had been marching, and of the men who had been leading them.

The battles of 1861–62 and of the winter of 1863 had
left the South still confident of success in securing her
independence and the North still fully resolved on
maintaining the integrity of the Union. In Virginia the
Confederates had won important victories at Bull Run,
in the seven days' battles around Richmond, at Harper's
Ferry, with the surrender of the Union forces to Jackson,
at second Manassas, at Fredericksburg, in the Valley,
and at Chancellorsville, and had claimed a drawn battle
at Sharpsburg—Antietam. Kirby Smith had marched
nearly across Kentucky, threatening Cincinnati, and success of more or less importance had attended Southern
arms in other localities.

In the West the Union arms had won at Fort Donelson, Fort Henry, and in the battle for the possession of

eastern Kentucky, where the Confederate commander Zollicoffer was killed, and the Union commander, George H. Thomas, won his first great victory. The Confederates had suffered severely at Pea Ridge in Arkansas, although no material advantage was gained on either side. McCulloch, the noted Texas ranger, fell, and the picturesque Albert Pike, with his two thousand Indians, lent additional interest to the scene. On both sides of the Mississippi the Union forces were advancing. Kentucky and all northern Tennessee and Missouri and northern Arkansas had been abandoned to Union occupation. The possession of the Mississippi River from its source to its mouth, and the cutting in twain of the Confederate territory, became for the Southwest the dominating policy of the Union authorities—the logical sequence of which would be to cut off Confederate food-supplies from Texas and the trans-Mississippi. The success of this policy was becoming assured by rapidly recurring and decisive blows. Island Number Ten, above Memphis, fell, forcing the evacuation of Fort Pillow and of Memphis, thus breaking Confederate control of this great waterway at every point north of Vicksburg. Farragut, the brilliant admiral, had battered his way through Confederate gunboats and forts from the Mississippi's mouth to New Orleans. This foremost genius of the Union navy, whose father was a friend of Andrew Jackson's, and whose mother was a North Carolina woman, had learned his first lesson in heroism from this Southern mother as she stood with uplifted axe in the door of their cabin home, defending her children from the red savages of the mountains.

General Benjamin F. Butler, who had advocated the nomination of Jefferson Davis for President in the Charleston Convention (1860), had marched his troops into New Orleans and taken possession of the city. Along the Atlantic coast, point after point held by Confederates was falling before the mighty naval armament of the United States. No Confederate navy existed to dispute its progress. General Burnside, in his expedition to North Carolina, had captured Fort Macon and New-bern. The cities of Fernandina and Jacksonville, Florida, were unable to stand against the fire from the fleet of Commodore Dupont. In Hampton Roads, Virginia, had occurred the first battle of perfected ironclads in the world's history, and one of the most furious in the annals of naval engagements. The Confederate *Virginia* and the United States *Monitor* in a few days had revolution-ized the theories of scientific seamen, and made the iron-clad the future monarch of the water. The United States frigate *Merrimac*, which had been scuttled and sunk by its former crew, was raised from its deep grave by the Con-federates and remodelled under the direction of Captain J. M. Brooke, of Virginia. It was covered with a sloping roof of railroad iron, plastered over with plumbago and tallow, and rechristened *Virginia*. From this roof of greased iron the heaviest solid shot of the most power-ful guns glanced like india-rubber balls from a mound of granite and whizzed harmlessly into the air. With its steel-pointed prow the *Virginia* crashed into the side of the United States war-ship *Cumberland*, tearing a huge hole through which the rushing waters poured into her hull, carrying her to the bottom with the gallant Fed-erals who had manned her. Under the belching fires of this floating volcano, with its crater near the water's surface and its base-line three feet below it, the United States frigate *Congress* was forced to surrender. The most thrilling scene, however, in this great struggle of naval monsters, was that witnessed when the Union ironclad *Monitor*, designed by Captain John Ericsson, engaged the ironclad *Virginia* at close quarters. The pointed beak of the *Virginia* could make no impression upon the armor of the *Monitor*. The heaviest shots of each bounded off from the sides of the other, doing no practical damage even when at closest range. These two heralds of the new era in naval construction and naval battles were buried at last in that element the warfare upon which they had completely revolutionized —the *Virginia* in the James River, the *Monitor* in the Atlantic off Hatteras.

The great military leaders on the two sides were just beginning to attract the attention of their countrymen and to fix the gaze of Christendom. George H. Thomas, who was regarded by Confederate officers as one of the ablest of the Union commanders, was steadily building that solid reputation the general recognition of which found at last popular expression in the sobriquet, "Rock of Chickamauga"—a title resembling that conferred upon Jackson at Bull Run, and for a similar service. Sheridan, who afterward became the most famous cavalryman of the North, was beginning to win the confidence of his commanders and of his Northern countrymen. McDowell, who was the classmate and friend at West Point of his opponent Beauregard, and whose ability as a soldier was recognized by Confederate leaders, had been defeated at Bull Run, the first great battle of the war, and had been supplanted by McClellan. It was my privilege to confer with General McClellan during the exciting and momentous period preceding the inauguration of President Hayes, and he impressed me then, as he had impressed his people in 1862, as a man of great personal magnetism and vivacious intellect. After the seven days' battles around Richmond, McClellan was replaced by General John Pope. That officer, who had ingloriously failed to make good his prophecy that his army would henceforth look only upon the backs of the enemy, and who, contrary to his prediction, found that even he must consider "lines of retreat" at second Manassas, had been sent to another field of service when General

McClellan was reinstated in command. President Lincoln, however, is said to have soon desired greater activity, and to have wittily suggested that if General McClellan had no special use for the army he would like to borrow it. Whether this characteristic suggestion was ever made by the President or not, it is certain that the army was later intrusted to General Burnside, with whom I served afterward in the Senate, and who was respected by all in that chamber for his stainless record as legislator and exalted character as man and patriot. General Burnside, after his defeat by Lee at Fredericksburg, had at his own request been relieved of the command of the army. General Hooker, his successor, who as long as the war lasted fought with heroism and devotion, and after it ended entertained his Southern friends with the lavish hand of a prince, had lost the great battle of Chancellorsville. Although this admirable officer, by his devotion to his duties as commander, had so enhanced the efficiency of his army in numbers and discipline that he felt justified in pronouncing it "the finest army on the planet," he also had asked to be relieved of chief command because of some conflict of authority. His successor was General George Gordon Meade, of whom I shall have more to say in another connection.

The reputations of Sherman and of Grant were now eclipsing those of other commanders. General Sherman, with Memphis as his base, was threatening to overrun the Confederate States on the east bank of the Mississippi, while Stephen D. Lee, a brilliant campaigner, pronounced by competent authority one of the most effective commanders on the Confederate side, was throwing his little army across General Sherman's lines of advance and retarding his progress. Sherman, however, was advancing and laying the foundations upon which he was to build the imposing structure of his future fame.

Grant was piling victory upon victory and steadily mounting to the heights to which destiny and his country were calling him.

On the Confederate side, a great light had gone out when Albert Sidney Johnston fell. In comparative youth he had rendered signal service to Texas in her struggle for independence. In the war with Mexico he had evoked from "Old Rough and Ready"—Zachary Taylor—the commanding general, praises that were neither few nor meagre. In Utah he had been the government's faithful friend and strong right arm. A Kentuckian by birth, he had in his veins some of the best of American blood. Like Washington and Lee, he combined those singularly attractive qualities which inspired and held the love and confidence of his soldiers, while commanding the respect and admiration of the sages of West Point. In him more than in any other man at that period were centred the hopes of the Southern people. He fell in the morning of his career, leading his steady lines through the woods at Shiloh, and in the very hour of apparently assured victory. As the rich life-current ebbed through the severed artery, he closed his eyes on this scene of his last conflict, confident of his army's triumph and with the exultant shouts of his advancing legions sounding a requiem in his ears.

The immediate successor of Albert Sidney Johnston was Pierre Gustave Toutant Beauregard, who was an officer of ability and sincerely patriotic. Had circumstances favored it, he would have found the broadest field for usefulness at some point where his great skill as an engineer could have been utilized. During the initiative period of the war, prior to the first great battle of Bull Run, it was my privilege to serve under General Beauregard and to learn something of those cheery, debonair characteristics which helped to make him the idol of the vivacious creoles of Louisiana. After the war a Virginian, an ardent admirer of General Lee, was extolling the great commander-in-chief in a conversation with one of Beauregard's devoted creole adherents. The Louisianian listened for a moment to the Virginian's praise of Lee, and then replied:

"Lee—Lee! Yes, seems to me I did hear Beauregard speak very well of Lee."

Louisiana furnished another successor to the lamented Albert Sidney Johnston in the person of General Braxton Bragg. This officer, who was one of President Davis's special favorites, becoming late in the war a military adviser of the Confederate President, was a noted artillerist, and would possibly have done greater execution in directing the movements of field batteries, which was a specialty, than in directing the movements of an army or handling it in battle. General Bragg was undoubtedly a man of ability, but his health was bad, and unfortunately his temper was no better. His reference, though in semi-private conversation, to one of his most prominent officers as "an old woman," and his declaration that he had few men under him capable of command, were in strange contrast to the confidence felt by the country in those officers, and were especially in contrast with the spirit of Lee in assuming for himself the responsibility for defeat, while giving the honors of success to his juniors. When General Bragg was indulging in these criticisms of his officers he had under him those brilliant soldiers, the accomplished, alert, and dashing E. C. Walthall, late United States senator from Mississippi; Patrick Cleburne, whose warm Irish blood and quick Irish intellect made him conspicuous in every fight, and who in the desperate charge at Franklin, Tennessee, was killed on the defences behind which the Union army had been posted; and W. H. T. Walker, who as a boy had won his spurs fighting Indians at Okeechobee, and who was afterward desperately wounded in

Mexico, recovering, as he said, "to spite the doctors." He lost his life at last in battle at Atlanta, and left a reputation for courage equal to that of Ney. There was also in Bragg's army at that time the accomplished and brave Bate, of Tennessee, who was repeatedly wounded, and finally maimed for life, and whose old war-horse, shot at the same time, followed his wounded owner to the hospital tent and died at its door, moaning his farewell to that gallant master. There were also Cheatham and Polk (of whom I have spoken in a former chapter), and a galaxy of able men of whom I would gladly write. There were also with Bragg the knightly cavalryman Joseph Wheeler, and N. B. Forrest, the "wizard of the saddle," who was one of the unique figures of the war, and who, in my estimation, exhibited more native untutored genius as a cavalry leader than any man of modern times. Like the great German emperor who thought the rules of grammar were not made for his Majesty, Forrest did not care whether his orders were written according to Murray or any other grammarian, so they meant to his troops "fight on, men, and keep fighting till I come."

Lieutenant-General Hardee was also one of Bragg's corps commanders. This officer, who was an accomplished tactician, had made a record which many thought indicated abilities of a high order, fitting him for chief command of the Western Army. Another of his corps commanders was the chivalrous John B. Hood, who, at Atlanta, in 1864, was named by President Davis to succeed General Joseph E. Johnston, who was removed from chief command. In commenting on the picturesque and high-spirited Hood a whole chapter might be consumed; but I shall confine myself to a few observations in regard to him. As division or corps commander, there were very few men in either army who were superior to Hood; but his most intimate associates and ardent admirers in the army never regarded him as endowed with those rare mental gifts essential in the man who was to displace General Joseph E. Johnston. To say that he was as brave and dashing as any officer of any age would be the merest commonplace tribute to such a man; but courage and dash are not the sole or even the prime requisites of the commander of a great army. There are crises, it is true, in battle, like that which called Napoleon to the front at Lodi, and caused Lee to attempt to lead his men on May 6 in the Wilderness, and again at Spottsylvania (May 12, 1864), when the fate of the army may demand the most daring exposure of the commander-in-chief himself. It is nevertheless true that care and caution in handling an army, the forethought which thoroughly weighs the advantages and disadvantages of instant and aggressive action, are as essential in a commander as courage in his men. In these high qualities his battles at Atlanta and later at Franklin would indicate that Hood was lacking. I am persuaded and have reason to believe that General Lee thought Joseph E. Johnston's tactics wiser, although they involved repeated retreats in husbanding the strength and morale of his army. Bosquet said of some brilliant episode in battle: "It is beautiful, but it is not war." Hood, like Jackson, thought battle a delightful excitement; but Jackson, with all his daring and apparent relish for the fray, was one of the most cautious of men. His terrible marches were inspired largely by his caution. Instead of hurling his troops on breastworks in front, which might have been "beautiful," he preferred to wage war by heavy marching in order to deliver his blow upon the flank. His declaration that it is better to lose one hundred men in marching than a thousand in fighting is proof positive of the correctness of the estimate I place on his caution. Ewell once said that he never saw one of Jackson's staff approaching without "expecting an order to storm the north pole"; but if Jackson had determined to take the north pole he would have first considered whether it could be more easily carried by assaulting in front or by turning its flank.

Hood had lost a leg in battle, and when the amputation was completed an attempt was made to console him by the announcement that a civil appointment was ready for him. With characteristic impetuosity, he replied: "No, sir; no bomb-proof place for me. I propose to see this fight out in the field." This undiminished ardor for military service calls to mind the many other soldiers of the Civil War, and of all history, whose loss of bodily activity in no way impaired their mental capacity. Ewell, with his one leg, not only rode in battle like a cow-boy on the plains, but in the whirlwind of the strife his brain acted with the precision and rapidity of a Gatling gun.

General Daniel E. Sickles, of New York, who was an able representative in Congress, continued his active and conspicuous service in the field long after he lost the leg which was shivered by a Confederate ball as the brave men in gray rushed up the steep of Little Round Top at Gettysburg. The United States Senate, since the war, has been a conspicuous arena for one-legged Confederates. The former illustrious senators of South Carolina, Hampton and Butler, and the combative and forceful Berry of Arkansas, each stood upon his single leg, an able and aggressive champion of Democratic faith; and it is certain that the brilliant oratory of Daniel, of Virginia, is none the less Websterian because the missile in the Wilderness mangled his leg and maimed him for life. Marshal Saxe, who ran away from home and joined the army at the age of twelve, and who became one of the most famous soldiers of his day, gathered for France and his own brow the glories of Fontenoy while he was

carried amidst his troops on a litter. The most illustrious patrician in the Republic of Venice, the sight-
less hero whom Lord Byron called "the blind old Dan-
dolo," achieved for his country its most brilliant naval
victories. No account, however, of the mental vigor
which has distinguished many maimed soldiers would
be complete without reference to a Union soldier who
lost both legs. My first meeting with "Corporal" Tanner,
to whom I allude, was many years ago, on the cars between Washington and Richmond. He was on his way
to the former capital of the fallen Confederacy. The exuberance of his spirits, the cordiality of his greeting,
and the catholicity of his sentiments arrested my attention and won my friendship at this first meeting. In
the course of the conversation I jocularly asked him if
he were not afraid to go to Richmond without a body-
guard? "Well," he said, "I left both my legs buried in
Virginia soil, and I think a man ought to be allowed
peaceably to visit his own graveyard." A few years
later I sat on a platform with Tanner before a great
audience in Cooper Institute, New York. This audience
had assembled for the purpose of considering ways and
means to aid in the erection of a Confederate Soldiers'
Home in Richmond. I had in my pocket a liberal contribution from General Grant, and after announcing this
fact, with a few additional words, I called for Tanner as
the speaker of the evening. He stood tremblingly on
the two wooden pins that served him as legs, and began
by saying: "My whole being is enlisted in this cause,
from the crown of my head down to the—as far as I go."
Those who were present at the great gathering of Confederates in the vast assembly-hall at Richmond during
the last days of June, 1895, will not soon forget his
speech on that occasion. This maimed Union veteran,
surrounded by Confederates, was pressed to the front of
the platform amidst the wildest acclamations of his

former foes. Every fibre of his body quivering with emotion, Tanner poured into the ears and hearts of his auditors a torrent of patriotic eloquence that evoked a demonstration such as rarely greets any man. In his case the loss of his legs seems to have added vigor to his brain and breadth to his heart.

The brief comments I have made upon General Hood's career as commander of an army are in no degree disparaging to his clear title to the gratitude of the Southern people. They are penned by as loyal a friend as he had in the Confederate army. No devoted Theban ever stood at the tomb of Epaminondas with keener appreciation of his great virtues than is mine of the high qualities of the great-hearted and heroic Hood. These views were not withheld from General Lee when the selection of a new commander for the Confederate army at Atlanta was in contemplation. When President Davis asked General Lee for an opinion as to the wisdom of removing General Johnston from the command of that army, General Lee did me the honor, as I presume he honored other corps commanders, to counsel with me as to the policy of such an act. I had served under General Johnston while he commanded the Army of Northern Virginia. I had learned by experience and observation how he could retreat day after day and yet retain the absolute confidence of his officers and men, who were ready at any moment to about face, and, with an enthusiasm born of that confidence, assume the offensive at his command. I therefore expressed the opinion that there was no one except General Lee himself who could take General Johnston's place without a shock to the morale of his troops that would greatly decrease the chances of checking General Sherman. Hood and others were discussed, and I ventured the suggestion that if the time should ever come for the removal of General Johnston, it would be after he had lost and not while he still retained, as he clearly did, the enthusiastic confidence of his army, from the commanders of corps to the privates in the ranks. I may here remark that General Lee was perhaps the most unassuming of great commanders. Responsibilities that clearly belonged to him as a soldier he met promptly and to the fullest extent; but he was the last man holding a commission in the Confederate army to assume authority about which there could be any question. Especially was this true when such authority was placed by the Constitution or laws in the hands of the President. Nothing could tempt him to cross the line separating his powers from those of the civil authorities. That line might be dim to others, but it was clear to him. This delicacy was exhibited again and again even during the desperate throes in the last death-struggle of his army. I cannot be mistaken, however, as to his opinion of the suggested removal of General Johnston and the promotion of General Hood or any one else to the chief command. While he avoided any direct reply to my suggestions, he said enough to indicate his opinions. I could not forget his expressions, and I give, I believe, the exact words he used. He said: "General Johnston is a patriot and an able soldier. He is upon the ground, and knows his army and its surroundings and how to use it better than any of us." This was the extent of his comment and ended the interview. He never again alluded to the subject. General Lee was influenced in this case, as always, by a possibly too extreme reluctance to assume powers vested in the head of the government. While there was more or less complaint and criticism of Mr. Davis's management (it could not be otherwise during the progress of so stupendous an enterprise), the confidence reposed in his ability and consecration was unshaken; and General Lee heartily shared in this confidence. The threadbare adage, "Uneasy lies the head that wears a crown," found a fit illustration of its truth in the experience of Jefferson Davis, as it did in that of George Washington and of Abraham Lincoln. In the case of Washington criticism ceased when he retired to Mount Vernon. In the case of Abraham Lincoln all carpings and all divisions were lost in the universal sorrow of the whole American people when he became the victim of the murderous bullet of an insane assassin. So Jefferson Davis when imprisoned became the representative martyr of his whole people. Every one of them was ready to share with him all responsibility for the struggle, to the chief conduct of which they had called him by their votes. I feel sure that so long as this vicarious suffering of Mr. Davis lasted, General Johnston himself would have been unwilling to publish any statements as to the controversy between them, though he might have deemed such statements necessary for his own vindication.

The strained relations between them originated in an honest difference of opinion as to the relative rank to which General Johnston was entitled among the five full generals. It is wholly immaterial to my present purpose to inquire which was right. The position of either could be sustained by forceful arguments. From my knowledge of both President Davis and General Johnston, I feel justified in saying that the spirit which prompted them differed essentially from that which impelled the Duke of Wellington and Talleyrand each to desire the first place in the picture in which the allied sovereigns were to appear. Personal ambition played a very small part in the conduct of the serious enterprise in which the South was embarked. I could not fail to be deeply concerned, as all Southerners were, as to the effect of this alienation between the President and one of the South's ablest commanders. Honored with the close personal friendship of both after the war, I had abundant opportunity for learning the peculiarities of each. That trenchant truism of Plato: " No man governs well who wants to govern," finds no illustration in the lives of these patriotic men. The high positions and responsibilities of both came to them unsought. Their characteristics were cast in similar moulds and were of the most inflexible metal. While courteous in intercourse, each was tenacious in holding and emphatic in expressing convictions. The breach, therefore, once made was never healed. President Davis wished General Johnston to assume the offensive, with Dalton as a base of operations. General Johnston felt that his army, which had been beaten back from Missionary Ridge in great confusion, could not safely inaugurate the movement. The President felt that it was his right as constitutional head of the Confederate Government to know when and where his general intended to make a stand. That general, who had made a retreat from Dalton to Atlanta in which he had lost no wagons, no material of any description except four pieces of artillery, and none of the enthusiastic confidence of his officers or men, with but few killed or wounded in the almost daily skirmishes and combats, failed to give to the government at Richmond such information of his plans and such assurances of his hopes of success as were expected. A man of great caution, but of towering capabilities, General Johnston had husbanded his army's strength and resources in this long retrograde movement so as to make it one of the most memorable in military annals; but I think he should have frankly and confidently stated where he intended to make a final stand, from which he expected most satisfactory results. Failing to do this, he will probably be judged by history as failing to meet in the fullest measure his duty to the President. On the other hand, President Davis, having placed in command this officer, who had few if any superiors in any age or in any army, should probably have imitated the example of Louis

XV, who said to the great marshal in command of his forces that he expected all to obey, " and I will be the first to set the example."

In the meantime, while these repeated changes in commanders were occurring in the Confederate Army of the West and in the Union Army of the East, Robert E. Lee was intrusted with supreme military control in Virginia. Once in command, he was destined to remain to the end. Supported by Jackson, by the two Hills and Hampton, by Longstreet and Stuart and the junior Lees, by Ewell and Early, by Breckenridge, Heth, Mahone, Hoke, Rodes, and Pickett; by Field and Wilcox, by Johnson, Cobb, Evans, Kershaw, and Ramseur; by Pendleton, Alexander, Jones, Long and Carter of the artillery, and by a long line of officers who have left their impress upon history, this great chieftain was concentrating largely in himself the hopes of the Southern people.

This cursory and necessarily imperfect review of some of the noted leaders on both sides would be still less satisfactory without some reference to the men of the ranks who stood behind them—or, rather, in front of them.

During the fall of 1896, on my tour in Ohio, a gallant officer of the Union army, after hearing some reference by me to the great debt of gratitude due the private soldiers, gave me an amusing account of a meeting held by privates and junior officers of the line in the Union camps. Brevet titles were being conferred upon many officers for meritorious conduct. A series of resolutions were passed at this meeting, with the usual *whereases*, by which it was declared, as the sense of the meeting, that every private who had bravely fought and uncomplainingly suffered was entitled to be brevetted as corporal, every corporal as sergeant, and every sergeant as captain. In that droll gathering some wag proposed an additional resolution, which, with solemn dignity, was unanimously adopted: "*Whereas*, the faithful mules of the army have worked hard without any complaint, each one of said mules should be promoted to the rank of horse."

General Lee evidenced his appreciation of the privates when he said to one of them who was standing near his tent, "Come in, captain, and take a seat."

"I 'm no captain, general; I 'm nothing but a private," said this modest soldier.

"Come in, sir," said Lee; "come in and take a seat. You ought to be a captain."

Although playfully uttered, these simple words reflected the real sentiment of the great chieftain. It is almost literally true that the intelligent privates in both the Confederate and Union armies were all competent to hold minor commissions after one year's service. They acquired well-defined opinions as to the wisdom and object of great movements.

No language would be too strong or eulogy too high to pronounce upon the privates who did their duty during that long and dreadful war, who manfully braved its dangers, patiently endured its trials, cheerfully obeyed the orders; who were ready to march and to suffer, to fight and to die, without once calling in question the wisdom of the orders or the necessity for the sacrifice.

CHAPTER XI

GETTYSBURG

Why General Lee crossed the Potomac—The movement into Pennsylvania—Incidents of the march to the Susquehanna—The first
day at Gettysburg—Union forces driven back—The key of the position—Why the Confederates did not seize Cemetery Ridge—A defence
of General Lee's strategy—The fight at Little Round Top—The immortal charge of Pickett's men—General Meade's deliberate pursuit—
Lee's request to be relieved.

FROM Gettysburg to Appomattox; from the zenith
of assurance to the nadir of despair; from the compact ranks, boundless confidence, and exultant hopes of
as proud and puissant an army as was ever marshalled—
to the shattered remnants, withered hopes, and final surrender of that army—such is the track to be followed
describing the Confederacy's declining fortunes and ultimate death. No picture can be drawn by human hand
vivid enough to portray the varying hues, the spasmodic
changes, the rapidly gathering shadows of the scenes
embraced in the culminating period of the great struggle.

A brief analysis of the reasons for General Lee's crossing of the Potomac is now in order. In the logistics of
defensive war, offensive movements are often the wisest
strategy. Voltaire has somewhere remarked that "to
subsist one's army at the expense of the enemy, to advance on their own ground and force them to retrace
their steps—thus rendering strength useless by skill—is
regarded as one of the masterpieces of military art."

It would be difficult to group together words more

concisely and clearly descriptive of General Lee's purposes in crossing the Potomac, both in '62 and '63. It must be added, however, that while the movement into Maryland in 1862, and into Pennsylvania in 1863, were each defensive in design, they differed in some particulars as to the immediate object which General Lee hoped to accomplish. Each sought to force the Union army to retrace its steps; "each sought to render strength useless by skill"; but in 1862 there was not so grave a necessity for subsisting his army on Union soil as in 1863. The movement into Maryland was of course a more direct threat upon Washington. Besides, at that period there was still a prevalent belief among Southern leaders that Southern sentiment was strong in Maryland, and that an important victory within her borders might convert the Confederate camps into recruiting-stations, and add materially to the strength of Lee's army. But the Confederate graves which were dug in Maryland's soil vastly outnumbered the Confederate soldiers recruited from her citizens. It would be idle to speculate as to what might have been the effect of a decisive victory by Lee's forces at South Mountain, or Boonsboro, or Antietam (Sharpsburg). The poignancy of disappointment at the small number recruited for our army was intensified by the recognition of the splendid fighting qualities of Maryland soldiers who had previously joined us.

The movement into Pennsylvania in 1863 was also, in part at least, a recruiting expedition. We did not expect, it is true, to gather soldiers for our ranks, but beeves for our commissary. For more than two years the effort to fill the ranks of the Southern armies had alarmingly reduced the ranks of Southern producers, with no appreciable diminution in the number of consumers. Indeed, the consumers had materially increased; for while we were not then seeking to encourage Northern immigration, we had a large number of visitors from that and other sections, who were exploring the country under such efficient guides as McClellan, Hooker, Grant, Sherman, Thomas, and others. We had, therefore, much need of borrowing supplies from our neighbors beyond the Potomac. The bill of fare of some commands was already very short and by no means appetizing. General Ewell, having exhausted the contents of his larder, thought to replenish it from the surrounding country by a personal raid, and returned after a long and dusty hunt with a venerable ox, which would not have made a morsel, on division, for one per cent. of his command. Ewell's ox had on him, however, that peculiar quality of flesh which is essential in feeding an army on short rations. It was durable—irreducible.

The whole country in the Wilderness and around Chancellorsville, where both Hooker's and Lee's armies had done some foraging, and thence to the Potomac, was well-nigh exhausted. This was true, also, of a large portion of the Piedmont region and of the Valley of Virginia beyond the Blue Ridge Mountains; while the lower valley, along the Shenandoah, had long been the beaten track and alternate camping-ground of both Confederate and Union armies. It had contributed to the support of both armies until it could contribute no more. How to subsist, therefore, was becoming a serious question. The hungry hosts of Israel did not look across Jordan to the vine-clad hills of Canaan with more longing eyes than did Lee's braves contemplate the yellow grain-fields of Pennsylvania beyond the Potomac.

Again, to defend Richmond by threatening Washington and Baltimore and Philadelphia was perhaps the most promising purpose of the Confederate invasion. Incidentally, it was hoped that a defeat of the Union army in territory so contiguous to these great cities would send gold to such a premium as to cause financial panic in the commercial centres, and induce the great business interests to demand that the war should cease. But the hoped-for victory, with its persuasive influence, did not materialize. Indeed, the presence of Lee's army in Pennsylvania seemed to arouse the North to still greater efforts, as the presence of the Union armies in the South had intensified, if possible, the decision of her people to resist to the last extremity.

The appearance of my troops on the flank of General Meade's army during the battle of Gettysburg was not our first approach into that little city which was to become the turning-point in the Confederacy's fortunes. Having been detached from General Lee's army, my brigade had, some days prior to the great battle, passed through Gettysburg on our march to the Susquehanna. Upon those now historic hills I had met a small force of Union soldiers, and had there fought a diminutive battle when the armies of both Meade and Lee were many miles away. When, therefore, my command — which penetrated farther, I believe, than any other Confederate infantry into the heart of Pennsylvania—was recalled from the banks of the Susquehanna to take part in the prolonged and stupendous struggle, I expressed to my staff the opinion that if the battle should be fought at Gettysburg, the army which held the heights would probably be the victor. The insignificant encounter I had had on those hills impressed their commanding importance upon me as nothing else could have done.

The Valley of Pennsylvania, through which my command marched from Gettysburg to Wrightsville on the Susquehanna, awakened the most conflicting emotions. It was delightful to look upon such a scene of universal thrift and plenty. Its broad grain-fields, clad in golden garb, were waving their welcome to the reapers and binders. Some fields were already dotted over with harvested shocks. The huge barns on the highest grounds meant to my sore-footed marchers a mount, a ride, and a rest on broad-backed horses. On every side, as far as our alert vision could reach, all aspects and conditions conspired to make this fertile and carefully tilled region a panorama both interesting and enchanting. It was a type of the fair and fertile Valley of Virginia at its best, before it became the highway of armies and the ravages of war had left it wasted and bare. This melancholy contrast between these charming districts, so similar in other respects, brought to our Southern sensibilities a touch of sadness. In both these lovely valleys were the big red barns, representing in their silent dignity the independence of their owners. In both were the old-fashioned brick or stone mansions, differing in style of architecture and surroundings as Teutonic manners and tastes differ from those of the Cavalier. In both were the broad green meadows with luxuriant grasses and crystal springs.

One of these springs impressed itself on my memory by its great beauty and the unique uses to which its owner had put it. He was a staid and laborious farmer of German descent. With an eye to utility, as well as to the health and convenience of his household, he had built his dining-room immediately over this fountain gushing from a cleft in an underlying rock. My camp for the night was near by, and I accepted his invitation to breakfast with him. As I entered the quaint room, one half floored with smooth limestone, and the other half covered with limpid water bubbling clear and pure from the bosom of Mother Earth, my amazement at the singular design was perhaps less pronounced than the sensation of rest which it produced. For many days we had been marching on the dusty turnpikes, under a broiling sun, and it is easier to imagine than to describe the feeling of relief and repose which came over me as we sat in that cool room, with a hot breakfast served from one side, while from the other the frugal housewife dipped cold milk and cream from immense jars standing neck-deep in water.

We entered the city of York on Sunday morning. A committee, composed of the mayor and prominent citizens, met my command on the main pike before we reached the corporate limits, their object being to make a peaceable surrender and ask for protection to life and property. They returned, I think, with a feeling of assured safety. The church bells were ringing, and the streets were filled with well-dressed people. The appearance of these church-going men, women, and children, in their Sunday attire, strangely contrasted with that of my marching soldiers. Begrimed as we were from head to foot with the impalpable gray powder which rose in dense columns from the macadamized pikes and settled in sheets on men, horses, and wagons, it is no wonder that many of York's inhabitants were terror-stricken as they looked upon us. We had been compelled on these forced marches to leave baggage-wagons behind us, and there was no possibility of a change of clothing, and no time for brushing uniforms or washing the disfiguring dust from faces, hair, or beard. All these were of the same hideous hue. The grotesque aspect of my troops was accentuated here and there, too, by barefooted men mounted double upon huge horses with shaggy manes and long fetlocks. Confederate pride, to say nothing of Southern gallantry, was subjected to the sorest trial by the consternation produced among the ladies of York. In my eagerness to relieve the citizens from all apprehension, I lost sight of the fact that this turnpike powder was no respecter of persons, but that it enveloped all alike—officers as well as privates. Had I realized the wish of Burns, that some power would "the giftie gie us, to see oursels as ithers see us," I might have avoided the slight panic created by my effort to allay a larger one. Halting on the main street, where the sidewalks were densely packed, I rode a few rods in advance of my troops, in order to speak to the people from my horse. As I checked him and turned my full dust-begrimed face upon a bevy of young ladies very near me, a cry of alarm came from their midst; but after a few words of assurance from me, quiet and apparent confidence were restored. I assured these ladies that the troops behind me, though ill-clad and travel-stained, were good men and brave; that beneath their rough exteriors were hearts as loyal to women as ever beat in the breasts of honorable men; that their own experience and the experience of their mothers, wives, and sisters at home had taught them how painful must be the sight of a hostile army in their town; that under the orders of the Confederate commander-in-chief both private property and non-combatants were safe; that the spirit of vengeance and of rapine had no place in the bosoms of these dust-covered but knightly men; and I closed by pledging to York the head of any soldier under my command who destroyed private property, disturbed the repose of a single home, or insulted a woman.

As we moved along the street after this episode, a little girl, probably twelve years of age, ran up to my horse and handed me a large bouquet of flowers, in the centre of which was a note, in delicate handwriting, purporting to give the numbers and describe the position of the Union forces of Wrightsville, toward which I was advancing. I carefully read and reread this strange note. It bore no signature, and contained no assurance of sympathy for the Southern cause, but it was so terse and explicit in its terms as to compel my confidence. The second day we were in front of Wrightsville, and from the high ridge on which this note suggested that I halt and examine the position of the Union troops, I eagerly scanned the prospect with my field-glasses, in order to verify the truth of the mysterious communication or detect its misrepresentations. There, in full view before us, was the town, just as described, nestling on the banks of the Susquehanna. There was the blue line of soldiers guarding the approach, drawn up, as indicated, along an intervening ridge and across the pike. There was the long bridge spanning the Susquehanna and connecting the town with Columbia on the other bank. Most important of all, there was the deep gorge or ravine running off to the right and extending around the left flank of the Federal line and to the river below the bridge. Not an inaccurate detail in that note could be discovered. I did not hesitate, therefore, to adopt its suggestion of moving down the gorge in order to throw my command on the flank, or possibly in the rear, of the Union troops and force them to a rapid retreat or surrender. The result of this movement vindicated the strategic wisdom of my unknown and—judging by the handwriting— woman correspondent, whose note was none the less martial because embedded in roses, and whose evident genius for war, had occasion offered, might have made her a captain equal to Catherine.

As I have intimated, the orders from General Lee for the protection of private property and persons were of the most stringent character. Guided by these instructions and by my own impulses, I resolved to leave no ruins along the line of my march through Pennsylvania; no marks of a more enduring character than the tracks of my soldiers along its superb pikes. I cannot be mistaken in the opinion that the citizens who then lived and still live on these highways will bear me out in the assertion that we marched into that delightful region, and then marched out of it, without leaving any scars to mar its beauty or lessen its value. Perhaps I ought to record two insignificant exceptions.

Going into camp in an open country and after dark,

it was ascertained that there was no wood to be had for even the limited amount of necessary cooking, and I was appealed to by the men for permission to use a few rails from an old-fashioned fence near the camp. I agreed that they might take the top layer of rails, as the fence would still be high enough to answer the farmer's purpose. When morning came the fence had nearly all disappeared, and each man declared that he had taken only the top rail! The authorized (?) destruction of that fence is not difficult to understand! It was a case of adherence to the letter and neglect of the spirit; but there was no alternative except good-naturedly to admit that my men had gotten the better of me that time.

The other case of insignificant damage inflicted by our presence in the Valley of Pennsylvania was the application of the Confederate "conscript law" in drafting Pennsylvania horses into service. That law was passed by the Confederate Congress in order to call into our ranks able-bodied men at the South, but my soldiers seemed to think that it might be equally serviceable for the ingathering of able-bodied horses at the North. The trouble was that most of these horses had fled the country or were in hiding, and the owners of the few that were left were not submissive to Southern authority. One of these owners, who, I believe, had not many years before left his fatherland and was not an expert in the use of English, attempted to save his favorite animal by a verbal combat with my quartermaster. That officer, however, failing to understand him, sent him to me. The "Pennsylvania Dutchman," as his class was known in the Valley, was soon firing at me his broken English, and opened his argument with the announcement: "You be's got my mare." I replied, "It is not at all improbable, my friend, that I have your mare, but the game we are now playing is what was called in my boyhood 'tit for tat'"; and I endeavored to explain to him that the country was at war, that at the South horses were being taken by the Union soldiers, and that I was trying on a small scale to balance accounts. I flattered myself that this statement of the situation would settle the matter; but the explanation was far more satisfactory to myself than to him. He insisted that I had not paid for his mare. I at once offered to pay him—in Confederate money; I had no other. This he indignantly refused. Finally I offered to give him a written order for the price of his mare on the President of the United States. This offer set him to thinking. He was quite disposed to accept it, but, like a dim ray of starlight through a rift in the clouds at night, there gradually dawned on him the thought that there might possibly be some question as to my authority for drawing on the President. The suggestion of this doubt exhausted his patience, and in his righteous exasperation, like his great countryman hurling the inkstand at the devil, he pounded me with expletives in so furious a style that, although I could not interpret them into English, there was no difficulty in comprehending their meaning. The words which I did catch and understand showed that he was making a comparison of values between his mare and his "t'ree vifes." The climax of his argument was in these words: "I 've been married, sir, t'ree times, and I vood not geef dot mare for all dose voomans."

With so sincere an admirer of woman as myself such an argument could scarcely be recognized as forcible; but I was also a great lover of fine horses, and this poor fellow's distress at the loss of his favorite mare was so genuine and acute that I finally yielded to his entreaties and had her delivered to him.

When General Early reached York a few days later, he entered into some business negotiations with the officials and prominent citizens of that city. I was not advised as to the exact character of those negotiations, but it was rumored through that portion of the army at the time that General Early wanted to borrow, or secure in some other way, for the use of his troops, a certain amount of greenbacks, and that he succeeded in making the arrangement. I learned afterward that the only promise to repay, like that of the Confederate notes, was at some date subsequent to the establishment of Southern independence.

It will be remembered that the note concealed in the flowers handed me at York had indicated a ravine down which I could move, reaching the river not far from the bridge. As my orders were not restricted, except to direct me to cross the Susquehanna, if possible, my immediate object was to move rapidly down that ravine to the river, then along its right bank to the bridge, seize it, and cross to the Columbia side. Once across, I intended to mount my men, if practicable, so as to pass rapidly through Lancaster in the direction of Philadelphia, and thus compel General Meade to send a portion of his army to the defence of that city. This programme was defeated, first, by the burning of the bridge, and second, by the imminent prospect of battle near Gettysburg. The Union troops stationed at Wrightsville had, after their retreat across it, fired the bridge which I had hoped to secure, and had then stood in battle line on the opposite shore. With great energy my men labored to save the bridge. I called on the citizens of Wrightsville for buckets and pails, but none were to be found. There was, however, no lack of buckets and pails a little later, when the town was on fire. The bridge might burn, for that incommoded, at the time, only the impatient Confederates, and these Pennsylvanians were not in sympathy with my expedition, nor anxious to facilitate the movement of such unwelcome visitors. But when the burning bridge fired the lumber-yards on the river's banks, and the burning lumber fired the town, buckets and tubs and pails and pans innumerable came from their hiding-places, until it seemed that, had the whole of Lee's army been present, I could have armed them with these implements to fight the rapidly spreading flames. My men labored as earnestly and bravely to save the town as they did to save the bridge. In the absence of fire-engines or other appliances, the only chance to arrest the progress of the flames was to form my men around the burning district, with the flank resting on the river's edge, and pass rapidly from hand to hand the pails of water. Thus, and thus only, was the advancing, raging fire met, and at a late hour of the night checked and conquered. There was one point especially at which my soldiers combated the fire's progress with immense energy, and with great difficulty saved an attractive home from burning. It chanced to be the home of one of the most superb women it was my fortune to meet during the four years of war. She was Mrs. L. L. Rewalt, to whom I refer in my lecture, " The Last Days of the Confederacy," as the heroine of the Susquehanna. I met Mrs. Rewalt the morning after the fire had been checked. She had witnessed the furious combat with the flames around her home, and was unwilling that those men should depart without receiving some token of appreciation from her. She was not wealthy, and could not entertain my whole command, but she was blessed with an abundance of those far nobler riches of brain and heart which are the essential glories of exalted womanhood. Accompanied by an attendant, and at a late hour of the night, she sought me, in the confusion which followed the destructive fire, to express her gratitude to the soldiers of my command and to inquire how long we would remain in Wrightsville. On learning that the village would be relieved of our presence at an early hour the following morning, she insisted that I should bring with me to breakfast at her house as many as could find places in her dining-room. She would take no excuse, not even the nervous condition in which the excitement of the previous hours had left her. At a bountifully supplied table in the early morning sat this modest, cultured woman, surrounded by soldiers in their worn, gray uniforms. The welcome she gave us was so gracious, she was so self-possessed, so calm and kind, that I found myself in an inquiring state of mind as to whether her sympathies were with the Northern or Southern side in the pending war. Cautiously, but with sufficient clearness to indicate to her my object, I ventured some remarks which she could not well ignore and which she instantly saw were intended to evoke some declaration upon the subject. She was too brave to evade it, too self-poised to be confused by it, and too firmly fixed in her convictions to hesitate as to the answer. With no one present except Confederate soldiers who were her guests, she replied, without a quiver in her voice, but with womanly gentleness: "General Gordon, I fully comprehend you, and it is due to myself that I candidly tell you that I am a Union woman. I cannot afford to be misunderstood, nor to have you misinterpret this simple courtesy. You and your soldiers last night saved my home from burning, and I was unwilling that you should go away without receiving some token of my appreciation. I must tell you, however, that, with my assent and approval, my husband is a soldier in the Union army, and my constant prayer to Heaven is that our cause may triumph and the Union be saved."

No Confederate left that room without a feeling of profound respect, of unqualified admiration, for that brave and worthy woman. No Southern soldier, no true Southern man, who reads this account will fail to render to her a like tribute of appreciation. The spirit of every high-souled Southerner was made to thrill over and over again at the evidence around him of the more than Spartan courage, the self-sacrifices and devotion, of Southern women, at every stage and through every trial of the war, as from first to last, they hurried to the front, their brothers and fathers, their husbands and sons. No Southern man can ever forget the words of cheer that came from these heroic women's lips, and their encouragement to hope and fight on in the midst of despair. When I met Mrs. Rewalt in Wrightsville, the parting with my own mother was still fresh in my memory. Nothing short of death's hand can ever obliterate from my heart the impression of that parting. Holding me in her arms, her heart almost bursting with anguish, and the tears running down her cheeks, she asked God to take care of me, and then said : " Go, my son; I shall perhaps never see you again, but I commit you freely to the service of your country." I had witnessed, as all Southern soldiers had witnessed, the ever-increasing consecration of those women to their cause. No language can fitly describe their saintly spirit of martyrdom, which grew stronger and rose higher when all other eyes could see the inevitable end of the terrific struggle slowly but surely approaching.

Returning from the banks of the Susquehanna, and meeting at Gettysburg, July 1, 1863, the advance of Lee's forces, my command was thrown quickly and squarely on the right flank of the Union army. A more timely arrival never occurred. The battle had been raging for four or five hours. The Confederate General Archer, with a large portion of his brigade, had been captured. Heth and Scales, Confederate generals, had been wounded. The ranking Union commander on the field, General Reynolds, had been killed, and Hancock was assigned to command. The battle, upon the issue of which hung, perhaps, the fate of the Confederacy, was in full blast. The Union forces, at first driven

back, now reënforced, were again advancing and pressing
back Lee's left and threatening to envelop it. The
Confederates were stubbornly contesting every foot of
ground, but the Southern left was slowly yielding. A
few moments more and the day's battle might have been
ended by the complete turning of Lee's flank. I was
ordered to move at once to the aid of the heavily
pressed Confederates. With a ringing yell, my command rushed upon the line posted to protect the Union
right. Here occurred a hand-to-hand struggle. That
protecting Union line once broken left my command
not only on the right flank, but obliquely in rear of it.
Any troops that were ever marshalled would, under like
conditions, have been as surely and swiftly shattered.
There was no alternative for Howard's men except to
break and fly, or to throw down their arms and surrender. Under the concentrated fire from front and
flank, the marvel is that any escaped. In the midst of
the wild disorder in his ranks, and through a storm of
bullets, a Union officer was seeking to rally his men for
a final stand. He, too, went down, pierced by a Minié
ball. Riding forward with my rapidly advancing lines,
I discovered that brave officer lying upon his back, with
the July sun pouring its rays into his pale face. He
was surrounded by the Union dead, and his own life
seemed to be rapidly ebbing out. Quickly dismounting
and lifting his head, I gave him water from my canteen,
asked his name and the character of his wounds. He
was Major-General Francis C. Barlow, of New York,
and of Howard's corps. The ball had entered his body
in front and passed out near the spinal cord, paralyzing
him in legs and arms. Neither of us had the remotest
thought that he could possibly survive many hours. I
summoned several soldiers who were looking after the
wounded, and directed them to place him upon a litter
and carry him to the shade in the rear. Before parting,

he asked me to take from his pocket a package of letters and destroy them. They were from his wife. He had but one request to make of me. That request was that if I should live to the end of the war and should ever meet Mrs. Barlow, I would tell her of our meeting on the field of Gettysburg and of his thoughts of her in his last moments. He wished me to assure her that he died doing his duty at the front, that he was willing to give his life for his country, and that his deepest regret was that he must die without looking upon her face again. I learned that Mrs. Barlow was with the Union army, and near the battle-field. When it is remembered how closely Mrs. Gordon followed me, it will not be difficult to realize that my sympathies were especially stirred by the announcement that his wife was so near him. Passing through the day's battle unhurt, I despatched at its close, under flag of truce, the promised message to Mrs. Barlow. I assured her that if she wished to come through the lines she should have safe escort to her husband's side. In the desperate encounters of the two succeeding days, and the retreat of Lee's army, I thought no more of Barlow, except to number him with the noble dead of the two armies who had so gloriously met their fate. The ball, however, had struck no vital point, and Barlow slowly recovered, though this fact was wholly unknown to me. The following summer, in battle near Richmond, my kinsman with the same initials, General J. B. Gordon of North Carolina, was killed. Barlow, who had recovered, saw the announcement of his death, and entertained no doubt that he was the Gordon whom he had met on the field of Gettysburg. To me, therefore, Barlow was dead; to Barlow, I was dead. Nearly fifteen years passed before either of us was undeceived. During my second term in the United States Senate, the Hon. Clarkson Potter, of New York, was a member of the House of Representatives. He invited me to dinner in Washington to meet a General Barlow who had served in the Union army. Potter knew nothing of the Gettysburg incident. I had heard that there was another Barlow in the Union army, and supposed, of course, that it was this Barlow with whom I was to dine. Barlow had a similar reflection as to the Gordon he was to meet. Seated at Clarkson Potter's table, I asked Barlow: " General, are you related to the Barlow who was killed at Gettysburg?" He replied: " Why, I am the man, sir. Are you related to the Gordon who killed me?" "I am the man, sir," I responded. No words of mine can convey any conception of the emotions awakened by those startling announcements. Nothing short of an actual resurrection from the dead could have amazed either of us more. Thenceforward, until his untimely death in 1896, the friendship between us which was born amidst the thunders of Gettysburg was greatly cherished by both.

No battle of our Civil War—no battle of any war—more forcibly illustrates the truth that officers at a distance from the field cannot, with any wisdom, attempt to control the movements of troops actively engaged. On the first day neither General Early nor General Ewell could possibly have been fully cognizant of the situation at the time I was ordered to halt. The whole of that portion of the Union army in my front was in inextricable confusion and in flight. They were necessarily in flight, for my troops were upon the flank and rapidly sweeping down the lines. The firing upon my men had almost ceased. Large bodies of the Union troops were throwing down their arms and surrendering, because in disorganized and confused masses they were wholly powerless either to check the movement or return the fire. As far down the lines as my eye could reach the Union troops were in retreat. Those at a distance were

still resisting, but giving ground, and it was only necessary for me to press forward in order to insure the same
results which invariably follow such flank movements.
In less than half an hour my troops would have swept
up and over those hills, the possession of which was of
such momentous consequence. It is not surprising, with
a full realization of the consequences of a halt, that I
should have refused at first to obey the order. Not until
the third or fourth order of the most peremptory character reached me did I obey. I think I should have
risked the consequences of disobedience even then but
for the fact that the order to halt was accompanied with
the explanation that General Lee, who was several miles
away, did not wish to give battle at Gettysburg. It is
stated on the highest authority that General Lee said,
sometime before his death, that if Jackson had been
there he would have won in this battle a great and possibly decisive victory.

The Rev. J. William Jones, D.D., writing of this statement of General Lee's, uses these words: "General Lee
made that remark to Professor James J. White and myself
in his office in Lexington one day when we chanced to go
in as he was reading a letter making some inquiries of
him about Gettysburg. He said, with an emphasis that I
cannot forget, and bringing his hand down on the table
with a force that made things rattle: 'If I had had
Stonewall Jackson at Gettysburg, I would have won that
fight, and a complete victory there would have given us
Washington and Baltimore, if not Philadelphia, and
would have established the independence of the Confederacy.'"

No soldier in a great crisis ever wished more ardently
for a deliverer's hand than I wished for one hour of
Jackson when I was ordered to halt. Had he been there,
his quick eye would have caught at a glance the entire
situation, and instead of halting me he would have urged

me forward and have pressed the advantage to the utmost, simply notifying General Lee that the battle was on and he had decided to occupy the heights. Had General Lee himself been present this would undoubtedly have been done. General Lee, as he came in sight of the battle-field that afternoon, sent Colonel Walter H. Taylor, of the staff (he makes this statement clearly in his book, "Four Years with Lee"), with an order to General Ewell to "advance and occupy the heights." General Ewell replied that he would do so, and afterward explained in his official report that he did not do so because of the report from General William Smith that the enemy was advancing on his flank and rear, the supposed enemy turning out to be General Edward Johnson's Confederate division. Absent as General Lee necessarily was, and intending to meet General Meade at another point and in defensive battle, he would still have applauded, when the facts were made known, the most aggressive movements, though in conflict with his general plan. From the situation plainly to be seen on the first afternoon, and from facts that afterward came to light as to the position of the different corps of General Meade's army, it seems certain that if the Confederates had simply moved forward, following up the advantages gained and striking the separated Union commands in succession, the victory would have been Lee's instead of Meade's.[1]

I should state here that General Meade's army at that hour was stretched out along the line of his march for

[1] I give here the numbers engaged. The figures are taken from the highest authorities:

FEDERAL.—Return, June 30, 1863, effective infantry and artillery (cavalry not reported), Army of the Potomac, 84,158 (Official Records, Vol. XXVII, Part I, p. 151). To which add cavalry (given by "Battles and Leaders" as 13,144), making a total of 97,302.

Estimates, at the battle: "Battles and Leaders," 93,500 (Vol. III, p. 440). Doubleday, 82,000 (he accepts estimate of the Count of Paris). Boynton, nearly thirty miles. General Lee's was much more concentrated. General Hancock's statement of the situation is true and pertinent: "The rear of our troops were hurrying through the town, pursued by Confederates. There had been an attempt to reform some of the Eleventh Corps as they passed over Cemetery Hill, but it had not been very successful." And yet I was halted!

My thoughts were so harrowed and my heart so burdened by the fatal mistake of the afternoon that I was unable to sleep at night. Mounting my horse at two o'clock in the morning, I rode with one or two staff officers to the red barn in which General Ewell and General Early then had their headquarters. Much of my time after nightfall had been spent on the front picket-line, listening to the busy strokes of Union picks and shovels on the hills, to the rumble of artillery wheels and the tramp of fresh troops as they were hurried forward by Union commanders and placed in position. There was, therefore, no difficulty in divining the scene that would break on our view with the coming dawn. I did not hesitate to say to both Ewell and Early that a line of heavy earthworks, with heavy guns and ranks of infantry behind them, would frown upon us at daylight. I expressed the opinion that, even at that hour, two o'clock, by a concentrated and vigorous night assault we could carry those heights, and that if we waited till morning it would cost us 10,000 men to take them. There was a disposition to yield to my suggestions, but

87,000. Meade, in testifying before Commission on Conduct of War, gives 95,000 (Second Series, Vol. I, p. 337). Livermore's "Numbers and Losses in Civil War," 83,000 pp. 102, 103).

CONFEDERATE.—Confederate returns, May 31, 1863, effective force, 68,352 (Official Records, Vol. XXV, Part I, pp. 845, 846).

Estimates, at the battle: "Battles and Leaders," 70,000 (Vol. IV, p. 440). Doubleday, 73,500 (he accepts estimate of the Count of Paris). Boynton, 80,000. Taylor's "Four Years with Lee," 62,000 (p. 113). Livermore's "Numbers and Losses," 75,054 (pp. 102, 103).

other counsels finally prevailed. Those works were never carried, but the cost of the assault upon them, the appalling carnage resulting from the effort to take them, far exceeded that which I had ventured to predict.

Late in the afternoon of this first day's battle, when the firing had greatly decreased along most of the lines, General Ewell and I were riding through the streets of Gettysburg. In a previous battle he had lost one of his legs, but prided himself on the efficiency of the wooden one which he used in its place. As we rode together, a body of Union soldiers, posted behind some buildings and fences on the outskirts of the town, suddenly opened a brisk fire. A number of Confederates were killed or wounded, and I heard the ominous thud of a Minié ball as it struck General Ewell at my side. I quickly asked: "Are you hurt, sir?" "No, no," he replied; "I'm not hurt. But suppose that ball had struck you: we would have had the trouble of carrying you off the field, sir. You see how much better fixed for a fight I am than you are. It don't hurt a bit to be shot in a wooden leg."

Ewell was one of the most eccentric characters, and, taking him all in all, one of the most interesting that I have ever known. It is said that in his early manhood he had been disappointed in a love affair, and had never fully recovered from its effects. The fair young woman to whom he had given his affections had married another man; but Ewell, like the truest of knights, carried her image in his heart through long years. When he was promoted to the rank of brigadier or major-general, he evidenced the constancy of his affections by placing upon his staff the son of the woman whom he had loved in his youth. The meddlesome Fates, who seem to revel in the romances of lovers, had decreed that Ewell should be shot in battle and become the object of solicitude and tender nursing by this lady, who had been for many years a widow—Mrs. Brown. Her gentle ministrations soothed his weary weeks of suffering, a marriage ensued, and with it came the realization of Ewell's long-deferred hope. It was most interesting to note the change that came over the spirit of this formerly irascible old bachelor. He no longer sympathized with General Early, who, like himself, was known to be more intolerant of soldiers' wives than the crusty French marshal who pronounced them the most inconvenient sort of baggage for a soldier to own. Ewell had become a husband, and was sincerely devoted to Mrs. Ewell. He never seemed to realize, however, that her marriage to him had changed her name, for he proudly presented her to his friends as "My wife, Mrs. Brown, sir."

Whatever differences of opinion may now or hereafter exist as to the results which might have followed a defeat of the Union arms at Gettysburg, there is universal concurrence in the judgment that this battle was the turning-point in the South's fortunes. The point where Pickett's Virginians, under Kemper, Garnett, and Armistead, in their immortal charge, swept over the rock wall, has been appropriately designated by the Government as "the high-water mark of the Rebellion." To the Union commander, General George Gordon Meade, history will accord the honor of having handled his army at Gettysburg with unquestioned ability. The record and the results of the battle entitle him to a high place among Union leaders. To him and to his able subordinates and heroic men is due the credit of having successfully met and repelled the Army of Northern Virginia in the meridian of its hope and confidence and power. This much seems secure to him, whether his failure vigorously to follow General Lee and force him to another battle is justified or condemned by the military critics of the future. General Meade's army halted, it is true, after having achieved a victory. The victory, however, was not of so decisive a character as to demoralize Lee's forces. The great Bonaparte said that bad as might be the condition of a victorious army after battle, it was invariably true that the condition of the defeated army was still worse. If, however, any successful commander was ever justified in disregarding this truism of Bonaparte's, General Meade was that commander; for a considerable portion of Lee's army, probably one third of it, was still in excellent fighting trim, and nearly every man in it would have responded with alacrity to Lee's call to form a defensive line and deliver battle.

It was my pleasure to know General Meade well after the war, when he was the Department Commander or Military Governor of Georgia. An incident at a banquet in the city of Atlanta illustrates his high personal and soldierly characteristics. The first toast of the evening was to General Meade as the honored guest. When this toast had been drunk, my health was proposed. Thereupon, objection was made upon the ground that it was "too soon after the war to be drinking the health of a man who had been fighting for four years in the Rebel army." It is scarcely necessary to say that this remark came from one who did no fighting in either army. He belonged to that curious class of soldiers who were as valiant in peace as they were docile in war; whose defiance of danger became dazzling after the danger was past. General Meade belonged to the other class of soldiers, who fought as long as fighting was in order, and was ready for peace when there was no longer any foe in the field. This chivalric chieftain of the Union forces at Gettysburg was far more indignant at the speech of the bomb-proof warrior than I was myself. The moment the objection to drinking my health was suggested, General Meade sprang to his feet, and with a compliment to myself which I shall not be expected to repeat, and a rebuke to the objector, he held high his glass and said, with significant emphasis: "I propose to drink, and drink now, to my former foe, but now my friend, General Gordon, of Georgia."

It will not be expected that any considerable space be devoted to the unseemly controversy over those brilliant but disastrous Confederate charges which lost the day at Gettysburg. I could scarcely throw upon the subject any additional light nor bring to its elucidation any material testimony not already adduced by those who have written on the one side or the other. A sense of justice, however, to say nothing of loyalty to Lee's memory, impels me to submit one observation; and I confidently affirm that nearly every soldier who fought under him will sympathize with the suggestion. It is this: that nothing that occurred at Gettysburg, nor anything that has been written since of that battle, has lessened the conviction that, had Lee's orders been promptly and cordially executed, Meade's centre on the third day would have been penetrated and the Union army overwhelmingly defeated. Lee's hold upon the confidence of his army was absolute. The repulse at Gettysburg did not shake it. I recall no instance in history where a defeated army retained in its retreating commander a faith so complete, and gave to him subsequent support so enthusiastic and universal.

General Longstreet is undoubtedly among the great American soldiers who attained distinction in our Civil War; and to myself, and, I am sure, to a large majority of the Southern people, it is a source of profound regret that he and his friends should have been brought into such unprofitable and ill-tempered controversy with the friends of his immortal chieftain.[1]

[1] It now seems certain that impartial military critics, after thorough investigation, will consider the following as established:

1. That General Lee distinctly ordered Longstreet to attack early the morning of the second day, and if he had done so, two of the largest corps

A third of a century has passed since, with Lee's
stricken but still puissant army, I turned my back upon
the field of Gettysburg, on which nearly 40,000 Americans
went down, dead or wounded, at the hands of fellow-
Americans. The commanders-in-chief and nearly all the
great actors upon it are dead. Of the heroes who fought
there and survived the conflict, a large portion have since
joined the ranks of those who fell. A new generation
has taken their places since the battle's roar was hushed,
but its thunders are still reverberating through my
memory. No tongue, nor pen, can adequately portray
its vacillating fortunes at each dreadful moment. As I
write of it now, a myriad thrilling incidents and rapidly
changing scenes, now appalling and now inspiring, rush
over my memory. I hear again the words of Barlow:
"Tell my wife that I freely gave my life for my country."
Yonder, resting on his elbow, I see the gallant young
Avery in his bloody gray uniform among his brave
North Carolinians, writing, as he dies: "Tell father that
I fell with my face to the foe." On the opposite hills,
Lee and Meade, surrounded by staff and couriers and

of Meade's army would not have been in the fight; but Longstreet delayed
the attack until four o'clock in the afternoon, and thus lost his opportunity
of occupying Little Round Top, the key to the position, which he might
have done in the morning without firing a shot or losing a man.

2. That General Lee ordered Longstreet to attack at daybreak on the
morning of the third day, and that he did not attack until two or three
o'clock in the afternoon, the artillery opening at one.

3. That General Lee, according to the testimony of Colonel Walter
Taylor, Colonel C. S. Venable, and General A. L. Long, who were present
when the order was given, ordered Longstreet to make the attack on the
last day, with the three divisions of his corps, and two divisions of A. P.
Hill's corps, and that instead of doing so he sent fourteen thousand men to
assail Meade's army in his strong position, and heavily intrenched.

4. That the great mistake of the halt on the first day would have been
repaired on the second, and even on the third day, if Lee's orders had been
vigorously executed, and that General Lee died believing (the testimony on
this point is overwhelming) that he lost Gettysburg at last by Longstreet's
disobedience of orders.

with glasses in hand, are surveying the intervening space. Over it the flying shells are plunging, shrieking, bursting. The battered Confederate line staggers, reels, and is bent back before the furious blast. The alert Federals leap from the trenches and over the walls and rush through this thin and wavering line. Instantly, from the opposite direction, with deafening yells, come the Confederates in countercharge, and the brave Federals are pressed back to the walls. The Confederate banners sweep through the riddled peach orchard; while farther to the Union left on the gory wheat-field the impacted forces are locked in deadly embrace. Across this field in alternate waves rolls the battle's tide, now from the one side, now from the other, until the ruthless Harvester piles his heaps of slain thicker than the grain shocks gathered by the husbandman's scythe. Hard by is Devil's Den. Around it and over it the deadly din of battle roars. The rattle of rifles, the crash of shells, the shouts of the living and groans of the dying, convert that dark woodland into a harrowing pandemonium. Farther to the Union left, Hood, with his stalwart Texans, is climbing the Round Tops. For a moment he halts to shelter them behind the great boulders. A brief pause for rest, and to his command, "Forward!" they mount the huge rocks reddened with blood—and Hood's own blood is soon added. He falls seriously wounded; but his intrepid Alabamians under Law press forward. The fiery brigades of McLaws move to his aid. The fiercest struggle is now for the possession of Little Round Top. Standing on its rugged summit like a lone sentinel is seen an erect but slender form clad in the uniform of a Union officer. It is Warren, Meade's chief of engineers. With practised eye, he sees at a glance that, quickly seized, that rock-ribbed hill would prove a Gibraltar amidst the whirling currents of the battle, resisting its heaviest shocks. Staff and couriers are summoned, who swiftly bear his messages to the Union leaders. Veterans from Hancock and Sykes respond at a "double-quick." Around its base, along its sides, and away toward the Union right, with the forces of Sickles and Hancock, the gray veterans of Longstreet are in herculean wrestle. Wilcox's Alabamians and Barksdale's Mississippians seize a Union battery and rush on. The Union lines under Humphreys break through a Confederate gap and sweep around Barksdale's left. Wright's Georgians and Perry's Floridians are hurled against Humphreys and break him in turn. Amidst the smoke and fury, Sickles with thighbone shivered, sickens and falls from his saddle into the arms of his soldiers. Sixty per cent. of Hancock's veterans go down with his gallant Brigadiers Willard, Zook, Cross, and Brooke. The impetuous Confederate leaders, Barksdale and Semmes, fall and die, but their places are quickly assumed by the next in command. The Union forces of Vincent and Weed, with Hazlett's artillery, have reached the summit, but all three are killed. The apex of Little Round Top is the point of deadliest struggle. The day ends, and thus ends the battle. As the last rays of the setting sun fall upon the summit, they are reflected from the batteries and bayonets of the Union soldiers still upon it, with the bleeding Confederates struggling to possess it. The embattled hosts sleep upon their arms. The stars look down at night upon a harrowing scene of pale faces all over the field, and of sufferers in the hospitals behind the lines—an army of dead and wounded numbering over twenty thousand.

The third day's struggle was the bloody postscript to the battle of the first and second. There was a pause. Night had intervened. It was only a pause for breath. Of sleep there was little for the soldiers, perhaps none for the throbbing brains of the great chieftains. Victory to Lee meant Southern independence. Victory to

Meade meant an inseparable Union. The life of the Confederacy, the unity of the Republic — these were the stakes of July 3. Meade decided to defend; Lee resolved to assault. The decisive blow at Meade's left centre was planned for the early morning. The morning came and the morning passed. The Union right, impatient at the Confederate delay, opens fire on Lee's left. The challenge is answered by a Confederate charge under Edward Johnson. The Union trenches are carried. Ruger's Union lines sweep down from the heights on Johnson's left and recover these trenches. High noon is reached, but the assault on the left centre is still undelivered. With every moment of delay, Lee's chances are diminishing with geometrical progression. At last the heavy signal-guns break the fatal silence and summon the gray lines of infantry to the charge. Pickett's Virginians are leading. The tired veterans of Heth and Wilcox and Pettigrew move with them. Down the long slope and up the next the majestic column sweeps. With Napoleonic skill, Meade's artillerists turn the converging, galling fire of all adjacent batteries upon the advancing Confederates. The heavy Southern guns hurl their solid shot and shell above the Southern lines and into the Union ranks on the summit. The air quivers and the hills tremble. Onward, still onward, the Southern legions press. Through a tempest of indescribable fury they rush toward the crest held by the compact Union lines. The Confederate leaders, Garnett, Trimble, and Kemper, fall in the storm — the first dead, the others down and disabled. On the Union side, Hancock and Gibbon are borne bleeding to the rear. Still onward press the men in gray, their ranks growing thinner, their lines shorter, as the living press toward the centre to fill the great gaps left by the dead. Nearly every mounted officer goes down. Riderless horses are flying hither and thither. Above the battle's roar is heard the familiar Southern yell. It proclaims fresh hope, but false hope. Union batteries are seen to limber up, and the galloping horses carry them to the rear. The Confederate shout is evoked by a misapprehension. These guns are not disabled. They do not fly before the Confederate lines from fear of capture. It is simply to cool their heated throats. Into their places quickly wheel the fresh Union guns. Like burning lava from volcanic vents, they pour a ceaseless current of fire into the now thin Confederate ranks. The Southern left is torn to fragments. Quickly the brilliant Alexander, his ammunition almost exhausted, flies at a furious gallop with his batteries to the support of the dissolving Confederate infantry. Here and there his horses and riders go down and check his artillery's progress. His brave gunners cut loose the dead horses, seize the wheels, whirl the guns into position, and pour the hot grape and canister into the faces of the Federals. The Confederates rally under the impulse, and rush onward. At one instant their gray jackets and flashing bayonets are plainly seen in the July sun. At the next they disappear, hidden from view as the hundreds of belching cannon conceal and envelop them in sulphurous smoke. The brisk west wind lifts and drives the smoke from the field, revealing the Confederate banners close to the rock wall. Will they go over? Look! They are over and in the Union lines. The left centre is pierced, but there is no Union panic, no general flight. The Confederate battle-flags and the Union banners are floating side by side. Face to face, breast to breast, are the hostile hosts. The heavy guns are silent. The roar of artillery has given place to the rattle of rifles and crack of pistol-shots, as the officers draw their side arms. The awful din and confusion of close combat is heard, as men batter and brain each other with clubbed muskets. The brave young Pennsylvanian, Lieutenant

Cushing, shot in both thighs, still stands by his guns. The Confederates seize them; but he surrenders them only with his life. One Southern leader is left; it is the heroic Armistead. He calls around him the shattered Southern remnants. Lifting his hat on the point of his sword, he orders " Forward! " on the second line, and falls mortally wounded amidst the culminating fury of Gettysburg's fires.

The collision had shaken the continent. For three days the tumult and roar around Cemetery Heights and the Round Tops seemed the echo of the internal commotion which ages before had heaved these hills above the surrounding plain.

It is a great loss to history and to posterity that General Lee did not write his own recollections as General Grant did. It was his fixed purpose to do so for some years after the war ended. From correspondence and personal interviews with him, I know that he was profoundly impressed with the belief that it was his duty to write, and he expended much time and labor in getting the material for such a work. From his reports, which are models of official papers, were necessarily excluded the free and full comments upon plans, movements, men, failures, and the reasons for such failures, as they appeared to him, and of which he was the most competent witness. To those who knew General Lee well, and who added to this knowledge a just appreciation of his generous nature, the assumption by him of entire responsibility for the failure at Gettysburg means nothing except an additional and overwhelming proof of his almost marvellous magnanimity. He was commander-in-chief, and as such and in that sense he was responsible; but in that sense he was also responsible for every act of every officer and every soldier in his army. This, however, is not the kind of responsibility under discussion. This is not the standard which history will erect and by which he will be judged. If by reason of repeated mistakes or blunders he had lost the confidence and respect of his army, and for this cause could no longer command its cordial and enthusiastic support, this fact would fix his responsibility for the failure. But no such conditions appertained. As already stated, the confidence in him before and after the battle was boundless. Napoleon Bonaparte never more firmly held the faith of Frenchmen, when thrones were trembling before him, than did Lee hold the faith of his devoted followers, amidst the gloom of his heaviest disasters.

If his plan of battle was faulty, then for this he is responsible; but if his general plan promised success, and if there was a lack of cheerful, prompt, and intelligent coöperation in its execution, or if there were delays that General Lee could not foresee nor provide against, and which delays or lack of coöperation enabled General Meade to concentrate his reserves behind the point of contemplated attack, then the responsibility is shifted to other shoulders.

There was nothing new or especially remarkable in General Lee's plans. Novelties in warfare are confined rather to its implements than to the methods of delivering battle. To Hannibal and Cæsar, to Frederick and Napoleon, to Grant and Lee, to all great soldiers, the plan was familiar. It was to assault along the entire line and hold the enemy to hard work on the wings, while the artillery and heaviest impact of infantry penetrated the left centre. Coöperation by every part of his army was expected and essential. However well trained and strong may be the individual horses in a team, they will never move the stalled wagon when one pulls forward while the other holds back. They must all pull together, or the heavily loaded wagon will never be carried to the top of the hill. Such coöperation at Gettysburg was only partial, and limited to comparatively small forces. Pressure—hard, general, and constant pressure—upon Meade's right would have called him to its defence and weakened his centre. That pressure was only spasmodic and of short duration. Lee and his plan could only promise success on the proviso that the movement was both general and prompt. It was neither. Moments in battle are pregnant with the fate of armies. When the opportune moment to strike arrives, the blow must fall; for the next instant it may be futile. Not only moments, but hours, of delay occurred. I am criticising officers for the lack of complete coöperation, not for unavoidable delays. I am simply stating facts which must necessarily affect the verdict of history. Had all the commands designated by General Lee coöperated by a simultaneous assault, thus preventing Meade from grouping his troops around his centre, and had the onset upon that centre occurred in the early morning, as intended by Lee, it requires no partiality to see that this great commander's object would have been assuredly achieved. That the plan involved hazard is undoubtedly true. All battles between such troops as confronted each other at Gettysburg are hazardous and uncertain. If the commanders of the Confederate and Union armies had waited for opportunities free of hazard and uncertainty, no great battle would have been fought and the war never would have ended. The question which history will ask is this: Was General Lee justified in expecting success? The answer will be that, with his experience in meeting the same Union army at Fredericksburg, at the second Manassas, in the seven-days' battles around Richmond, and at Chancellorsville; with an army behind him which he believed well-nigh invincible, and which army believed its commander well-nigh infallible; with a victory for his troops on the first day at Gettysburg, the completeness of which had been spoiled only by an untimely and fatal halt; with the second day's battle ending with alternate successes and indecisive results; and with the expectation of prompt action and vigorous united coöperation, he was abundantly justified in confidently expecting success.

Wellington at Waterloo and Meade at Gettysburg, each held the highlands against his antagonist. Wellington on Mont-Saint-Jean, and Meade on Cemetery Ridge, had the bird's-eye view of the forces of attack. The English batteries on the plateau and the Union batteries on Cemetery Heights commanded alike the intervening undulations across which the charging columns must advance. Behind Mont-Saint-Jean, to conceal Wellington's movements from Napoleon's eye, were the woodlands of Soignies. Behind Cemetery Ridge, to conceal Meade's movements from the field-glasses of Lee, was a sharp declivity, a protecting and helpful depression. As the French under Napoleon at Waterloo, so the Confederates under Lee at Gettysburg, held the weaker position. In both cases the assailants sought to expel their opponents from the stronger lines. I might add another resemblance in the results which followed. Waterloo decreed the destiny of France, of England, of Europe. Gettysburg, not so directly or immediately, but practically, decided the fate of the Confederacy.

There were points of vast divergence. The armies which met at Waterloo were practically equal. This was not true of the armies that met at Gettysburg.[1] Napoleon's artillery far exceeded that of Wellington. Lee's was far inferior to Meade's, in the metal from which the

---

[1] General Lee's army at Gettysburg, according to most reliable estimates [see note, pp. 155 and 156], was about 60,000 or 62,000; General Meade's is placed by different authorities at figures ranging from 82,000 to 105,000. Appleton's Cyclopedia of American Biography places the numbers of Lee at 69,000 and Meade's between 82,000 and 84,000.

guns were moulded, as well as in number. Waterloo was a rout, Gettysburg a repulse. Napoleon, in the ensuing panic, was a deserted fugitive. Lee rode amidst his broken lines calmly majestic, the idol of his followers. With no trace of sympathy for Napoleon's selfish aims, with righteous condemnation of his vaulting ambition, one cannot fail to realize the profound pathos of his position on that dismal night of wildest panic and lonely flight. Abandoned by fortune, deserted by his army, discrowned and doomed, he is described by Hugo as having not an organized company to comfort him, not even his faithful Old Guard to rally around him. In Lee's army there was neither panic nor precipitate retreat. There was no desertion of the great commander. Around him still stood his heroic legions, with confidence in him unshaken, love for him unabated, ready to follow his lead and to fight under his orders to the last extremity.

General Meade evidently, perhaps naturally, expected far greater confusion and disorganization in Lee's army, from the terrific repulse to which it had been subjected. He wisely threw his cavalry upon Lee's flank in order to sweep down upon the rear and cut to pieces or capture the fragments of Southern infantry, in case of general retreat or demoralization. As the Union bugles sounded the charge, however, for the gallant horsemen under Farnsworth, Lee's right was ready to receive them. Proudly they rode, but promptly were they repulsed. Many saddles were emptied by Confederate bullets. The intrepid commander, General Farnsworth himself, lost his life in the charge. On the other flank, and with similar design, Lee had placed Stuart with his dashing Confederate riders. Stuart was to attack when Lee's infantry had pierced Meade's centre, and when the Union army was cut in twain and in rapid retreat. This occasion never came to Stuart, but he found all the opportunity he could reasonably desire for the exercise of his men and horses in a furious combat with Gregg's five thousand Union troopers.

The introduction of gunpowder and bullets and of long-range repeating rifles has, in modern warfare, greatly lessened the effectiveness of cavalry in general battle with infantry, and deprived that great arm of the service of the terror which its charges once inspired. In wars of the early centuries, the swift horsemen rode down the comparatively helpless infantry and trampled its ranks under the horses' feet. For ages after the dismemberment of the Roman Empire, it was the vast bodies of cavalry that checked and changed the currents of battles and settled the fate of armies and empires. This is not true now — can never be true again; but a cavalry charge, met by a countercharge of cavalry, is still, perhaps, the most terrible spectacle witnessed in war. If the reader has never seen such a charge, he can form little conception of its awe-inspiring fury. Imagine yourself looking down from Gettysburg's heights upon the open, wide-spreading plain below, where five thousand horses are marshalled in battle line. Standing beside them are five thousand riders, armed, booted and spurred, and ready to mount. The bugles sound the "Mount!" and instantly five thousand plumes rise above the horses as the riders spring into their saddles. In front of the respective squadrons the daring leaders take their places. The fluttering pennants or streaming guidons, ten to each regiment, mark the left of the companies. On the opposite slope of the same plain are five thousand hostile horsemen clad in different uniforms, ready to meet these in countercharge. Under those ten thousand horses are their hoofs, iron-shod and pitiless, beneath whose furious tread the plain is soon to quiver. Again on each slope of the open field the bugles sound. Ten thousand sabres leap from scabbards and glisten in the sun. The trained horses chafe their restraining bits, and, as the bugle notes sound the charge, their nostrils dilate and their flanks swell in sympathetic impulse with the dashing riders. " Forward ! " shouts the commander. Down the lines and through the columns in quick succession ring the echoing commands," Forward, forward ! " As this order thrills through eager ears, sabres flash and spurs are planted in palpitating flanks. The madly flying horses thunder across the trembling field, filling the air with clouds of dust and whizzing pebbles. Their iron-rimmed hoofs in remorseless tread crush the stones to powder and crash through the flesh and bones of hapless riders who chance to fall. As front against front these furious riders plunge, their sweeping sabres slashing edge against edge, cutting a way through opposing ranks, gashing faces, breaking arms, and splitting heads, it is a scene of wildest war, a whirling tempest of battle, short-lived but terrible.

Ewell's Corps, of which my command was a part, was the last to leave Gettysburg, and the only corps of either army, I believe, that forded the Potomac. Reaching this river, we found it for the time an impassable barrier against our further progress southward. The pontoons had been destroyed. The river was deep and muddy, swollen and swift. We were leaving Pennsylvania and the full granaries that had fed us. Pennsylvania was our Egypt whither we had "gone to buy corn." We regretted leaving, although we had found far less favor with the authorities of this modern Egypt than had Joseph and his brethren with the rulers of the ancient land of abundance.

The fording of the Potomac in the dim starlight of that 13th of July night, and early morning of the 14th, was a spectacular phase of war so quaint and impressive as to leave itself lastingly daguerreotyped on the memory. To the giants in the army the passage was comparatively easy, but the short-legged soldiers were a source of anxiety to the officers and of constant amusement to their long-legged comrades. With their knapsacks high up on their shoulders, their cartridge-boxes above the knapsacks, and their guns lifted still higher to keep them dry, these little heroes of the army battled with the current from shore to shore. Borne down below the line of march by the swiftly rolling water, slipping and sliding in the mud and slime, and stumbling over the boulders at the bottom, the marvel is that none were drowned. The irrepressible spirit for fun-making, for jests and good-natured gibes, was not wanting to add to the grotesque character of the passage. Let the reader imagine himself, if he can, struggling to hold his feet under him, with the water up to his armpits, and some tall, stalwart man just behind him shouting, "Pull ahead, Johnny; General Meade will help you along directly by turning loose a battery of Parrott guns on you." Or another, in his front, calling to him: "Run here, little boy, and get on my back, and I 'll carry you over safely." Or still another, with mock solemnity, proposing to change the name of the corps to "Lee's Waders," and this answered by a counter-proposition to petition the Secretary of War to imitate old Frederick the Great and organize a corps of "Six-footers" to do this sort of work for the whole army. Or still another offering congratulations on this opportunity for being washed, "The first we have had, boys, for weeks, and General Lee knows we need it."

Most of our wounded and our blue-coated comrades who accompanied us as prisoners were shown greater consideration—they were ferried across in boats. The only serious casualty connected with this dangerous crossing occurred at the point least expected. From the pontoon-bridge, which had been repaired, and which was regarded as not only the most comfortable but by far the safest method of transit, the horses and a wagon loaded with sick and wounded were plunged into the river. By well-directed effort they were rescued, not one of the men, I believe, being lost.

General Meade was deliberate in his pursuit, if not considerate in his treatment of us. He had induced us to change our minds. Instead of visiting Philadelphia on this trip, he had persuaded us to return toward Richmond. He doubtless thought that the last day's fight at Gettysburg was fairly good work for one campaign, and that if he attempted to drive us more rapidly from Pennsylvania, the experiment might prove expensive. As previously intimated, he was probably correct in this opinion. Had he left his strong position while Lee stood waiting for him to come out on the Fourth of July at Gettysburg and to assume the offensive, the chances are at least even that his assault would have been repelled and might have led to a Union disaster. One of the wisest adages in war is to avoid doing what your antagonist desires, and it is beyond dispute that, from General Lee down through all the grades, even to the heroic privates in the ranks, there was a readiness if not a desire to meet General Meade should he advance upon us. Meade's policy after the Confederate repulse at Gettysburg did not differ materially from that of Lee after the Union repulse at Fredericksburg. General Halleck, as he surveyed the situation from Washington, did not like. General Meade's deliberation and pelted him with telegrams extremely nettling to that proud soldier's sensibilities. In the citadel of the War Office at Washington, General Halleck could scarcely catch so clear a view of the situation as could General Meade from the bloody and shivered rocks of the Round Tops. No one doubts General Halleck's ability or verbal impetuosity. To Southern apprehension, however, there was far more serious work to be expected from the silent Grant and the undemonstrative Meade than from the explosive Halleck or fulminating Pope.

It is one of the curious coincidences of the war that the results at Gettysburg furnished the occasion for the tender of resignation by each of the commanders-in-chief. Lee offered to resign because he had not satisfied himself; Meade because he had not satisfied his Government. Lee feared discontent among his people; Meade found it with General Halleck. Relief from command was denied to Lee; it was granted at last to Meade.

It would have been a fatal mistake, a blunder, to have accepted General Lee's resignation. There was no other man who could have filled his place in the confidence, veneration, and love of his army. His relief from command in Virginia would have brought greater dissatisfaction, if not greater disaster, than did the removal from command of General Joseph E. Johnston in Georgia. The Continental Congress might as safely have dispensed with the services of Washington as could the Confederacy with those of Lee. Looking back now over the records of that Titanic sectional struggle in the light of Lee's repeated successes prior to the Gettysburg battle and of his prolonged resistance in 1864–65, with depleted ranks and exhausted resources, how strangely sounds the story of his self-abnegation and desire to turn over his army to some "younger and abler man"! How beautiful and deeply sincere the words, coming from his saddened heart, in which he characterized his devoted followers in that official letter tendering his resignation! Speaking of the new commander, whose selection he was anxious should at once be made, he said: "I know he will have as gallant and brave an army as ever existed to second his efforts, and it will be the happiest day of my life to see at its head a worthy leader—one who can accomplish more than I can hope to perform, and all that I have wished." He urged with characteristic earnestness as his reason for asking the selection of another commander, "the desire to serve my country, and to do all in my power to insure the success of her righteous cause." He had no grievances to ventilate; no scapegoat to bear the burden of his responsibilities; no puerile repinings at the fickleness of Fortune; no complaints to lodge against the authorities above him for the paucity of the resources they were able to provide. Of himself, and of himself only, did he complain; and he was the only man in his army who would have made such complaint. General Lee might criticise himself, but criticisms of him by any other officer would have been answered by an indignant and crushing rebuke from the whole Confederate army. The nearest approach he made to fault-finding was his statement that his own sight was not perfect, and that he was so dull that, in attempting to use the eyes of others, he found himself often misled.

To General Lee's request to be relieved, and to have an abler man placed in his position, Mr. Davis very pointedly aud truthfully replied that to request him to find some one "more fit for command, or who possessed more of the confidence of the army, or of the reflecting men of the country, is to demand an impossibility."

CHAPTER XII

VICKSBURG AND HELENA

The four most crowded and decisive days of the war—Vicksburg the culmination of Confederate disaster — Frequent change of commanders in the Trans-Mississippi Department—General Grant's tunnel at Fort Hill—Courage of Pemberton's soldiers—Explosion of the mine—Hand-to-hand conflict—The surrender.

IF called upon to select in the four years of war, from April, 1861, to April, 1865, four consecutive days into which were crowded events more momentous and decisive than occurred in any other like period, I should name the 1st, 2d, 3d, and 4th of July, 1863. During the first three we were engaged at Gettysburg in a struggle which might decide the fate of the Federal capital, of Baltimore, and possibly of Philadelphia, if not of the Union itself. On the 4th General Grant received the surrender at Vicksburg of 35,000 Confederates under General Pemberton.

There were other days which will always be conspicuous in the records of that war; but I do not believe that any other four days, consecutive or isolated, so directly and decidedly dashed the hopes of the Southern people. The double disaster to our arms—the Gettysburg failure and the fall of Vicksburg—occurring at distant points and almost simultaneously, was a blow heavy enough to have effectually dispirited any army that was ever marshalled. It is, however, a remarkable fact that the morale of the Confederate army was not affected—at

177

least, was not perceptibly lowered by it. The men endured increasing privations with the same cheerfulness and fought with the same constancy and courage after those events as they did before. In proof, I need only summon as witnesses the fields of Chickamauga, Resaca, Atlanta, and Jonesboro in Georgia; Franklin in Tennessee; Monocacy in Maryland; and the Wilderness, Spottsylvania, Cold Harbor, Bermuda Hundred, and Petersburg in Virginia. To Southern thought this wonderfully persistent courage of the Southern troops is easily understood on the theory that the independence of the South was as consecrated a cause as any for which freemen ever fought; but it is probably true that such steadfastness and constancy under such appalling conditions will remain to analytical writers of later times one of the unsolved mysteries of that marvellous era of internecine strife.

The capture by General Grant of Pemberton and his men at Vicksburg was preceded by no great victories in the West for either side. The Confederates, however, had been successful in their efforts to hold some points on the Mississippi River, thus preventing its entire control by the Union army and the complete isolation of the Confederate forces in the Trans-Mississippi Department. On the very day (Fourth of July, 1863) when General Grant was receiving the surrender of Vicksburg and its starving army, the Confederates on the other side of the Mississippi were fighting for the possession of the river at Helena, Arkansas. General Sterling Price ("Old Pap," as he was affectionately called by his men, who felt for him the devotion of children for a father) had captured one of the leading forts which crowned the hill at Helena, and was halting in the fort for Generals Joe Shelby and Walker, under Marmaduke, to capture the most northern fort and then sweep down upon the Union lines held by Colonel Clayton. Shelby was wounded, and Walker did not assail the Union lines because he was waiting under orders until the fort was captured by Shelby. Out of this affair grew that unfortunate quarrel between Generals Walker and Marmaduke which ended in a challenge to a duel, and the killing of Walker by Marmaduke.

While Price was thus waiting for the movement under Marmaduke, General Holmes, who was the commander-in-chief of the Confederate forces, rode to the captured fort. He ordered General Price at once to assault an infinitely stronger fort, one heavily manned and practically impregnable. The forces which Price could bring against it were utterly inadequate, and the assault failed, disastrously failed, adding to the discomfiture of the Confederacy.

As illustrating the trials which beset both the Confederate and United States governments in their efforts to select able and efficient chiefs for their armies, I may note the fact that the Trans-Mississippi Department changed commanders about as often as the Union army in Virginia changed leaders in its repeated marches upon Richmond. General Holmes was not successful in his effort to command the support or the good-will of his officers and men. Disagreements with his officers were not rare, and arrests were not infrequent. On a notable occasion General Joe Shelby, of Missouri, one of the noted cavalry officers of the Civil War, was placed under arrest and ordered to report to the Commanding General. Shelby, in his cavalry operations, was compelled to depend largely upon his own efforts among the people to furnish supplies for his men and horses. Necessarily, under such circumstances, there were occasional collisions between his appointed foragers and the suffering citizens. Such disagreements could not be avoided, although the citizens were patriotic and generous, and the large body of Shelby's men were of the law-abiding and leading classes of northern Missouri. When these disagreements occurred between the soldiers and the citizens, complaints were made to General Holmes. Without waiting to investigate the charges, he at once ordered Shelby under arrest. When the dashing cavalryman appeared before his commanding general to learn the reason for his arrest, the irascible General Holmes opened upon him a battery of invective. His first discharge was: "General Shelby, you are charged with being a robber, sir, and your men with being thieves."

"Who made these charges, General Holmes?"

"Everybody, sir; everybody!"

"And you believe them, do you, General Holmes?"

"Certainly I do, sir. How can I help believing them?"

Joe Shelby, justly proud of his splendid command, was deeply indignant at the wrong done both to himself and his high-spirited men. He was also not a little amused by this remarkable procedure and by the fiery invectives of the aged commander. He quietly replied:

"Well, General Holmes, I will be more just to you than you have been to me and my men. Everybody says that you are a damned old fool; but I do not believe it."

This ended the interview, and in the ensuing battles nothing more was heard of the arrest or the charges. General Shelby died recently while holding the office of United States Marshal for his State and the position of Commander of the United Confederate Veterans of Missouri.

Among these Missouri Confederates was Dick Lloyd, a private in Price's command who deserves a place among American heroes. In a furious battle Dick Lloyd had both arms shot off below the elbow. He recovered, however, and refused to be retired from service. Without hands he still did his duty as a soldier to the end of the war, acting as courier, and guiding and successfully managing his horse by tying the bridle-reins around the crook in his elbow. He lives now in

Helena, and has supported his family for years by riding horseback, carrying mail through country districts.

The commander of the Union forces at Helena on this fourth day of July, 1863, was the gallant General Prentiss, who made so enviable a record at Shiloh, where he was captured. In that battle the position which for hours was held by his men was raked by so deadly a fire that it was called by the Federals " The Hornet's Nest " and he " The Hero of the Hornet's Nest." At Helena, July, 1863, he repulsed Shelby at the flanking fort, Feagin at Fort Hindman, and Price at Fort Curtis, after that brave old Missourian had captured the fortress upon Graveyard Hill. Prentiss was, therefore, enabled to join General Grant in celebrating the Fourth of July over another victory for the Union armies. The roaring guns on the opposite banks of the Mississippi proclaimed the opening of the river from the source to its mouth—news as depressing to the Confederates as it was inspiring to the Union armies. To the Southern heart and hope this final capture and complete control of the great waterway severing the Confederate territory and isolating the great storehouse beyond the Mississippi, while recognized as a great calamity, was perhaps less depressing and galling than the surrender at Vicksburg of Pemberton's splendid army of 35,000 men. The imperial Roman, Cæsar Augustus, after the crushing defeat of his vicegerent Varus in Germany, which involved the destruction of his army and the dragging of his proud Eagles in the dust, lamented more the loss of that valiant body of Roman soldiery than he did the breaking of his dominion over German territory. In his grief over this irreparable disaster, Augustus is said to have murmured to himself as he gazed into vacancy, " Varus, Varus, give me back my legions." It is no exaggeration to say that if General Pemberton could have saved his army, could have given back to the Confederacy those splendid "legions" which had so long and so bravely fought and starved in the trenches around Vicksburg, the fall of that Mississippi city would have been stripped of more than half its depressing effects. General Grant knew this. He knew that the Confederate government could not replace those soldiers, who were among its best; and he decided, therefore, to circumvent, if possible, all efforts at escape and every movement to rescue them.

General Johnston, then chief in command of the Army of the West, had anticipated the siege of Vicksburg and had persistently endeavored to prevent General Pemberton being hemmed in. But there was no other avenue open to General Pemberton, as General Grant had closed all other lines of retreat.

The shock of Vicksburg's fall was felt from one end of the Confederacy to the other. Following so closely on the repulse of the Confederates at Gettysburg, it called from the press and people thoughtless and unfair criticisms. In a peculiarly sensitive mood, the public sought some other explanation than the real one, and great injustice was done General Pemberton. But this brave officer's loyalty and devotion were tested — thoroughly tested. At a sacrifice almost measureless, he had separated from his own kindred, and in obedience to his profound convictions had drawn his sword for Southern independence. He did not cut his way out of Vicksburg because his army was not strong enough; he did not hold the city longer because his troops and the population could not live without food. That great soldier, General Joseph E. Johnston, with all his skill in manœuvre and as strategist, failed to afford the needed relief. At Raymond, on May 12, General Johnston had been forced back upon Jackson, Mississippi. On the 14th he fought the heavy battle of Jackson. On the 16th,

Pemberton moved out and fought, grandly fought, at Champion Hill. Three days later he made another stand against Grant's advance at Black River; holding the weaker lines and with inferior forces, he was driven into the trenches at Vicksburg. On the 22d of May, three days later, General Grant invested the fated city. Thenceforward to July 4th Pemberton and his men held those works against the combined fire of small arms, artillery, and gunboats, sinking a Union monitor on the river, making sorties to the front, resisting efforts to scale the works, rallying around the breach made by the explosion at Fort Hill, rushing upon and crushing the Union columns as they pressed into that breach, and holding the city against every assault, save that of starvation.

Scarcely had General Grant settled in his lines around the city when his intrepid men were standing in the dim starlight on the margin of the ditches which bordered the Confederate earthworks. With scaling-ladders on their shoulders, they made ready to mount the parapets and fight hand to hand with the devoted Confederate defenders. These great ditches were deep and wide; the scaling-ladders were too short. Upon the top of the earthworks stood Pemberton's men, pouring a galling fire down on the Union heads below. Under that fire the Union ranks melted, some falling dead upon the bank, others tumbling headlong into the ditches, still others leaping voluntarily sixteen feet downward to its bottom to escape the consuming blast, and the remainder abandoning the futile effort in precipitate retreat.

The commanding position along the line of defensive works was the fortress on the lofty eminence called Fort Hill. Toward this fortress, with the purpose of undermining it and blowing it skyward, General Grant began early in June to drive his zigzag tunnel. The task was not herculean in the amount of labor required to accomplish it, but was a most tedious one, as but few men could be employed at the work, and every pound of earth had to be carried out at the tunnel's mouth. Day and night the work was pressed. Nearer and nearer the tunnel approached the point where mother earth was to receive into her innocent bosom the explosives that would hurl the fort high into the air and bury in the ruins the brave men who defended it. While such explosions failed to accomplish important results during this war, the knowledge that they were to occur, and the uncertainty as to when or where, filled the minds of soldiers with an indescribable apprehension. The high-spirited volunteers of both armies could meet without a tremor the most furious storms and agony of battle in the open field, where they could see the foe and meet fire with fire; if need be, they could face the pelting hail of bullets without returning a shot, and meet death as Napoleon's great marshal proposed to meet it when, in the endeavor to hold his troops in a withering fire without returning it, he stepped to their front and, folding his arms, said to them, " Soldiers of France, see how a marshal can die in discharge of his duty!" But to walk the silent parapets in the gloom of night, above the magazine of death which they knew was beneath them, to stand in line along the threatened battlements, with only the dull tread of the sentinel sounding in the darkness, while the imagination pictured the terrors of the explosion which was coming perhaps that night, perhaps that hour or that moment, or the next: this was a phase of war which taxed the nerve of any soldier, even the most phlegmatic.

Pemberton's soldiers, faint with hunger and in full knowledge that they were standing above a death-dealing magazine, endured such harrowing suspense night after night for weeks. As each regiment was successively assigned to the awful duty, they wondered whether the tunnel was yet complete, whether the barrels of powder had been placed beneath them, whether it was to be their fate or the fate of the next regiment to be whirled upward with tons of earth and torn limb from limb. Bravely, grandly, they took their posts without a murmur. No hyperbole can exaggerate the loftiness of spirit that could calmly await the moment and manner of such a martyrdom. Every one of those emaciated Southern soldiers who trod that fated ground should have his name recorded in history. Beside them in American war annals should be placed the names of those Union soldiers who, amidst the explosions and conflagration at Yorktown, Virginia, in December, 1863, won the gratitude of their people. During those trying scenes, in the effort to prevent the escape of the Confederate prisoners, Private Michael Ryan of the Sixteenth New York, his leg shivered by a shell, remained on his knees at his post with his musket in hand. Private Healey, One Hundred and Forty-eighth New York, stood at the gate, almost parched by the flames, until the explosion hurled the gate and his own body high into the air.

On the night of June 26, 1863, the long-dreaded hour came to Pemberton's faithful and fated watchers. General Grant had finished his tunnel. Under the fortress at Fort Hill he had piled the tons of powder, and had run through this powder electric wires whose sparks of fire were to wake the black Hercules to the work of death. As Pemberton's Confederates stood around the silent battlements, the moments were lengthened into hours by the intensity of their apprehension; and as Grant's veterans crept and formed in the darkness behind the adjacent hills, waiting for the earthquake shock to summon them to the breach, the clock in the sleeping city struck the hour of ten. The electric messengers flew along the wires. The loaded magazines responded with the convulsive roar of a thousand unchained thunderbolts. The hills quivered, shaking from roof to foundation-stone every Vicksburg home. High above its highest turret flew the trampled floor of the fortress, with the bodies of its gray-clad defenders. Into its powder-blackened and smoking ruins quickly rushed the charging columns of Grant, led by the Thirty-second Regiment of Illinois; Pemberton's Confederates from the right and left and rear of the demolished fort piled into the breach at the same instant. Hand to hand over the upheaved and rugged earth they grappled with the invaders in the darkness. This Illinois regiment, after desperately fighting and holding the breach for two hours, was overpowered. Again and again in rapid succession came the Union charges. Pemberton's veterans, from the broken rim of the fortress, poured upon them an incessant fire from small arms, and, carrying loaded shells with burning fuses in their hands, rolled them down the crater's banks to explode among the densely packed attacking forces. For six hours this furious combat raged in the darkness. From ten at night till four in the morning the resolute Federals held the breach, but could make no headway against the determined Confederate resistance. The tunnel had been driven, the magazine exploded, and the fort demolished. The long agony of Confederate suspense was over. The desperate effort of the Union commander to force his column through the breach had failed. The heaps of his dead and wounded, more than a thousand in number, piled in that narrow space, had given to this spot among his surviving men the name of "Logan's Slaughter Pen." In the terrific explosion a Confederate negro, who chanced to be in the fort at the time, was thrown a considerable distance toward the Union line without being fatally hurt. Picking himself up half dead, half alive, he found around him the Union soldiers moving on the smoking crater.

" How did you get here ? " he was asked.

" Don't know, boss.   Yestidy I was in de Confed'acy ; but, bless de Lawd, last night somethin' busted and blowed me plum' into de Union."

CHAPTER XIII

FROM VICKSBURG AND GETTYSBURG TO CHICKAMAUGA

Lee's army again headed toward Washington—He decides not to cross the Potomac at the opening of winter—Meade's counter-attack—Capture of a redoubt on the Rappahannock—A criticism of Secretary Stanton—General Bragg's strategy—How Rosecrans compelled the evacuation of Chattanooga.

IN the autumn of 1863 both Lee's and Meade's armies had returned from Pennsylvania and were again camping or tramping on the soil of Virginia. The Union forces were in complete and easy communication with the great storehouses and granaries of the North and West. The Confederates were already in a struggle for meagre subsistence. Meade began another march on Richmond. Lee patched up his army as best he could, threw it across Meade's path, and halted him at the Rapidan. Thenceforward for weeks and months, these two commanders were watching each other from opposite sides of the Rapidan, moving up and down the river and the roads, seeking an opportunity for a blow and never finding it. Lee made the first move. On October 9, 1863, he headed his army again toward Washington and the Potomac, passing Meade's right, and threatening to throw the Confederates between the Union forces and the national capital. Lee at one time was nearer to Washington than Meade, but as there was no longer any green corn in the fields for the Southern soldiers to subsist upon, the difficulty of feeding them checked Lee's march

188

and put Meade ahead of him and nearer to the defences around Washington. Lee then debated whether he should assail Meade on or near the old field of Bull Run or recross the Potomac into Maryland and Pennsylvania. He decided not to attack, because he found Meade's position too strong and too well intrenched. He declined to cross again the Potomac at the opening of winter, because, as he said, "Thousands of our men are barefooted, thousands with fragments of shoes, all without overcoats, blankets, or warm clothing. I cannot bear to expose them to certain suffering on an uncertain issue." We were not able then, as formerly, to furnish to each soldier strips of rawhide, which he might tie on, with the hair side next his feet, and thus make rude sandals; and these picturesque foot-coverings, if obtainable, would scarcely have been sufficient for long marches in the coming freezes. So Lee returned to his camps behind the Rapidan and Rappahannock.

Some spirited engagements of minor importance occurred between detached portions of the two armies, in which the honors were about equally divided between the two sides. Stuart's Southern horsemen had the better of the fight at Buckland, and the Confederates were successful on the Rapidan; but Warren's Union forces captured five pieces of artillery and between four and five hundred prisoners from A. P. Hill.

As Lee moved back, Meade followed, and the programme of marching after each other across the river was resumed. Just one month, lacking two days, after Lee's move toward Washington, Meade turned his columns toward Richmond. His first dash, made at a redoubt which stood in his way on the north bank of the Rappahannock, was a brilliant success. The redoubt was occupied by a portion of Early's troops, and was carried just before nightfall by a sudden rush. I sat on my horse, with a number of officers, on the opposite side of the little river, almost within a stone's throw of the spot. General Early did not seem to consider it seriously threatened, nor did any one else, although the Union artillery was throwing some shells, one of which lowered the perch of a visiting civilian at my side by shortening the legs of his horse. The dash upon the redoubt was made by Maine and Wisconsin regiments—troops of Russell and Upton, under Sedgwick, who was regarded by the Confederates as one of the best officers in the Union army. Personally I had great reason to respect Sedgwick, for it was my fortune in the ensuing campaign to be pitted against him on several occasions. Though nothing like so serious to the Confederates in its results, this brilliant little episode on the Rappahannock resembled in character the subsequent great charge of Hancock over the Bloody Angle at Spottsylvania on May 12, 1864. Both assaults were so unexpected and made with such a rush that the defending troops had no time to fire. Only a few shots were discharged at Hancock's men at Spottsylvania, and in the capture of this redoubt by Russell and Upton only six Union men were killed. It was justly considered by General Meade as most creditable to his troops; and he sent General Russell himself to bear the eight captured Confederate flags to Washington. Mr. Stanton may have been a great Secretary of War, and I must suppose him such; but if he treated General Russell as he is reported to have treated him, he had as little appreciation of the keen sensibilities of a high-strung soldier as old Boreas has for the green summer glories of the great oak. The Secretary, it is said, was "too busy" to see General Russell. The proposition will scarcely be questioned, I think, that a Secretary of War, who is not called upon to endure the hardships of the field and meet the dangers of battle, should never be "too busy" to meet a gallant soldier who is defending his flag at the front, and who calls to lay before him the trophies of victory. Perhaps the Secretary thought that General Russell and his men had only done their duty. So they had; but "Light Horse Harry" Lee, the father of General Robert E. Lee, only did his duty when he planned and executed the brilliant dash upon Paulus Hook and captured it. The Continental Congress, however, thought it worth its while to turn from its regular business and make recognition of the handsome work done by voting the young officer a gold medal. All the wreaths ever conferred at the Olympic games, all the decorations of honor ever bestowed upon the brave, all the swords and the thanks ever voted to a soldier, were designed to make the same impress upon their recipients which three minutes of the busy Secretary's time and a few gracious words would have produced on the mind and spirit of General Russell and his comrades.

General Meade crossed the Rappahannock and then recrossed it. He found Lee strongly posted behind Mine Run, and suddenly returned to his winter quarters. General Lee moved back to his encampment on the border of the Wilderness and along the historic banks of the Rapidan.

Meantime, in the months intervening between the Gettysburg campaign and the hibernation of the two armies in 1863–64, a portion of Lee's forces had been sent under Longstreet to aid Bragg in his effort to check the further advance of the Union army under Rosecrans at Chickamauga. My troops were not among those sent to Georgia, and therefore took no part in that great battle which saturated with blood the soil of my native State.

A chapter full of interest to the military critic and to the student of strategy might be written of the two armies commanded respectively by Rosecrans and Bragg, and of their movements prior to the clash in the woodlands at Chickamauga.

The antecedent campaign runs back in a connected chain to the battle of Murfreesboro, Tennessee, in the preceding December. Under General Bragg, at Murfreesboro, as one of his division commanders, was an ex-Vice-President of the United States, who had also been a prominent candidate for the Presidency in the campaign of 1860, and had presided over the joint session of the two houses of Congress when Abraham Lincoln was declared duly elected. This illustrious statesman, who was fast winning his way to distinction in his new rôle of Confederate soldier, was John C. Breckinridge of Kentucky. Tall, erect, and commanding in physique, he would have been selected in any martial group as a typical leader. In the campaign in the Valley of Virginia, where I afterward saw much of him, he exhibited in a marked degree the characteristics of a great commander. He was fertile in resource, and enlisted and held the confidence and affection of his men, while he inspired them with enthusiasm and ardor. Under fire and in extreme peril he was strikingly courageous, alert, and self-poised. No man in the Confederate army had surrendered a brighter political future, sacrificed more completely his personal ambition, or suffered more keenly from the perplexing conditions in his own State. With all his other trials, and before he had fairly begun his career as a soldier, General Breckinridge had been strongly tempted to challenge to personal combat his superior officer, General Bragg, who at the time was commander-in-chief of the Confederate forces in the Department of Tennessee and the West. At the battle of Murfreesboro, Tennessee (December, 1862), this brilliant soldier from the blue-grass region had led his gallant Kentuckians through a consuming fire on both flanks, losing about thirty-six per cent. of his men in less than half an hour. General Bragg, who, it seems, was not present at the point where this movement was made, had in some way been misinformed as to the conduct of General Breckinridge's troops, and sent to Richmond a disparaging despatch.

These high-bred sons of Kentucky who had left home and kindred behind them had already made a record of devotion and daring, which grew in lustre to the end of the war, and which any troops of any army might envy. At this battle of Murfreesboro they had waded the river in chilly December, had charged and captured the first heights and doubled back one wing of their stubbornly fighting antagonists. They had, however, been repelled with terrific slaughter in the impossible effort to capture the still more commanding hill. In this fearful assault they had marched between converging lines of fire drawn up in the shape of the letter V, the apex of those lines formed by hills crowned with batteries. Among their killed was the dashing General Hanson, one of the foremost soldiers of Bragg's army. No troops that were ever marshalled could have succeeded under such conditions and against such odds. Had they persisted in the effort, they would simply have invited annihilation. Smarting under a sense of the injustice done themselves and their dead comrades by the commanding general's despatch to Richmond, and realizing their own inability to have the wrong righted, they appealed to General Breckinridge, their own commander, to resent the insult. Resolutions and protests were powerless to soothe their smarting sensibilities or to assuage their burning wrath. They urged General Breckinridge to resign his position in the army and call General Bragg to personal account—to challenge him to single-handed combat. General Breckinridge must have felt as keenly as they the wrong inflicted, but he was more self-contained. He sought to appease them by reminding them of the exalted motives which had impelled them to enlist in the army as volunteers, of the self-sacrifice which they had exhibited, and of their duty as soldiers to endure any personal wrong for the sake of the common cause. His appeal was not in vain; and when he added that if both he and General Bragg should live to the end of the war, he would not forget their request to call the commanding general to account, they gladly went forward, enduring and fighting to the end.

The Fabian policy of General Bragg, adopted after the bloody encounter at Murfreesboro, his retreat to Chattanooga and beyond it, called from press and people fewer and milder protests than those afterward made against General Joseph E. Johnston for a like policy. It would seem that the persistent criticisms of General Johnston for not meeting General Sherman between Dalton and Atlanta in determined battle, might have been applied with equal force to General Bragg for surrendering the strong positions in the gaps of the Cumberland Mountains and the line of the Tennessee River to General Rosecrans, without more resolute resistance. It is much easier, however, to criticise a commander than to command an army. In both these cases the strong positions alluded to could have been successfully flanked and the Confederate commanders forced to retire, as the Union troops moved around toward the rear and threatened the Southern lines of communication and supplies. General Rosecrans was too able a soldier and too wise a strategist to assail General Bragg in his selected stronghold when the country was open to him on either flank. His policy, therefore, was to cross the Tennessee River, not in front of Chattanooga, where Bragg was ready to meet him, but at a distance either above or below it. Both were practicable; and he set his army in motion toward points both above and below the city, thus leaving General Bragg in doubt as to his real purpose. He sent a force to the hills just opposite Chattanooga, and opened heavy fire with his batteries upon Bragg's position. He sent still larger forces up the right bank of the Tennessee to a point more than forty miles above Chattanooga. Camp-fires were built along the brows of the mountains and on hillsides, in order to attract Bragg's attention and create the belief that the great body of the Union army was above the city. Troops were marched across open spaces exposed to view, then countermarched behind the hills, and passed again and again through the same open spaces, thus deepening the impression that large forces were marching up the river. To still further strengthen this impression upon the Confederate commander, Union drums were beat and bugles sounded for great distances along the mountain-ranges. Union axes, saws, and hammers were loud in their demonstrations of boat-building; but they were only demonstrations. The real work, the real preparation, was going forward fully fifty miles south of this noisy point. The apparent movement above Chattanooga, and the real preparation for crossing far below, were admirably planned and consummately executed by General Rosecrans, and showed a strategic ability perhaps not surpassed by any officer during the war. Behind the woods and hills men were drilled in the work of laying bridges. Trains of cars loaded with bridges and boats were unloaded at a point entirely pro-tected from the view of the Confederate cavalry on the opposite banks of the river. Fifty of these boats, each with a capacity of fifty men, were hurried in the early morning to the river-bank and launched upon the water. This formidable fleet, carrying 2500 armed men, pulled for the other shore, which was guarded only by Confed-erate cavalry pickets. With this strong force of Union infantry landed on the southern bank, the pontoon-bridge soon spanned the stream. Across it were hurried all the Union infantry and artillery that could be crowded upon it. At other points canoes of enormous size were hewn out of tall poplars that grew in the lowlands. Logs were rolled into the stream and fastened together, and as these improvised flotillas, loaded with soldiers, were pushed from the shore, athletic swimmers, left behind, caught the enthusiasm, and piling their clothing, arms, and accoutrements upon rails lashed together, leaped into the stream and swam across, pushing the loaded rails before them. At still another point the Union cavalry rode into the river and spurred their hesitating horses into the deep water for a long swim to the other shore. As thousands of struggling, snorting horses bore these human forms sitting upright upon their backs, nothing seen above the water's surface except the erect upper portions of the riders' bodies and the puffing nostrils of the horses with their bushy tails spread out behind them, the scene must have presented the appearance of a mass of moving centaurs rather than an army of mounted soldiers. Such scenes, however, were not infrequent during the war—especially with the noted Confederate raiders of John Morgan, Jeb Stuart, Bedford Forrest, and Mosby. With his army safely across the river, General Rosecrans pushed heavy columns across Raccoon and Lookout mountains and the intervening valley, completely turned General Bragg's position, and compelled the evacuation of Chattanooga without a skirmish.

It would be the grossest injustice to General Bragg to hold him responsible for the failure to prevent General Rosecrans crossing the Tennessee. An army double the size of the one he commanded would have been wholly insufficient to cover the stretch of more than one hundred miles of river-frontage. The Union commander could have laid his pontoons and forced a passage at almost any point against so attenuated a line of resistance. General Bragg was not only one of the boldest fighters in the Confederate army, but he was an able commander. Retreat from Chattanooga was his only resource. This movement was made not an hour too soon. Rosecrans's columns were sweeping down from the eastern Lookout Bluffs, and would speedily have grasped Bragg's only line of railroad and held his only avenues of escape. As the Union officers Thomas and McCook came down the eastern slopes of the mountain and Crittenden came around its point and into Chattanooga, Bragg placed his army in position for either resisting, retreating, or advancing. He decided to assume the offensive and to attack the Union forces in their isolated positions, and crush them, if possible, in detail. Longstreet had not yet arrived; but had Bragg's plan of assault been vigorously executed, it now seems certain that he would have won a great triumph before the Union army could have been concentrated along the western bank of the Chickamauga. General Rosecrans himself and his corps commanders were fully alive to the hazardous position of his army. Bragg's aggressive front changed the policy of the Union commander from one of segregation for pursuit to one of concentration for defence. Rapidly and skilfully was that concentration effected. Boldly and promptly did the Confederates advance. The next scene on which the curtain rose was the collision, the crash, the slaughter at Chickamauga.

CHAPTER XIV

CHICKAMAUGA

One of the bloodiest battles of modern times—Comparison with other great battles of the world—Movements of both armies before the collision—A bird's-eye view—The night after the battle—General Thomas's brave stand—How the assault of Longstreet's wing was made—Both sides claim a victory.

REARED from childhood to maturity in North Georgia, I have been for fifty years familiar with that historic locality traversed by the little river Chickamauga, which has given its name to one of the bloodiest battles of modern times. Not many years after the Cherokee Indians had been transferred to their new Western home from what was known as Cherokee Georgia, my father removed to that portion of the State. Here were still the fresh relics of the redskin warriors, who had fished in Chickamauga's waters and shot the deer as they browsed in herds along its banks. Every locality now made memorable by that stupendous struggle between the Confederate and Union armies was impressed upon my boyish memory by the legends which associated them with deeds of Indian braves. One of the most prominent features of the field was the old Ross House, built of hewn logs, and formerly the home of Ross, a noted and fairly well-educated Cherokee chief. In this old building I had often slept at night on my youthful journeyings with my father through that sparsely settled region. Snodgrass Hill,

Gordon's and Lee's Mills, around which the battle raged, the La Fayette road, across which the contending lines so often swayed, and the crystal Crawfish Spring, at which were gathered thousands of the wounded, have all been so long familiar to me that I am encouraged to attempt a brief description of the awful and inspiring events of those bloody September days in 1863. Words, however, cannot convey an adequate picture of such scenes; of the countless costly, daring assaults; of the disciplined or undisciplined but always dauntless courage; of the grim, deadly grapple in hand-to-hand collisions; of the almost unparalleled slaughter and agony.

An American battle which surpassed in its ratio of carnage the bloodiest conflicts in history outside of this country ought to be better understood by the American people. Sharpsburg, or Antietam, I believe, had a larger proportion of killed and wounded than any other single day's battle of our war; and that means larger than any in the world's wars. Chickamauga, however, in its two days of heavy fighting, brought the ratio of losses to the high-water mark. Judged by percentage in killed and wounded, Chickamauga nearly doubled the sanguinary records of Marengo and Austerlitz; was two and a half times heavier than that sustained by the Duke of Marlborough at Malplaquet; more than double that suffered by the army under Henry of Navarre in the terrific slaughter at Coutras; nearly three times as heavy as the percentage of loss at Solferino and Magenta; five times greater than that of Napoleon at Wagram, and about ten times as heavy as that of Marshal Saxe at Bloody Raucoux. Or if we take the average percentage of loss in a number of the world's great battles—Waterloo, Wagram, Valmy, Magenta, Solferino, Zurich, and Lodi—we shall find by comparison that Chickamauga's record of blood surpassed them nearly three for one. It will not do to say

that this horrible slaughter in our Civil War was due to
the longer range of our rifles nor to the more destructive character of any of our implements of warfare;
for at Chickamauga as well as in the Wilderness and at
Shiloh, where these Americans fell at so fearful a rate,
the woodlands prevented the hostile lines from seeing
each other at great distances and rendered the improved
arms no more effective than would have been rifles of
short range. Some other and more reasonable explanation must be found for this great disparity of losses in
American and European wars. There is but one possible explanation—the personal character and the consecrated courage of American soldiers. At Chickamauga
thousands fell on both sides fighting at close quarters,
their faces at times burnt by the blazing powder at the
very muzzles of the guns.

The Federal army under Rosecrans constituted the
center of the Union battle line, which, in broadest military sense, stretched from Washington City to New
Orleans. The fall of Vicksburg had at last established
Federal control of the Mississippi along its entire length.
The purpose of Rosecrans's movement was to penetrate
the South's centre by driving the Confederates through
Georgia to the sea. Bragg, to whom was intrusted for
the time the task of resisting this movement, had retired
before the Union advance from Chattanooga to a point
some miles south of the Chickamauga, and the Union
forces were pressing closely upon his rear. Bragg had,
however, halted and turned upon Rosecrans and compelled him to retrace his steps to the north bank of the
Chickamauga, which, like the Chickahominy in Virginia, was to become forever memorable in the Republic's annals.

In order to obtain a clear and comprehensive view of
the ever-shifting scenes during the prolonged battle,
to secure a mental survey of the whole field as the

marshalled forces swayed to and fro, charging and countercharging, assaulting, breaking, retreating, reforming, and again rushing forward in still more desperate assault, let the reader imagine himself on some great elevation from which he could look down upon that wooded, undulating, and rugged region.

For forty-eight hours or more the marching columns of Bragg were moving toward Chattanooga and along the south bank of the Chickamauga in order to cross the river and strike the Union forces on the left flank. At the same time Rosecrans summoned his corps from different directions and concentrated them north of the river. Having passed, as was supposed, far below the point where the Union left rested, Bragg's columns, in the early hours of the 19th of September, crossed the fords and bridges, and prepared to sweep by left wheel on the Union flank. During the night, however, George H. Thomas had moved his Union corps from the right to this left flank. Neither army knew of the presence of the other in this portion of the woodland. As Bragg prepared to assail the Union left, Thomas, feeling his way through the woods to ascertain what was in his front, unexpectedly struck the Southern right, held by Forrest's cavalry, and thus inaugurated the battle. Forrest was forced back; but he quickly dismounted his men, sent the horses to the rear, and on foot stubbornly resisted the advance of the Union infantry. Quickly the Confederates moved to Forrest's support. The roar of small arms on this extreme flank in the early morning admonished both commanders to hurry thither their forces. Bragg was forced to check his proposed assault upon another portion of the Union lines and move to the defence of the Confederate right. Rapidly the forces of the two sides were thrown into this unexpected collision, and rapidly swelled the surging current of battle. The divisions of the Union army before whom Forrest's cavalry had yielded were now driven back; but other Federals suddenly rushed upon Forrest's front. The Southern troops, under Cheatham and Stewart, Polk, Buckner, and Cleburne, hurried forward in a united assault upon Thomas. Walthall's Mississippians at this moment were hurled upon King's flank, and drove his brigade in confusion through the Union lines; and as Govan's gray-clad veterans simultaneously assailed the Union forces under Scribner, that command also yielded. The Federal battery was captured, and the tide of success seemed at the moment to be with the Confederates. Fortune, however, always fickle, was especially capricious in this battle. The Union forces farther to westward held their ground with desperate tenacity. General Rosecrans, the Federal commander-in-chief, rode amidst his troops as they hurried in converging columns to the point of heaviest fire, and in person hurled them fiercely against the steadfast Confederate front. The shouts and yells and the roll of musketry swelled the din of battle to a deafening roar. The fighting was terrific. Walthall's Mississippians at this point contended desperately with attacks in front and on their flank. The Ninth Ohio, at double quick and with mighty shout, rushed upon the captured Union battery and recovered it. The Confederate gunners were killed by bayonets as they bravely stood at their posts. Hour after hour the battle raged, extending the area of its fire and the volume of its tremendous roar. Here and there along the lines a shattered command, its leading officers dead or wounded, was withdrawn, reorganized, and quickly returned to its bloody work. Still farther toward the Confederate right, Forrest again essayed to turn the Union left. Charging as infantry, he pressed forward through a tempest of shot and neared the Union flank, when the Federal batteries poured upon his entire line rapid discharges of grape, canister, and shell. Round after round on flank and front, these deadly volleys came until Forrest's dissolving lines disappeared, leaving heaps of dead near the mouths of the Union guns. Reforming his broken ranks, Forrest, with Cheatham's support, again rushed upon the Union left, the impetuous onset bringing portions of the hostile lines to a hand-to-hand struggle. Still there was no decisive break in the stubborn Union ranks. Coming through woods and fields from the other wings, the flapping ensigns marked the rapid concentration of both armies around this vortex of battle. As the converging columns met, bayonet clashed with bayonet and the trampled earth was saturated with blood. Here and there the Union line was broken by the charges of Cheatham, Stewart, and Johnson, but was quickly reformed and reestablished by the troops under Reynolds. The Union commands of Carlin and Heg were swept back before the fire at short range from the Southern muskets; but as the Confederate lines again advanced and leaped into the Union trenches, they were met and checked by a headlong countercharge.

The La Fayette road along or near which the broken lines of each army were rallied and reformed, and across which the surging currents of fire had repeatedly rolled, became the "bloody lane" of Chickamauga.

The remorseless war-god at this hour relaxed his hold on the two armies whose life-blood had been flowing since early morning. Gradually the mighty wrestlers grew weary and faint, and silence reigned again in the shell-shivered forest. It was, however, only a lull in the storm. On the extreme Union left the restless Confederates were again moving into line for a last and tremendous effort. The curtain of night slowly descended, and the powder-blackened bayonets and flags over the hostile lines were but dimly seen in the dusky twilight. Wearily the battered ranks in gray moved again through the bullet-scarred woods, over the dead bodies of their brothers who fell in the early hours and whose pale faces told the living of coming fate. Nature mercifully refused to lend her light to guide the unyielding armies to further slaughter. But the blazing muzzles of the rifles now became their guides, and the first hour of darkness was made hideous by resounding small arms and their lurid flashes. Here might follow a whole chapter of profoundly interesting personal incidents. The escape of officers of high rank, who on both sides rode with their troops through the consuming blasts, was most remarkable; but here and there the missiles found them. General Preston Smith, of Tennessee, my friend in boyhood, was among the victims. A Minié ball in search of his heart struck the gold watch which covered it. The watch was shivered, but it only diverted the messenger of death to another vital point. The inverted casing, whirled for a great distance through the air, fell at the feet of a Texan, who afterward sent it to the bereaved family. Near by was found the Union General Baldwin, his blue uniform reddened with his own blood and the blood of his dead comrades around him. The carnage was appalling and sickening. "Enough of blood and death for one day!" was the language of the bravest hearts which throbbed with anguish at the slaughter of the 19th and with anxiety as to the morrow's work.

Night after the battle! None but a soldier can realize the import of those four words. To have experienced it, felt it, endured it, is to have witnessed a phase of war almost as trying to a sensitive nature as the battle itself. The night after a battle is dreary and doleful enough to a victorious army cheered by triumph. To the two armies, whose blood was still flowing long after the sun went down on the 19th, neither of them victorious, but each so near the other as to hear the groans of the wounded and dying in the opposing ranks, the scene was indescribably oppressive. Cleburne's Confederates had waded the river with the water to their arm-pits. Their clothing was drenched and their bodies shivering in the chill north wind through the weary hours of the night. The noise of axe-blows and falling trees along the Union lines in front plainly foretold that the Confederate assault upon the Union breastworks at the coming dawn was to be over an abatis of felled timber, tangled brush, and obstructing tree-tops. The faint moonlight, almost wholly shut out by dense foliage, added to the weird spell of the sombre scene. In every direction were dimly burning tapers, carried by nurses and relief corps searching for the wounded. All over the field lay the unburied dead, their pale faces made ghastlier by streaks of blood and clotted hair, and black stains of powder left upon their lips when they tore off with their teeth the ends of deadly cartridges. Such was the night between the battles of the 19th and 20th of September at Chickamauga.

At nine o'clock on that Sabbath morning, September 20, as the church bells of Chattanooga summoned its children to Sunday-school, the signal-guns sounding through the forests at Chickamauga called the bleeding armies again to battle. The troops of Longstreet had arrived, and he was assigned to the command of the Confederate left, D. H. Hill to the Confederate right. On this latter wing of Bragg's army were the troops of John C. Breckinridge, W. H. T. Walker, Patrick Cleburne, and A. P. Stewart, with Cheatham in reserve. Confronting them and forming the Union left were the blue-clad veterans under Baird, Johnson, Palmer, and Reynolds, with Gordon Granger in reserve. Beginning on the other end of the line forming the left wing of Bragg's battle array were Preston, Hindman, and Bushrod Johnson, with Law and Kershaw in reserve. Confronting these, beginning on the extreme Union right and forming the right wing of Rosecrans's army, were

Sheridan, Davis, Wood, Negley, and Brannan, with Wilder and Van Cleve in reserve.

The bloody work was inaugurated by Breckinridge's assault upon the Union left. The Confederates, with a ringing yell, broke through the Federal line. The Confederate General Helm, with his gallant Kentuckians, rushed upon the Union breastworks and was hurled back, his command shattered. He was killed and his colonels shot down. Again rallying, again assaulting, again recoiling, this decimated command temporarily yielded its place in line. The Federals, in furious countercharge, drove back the Confederates under Adams, and his body was also left upon the field.

The Chickamauga River was behind the Confederates; Missionary Ridge behind the Federals. On its slopes were Union batteries pouring a storm of shell into the forests through which Bragg's forces were bravely charging. As the Confederates under Adams and Helm were borne back, the clear ring of Pat Cleburne's "Forward!" was heard; and forward they moved, their alignment broken by tree-tops and tangled brush and burning shells. His superb troops pressed through the storm, only to recoil under the concentrated fire of artillery and the blazing muzzles of small arms from the Federals behind their breastworks. The whole Confederate right, brigade after brigade, in successive and repeated charges, now furiously assailed the Union breastworks, only to recoil broken and decimated. Walthall, with his fiery Mississippians, was repulsed, with all his field officers dead or wounded and his command torn into shreds. The gallant Georgians at once rushed into the consuming blasts, and their brilliant leader, Peyton Colquitt, fell, with many of his brave boys around him, close to the Union breastworks. The Confederates under Walker, Cleburne, and Stewart with wild shouts charged the works held by the determined forces of Reynolds, Bran-

nan, and Baird. Bravely these Union troops stood to
their posts, but the Southern forces at one point broke
through their front as Breckinridge swept down upon
flank and rear. George H. Thomas, the "Rock of
Chickamauga," with full appreciation of the crisis, called
for help to hold this pivotal position of the Union left.
Van Derveer's moving banners indicated the quick step of
his troops responding to Thomas's call; and raked by
flanking fire, this dashing officer drove Breckinridge back
and relieved the Union flank. At double quick and with
ringing shout, the double Union lines pressed forward
until, face to face and muzzle to muzzle, the fighting became fierce and desperate. Charging columns of blue and
gray at this moment rushed against each other, and both
were shivered in the fearful impact. The superb Southern leader, Deshler, fell at the head of his decimated command. Govan's Mississippians and Brown's Tennesseeans
were forced back, when Bate, also of Tennessee, pressed
furiously forward, captured the Union artillery, and
drove the Federals to their breastworks. Again and
quickly the scene was changed. Fresh Union batteries
and supporting infantry with desperate determination
overwhelmed and drove back temporarily the Confederates led by the knightly Stewart. Still farther westward, Longstreet drove his column like a wedge into the
Union right center, ripping asunder the steady line of
the Federal divisions. In this whirlwind of battle,
amidst its thunders and blinding flashes, the heroic
Hood rode, encouraging his men, and fell desperately
wounded. His leading line was shattered into fragments,
but his stalwart supports pressed on over his own and
the Union dead, capturing the first Union line. Halting
only to reform under fearful fire, they started for the
second Union position. Swaying, reeling, almost breaking, they nevertheless captured that second line, and
drove up the ridge and over it the Federal fighters, who

bravely resisted at every step. Whizzing shells from opposing batteries crossed each other as they tore through the forest, rending saplings and tumbling severed limbs and tree-tops amidst the surging ranks. Wilder's mounted Union brigade in furious charge swept down upon Manigault's Confederates, flank and rear, and drove them in wild confusion; but the Union horsemen were in turn quickly driven from the field and beyond the ridge. Battery after battery of Union artillery was captured by the advancing Confederates. The roaring tide of battle, with alternate waves of success for both sides, surged around Snodgrass House and Horseshoe Ridge. Before a furious and costly Confederate charge the whole extreme Union right was broken and driven from the field. Negley's shattered lines of blue abandoned the position and retreated to Rossville with the heavy batteries. Davis, with decimated Union lines under Carlin and Heg, moved into Negley's position; but these were driven to the right and rear. Onward, still onward, swept the Confederate columns; checked here, broken there, they closed the gaps and pressed forward, scattering Van Cleve's veterans in wild disorder. Amidst the shouting Confederates rode their leaders, Stewart, Buckner, Preston, Kershaw, and Johnson. The gallant McCook led in person a portion of Sheridan's troops with headlong fury against the Southern front; and Sheridan himself rode among his troops, rallying his broken lines and endeavoring to check the resistless Southern advance. The brave and brilliant Lytle of the Union army, soldier and poet, at this point paid to valor and duty the tribute of his heart's blood. The Confederate momentum, however, scattered these decimated Union lines and compelled them to join the retreating columns, filling the roads in the rear.

Rosecrans, McCook, and Crittenden rode to Chattanooga to select another line for defence. In the furious tempest there now came one of those strange, unexpected lulls; but the storm was only gathering fresh fury. In the comparative stillness which pervaded the field its mutterings could still be heard. Its lightnings were next to flash and its thunders to roll around Horseshoe summit. Along that crest and around Snodgrass House the remaining troops of Rosecrans's left wing planted themselves for stubborn resistance—one of the most stubborn recorded in history. To meet the assault of Longstreet's wing, the brave Union General Brannan, standing upon this now historic crest, rallied the remnants of Croxton, Wood, Harker, Beatty, Stanley, Van Cleve, and Buell; but up the long slopes the exulting Confederate ranks moved in majestic march. As they neared the summit a sheet of flame from Union rifles and heavy guns blazed into their faces. Before the blast the charging Confederates staggered, bent and broke; reforming at the foot of the slope, these dauntless men in gray moved again to still more determined assault upon the no less dauntless Union lines firmly planted on the crest. Through the blinding fires they rushed to a hand-to-hand conflict, breaking here, pushing forward there, in terrible struggle. Through clouds of smoke around the summit the banners and bayonets of Hindman's Confederates were discovered upon the crest; when Gordon Granger and Steedman, with fresh troops, hurried from the Union left and, joining Van Derveer, hurled Hindman and his men from this citadel of strength and held it till the final Union retreat. With bayonets and clubbed muskets the resolute Federals pierced and beat back the charging Confederates, covering the slopes of Snodgrass Hill with Confederate dead. Roaring like a cyclone through the forest, the battle-storm raged. Battery answered battery, deepening the unearthly din and belching from their heated throats the consuming iron hail. The woods caught fire from the flaming shells and scorched the bodies of dead and dying. At the close of the day the Union forces had been driven from every portion of the field except Snodgrass Hill, and as the sun sank behind the cliffs of Lookout Mountain, hiding his face from one of the bloodiest scenes enacted by human hands, this heroic remnant of Rosecrans's army withdrew to the rear and then to the works around Chattanooga, leaving the entire field of Chickamauga to the battered but triumphant and shouting Confederates.

It is not my purpose to enter the controversy as to numbers brought into action by Bragg and Rosecrans respectively. General Longstreet makes the strength of the two armies practically equal; General Boynton's figures give to Bragg superiority in numbers. It is sufficient for my purpose to show that the courage displayed by both sides was never surpassed in civilized or barbaric warfare; that there is glory enough to satisfy both; that the fighting from first to last was furious; that there was enough precious blood spilt by those charging and recoiling columns in the deadly hand-to-hand collisions on the 19th and 20th of September to immortalize the prowess of American soldiery and make Chickamauga a Mecca through all the ages.[1]

The fact that both sides claim a victory is somewhat remarkable. General H. V. Boynton, who fought under General Rosecrans, to whose vigorous pen and wise labors much credit is due for the success of the great battle park at Chickamauga, and who is one of the ablest and fairest of the commentators upon this memorable struggle, has devoted much time and labor to prove that the victory was with the Union arms. With sincere

[1] Despatch of C. A. Dana: "Chickamauga is as fatal a name in our history as Bull Run." (See page 111, Confederate Military History, Vol. VIII, Tennessee; also page 179, Confederate Military History, Vol. IX, Kentucky; also page 358, Confederate Military History, Vol. X, Arkansas.)

friendship for General Boynton as a man and a soldier, and with full appreciation of his ability and sense of justice, I must be permitted to suggest that his reasoning will scarcely stand the test of unbiassed historical criticism. His theory is that although General Rosecrans abandoned the field after two days of determined and desperate fighting in the effort to hold it, yet his retirement was not a retreat, but an advance. "At nightfall," says General Boynton, "the army advanced to Chattanooga. The Army of the Cumberland was on its way to Chattanooga, the city it set out to capture. Every foot of it [the march] was a march in advance and not retreat." History will surely ask how this retrograde movement into the trenches at Chattanooga can fairly be considered an advance, the object of which was "to capture" the city, when that city had been evacuated by Bragg and occupied by Rosecrans ten days before; when it was held by the Union forces already; and when that city was then, and had been for many days, the base of Union supplies and operations. General Boynton ignores the dominating fact that before the battle the faces of the Union army were toward Atlanta and their backs were upon Chattanooga. The battle induced Rosecrans to "about face" and go in the opposite direction. The same reasoning as that employed by General Boynton would give to McClellan the victory in the seven days' battles around Richmond; for he, too, had beaten back the Confederates at certain points, and had escaped with his army to the cover of his gunboats at Harrison's Landing. From like premises the Confederates might claim a victory for Lee at Gettysburg, and that his movement to the rear was an advance. General Pope might in like manner claim that the rout at second Manassas was a victory, and his retreat to Washington an advance which saved the Capitol. To my thought, such victories are similar to that achieved by the doctor who was asked: "Well, doctor, how is the mother and the new baby?" "They are both dead," replied the doctor; "but I have saved the old man." The advance on Atlanta was checked; Chickamauga was lost; but, like the doctor's old man, Chattanooga was saved. General Boynton is too sensitive in this matter. All great commanders in modern times, the most consummate and successful, have had their reverses. General Rosecrans had unfortunate opposition at Washington, and his record as commander under such conditions is brilliant enough to take the sting out of his defeat at Chickamauga. His ability as strategist, his skill in manœuvre, and his vigor in delivering battle are universally recognized. The high court of history will render its verdict in accordance with the facts. These facts are simple and indisputable. First, Bragg threw his army across Rosecrans's front, checked his advance, and forced him to take position on the north bank of the Chickamauga. Second, Bragg assailed Rosecrans in his chosen stronghold, drove him from the entire field, and held it in unchallenged possession. Third, at the end of the two days' battle, which in courage and carnage has scarcely a parallel, as the two wings of the Confederate army met on the field, their battle-flags waved triumphantly above every gory acre of it; and their ringing shouts rolled through Chickamauga's forests and rose to heaven, a mighty anthem of praise and gratitude to God for the victory.

CHAPTER XV

MISSIONARY RIDGE—TRIUNE DISASTER

Why General Bragg did not pursue Rosecrans after Chickamauga—
Comparison of the Confederates at Missionary Ridge with the Greeks
at Marathon—The Battle above the Clouds—Heroic advance by
Walthall's Mississippians—General Grant's timely arrival with reënforcements—The way opened to Atlanta.

GENERAL LEE was not a believer in the infallibility
of newspapers as arbiters of military movements.
With full appreciation of their enormous power and
vital agency in arousing, guiding, and ennobling
public sentiment, his experience with them as military
critics of his early campaigns in the West Virginia
mountains had led him to question the wisdom of some
of their suggestions. In a letter to Mrs. Lee he once
wrote, in half-serious, half-jocular strain, that he had
been reading the papers, and that he would be glad if
they had entire control and could fix matters to suit
themselves, adding, "General Floyd has three editors
on his staff, and I hope something may be done to
please them."

General Bragg had been subjected to a somewhat
similar fire from the rear for not following General
Rosecrans, after the battle of Chickamauga, and driving
him into the river or across it. That he did not do so,
and thus make the battle of Missionary Ridge impossible and save his army from its crushing defeat there,
was a disappointment not only to the watchful and ex-

pectant press, but to the Southern people, and to some of the leaders who fought under him at Chickamauga. A calm review of the situation, and the facts as they existed at the time, will demonstrate, I think, that his failure to follow and assault General Rosecrans in his strong works at Chattanooga was not only pardonable, but prudent and wise. The Confederate victory at Chickamauga, which was the most conspicuous antecedent of Missionary Ridge, was achieved after two days of desperate fighting and at tremendous cost. While the Confederates had inflicted heavy losses upon the Union army, they had also suffered heavy losses. Of the thirty-three thousand dead and wounded, practically one half wore gray uniforms. For every Union regiment broken and driven in disorder from the field, there was a Confederate regiment decimated and shattered in front of the breastworks. The final retreat of the Union army was immediately preceded by successful repulses and countercharges, and by the most determined stand against the desperate and repeated Confederate assaults on Snodgrass Hill. General Bragg's right wing had been partially shattered in front of the Union field works in the woods at Chickamauga, and his left wing held in check till near nightfall at Snodgrass Hill. It seems to me, therefore, that these facts constitute almost a mathematical demonstration—at least a moral assurance—that his army must have failed in an immediate march across the open plain through the network of wire spread for Confederate feet, in the face of wide-sweeping Union artillery, and against the infinitely stronger works at Chattanooga. In whatever other respects General Bragg may be regarded by his critics as worthy of blame, it seems manifestly unfair to charge that he blundered in not pursuing Rosecrans after Chickamauga. Far more just would be criticisms of General McClellan for his refusal to renew the attack in the

open after Sharpsburg (Antietam), or of General Meade
for not accepting the gauge of battle tendered him by
Lee after the repulse of Gettysburg; or of General Lee
himself for not pressing Burnside after Fredericksburg,
Hooker after Chancellorsville, and Pope after the rout at
second Manassas.

These reflections are submitted in the interest of truth
and in justice to General Bragg's memory. They are
submitted after the most patient and painstaking investigation, and I must confess that they are in direct
conflict with the impressions I had myself received and
the opinions which I entertained before investigation.

One other remark as to General Bragg's halt after the
Confederate victory at Chickamauga. His beleaguering
of the Union army for a whole month in its stronghold
at Chattanooga is by no means conclusive evidence that
he blundered in his failure to immediately assault General
Rosecrans in his intrenchments. While admitting that,
however shattered the ranks of the victor, the ranks of
the beaten army are always in still worse condition, it
must be remembered that assaults against breastworks,
as a rule, are most expensive operations. Pemberton
had been beaten in a series of engagements before he
was driven into his works at Vicksburg; yet with his
small force he successfully repelled for months every assault made upon those breastworks by General Grant.
General Lee's hitherto victorious veterans recoiled before
the natural battlements of the Round Tops and Cemetery
Ridge at Gettysburg. On June 27, 1864, General
Sherman assaulted with tremendous power the strong
position held by General Joseph E. Johnston's retreating
army; but General Sherman's loss was nearly ten for
every Confederate killed or wounded. The experience
of General Nathaniel P. Banks in his assault upon the
Confederate forces behind their breastworks at Port
Hudson furnishes possibly a still more convincing proof

of this truth. Page after page of similar illustrations might be taken from the records of our Civil War. It may be true that Chickamauga had brought temporary demoralization to portions of Rosecrans's army; it may be true that General Grant did say to General Sherman at Chattanooga, "The men of Thomas's army have been so demoralized by the battle of Chickamauga that I fear they cannot be got out of their trenches to assume the offensive." But when he witnessed their superb assault upon Missionary Ridge he must have changed his opinion. It may be true — it is true—that had General Bragg assailed the Union army after Chickamauga, he would have had the advantage of the momentum and ardor imparted to a column in a charge; but he would also have been compelled to overcome the feeling of security imparted to troops protected by heavy breastworks and the increased effectiveness of their fire. General Longstreet assailed the breastworks at Knoxville after the Chickamauga battle; but his superb battalions were powerless before them.

General Bragg's mistake, therefore, it seems to me, was not his decision to besiege rather than assault the Union army in Chattanooga, but it was the weakening of his lines by detaching for other service such large bodies as to reduce his army to a mere skeleton of its former strength. While Bragg was reducing his troops to an estimated force of about 25,000 men by sending off Longstreet and Buckner and the Confederate cavalry, General Grant, who had displaced Rosecrans and assumed command at Chattanooga, was increasing his army in and around that city to 100,000 or more. By his official report it seems that after the arrival of his two corps from the East and General Sherman's army from the West, he had on the 25th of November, when the advance was ordered, about 86,000 men, armed and equipped, ready for the assault. I recall no instance in the history of our war, and few in any other war, where, on so contracted a field, was marshalled for battle so gigantic and puissant an army.

More than two thousand years ago occurred a scene which Missionary Ridge recalls. On the plains of Marathon, Datis, under the orders of King Darius, assembled his army of Persian warriors, whose number did not differ widely from those commanded at Chattanooga by General Grant. Confronting Datis was the little army of the Greeks under Miltiades, the great Athenian, in whose veins ran the blood of Hercules. Posted along the Attican range of mountains, this little army of Athenians looked down upon the vast hosts assembled against them on the Marathon plain below as Bragg's small force of Confederates stood on Missionary Ridge and the slopes of Lookout Mountain, contemplating the magnificent but appalling panorama of Grant's overwhelming legions moving from their works and wheeling into lines of battle. The two scenes — the one at Marathon, the other at Chattanooga—present other strikingly similar features. The ground on which the respective armies under Datis and Grant were assembled bore a close resemblance the one to the other. Crescent-shaped Marathon, washed by the winding bay, had its counterpart in that crescent formed at Chattanooga by the Tennessee as it flows around the city.

The Greeks at Marathon and the Confederates at Missionary Ridge were each moved by a kindred impulse of self-defence. The Athenian Republicans under Miltiades, as they stood upon the bordering hills around Marathon, realized that the spirits of departed Grecian heroes were hovering above them, and resolved not to survive the loss of Athenian freedom or the enslavement of their people. They were the foremost men of their time. The mountain on which they stood was sacred ground; every stone and scene was an inspiration.

The American Republicans of Southern birth and training who stood with Bragg on Missionary Ridge were imbued with an ardor none the less strong and sacred. At this point, however, appear vast contrasts. The Grecian commander was to fight Persians: the Southern leader was to meet Americans. The hireling hordes which swarmed on the plains of Marathon served not from choice but from compulsion. The Persian array was a vast conglomeration of incohesive elements, imposing in aspect but weak in determined battle: the army which Bragg was to meet was composed of patriotic volunteers, every man impelled by a thorough belief in the righteousness of his cause. At Marathon it was the resolute, compact, and self-sacrificing Grecian phalanxes against the uncertain, disjointed, and self-seeking hordes of Persian plunderers. It was heroes against hirelings, the glorious sons of Athenian freedom against the submissive serfs of triumphant wrong and of kingly power. At Missionary Ridge it was patriot against patriot, inherited beliefs against inherited beliefs, liberty as embodied in the sovereignty of the States against liberty as embodied in the perpetuity of the Union. The Persians represented organized vindictiveness. The haughty monarch Darius had resolved to wreak his vengeance on the free people of Athens. In his besotted pride and blasphemy, he implored the gods to give him strength to punish these freemen of Greece. His servants were instructed constantly to repeat to him as he gorged himself with costly viands, "Sire, remember the Athenians!" The army and commanders whom he sent to Marathon were fit agents for the execution of so diabolical a purpose. Numbers, therefore, did not count for much in the conflict with such men as Miltiades led against them. The Federals and Confederates, however, who met each other at Missionary Ridge, were of the same race and of kindred impulse. They gathered their strength and ardor from the memories and example of the same rebelling fathers. In such a contest numbers did tell, and gave to General Grant the moral assurance of victory even before the battle was joined.

The Union assault on Missionary Ridge was heralded by the "Battle above the Clouds," as the fight on Lookout Mountain is called. Important events had transpired which precipitated that conflict amidst the heavy vapors around Lookout Mountain. These events rendered the capture of that citadel of strength possible, if not easy. Nearly 10,000 Federals under General Hooker had forced a passage of the Tennessee below Lookout Point, driving back the two Confederate regiments, numbering about 1000 men, commanded by the gallant Colonel Oates, of Alabama, who fell severely wounded while making a most stubborn resistance. The night battle at Wauhatchie had also been fought and the small Confederate force had been defeated. It was in this fire in the darkness that the brave little Billy Bethune of Georgia made his début as a soldier and his exit on an Irishman's shoulder. The Irishman who was carrying Billy off the field was asked by his major, "Who is that you are carrying to the rear?" "Billy Bethune, sir." "Is he wounded?" "Yis, sir; he's shot in the back, sir." This was more than Billy could endure, and he shouted his indignant answer to the Irishman, "Major, he's an infernal liar; I am shot across the back, sir."

The Hon. John Russell Young, in his book "Around the World with General Grant," states that this great Union general once said: "The battle of Lookout Mountain (the 'Battle above the Clouds') is one of the romances of the war. There was no such battle, and no action worthy to be called a battle, on Lookout Mountain. It is all poetry."

I shall not enter into the controversy as to the rank which should be assigned to that brief but noted conflict. Whatever may be its proper designation, it was a most creditable affair to both sides. Reared among the mountains, I can readily appreciate the peculiar atmospheric conditions and the impressive character of the scenes which met those contending forces on the rugged mountain-side. Many times in my boyhood I have stood upon those mountain-tops in the clear sunlight, while below were gathered dense fogs and mists, sometimes following the winding courses of the streams, often covering the valleys like a vast sea and obscuring them from view. As stated in another chapter, General Hooker was probably not apprised of the fact that there confronted him in the forenoon only Walthall's Mississippians,—less than 1500 men against 10,000,—and in the afternoon only the shattered remnants of this brave little brigade, joined by three regiments of Pettus and the small brigade of Moore, in all probably not more than 2500 men. The conception of moving upon an unknown force located in such a stronghold was bold and most creditable to the high soldierly qualities of General Hooker and the gallant men who moved at his command through the fogs and up the steeps, where gorges and boulders and jutting cliffs made almost as formidable barriers as those which opposed the American soldiers at Chapultepec. General Walthall, who commanded the little band of resisting Confederates, was compelled to stretch them out along the base and up the sides of the mountain until his command covered a front so long as to reduce it practically to a line of skirmishers. Far beyond the west flank of this attenuated line, Hooker's plan of battle for this unique field had placed a heavy force under enterprising and daring leaders. Up the mountain-side the troops worked their way, clutching bushes and the branches of trees in order to lift themselves over the rugged ledges, firing as they rose, capturing small bodies here and there, and driving back the stubborn little band of Confederates. The Union lines in front and on Walthall's right threatened to make prisoners of his men, who retreated from ledge to ledge, pouring their fire into Hooker's troops and directing their aim only at the flashes of the Union rifles as they gleamed through the dense fog.

The resistance of Walthall's Mississippians was pronounced by the distinguished Union leader, General George H. Thomas, "obstinate"; by General Bragg, the Confederate commander-in-chief, as "desperate," and by the brave Steedman, of the Union army, as "sublimely heroic." More emphatic than all of these well-merited tributes was the eloquent fact that but 600 were left of the 1500 carried into the fight.

General Grant's arrival at Chattanooga with his reënforcements was as timely a relief for Thomas and his troops as the coming of Buell's forces had previously been for the succor of General Grant's army at Pittsburg Landing or Shiloh.

The interchange of courtesies which became so common during the war at no time interfered with the stern demands of duty. As General Manderson, one of the most gallant officers of the Union army, rode near the Confederate picket-lines in front of Chattanooga, he received a salutation almost as courteous as they would have given to one of their Confederate generals; yet they were ready to empty their deadly rifles into the bosoms of his troops when they moved in battle array against them. General Manderson himself in these words gives account of the Confederate courtesy shown him: "A feeling of amity, almost fraternization, had existed between the picket-lines in front of Wood's division for many days. In the early morning of that day, being in charge of the left of our picket-line

[Union], I received a turnout and salute from the Confederate reserve as I rode the line." This was on the very day of the great battle. On the river below, the Confederates would gladly have divided their own meagre rations with any individual soldier in Thomas's army, yet they were attempting to shoot down every team and sink every boat which sought to bring the needed supplies to the beleaguered and hungry commands suffering in the city.

Major Nelson of Indiana, who, like all truly brave soldiers, has exhibited in peace the same high qualities which distinguished him in war, gave me the following incident, which occurred at another point, and admirably illustrates the spirit of the best men in the two armies. Major Nelson was himself in command of the Union picket-lines. The Confederate officer who stood at night in the opposing lines near him called out:

"Hello there, Yank! Have you got any coffee over there?"

"Yes," replied Major Nelson. "Come over and get some."

"We would like to come, but there are fourteen of us on this post."

"All right, Johnny; bring them all along. We'll divide with you. Come over, boys, and get your coffee."

The Johnnies accepted. At two o'clock in the morning they sat down in the trenches with the boys in blue, and told war jokes on each other while drinking their coffee together. Looking at his watch, the major said:

"It's time for you Johnnies to get away from here. The inspector will be along soon, and he will put every one of you in prison, and me, too, if he catches us at this business."

The Confederates at once sprang to their feet and left with this salutation:

"Good night, Yanks; we are greatly obliged to you. We have had a nice visit and enjoyed your coffee very much. We hope you will get a good rest to-night; we are going to give you hell to-morrow."

When General Grant arrived at Chattanooga and had surveyed the field, he sent an order to General Sherman, who was rebuilding the Memphis and Charleston Railroad, to stop this work and move his army rapidly eastward toward Chattanooga. This order, it is said, was carried in a canoe down the Tennessee River, over Muscle Shoals, and for a distance of probably two hundred miles. The daring soldier who bore it was Corporal Pike, a noted scout. On the very day of Sherman's crossing the Tennessee at Chattanooga, Grant ordered the advance upon Missionary Ridge. To this ridge the Confederates had been withdrawn from their eyry on Point Lookout, and the forces of Hooker swept down upon Bragg's left flank. Against Bragg's other flank General Sherman's army was concentrated. In General Grant's admirable plan of the battle, the movement by Hooker against the Confederate left, and the attack by Thomas upon its centre, were intended as mere demonstrations, while the heavy columns of Sherman were to turn its right flank and completely envelop it, thus making the capture of the bulk of Bragg's small army probable, or rendering his retreat extremely hazardous. But, as is often the case in battle, the unexpected transpired. Across the line of Sherman's advance, from which the greatest results were expected, was a railroad cut and tunnel from which the Confederates suddenly rushed upon the head of the Union column, checking, breaking, and routing it. In the meanwhile, Grant, who stood on Orchard Knob opposite the Confederate centre, had ordered Thomas to move at a given signal and seize the Confederate rifle-pits at the base of the ridge. As the six shots from Orchard Knob sounded the signal for the advance, the blue line of Thomas swept across the plain and into the rifle-pits, making prisoners of many of the advanced Confederate skirmishers. This movement, as above stated, like Hooker's upon Lookout Mountain on the previous day, was intended by General Grant only as a "demonstration," the purpose being only to take the rifle-pits as a diversion to aid Sherman in his attack upon Bragg's right. The seasoned veterans of Thomas, however, weré wiser in this instance, or at least bolder, than the generals. Was it a misapprehension of orders, was it recklessness, or was it the habit acquired in battle of never halting when ordered forward under fire until their lines were broken against the solid fronts of opposing forces? General Grant was amazed when he saw those lines pass the rifle-pits in furious charge toward the crest of Missionary Ridge. Both Thomas and Granger denied having given the order for such a movement. It was, however, too late to halt the troops; and most fortunate was it for the Union army that the movement could not be recalled. Those brave men, without orders, mounted to the summit of Missionary Ridge, leaped into Bragg's intrenchments, piercing his lines in the centre, doubling them to the right and left, and forcing the front in confusion to the rear. The capture of 6000 Southern prisoners, several pieces of artillery, and many thousand stands of small arms was an irreparable loss to the Confederacy. In its exhausted condition these could not be replaced by new levies and new guns. Infinitely greater, however, was the loss of the prestige which Bragg's army had gained by the brilliant victory at Chickamauga just two months and five days before. Still greater was the loss which Missionary Ridge inflicted upon the Southern cause by opening the way to Atlanta. The bold and successful stand made after Missionary Ridge by Bragg's forces at Ringgold was but a temporary check to the advance of the Union forces.

As Hooker's forces moved from the mountain-top up Bragg's left, a Confederate officer, on his Kentucky thoroughbred, galloped into this portion of the Union line. It was young Breckinridge, looking for his father, General John C. Breckinridge, who was commanding a division of Confederates. Instead of his father, he found General James A. Williamson commanding Union troops. He lost his Kentucky racer and exchanged his staff position for that of prisoner of war.

General Bragg, with patriotic purpose, and with the hope that some other commander might serve the cause more efficiently, asked to be relieved from the command of the army, and his request was granted. General Rosecrans had perhaps a still more pathetic fate. He had inaugurated and conducted against General Bragg during the summer a strategic campaign, pronounced by General Meigs "the greatest operation in our war." During the progress of this campaign General George H. Thomas and the corps commanders of the Union army seemed unanimous and enthusiastic in the commendation and support of it. Yet after its culmination General Rosecrans was removed from the command of his army. From the standpoint of unbiassed criticism the future historian will probably have some trouble in finding sufficient reasons for this removal. It is not my province to participate in the discussion of this interesting question. As a soldier, however, who fought on the Southern side, and who has studied with much interest this campaign of General Rosecrans, I wish to leave upon record two or three inquiries which it seems to me history must necessarily make.

First, how was it possible for the transfer of Longstreet's troops from Lee to Bragg to have escaped the attention of Secretary Stanton or General Halleck? This movement was reported to General Rosecrans by General Peck of the Union army stationed in North Carolina.

It was suggested as probable by the Hon. Murat Halstead in the columns of his paper. General H. V. Boynton states in the most positive terms that Colonel Jacques, of the Seventy-third Illinois, tried in vain for ten days to gain admittance in Washington to communicate the fact of Longstreet's movements to Halleck and Stanton, and then, without accomplishing it, returned in time to fight with his regiment at Chickamauga.

Another question which history will probably ask is why no reënforcements were sent to the Union army while Rosecrans was in command and when Longstreet was moving to strengthen General Bragg, and yet after Rosecrans's removal immense reënforcements were sent, although both Longstreet and Buckner had then been detached from that immediate vicinity.

The heavy concentration of Union forces at Chattanooga, and the consequent defeat of Bragg's army at Missionary Ridge, was a master stroke; but justice to General Rosecrans seems to demand the above reflections. In the light of his previous strategic campaign and of his fight at Chickamauga, where, without reënforcements, he so stubbornly resisted Bragg's assaults while both Longstreet and Buckner were present, history will surely ask: "What would General Rosecrans probably have accomplished with his own army heavily reënforced, while Bragg's was reduced by the absence of both Longstreet's and Buckner's commands?"

Missionary Ridge had added its quota of cloud to the Confederate firmament, and intensified the gloom of the succeeding winter. It had laid bare the Confederacy's heart to the glistening points of Union bayonets, and vastly increased the sufferings of the Confederate armies. Vicksburg, Gettysburg, Missionary Ridge! Distinct defeats to different armies in distant sections, they nevertheless constituted a common, a triune disaster to the Confederate cause. The great crevasses in the Mississippi's levees constitute one agency of ruin when they unite their floods and deluge the delta. So these breaks in the gray lines of defence constituted, I repeat, one common defeat to Southern arms. There is, however, this noteworthy defect in the completeness of the simile: The Mississippi levees could be rebuilt; the material for reconstructing them was inexhaustible; and the waters would soon disappear without any human effort to drive them back. The Confederacy's lines, on the contrary, could not be rebuilt. The material for reconstructing them was exhausted. The blue-crested flood which had broken those lines was not disappearing. The fountains which supplied it were exhaustless. It was still coming with an ever-increasing current, swelling higher and growing more resistless. This triune disaster was especially depressing to the people because it came like a blight upon their hopes which had been awakened by recent Confederate victories. The recoil of Lee's army from its furious impact against the blue barrier of Meade's lines at Gettysburg was the first break in the tide of its successes. Beginning with the marvellous panic and rout of McDowell's troops at Bull Run in 1861, there followed in almost unbroken succession wave after wave of Confederate triumph. The victory of Joseph E. Johnston over General McClellan at Seven Pines, or Fair Oaks; the rapidly recurring victories of Lee in the seven days' battles around Richmond over the same brilliant commander; the rout of General Pope's army at second Manassas, or second Bull Run; the bloody disaster inflicted by Lee upon Burnside's forces at Fredericksburg and upon Hooker's splendid army at Chancellorsville, together with Stonewall Jackson's Napoleonic campaign in the Valley of Virginia, had constituted a chain of Confederate successes with scarcely a broken link. Even at Sharpsburg, or Antietam, in 1862, the result was of so indecisive a character as to leave that battle among those that are in dispute. The Federals claim it as a Union victory on the ground that Lee finally abandoned the field to McClellan. The Confederates place it among the drawn battles of the war, and base their claim on these facts: that McClellan was the aggressor, and declined to renew his efforts, although the Confederates invited him to do so by flying their flags in his front during the whole of the following day; that although the battle-tide swayed to and fro, with alternate onsets and recoils on the different hotly contested portions of the field, yet in the main the Federal assaults were successfully repelled; that McClellan failed to drive Lee from his general line, and that whatever advance he made against Lee was more than counterbalanced by Jackson's capture of the entire Union forces which held the left of the Union army at Harper's Ferry.

CHAPTER XVI

WINTER ON THE RAPIDAN

In camp near Clark's Mountain—Religious awakening—Revival services
throughout the camps—General Lee's interest in the movement—
Southern women at work—Extracts from General Lee's letters to his
wife—Influence of religion on the soldiers' character.

THE winter of 1863–64 on the banks of the Rapidan
was passed in preparation by both armies for that
wrestle of giants which was to begin in May in the Wilderness and end at Appomattox in the following April.

My camp and quarters were near Clark's Mountain,
from the top of which General Lee so often surveyed
with his glasses the white-tented city of the Union army
spread out before us on the undulating plain below. A
more peaceful scene could scarcely be conceived than
that which broke upon our view day after day as the
rays of the morning sun fell upon the quiet, wide-spreading Union camp, with its thousands of smoke columns
rising like miniature geysers, its fluttering flags marking, at regular intervals, the different divisions, its stillness unbroken save by an occasional drum-beat and
the clear ringing notes of bugles sounding the familiar
calls.

On the southern side of the Rapidan the scenes were,
if possible, still less warlike. In every Confederate camp
chaplains and visiting ministers erected religious altars,
around which the ragged soldiers knelt and worshipped
the Heavenly Father into whose keeping they committed

229

themselves and their cause, and through whose all-wise guidance they expected ultimate victory. The religious revivals that ensued form a most remarkable and impressive chapter of war history. Not only on the Sabbath day, but during the week, night after night for long periods, these services continued, increasing in attendance and interest until they brought under religious influence the great body of the army. Along the mountain-sides and in the forests, where the Southern camps were pitched, the rocks and woods rang with appeals for holiness and consecration, with praises for past mercies and earnest prayers for future protection and deliverance. Thousands of these brave followers of Southern banners became consistent and devoted soldiers of the cross. General Lee, who was a deeply pious man, manifested a constant and profound interest in the progress of this religious work among his soldiers. He usually attended his own church when services were held there, but his interest was confined to no particular denomination. He encouraged all and helped all.

Back of the army on the farms, in the towns and cities, the fingers of Southern women were busy knitting socks and sewing seams of coarse trousers and gray jackets for the soldiers at the front. From Mrs. Lee and her daughters to the humblest country matrons and maidens, their busy needles were stitching, stitching, stitching, day and night. The anxious commander thanked them for their efforts to bring greater comfort to the cold feet and shivering limbs of his half-clad men. He wrote letters expressing appreciation of the bags of socks and shirts as they came in. He said that he could almost hear, in the stillness of the night, the needles click as they flew through the meshes. Every click was a prayer, every stitch a tear. His tributes were tender and constant to these glorious women for their labor and sacrifices for Southern independence. His unselfish solicitude for his men was marked and unvarying. He sent to the suffering privates in the hospitals the delicacies contributed for his personal use from the meagre stores of those who were anxious about his health. If a handful of real coffee came to him, it went in the same direction, while he cheerfully drank from his tin cup the wretched substitute made from parched corn or beans. He was the idolized commander of his army and at the same time the sympathizing brother of his men.

General Fitzhugh Lee, the brilliant nephew of the great chieftain, gives extracts from his private letters, some of which I insert in this connection because they illustrate the character of Robert E. Lee as a man. These excerpts are of greater value because they are taken from letters addressed to Mrs. Lee and meant for her eyes alone.

In 1861, from West Virginia, General Lee concluded a letter to Mrs. Lee in these words:

I travelled from Staunton on horseback. A part of the road I traveled over in the summer of 1840 on my return from St. Louis after bringing you home. If any one had told me that the next time I travelled that road would have been on my present errand I should have supposed him insane. I enjoyed the mountains as I rode along. The valleys are peaceful, the scenery beautiful. What a glorious world Almighty God has given us! How thankless and ungrateful we are!

Denied the privilege of being with his family at the Christmas reunion, he wrote:

I shall pray the great God to shower His blessings upon you and unite you all in His courts above. . . . Oh, that I were more worthy and more thankful for all that he has done and continues to do for me!

From the southern coast in February, 1862, he wrote Mrs. Lee:

My constant prayer is to the Giver of all victory. . . . The contest must be long and the whole country has to go through much suffering. It is necessary we should be more humble, less boastful, less selfish, and more devoted to right and justice to all the world. . . . God, I hope, will shield us and give us success.

After his brilliant victory over McClellan in the seven days' battles around Richmond, he wrote Mrs. Lee:

I am filled with gratitude to our Heavenly Father for all the mercies he has extended to us. Our success has not been as complete as we could desire, but God knows what is best for us.

If Wellington, the Iron Duke, ever said, as is reported: " A man of fine Christian sensibilities is totally unfit for the position of a soldier," he must have had in contemplation the mere soldier of fortune—the professional soldier, and not the class of men who fight only because duty compels them to fight. The lofty Christian character, the simple, earnest Christian faith, the consistent, unostentatious Christian life and humility of spirit of both Lee and Jackson, furnish an eloquent and crushing rebuke to Wellington's suggestions. Jackson fought while praying and prayed while planning. Lee's heart was full of supplication in battle, while his lips were silent. In sunshine and in storm, in victory and in defeat, his heart turned to God. Chapter after chapter might be filled with these extracts from his private letters and with accounts of acts consistent with his letters, illustrating the fact that great soldiers may be the tenderest men and the truest Christian believers. The self-denial, the stainless manhood, the unfaltering faith in the saving truths of the Bible, the enormous will power, submissive as a child to God's will, — the roundness and completeness of such a life, should be a model and an inspiration to the young men of our whole country.

Christian men and women, indeed all who truly love this country and realize how essential to its permanence and freedom is the character of its citizenship, must find no little comfort in the facts recorded in the last few paragraphs. The reward promised by mythology to the brave who fell in battle was a heaven, not of purity and peace, but of continued combat with their foes and a life of eternal revelry. Such a religion could only degrade the soldiers who fought and increase the depravity of the people. It was a religion of hate, of vindictiveness, of debauchery. The religious revivals which occurred in the Southern camps, on the contrary, while banishing from the heart all unworthy passions, prepared the soldiers for more heroic endurance; lifted them, in a measure, above their sufferings; nerved them for the coming battles; exalted them to a higher conception of duty; imbued them with a spirit of more cheerful submission to the decrees of Providence; sustained them with a calmer and nobler courage; and rendered them not insensible to danger, but superior to it. The life we now live is not the only life; what we call death is, not an eternal sleep; the soldier's grave is not an everlasting prison, but the gateway to an endless life beyond: and this belief in immortality should be cultivated in armies, because of the potent influence it must exert in developing the best characteristics of the soldier. Aside from any regard for the purely spiritual welfare of the men, the most enlightened nations of Europe have shown a commendable worldly wisdom in making religious literature an important part of an army's equipment.

No one, who calmly and fairly considers the conditions which surrounded the soldiers of the Confederate armies when they were disbanded and the manner in which these men met those conditions, can doubt that their profound religious convictions, which were deep-

ened in the camps, had a potent influence upon their
conduct in the trying years which followed the war.
Reared under a government of their own choosing,
born and bred under laws, State and federal, enacted
by their own representatives, habituated for four years
to the watchful eyes and guarding bayonets of army
sentinels, accustomed to the restraints of the most rigid
regulations, they found themselves at the close of the war
suddenly confronted by conditions radically, totally
changed. Their State governments were overthrown;
State laws were in abeyance; of chosen representatives
they had none. Sheriffs, other officers of the court, and
the courts themselves were gone. Penniless and home-
less as thousands of them were, with the whole financial
system in their States obliterated, the whole system of
labor revolutionized, without a dollar or the possibility
of borrowing, they went bravely and uncomplainingly
to work. They did not rob, they did not steal, they did
not beg, they did not murmur at their fate. With all
the restraints to which they had been subjected, both
as citizens and soldiers, not only relaxed but entirely
removed, they kept the peace, lived soberly and circum-
spectly, each ready to lend a helping hand to maimed
and helpless comrades or to fight again for the enforce-
ment of law or in defence of the restored Republic.
Who will deny that these facts, which are in no particular and in no degree over-stated, but fall far short of
the reality, demonstrate the power of religious convictions over the conduct of these disbanded soldiers
transformed into citizens under conditions so changed,
so trying, so desperate?

CHAPTER XVII

THE WILDERNESS—BATTLE OF MAY 5

Beginning of the long fight between Grant and Lee—Grant crosses the Rapidan—First contact of the two armies—Ewell's repulse—A rapid countercharge—A strange predicament—The Union centre broken—Unprecedented movement which saved the Confederate troops.

L EE and Grant, the foremost leaders of the opposing armies, were now to begin a campaign which was to be practically a continuous battle for eleven months. Grant had come from his campaigns in the Southwest with the laurels of Fort Donelson, Shiloh, Vicksburg, and Missionary Ridge on his brow. Lee stood before him with a record as military executioner unrivalled by that of any warrior of modern times. He had, at astoundingly short intervals and with unvarying regularity, decapitated or caused the official "taking off" of the five previously selected commanders-in-chief of the great army which confronted him.

A more beautiful day never dawned on Clark's Mountain and the valley of the Rapidan than May 5, 1864. There was not a cloud in the sky, and the broad expanse of meadow-lands on the north side of the little river and the steep wooded hills on the other seemed " apparelled in celestial light " as the sun rose upon them. At an early hour, however, the enchantment of the scene was rudely broken by bugles and kettledrums calling Lee's veterans to strike tents and "fall into line." The advent of spring brought intense relief to the thinly clad and poorly fed Confederates. The Army of Northern Virginia had suffered so much during the preceding winter that there was general rejoicing at its close, although every man in that army knew that it meant the opening of another campaign and the coming of Grant's thoroughly equipped and stalwart corps. The reports of General Lee's scouts were scarcely necessary to our appreciation of the fact that the odds against us were constantly and rapidly increasing: for from the highland which bordered the southern banks of the Rapidan one could almost estimate the numbers that were being added to Grant's ranks by the growth of the city of tents spreading out in full view below. The Confederates were profoundly impressed by the situation, but they rejected as utterly unworthy of a Christian soldiery the doctrine that Providence was on the side of the heaviest guns and most numerous battalions. To an unshaken confidence in their great leader and in each other there had been added during the remarkable religious revivals to which I have referred a spiritual vitality which greatly increased among Lee's soldiers the spirit of self-sacrifice and of consecration. Committing themselves and their cause to God, with honest and fervent prayers for His protection and guidance, they hopefully and calmly awaited the results of the coming battle.

On the morning of May 4, 1864, shortly after midnight, General Grant began the movement which was soon to break the long silence of that vast and dense woodland by the roaring tumult of battle. This advance by General Grant inaugurated the seventh act in the " On to Richmond " drama played by the armies of the Union. The first advance, led by General McDowell, had been repelled by Beauregard and Johnston at Bull Run; the next five, under the leadership respectively of

McClellan, Pope, Burnside, Hooker, and Meade, had been repelled by Lee. He had not only defeated these noted leaders, but caused their removal from command of the Union army.

Crossing the Rapidan with but little resistance, General Grant spent the 4th of May in placing his army in position. Pushing toward Richmond the head of his column, which was to form the left of his battle line, in order to throw himself, if possible, between Lee and the Confederate capital, General Grant promptly faced his army in the direction from which Lee must necessarily approach and moved to the front as rapidly as the tangled wilderness would permit. Lee, in the meantime, was hurrying his columns along the narrow roads and throwing out skirmish-lines, backed by such troops as he could bring forward quickly in order to check Grant's advance and to ascertain whether the heaviest assault was to be made upon the Confederate centre or upon the right or left flank. Field-glasses and scouts and cavalry were equally and almost wholly useless in that dense woodland. The tangle of underbrush and curtain of green leaves enabled General Grant to concentrate his forces at any point, while their movements were entirely concealed. Overlapping the Confederate lines on both flanks, he lost no time in pushing to the front with characteristic vigor.

My command brought up the rear of the extreme left of Lee's line, which was led by Ewell's corps. Long before I reached the point of collision, the steady roll of small arms left no doubt as to the character of the conflict in our front. Despatching staff officers to the rear to close up the ranks in compact column, so as to be ready for any emergency, we hurried with quickened step toward the point of heaviest fighting. Alternate confidence and apprehension were awakened as the shouts of one army or the other reached our ears. So distinct in character were these shouts that they were easily discernible. At one point the weird Confederate "yell" told us plainly that Ewell's men were advancing. At another the huzzas, in mighty concert, of the Union troops warned us that they had repelled the Confederate charge; and as these ominous huzzas grew in volume we knew that Grant's lines were moving forward. Just as the head of my column came within range of the whizzing Miniés, the Confederate yells grew fainter, and at last ceased; and the Union shout rose above the din of battle. I was already prepared by this infallible admonition for the sight of Ewell's shattered forces retreating in disorder. The oft-repeated but spasmodic efforts of first one army and then the other to break through the opposing ranks had at last been ended by the sudden rush of Grant's compact veterans from the dense covert in such numbers that Ewell's attenuated lines were driven in confusion to the rear. These retreating divisions, like broken and receding waves, rolled back against the head of my column while we were still rapidly advancing along the narrow road. The repulse had been so sudden and the confusion so great that practically no resistance was now being made to the Union advance; and the elated Federals were so near me that little time was left to bring my men from column into line in order to resist the movement or repel it by countercharge. At this moment of dire extremity I saw General Ewell, who was still a superb horseman, notwithstanding the loss of his leg, riding in furious gallop toward me, his thoroughbred charger bounding like a deer through the dense underbrush. With a quick jerk of his bridle-rein just as his wooden leg was about to come into unwelcome collision with my knee, he checked his horse and rapped out his few words with characteristic impetuosity. He did not stop to explain the situation; there was no need of explanation. The disalignment, the confusion, the

JOHN B. GORDON
Drawn by George T. Tobin from a daguerreotype taken at
the age of twenty-two.

SENATOR JOHN B. GORDON
From a photograph taken in 1896, when he represented Georgia in
the United States Senate.

rapid retreat of our troops, and the raining of Union bullets as they whizzed and rattled through the scrub-oaks and pines, rendered explanations superfluous, even had there been time to make them. The rapid words he did utter were electric and charged with tremendous significance. "General Gordon, the fate of the day depends on you, sir," he said. "These men will save it, sir," I replied, more with the purpose of arousing the enthusiasm of my men than with any well-defined idea as to how we were to save it. Quickly wheeling a single regiment into line, I ordered it forward in a countercharge, while I hurried the other troops into position. The sheer audacity and dash of that regimental charge checked, as I had hoped it would, the Union advance for a few moments, giving me the essential time to throw the other troops across the Union front. Swiftly riding to the centre of my line, I gave in person the order: "Forward!" With a deafening yell which must have been heard miles away, that glorious brigade rushed upon the hitherto advancing enemy, and by the shock of their furious onset shattered into fragments all that portion of the compact Union line which confronted my troops.

At that moment was presented one of the strangest conditions ever witnessed upon a battle-field. My command covered only a small portion of the long lines in blue, and not a single regiment of those stalwart Federals yielded except those which had been struck by the Southern advance. On both sides of the swath cut by this sweep of the Confederate scythe, the steady veterans of Grant were unshaken and still poured their incessant volleys into the retreating Confederate ranks. My command had cut its way through the Union centre, and at that moment it was in the remarkably strange position of being on identically the same general line with the enemy, the Confederates facing in one direction, the Federals in the other. Looking down that line from

Grant's right toward his left, there would first have been
seen a long stretch of blue uniforms, then a short stretch
of gray, then another still longer of blue, in one continuous line. The situation was both unique and alarming.
I know of no case like it in military history; nor has
there come to my knowledge from military text-books
or the accounts of the world's battles any precedent for
the movement which extricated my command from its
perilous environment and changed the threatened capture or annihilation of my troops into victory. The solid
and dotted portions of the line, here given, correctly represent the position of my troops in relation to the Federals
at this particular juncture: the Union forces are indicated by a solid line, the Confederates (my command)
by a dotted line, and the arrows indicate the direction in
which the forces were facing.

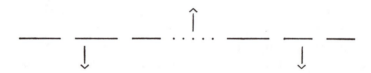

It will be seen that further movement to Grant's rear
was not to be considered; for his unbroken lines on each
side of me would promptly close up the gap which my
men had cut through his centre, thus rendering the capture of my entire command inevitable. To attempt to retire by the route by which we had advanced was almost, if
not equally, as hazardous; for those same unbroken and
now unopposed ranks on each side of me, as soon as such
retrograde movement began, would instantly rush from
both directions upon my retreating command and quickly
crush it. In such a crisis, when moments count for
hours, when the fate of a command hangs upon instan-
taneous decision, the responsibility of the commander is
almost overwhelming; but the very extremity of the

danger electrifies his brain to abnormal activity. In
such peril he does more thinking in one second than he
would ordinarily do in a day. No man ever realized
more fully than I did at that dreadful moment the truth
of the adage: "Necessity is the mother of invention."
As soon as my troops had broken through the Union
ranks, I directed my staff to halt the command; and before the Union veterans could recover from the shock,
my regiments were moving at double-quick from the
centre into file right and left, thus placing them in two
parallel lines, back to back, in a position at a right angle
to the one held a moment before. This quickly executed
manœuvre placed one half of my command squarely
upon the right flank of one portion of the enemy's unbroken line, and the other half facing in exactly the
opposite direction, squarely upon the left flank of the
enemy's line. This position is correctly represented by
the solid (Federal) and dotted (Confederate) lines here
shown.

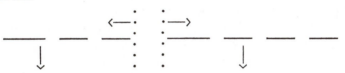

This done, both these wings were ordered forward,
and, with another piercing yell, they rushed in opposite
directions upon the right and left flanks of the astounded
Federals, shattering them as any troops that were ever
marshalled would have been shattered, capturing large
numbers, and checking any further effort by General
Grant on that portion of the field.

Meantime, while this unprecedented movement was
being executed, the Confederates who had been previously
driven back, rallied and moved in spirited charge to the
front and recovered the lost ground. Both armies rested
for the night near the points where the first collisions of

the day had occurred. It would be more accurate to say they *remained* for the night; for there was little rest to the weary men of either army. Both sides labored all night in the dark and dense woodland, throwing up such breastworks as were possible—a most timely preparation for the next day's conflicts. My own command was ordered during the night to the extreme left of Lee's lines, under the apprehension that Grant's right overlapped and endangered our left flank.

Thus ended the 5th of May, which had witnessed the first desperate encounter between Grant and Lee. The fighting had not involved the whole of either army, but it was fierce and bloody. It would be unjust to claim that either of the famous leaders had achieved a signal victory. Both sides had left their dead scattered through the bullet-riddled underbrush. The Confederates drew comfort from the fact that in the shifting fortunes of the day theirs was the last advance, that the battle had ended near where it had begun, and that the Union advance had been successfully repulsed.

It was impossible to know what changes in the disposition of his forces General Grant would make during the night. It was useless to speculate as to whether he would mass his troops for still heavier assault upon the positions we then held or would concentrate against Lee's right or left flank. All that could be done was to prepare as best we could for any contingency, and await the developments which the morrow would bring.

CHAPTER XVIII

THE WILDERNESS — BATTLE OF MAY 6

The men ordered to sleep on their arms — Report of scouts — Sedgwick's exposed position — A plan proposed to flank and crush him — General Early's objections to it — Unfounded belief that Burnside protected Sedgwick — General Lee orders a movement in the late afternoon — Its success until interrupted by darkness — The Government official records prove that Early was mistaken.

THE night of the 5th of May was far spent when my command reached its destination on the extreme Confederate left. The men were directed to sleep on their arms during the remaining hours of darkness. Scouts were at once sent to the front to feel their way through the thickets and ascertain, if possible, where the extreme right of Grant's line rested. At early dawn these trusted men reported that they had found it: that it rested in the woods only a short distance in our front, that it was wholly unprotected, and that the Confederate lines stretched a considerable distance beyond the Union right, overlapping it. I was so impressed with the importance of this report and with the necessity of verifying its accuracy that I sent others to make the examination, with additional instructions to proceed to the rear of Grant's right and ascertain if the exposed flank were supported by troops held in reserve behind it. The former report was not only confirmed as to the exposed position of that flank, but the astounding information was brought that there was not a supporting force within several miles of it.

243

Much of this scouting had been done in the late hours of the night and before sunrise on the morning of the 6th. Meantime, as this information came my brain was throbbing with the tremendous possibilities to which such a situation invited us, provided the conditions were really as reported. Mounting my horse in the early morning and guided by some of these explorers, I rode into the unoccupied woodland to see for myself. It is enough to say that I found the reports correct in every particular. Riding back toward my line, I was guided by the scouts to the point near which they had located the right of the Union army. Dismounting and creeping slowly and cautiously through the dense woods, we were soon in ear-shot of an unsuppressed and merry clatter of voices. A few feet nearer, and through a narrow vista, I was shown the end of General Grant's temporary breastworks. There was no line guarding this flank. As far as my eye could reach, the Union soldiers were seated on the margin of the rifle-pits, taking their breakfast. Small fires were burning over which they were boiling their coffee, while their guns leaned against the works in their immediate front.

No more time was consumed in scouting. The revelations had amazed me and filled me with confident anticipations of unprecedented victory. It was evident that General Grant had decided to make his heaviest assaults upon the Confederate right, and for this purpose had ordered his reserves to that flank. By some inconceivable oversight on the part of his subordinates, his own right flank had been left in the extremely exposed condition in which my scouts had found it. Undoubtedly the officer who located that battle line for General Grant or for General Sedgwick was under the impression that there were no Confederates in front of that portion of it; and this was probably true at the time the location was made. That fact, however, did not justify the officer in leaving his flank (which is the most vulnerable part of an army) thus unguarded for a whole night after the battle.

If it be true that in peace " eternal vigilance is the price of liberty," it is no less true that in war, especially war in a wilderness, eternal vigilance is the price of an army's safety. Yet, in a woodland so dense that an enemy could scarcely be seen at a distance of one hundred yards, that Union officer had left the right flank of General Grant's army without even a picket-line to protect it or a vedette to give the alarm in case of unexpected assault. During the night, while the over-confident Union officer and his men slept in fancied security, my men stole silently through the thickets and planted a hostile line not only in his immediate front, but overlapping it by more than the full length of my command. All intelligent military critics will certainly agree that such an opportunity as was here presented for the overthrow of a great army has rarely occurred in the conduct of a war. The failure to take advantage of it was even a greater blunder than the " untimely discretion " which checked the sweep of the Confederate lines upon the Union right on that first afternoon at Gettysburg, or the still more fatal delay on the third day which robbed Lee of assured victory.

As soon as all the facts in regard to the situation were fully confirmed, I formed and submitted the plan which, if promptly adopted and vigorously followed, I then believed and still believe would have resulted in the crushing defeat of General Grant's army. Indeed, the plan of battle may almost be said to have formed itself, so naturally, so promptly and powerfully did it take hold of my thoughts. That plan and the situation which suggested it may be described simply and briefly:

First, there was Grant's battle line stretching for miles through the Wilderness, with Sedgwick's corps on the right and Warren's next, while far away on the left was Hancock's, supported by the great body of the Union reserves.

Second, in close proximity to this long stretch of Union troops, and as nearly parallel to it as circumstances would permit, was Lee's line of Confederates.

Third, both of these lines were behind small breastworks which had been thrown up by the respective armies during the night of the 5th. On Lee's left and confronting Sedgwick was Ewell's corps, of which my command was a part. In my immediate front, as above stated, there was no Union force whatever. It was perfectly practicable, therefore, for me to move out my command and form at right angles to the general line, close to Sedgwick's unprotected flank and squarely across it.

Fourth, when this movement should be accomplished there would still remain a brigade of Confederates confronting each brigade of Federals along the established battle line. Thus the Union troops could be held to their work along the rifle-pits, while my command would sweep down upon the flank and obliquely upon their rear.

As later developments proved, one brigade on the flank was all that was needed for the inauguration of the plan and the demonstration of its possibilities. The details of the plan were as follows: While the unsuspecting Federals were drinking their coffee, my troops were to move quickly and quietly behind the screen of thick underbrush and form squarely on Sedgwick's strangely exposed flank, reaching a point far beyond that flank and lapping around his rear, so as to capture his routed men as they broke to the rear. While my command rushed from this ambush a simultaneous demonstration was to be made along his front. As each of Sedgwick's brigades gave way in confusion, the corresponding Confederate brigade, whose front was thus cleared on the general line, was to swing into the column of attack on the flank, thus swelling at each step of our advance the numbers, power, and momentum of the Confederate forces as they swept down the line of works and extended another brigade's length to the unprotected Union rear. As each of the Union brigades, divisions, and corps were struck by such an absolutely resistless charge upon the flank and rear, they must fly or be captured. The effective force of Grant's army would be thus constantly diminished, and in the same proportion the column of attack would be steadily augmented.

Add to this inestimable Confederate advantage the panic and general demoralization that was inevitable on the one side, and the corresponding and ever-increasing enthusiasm that would be aroused upon the other, and it will be admitted that I do not overestimate the opportunity when I say that it has been rarely equalled in any war.

As far as could be anticipated, the plan was devised to meet every contingency. For example, as Sedgwick had no reserves in support behind him, all having been sent to the Union left, his only chance of meeting the sudden assault on his right and rear was to withdraw from his intrenchments under the fire of this flanking force and attempt to form a new line at right angle to his works, and thus perhaps arrest the headlong Confederate charge.

But it will be seen that his situation would then be rendered still more hopeless, because as he changed front and attempted to form a new line the Confederates in front of his works were to leap from their rifle-pits and rush upon his newly exposed flank. He would thus be inevitably crushed between the two Confederate forces.

When Sedgwick's corps should thus be destroyed, the fate of the next Union corps (Warren's) would surely be sealed, for in its front would be the Confederate corps, led by that brilliant soldier, A. P. Hill, ready to assault from that direction, while upon its flank would be not only my two brigades, as in the case of Sedgwick, but Ewell's entire corps, adding to the column of attack. In practically unobstructed march around Warren's flank Ewell would speedily envelop it, and thus the second Union corps in the battle line would be forced to precipitate flight; or if it attempted, however bravely, to stand its ground, it would be inevitably crushed or captured as Ewell assailed it in rear while Hill assaulted in front.

And so of the next corps and the next. Had no part of this plan ever been tested, the vast results which must have attended its execution could scarcely be doubted by any experienced soldier. Fortunately, however, for the removal of all doubt in the premises, it was tested—tested at an hour most unfavorable to its success and after almost the entire day had been wasted; tested on General Lee's approval and by his personal order and almost in his immediate presence. The test, unfair as it was, furnished the plainest and most convincing proof that had it been made at an early hour in the day instead of at sundown, the 6th of May would have ended in the crushing defeat of General Grant's army.

Here is the test and here the results. With my own Georgia brigade and General Robert Johnson's North Carolinians moving by the left flank, so that we should have nothing to do, when the proper point was reached, except to close up, to front face and forward, we pressed through the woods as rapidly and noiselessly as possible and halted at the point immediately opposite Sedgwick's flank.

The solid and dotted lines here given sufficiently

indicate the approximate positions occupied by the respective armies at the beginning of my flank attack.

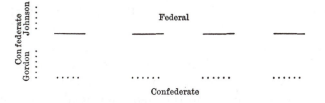

The Georgia brigade (Gordon's) was directed to make the assault, and the North Carolina brigade (Johnson's) was ordered to move farther to the Union rear and to keep as nearly as possible in touch with the attacking force and to gather up Sedgwick's men as they broke to the rear. As the sun went down these troops were ordered forward. In less than ten minutes they struck the Union flank and with thrilling yells rushed upon it and along the Union works, shattering regiments and brigades, and throwing them into wildest confusion and panic. There was practically no resistance. There could be none. The Georgians, commanded by that intrepid leader, Clement A. Evans, were on the flank, and the North Carolinians, led by a brilliant young officer, Robert Johnson, were sweeping around to the rear, without a shot in their front. There was nothing for the brave Federals to do but to fly. There was no time given them to file out from their works and form a new line of resistance. This was attempted again and again; but in every instance the swiftly moving Confederates were upon them, pouring a consuming fire into their half-formed ranks and shivering one command after another in quick succession. The gallant Union leaders, Generals Seymour and Shaler, rode among their panic-stricken troops in the heroic endeavor to form them into a new line. Their brave efforts were worse than unavailing, for both of these superb officers, with large numbers of their brigades, were quickly gathered as prisoners of war in the Confederate net; and nearly the whole of Sedgwick's corps was disorganized.

It is due to both General Ewell and General Early to say that they did all in their power to help forward the movement when once begun. There was, however, little need for help, for the North Carolina brigade, which was in the movement, had not found an opportunity to fire or to receive a shot; and the Georgia brigade as a whole had not been checked for a single moment nor suffered any serious loss. These men were literally revelling in the chase, when the unwelcome darkness put an end to it. They were so enthused by the pursuit, which they declared to me, as I rode among them, was the "finest frolic" they had ever been engaged in, that it was difficult to halt them even when it became too dark to distinguish friend from foe. With less than sixty casualties, this brigade almost single-handed had achieved these great results during the brief twilight of the 6th of May. And possibly one half of the small loss that occurred was inflicted after nightfall by Confederates who enthusiastically charged from the front upon the Union breastworks, firing as they came, and not realizing that my command in its swift movement down the flank had reached that point on Sedgwick's line. The brave and brilliant John W. Daniel, now United States senator from Virginia, was then serving on the staff of General Early. As he rode with me in the darkness, he fell, desperately wounded, with his thigh-bone shattered. He narrowly escaped death from this wound, which has maimed him for life.

It will be seen that my troops were compelled to halt at last, not by the enemy's resistance, but solely by the darkness and the cross-fire from Confederates. Had daylight lasted one half-hour longer, there would not have been left an organized company in Sedgwick's corps. Even as it was, all accounts agree that his whole command was shaken. As I rode abreast of the Georgians, who were moving swiftly and with slight resistance, the last scene which met my eye as the curtain of night shut off the view was the crumbling of the Union lines as they bravely but vainly endeavored to file out of their works and form a new line under the furious onset and withering fire of the Confederates.

General Horace Porter, who served with distinction on General Grant's staff, speaking in his book of this twilight flank attack on the 6th of May, says: "It was now about sundown; the storm of battle which had raged with unabated fury from early dawn had been succeeded by a calm. . . . Just then the stillness was broken by heavy volleys of musketry on our extreme right, which told that Sedgwick had been assaulted and was actually engaged with the enemy. The attack against which the general-in-chief during the day had ordered every precaution to be taken had now been made. . . . Generals Grant and Meade, accompanied by me and one or two other staff officers, walked rapidly over to Meade's tent, and found that the reports still coming in were bringing news of increasing disaster. It was soon reported that General Shaler and part of his brigade had been captured; then that General Seymour and several hundred of his men had fallen into the hands of the enemy; afterward that our right had been turned, and Ferrero's division cut off and forced back upon the Rapidan. . . . Aides came galloping in from the right, laboring under intense excitement, talking wildly and giving the most exaggerated reports of the engagement. Some declared that a large force had broken and scattered Sedgwick's entire corps. Others insisted that the enemy had turned our right completely and captured the wagon-train. . . . A general officer came in from his command at this juncture and said to the general-in-chief, speaking rapidly and laboring under considerable excitement: 'General Grant, this is a crisis that cannot be looked upon too seriously; I know Lee's methods well by past experience; he will throw his whole army between us and the Rapidan and cut us off completely from our communications.'"

This extract from General Porter's book is given merely to show what consternation had been carried into the Union ranks by this flank attack, which had been delayed from early morning to sundown. The question is pertinent: What would have been the result of that flank movement had the plan of battle suggested been promptly accepted in the early morning and vigorously executed, as was urged?

If we carefully and impartially consider all the facts and circumstances, there cannot be much disagreement as to the answer. If that one Georgia brigade, supported by the North Carolinians, could accomplish such results in such brief space of time, it is beyond question that the Confederate column of attack, constantly augmented during an entire day of battle, would have swept the Union forces from the field. Indeed, had not darkness intervened, the Georgia and North Carolina brigades alone would have shattered Sedgwick's entire corps; and the brigades and divisions of Ewell, which confronted those of Sedgwick on the general line, would have marched steadily across to join the Georgians and North Carolinians, instead of rushing across in the darkness, firing as they came, and inflicting more damage upon my men than upon the enemy.

General Porter, speaking of General Grant's promptness after dark in "relieving the situation," says: "Reenforcements were hurried to the point attacked, and preparations made for Sedgwick's corps to take up a new line with the front and right thrown back." These movements were such as were to be expected from so able a commander as General Grant. But it will be seen that neither of them could have been accomplished had this flank assault been made at an early hour of the day. General Grant's army on the other flank was so pressed that he could not have safely weakened his force there to aid Sedgwick. Both armies on that flank were strained to the utmost, and Lee and Grant were both there in person, superintending the operations of their respective forces. When night came and put an end to the fighting on his left flank, then, and not till then, was General Grant in position to send reënforcements to Sedgwick. Moreover, had the plan of battle proposed to Early and Ewell been accepted, Lee, of course, would have been fully advised of it, and of every stage of its progress. He would, therefore, have made all his arrangements auxiliary to this prime movement upon General Grant's exposed right. The simple announcement to Lee of the fact that this right flank of the Union army was entirely unprotected, and that it was in close proximity to his unemployed troops, would have been to that great Southern soldier the herald of victory. He would have anticipated at once every material and commanding event which must necessarily have followed the embracing of so unexampled an opportunity. As soon as he had learned that his troops were placed secretly and squarely across Sedgwick's right, Lee could have written in advance a complete description of the resistless Confederate charge—of the necessary flight or capture in quick succession of the hopelessly flanked Union commands, of the cumulative power of the Confederate column at every step of its progress, compelling General Grant to send large bodies of men to his right, thus weakening his left. In front of that left was Lee in person. With a full knowledge of the progress made by his own flanking columns, and appreciating the extremity in which such a movement would place the Union commander, Lee would have lost no time in availing himself of all the advantages of the anomalous situation. Knowing that General Grant would be compelled to send a large part of his army to meet the Confederate column, which had completely turned his flank and was pressing his rear, Lee would either have driven back the forces left in his front, thus bringing confusion to that wing also, or he would have detached a portion of the troops under his immediate command and sent them to Ewell to swell the column of Confederates already in Grant's rear, forcing him to change front and reform his whole battle line under the most perilous conditions.

After weighing the unparalleled advantage which such a situation would have given to such a commander as Lee, can any impartial military critic suggest a manœuvre which could possibly have saved General Grant's army from crushing defeat? If so, he will have solved the embarrassing problem which a completely flanked and crumbling army must always meet.

The simple truth is that an army which is expending all its strength, or even the major part of it, in repelling attacks along its front, and permits itself to be completely flanked, is in the utmost extremity of peril. Among the highest military authorities there will be no dispute, I think, as to the correctness of the proposition that when opposing battle lines are held by forces of even approximate strength and of equal fighting qualities, and are commanded by officers of equal ability, the one or the other is in a practically hopeless condition if, while met at every point on its front, it is suddenly startled by a carefully planned and vigorous assault upon either its flank or rear. Its situation is still more desperate if assaulted both in flank and rear. This is especially true when the plan of attack is based upon the certainty of rapidly accumulating strength in the assaulting column. It is not too much to say that the position of an army so flanked is absolutely hopeless unless, as in this case, the coming of darkness intervenes to save it.

Another inquiry to which I feel compelled, in the interest of history, to give a full and frank answer is this: Who was responsible for the delay of nine hours or more while that exposed Union flank was inviting our attack?

When the plan for assault was fully matured, it was presented, with all its tremendous possibilities and with the full information which had been acquired by scouts and by my own personal and exhaustive examination. With all the earnestness that comes from deep conviction, the prompt adoption and vigorous execution of the plan were asked and urged. General Early at once opposed it. He said that Burnside's corps was immediately behind Sedgwick's right to protect it from any such flank attack; that if I should attempt such movement, Burnside would assail my flank and rout or capture all my men. He was so firmly fixed in his belief that Burnside's corps was where he declared it to be that he was not perceptibly affected by the repeated reports of scouts, nor my own statement that I myself had ridden for miles in rear of Sedgwick's right, and that neither Burnside's corps nor any other troops were there. General Ewell, whose province it was to decide the controversy, hesitated. He was naturally reluctant to take issue with my superior officer in a matter about which he could have no personal knowledge, because of the fact that his headquarters as corps-commander were located at considerable distance from this immediate locality. In view of General Early's protest, he was unwilling to order the attack or to grant me permission to make it, even upon my proposing to assume all responsibility of disaster, should any occur.

Meantime the roaring battle to our right was punctuating with tremendous emphasis the folly of our delay. A. P. Hill, in impetuous assault, had broken and hurled back almost upon General Grant's headquarters a portion of Warren's corps. The zone of the most furious fighting was, however, still farther off and on the extreme right of our line, where the heaviest forces of both armies were gathered. The almost incessant roll of musketry indicated that the fighting was tremendous. From 4:30 o'clock in the morning, through the entire forenoon, and until late in the day, there had been at different points along the lines to our right alternate and desperate assaults by the two armies, with varying success; but not a shot was being fired near us. My troops and the other portions of Ewell's corps were comparatively idle during the greater part of the day, while the bloody scenes to our right were being enacted. It is most remarkable that the desperate struggle on that far-off flank, coupled with the stillness on ours, failed to impress my superior officers as significant. In the early hours of the day Hancock had pressed back the Confederate right, doubling it up and driving it, as was asserted, for a mile or more. Meantime Longstreet arrived with his superb corps. Hancock was checked, and General Grant's forces, in turn, were hurled back by the Confederate assaults. Like an oscillating pendulum, victory was vibrating between the two armies through all of that eventful day, while at any hour of it the proposed movement on Sedgwick's flank by Ewell's idle Confederates was not only perfectly feasible, but full of promise to the Confederate army.

After Jenkins was killed and Longstreet had been carried back on a litter, seriously wounded, General Lee's attention was necessarily confined to that portion of the field where General Grant was superintending his own aggressive operations. This was one of the crises when General Lee took personal command of his troops; and as Gregg's superb brigade of Texans pressed to the front, the commander-in-chief spurred his horse through a gap in the trenches and attempted to go with them. As these brave men recognized General Lee, a ringing protest ran down the line, and they at last compelled him to yield to their entreaties: " Go back, General Lee; go back!"

General Grant during that day was full of apprehension that Ewell would attempt some offensive tactics against Sedgwick, while Lee was wondering why it was not done. Lee knew that it ought to be done, as will appear later, if for no other object than to divert Grant's attention from his prime purpose and thus bring incidental relief to Longstreet and the other heavily pressed Confederates far off to our right. General Horace Porter, in his " Campaigning with Grant," more than once refers to General Grant's uneasiness about Sedgwick. He says: " The general-in-chief was devoting a good deal of thought to our right, which had been weakened." Well might General Grant be apprehensive. Had he been fully apprised of that strangely exposed flank of his army, he would have been impelled to send troops to protect Sedgwick's right. On the other hand, had Lee been advised, as he should have been, of the reports of my scouts and of myself, he would not have delayed the proposed movement against Sedgwick's flank a moment longer than was necessary to give an order for its execution. The correctness of this opinion as to what Lee would have done is based not merely upon the knowledge which every officer in his army possessed of his mental characteristics, but upon his prompt action when at last he was informed of the conditions as they had existed for more than nine hours.

Both General Early and I were at Ewell's headquarters when, at about 5:30 in the afternoon, General Lee rode up and asked: "Cannot something be done on this flank to relieve the pressure upon our right?" After listening for some time to the conference which followed this pointed inquiry, I felt it my duty to acquaint General Lee with the facts as to Sedgwick's exposed flank, and with the plan of battle which had been submitted and urged in the early hours of the morning and during the day. General Early again promptly and vigorously protested as he had previously done. He still steadfastly maintained that Burnside's corps was in the woods behind Sedgwick's right; that the movement was too hazardous and must result in disaster to us. With as much earnestness as was consistent with the position of junior officer, I recounted the facts to General Lee, and assured him that General Early was mistaken; that I had ridden for several miles in Sedgwick's rear, and that neither Burnside's corps nor any other Union troops were concealed in those woods. The details of the whole plan were laid before him. There was no doubt with him as to its feasibility. His words were few, but his silence and grim looks while the reasons for that long delay were being given, and his prompt order to me to move at once to the attack, revealed his thoughts almost as plainly as words could have done. Late as it was, he agreed in the opinion that we could bring havoc to as much of the Union line as we could reach before darkness should check us. It was near sunset, and too late to reap more than a pittance of the harvest which had so long been inviting the Confederate sickle.

Where was General Burnside on the morning of the 6th? Where was he during the entire day?

General Early never yielded his convictions that had I been permitted to attack Sedgwick's exposed right flank in the morning, the movement would have led to Confed-

erate disaster, because of the presence of Burnside behind that flank. He was so thoroughly satisfied of this
that in his book, written and published since the war, he
insists: "Burnside's corps was in rear of the enemy's
flank on which the attack was suggested." In the years
that have passed I have made no effort to controvert General Early's opinions in this matter. Now, however, the
time has come when the publication of my own reminiscences makes it necessary for me to speak. The recent
printing by the Government of the War Records makes
public the official reports of the Federal officers who
fought in the Wilderness on that 6th of May. I shall
quote only from Federal officers or Northern history.

In his report General Hancock says: "I am not aware
what movements were made by General Burnside near
Parker's store on the morning of the 6th, but I experienced no relief from the attack I was informed he would
make across my front—a movement long and anxiously
waited for. . . . During the night of the 5th I received orders to move on the enemy again at 5 A.M. on
the 6th." He adds that his orders informed him that
his right would be relieved by an attack of other troops,
among them "two divisions . . . under General Burnside." It will be remembered that Hancock held the
extreme left of Grant's army. Burnside was there with
Hancock. This officer describes the places and times
where and when Burnside was to move, and adds: "The
same despatch directed me to attack simultaneously with
General Burnside."

This was during the morning hours. Later in the day
General Meade locates him thus: "Soon after Hancock
fell back, about 2 P.M., Burnside attacked toward the
Orange plank road to the right and in advance of Hancock's position."

General Grant himself (speaking of Burnside's movements) says in his official report: "By six o'clock of the

morning of the 6th he was leading his corps into action near Wilderness Tavern," etc.

Swinton, in his history of " The Army of the Potomac," says: " The Union line as formed by dawn of the 6th was therefore in the order of Sedgwick on the right, next Warren, and Burnside and Hancock on the left."

General Porter says: " At four o'clock the next morning, May 6, we were awakened in our camp by the sound of Burnside's men moving along the Germanna road. They had been marching since 1 A.M., hurrying on to reach *the left of Warren.*" He adds: " The general now instructed me to ride out to Hancock's front, inform him of the progress of Burnside's movement," etc. This was early on the morning of the 6th, and Hancock and Burnside were on the extreme left. It is established, therefore, beyond question that Burnside was not in rear of Sedgwick when I insisted upon attacking that exposed right flank in the early morning. He was not there at all during the entire day. He was on the other flank of Grant's army morning, noon, and evening. The Federal reports so locate him, and there can be no longer any dispute as to Burnside's locality, upon which the entire controversy rests.

General Early, in his book, states that General Ewell agreed with him as to the impolicy of making the morning flank attack which I so earnestly urged. Alas! he did; and in the light of revelations subsequently made by Union officers, no intelligent military critic, I think, will fail to sympathize with my lament, which was even more bitter than at Gettysburg, over the irreparable loss of Jackson. But for my firm faith in God's Providence, and in His control of the destinies of this Republic, I should be tempted to imitate the confident exclamation made to the Master by Mary and Martha when they met Him after the death of Lazarus: " Hadst thou been here, our brother had not died." Calmly reviewing the indisputable facts which made the situation at Gettysburg and in the Wilderness strikingly similar, and considering them from a purely military and worldly standpoint, I should utter my profoundest convictions were I to say: "Had Jackson been there, the Confederacy had not died." Had he been at Gettysburg when a part of that Second Corps which his genius had made famous had already broken through the protecting forces and was squarely on the Union right, which was melting away like a sand-bank struck by a mountain torrent; when the whole Union battle line that was in view was breaking to the rear; when those flanking Confederates in their unobstructed rush were embarrassed only by the number of prisoners—had Jackson been there then, instead of commanding a halt, his only order would have been, "Forward, men, forward!" as he majestically rode in their midst, intensifying their flaming enthusiasm at every step of the advance.

Or had he been in the Wilderness on that fateful 6th of May, when that same right flank of the Union army was so strangely exposed and was inviting the assault of that same portion of his old corps, words descriptive of the situation and of the plan of attack could not have been uttered fast enough for his impatient spirit. Jackson's genius was keener-scented in its hunt for an enemy's flank than the most royally bred setter's nose in search of the hiding covey. The fleetest tongue could not have narrated the facts connected with Sedgwick's position before Jackson's unerring judgment would have grasped the whole situation. His dilating eye would have flashed, and his laconic order, "Move at once, sir," would have been given with an emphasis prophetic of the energy with which he would have seized upon every advantage offered by the situation. But Providence had willed otherwise. Jackson was dead, and Gettysburg was lost. He was not now in the Wilderness, and the greatest opportunity ever presented to Lee's army was permitted to pass.

CHAPTER XIX

RESULTS OF THE DRAWN BATTLES

General Grant the aggressor—Failure to dislodge Lee—An exciting
night ride—Surrounded by Federal troops—A narrow escape in the
darkness—General Lee's comments on the assault upon Sedgwick—
A remarkable prediction as to General Grant's next movement.

IN the thirty hours, more or less, which elapsed from
the beginning of the struggle on the 5th of May to
its close after dark on the 6th, there was, during the
night which intervened, a period of about eleven hours
in which the fighting was suspended. In addition to
this, the intervals between the successive assaults and
the skirmishing consumed, perhaps, in all, some eight or
nine hours, leaving in round numbers about ten hours
of uninterrupted, continuous battle. When it is remembered that the aggregate losses on the two sides
amounted in killed and wounded to twenty thousand, it
will be seen that these Americans were shooting each
other down at the rate of two thousand per hour; and
yet at no time or place during these hours was one half
of the two lines in actual strenuous battle.

As at Gettysburg, so in this prolonged struggle of the
5th and 6th of May, there was a series of desperate battles; but, unlike Gettysburg, this engagement brought
to neither army any decided advantage. Both had successes, both corresponding reverses.

The critical student, however, who wishes to make a

more complete analysis of the two days' happenings on those battle lines, and to consider the resulting situation on the night of the 6th, will, in order to determine on which side was the weight of victory, take into account the following facts: namely, that General Grant was the aggressor; that his purpose was to drive Lee before him; that this was not accomplished; that both armies camped on the field; that Lee only left it when Grant moved to another field; and that both days ended with a Confederate victory won by the same Confederate troops.

His gifted staff officer states that General Grant, during this last day of alternate successes and reverses, smoked twenty large, strong Havana cigars. In after years, when it was my privilege to know General Grant well, he was still a great smoker; but if the nervous strain under which he labored is to be measured by the number of cigars consumed, it must have been greater on the 6th of May than at any period of his life, for he is said never to have equalled that record. As General Lee did not smoke, we have no such standard by which to test the tension upon him. I apprehend, however, that his pulses also were beating at an accelerated pace, for he and General Grant were for the first time testing each other's mettle.

The night of the 6th passed without alarms on the picket-lines or startling reports from scouts; but a short time after darkness had brought an end to my attack on Sedgwick's corps, I myself had an exceptionally exciting experience — a cautious ride to the front and a madcap ride to the rear. I had ordered a force to move a short distance nearer to the enemy and deploy a protecting line of pickets across my front. This movement was so difficult in that dense thicket at night that the task was both dangerous and slow. The officer in charge was to notify me when the line was in position.

I waited impatiently for this notification, and as it did not reach me as soon as expected, I decided to ride slowly to the front and in person superintend the deployment.

Taking with me but one courier, William Beasley of Lagrange, Georgia, who had been in his boyhood the constant companion of his father, Dr. Beasley, in the fox chase, and who had thus become an experienced woodsman, I rode cautiously in the general direction taken by my picket force. There was no moonlight, but the night was cloudless and the stars furnished enough light for us to ride without serious difficulty through the woods. It was, however, too dark for us readily to distinguish the color of uniforms. Before we had proceeded far we rode into a body of men supposed to be the troops whom I had sent out on picket. There was no sort of deployment or alignment, and I was considerably annoyed by this appearance of carelessness on the part of the officer, to whom I had given special instructions. But before I had time to ascertain what this indifference to orders meant, my trusted courier, whose sight was clearer than mine at night, said to me in a whisper, "General, these are not our men; they are Yankees." I replied, "Nonsense, Beasley," and rode on, still hoping to ascertain the reason for this inexcusable huddling of my pickets. Beasley, however, was persistent, and, taking hold of my arm, asserted in the most emphatic manner, "I tell you, General, these men are Yankees, and we had better get away from here." His earnestness impressed me, especially as he strengthened his assertion by calling my attention to the fact that even in the dim starlight the dark blue of the uniforms around us presented a contrast with those we were wearing. I cautioned him to be quiet and keep close to me as I began to turn my horse in the opposite direction. Meantime, and at the moment we discovered

our alarming position, we heard the startling calls from
Union officers close by us, who were endeavoring to
disentangle the confused mass of men: " Rally here,
—— New York." " Let all the men of the —— Regiment of Pennsylvania form here." Up to this moment
not the slightest suspicion seemed to have been entertained by these men that Beasley and I were Confederates; and, apparently for the sole purpose of ascertaining
to what Union command we belonged, an officer with
his sword in his hand asked in the most courteous
manner to what brigade we were attached, evidently
hoping to aid us in finding it. Both Beasley and I were,
of course, deaf to his inquiry, and continued to move on
without making any reply, turning our horses' heads
toward the gray lines in which we would feel more at
home. Either our strange silence or our poorly concealed purpose to get away from that portion of the
Wilderness aroused his suspicions, and the officer called
to his comrades as we rode away from him, " Halt those
men! " His orders were scarcely uttered when the
" boys in blue " rushed around us, shouting, " Halt,
halt! " But the company in which we found ourselves
was not congenial and the locality was not at that
moment a good place for us to halt. We had to go, and
go instantly, back to our own lines or to a Northern
prison. I instantly resolved to take the risk of escape,
though we might be shot into mincemeat by the hundreds of rifles around us. Beasley was well mounted,
and I was riding a thoroughbred stallion, the horse
General Shaler rode when he was made prisoner a few
hours previous. Both Beasley and I were fairly good
riders. Instantly throwing my body as far down on
my horse's side as possible, my right foot firmly fixed
in the stirrup, my left leg gripping the saddle like an
iron elbow, I seized the bridle-rein under my horse's
neck, planted my spur in his flank, and called, " Fol-

low me, Beasley!" This courier had intuitively followed the motion of my body, and was clinging like an experienced cowboy to the side of his horse. As the superb animal which I rode felt the keen barb of the spur, he sprang with a tremendous bound through the dense underbrush and the mass of startled soldiers. It seems probable that the Union men were in almost as much danger from the hoofs of our horses as we were from the Union rifles.

Strange as our escape may seem, it will be readily understood when it is remembered that the whole affair, like a sudden flash in the darkness, was so unexpected and so startling as completely to bewilder these men, and that they were crowded so closely together that it was difficult to shoot at us without shooting each other. In our flight we seemed to outstrip the bullets sent after us; for neither Beasley nor myself nor our horses were hit, although the roll of musketry was like that from a skirmish line. With the exception of bruises to shins and scalps, the only serious damage done was that inflicted upon our clothing by the bristling chinquapins and pines, through which we plunged at so furious a rate.

The impressive feature of that memorable night was the silence that succeeded the din of battle. The awe inspired by the darkness and density of the woods, in which two great armies rested within hailing distance of each other, was deepened by the low moans of the wounded, and their calls for help, as the ambulance corps ministered to blue and gray alike. And yet these harrowing conditions, which can never be forgotten, did not compare in impressiveness with those at the other end of the lines. As already explained, the battle's storm-centre was on our right flank. The diameter of its circling and destructive currents did not exceed, perhaps, one and a half miles; but the amount of blood spilt has not often been equalled in so circumscribed an area. The conditions were not favorable for the use of artillery; but the few batteries used left their impress on the forest and the imaginations of the men. The solid shot slashed the timber, and the severed tree-tops or branches dropped upon the surging lines, here and there covering, as they fell, the wounded and the dead. The smaller underbrush in that zone of fire was everywhere cut and scarred, and in some places swept down by the terrific hail from small arms. Bloody strips from soldiers' shirts hung upon the bushes, while, to add to the accumulation of horrors, the woods caught fire, as at Chickamauga, and the flames rapidly spread before a brisk wind, terrifying the disabled wounded and scorching the bodies of the slain.

On the morning of May 7, I was invited by the commanding general to ride with him through that portion of the sombre woodland where the movement of my troops upon the Union right had occurred on the previous evening. It will be remembered that the plan of that battle was entirely my own, and that its execution had been delayed until my statement of the facts to General Lee, in the presence of Generals Ewell and Early, secured from the commander-in-chief the order for the movement. The reasons which impel me to refrain from giving General Lee's comments in this connection will therefore be appreciated. I shall be pardoned, however, and, I think, justified by all fair-minded men if I say that although nothing could compensate the Confederate cause for that lost opportunity, yet his indorsement of the plan was to me personally all that I could desire.

It would be a matter of profound interest if all that General Lee said on this ride could be placed upon record. This I could not venture to undertake; but I may state, without fear of misleading, that his comments upon the situation were full and free. He discussed the dominant characteristics of his great antagonist: his indomitable will and untiring persistency; his direct method of waging war by delivering constant and heavy blows upon the enemy's front rather than by seeking advantage through strategical manœuvre. General Lee also said that General Grant held so completely and firmly the confidence of the Government that he could command to any extent its limitless resources in men and materials, while the Confederacy was already practically exhausted in both. He, however, hoped—perhaps I may say he was almost convinced—that if we could keep the Confederate army between General Grant and Richmond, checking him for a few months longer, as we had in the past two days, some crisis in public affairs or change in public opinion at the North might induce the authorities at Washington to let the Southern States go, rather than force their retention in the Union at so heavy a cost.

I endeavored to learn from General Lee what movements he had in contemplation, or what he next expected from General Grant. It was then, in reply to my inquiry, that I learned for the first time of his intention to move at once to Spottsylvania. Reports had reached me to the effect that General Grant's army was retreating or preparing to retreat; and I called General Lee's attention to these rumors. He had heard them, but they had not made the slightest impression upon his mind. He admitted that his own scouts had made to him some such statement, but said that such rumors had no foundation, except in the moving to the rear of General Grant's ambulances and wagon-trains, with the necessary forces for protection. Indeed, he said in so many words: " General Grant is not going to retreat. He will move his army to Spottsylvania."

I asked him if he had information of such contemplated change by General Grant, or if there were special evidences of such purpose. "Not at all," said Lee, "not at all; but that is the next point at which the armies will meet. Spottsylvania is now General Grant's best strategic point. I am so sure of his next move that I have already made arrangements to march by the shortest practicable route, that we may meet him there." If these are not his exact words, they change in no sense the import of what he did say. These unhesitating and emphatic statements as to Grant's purposes were made by Lee as if based on positive knowledge and not upon mere speculation; and the reasons given by him for his conclusions as to Grant's next move illustrate the Confederate chieftain's wonderful foresight as well as his high estimate of the Union commander as a soldier.

General Horace Porter, of General Grant's staff, says: "At 6:30 the general issued his orders to prepare for a night march of the entire army toward Spottsylvania Court-house."

Let it be remembered that this announcement by General Grant of his purpose was made at 6:30 A.M. on the 7th, and that General Lee's prediction was uttered on the same morning and at nearly the same hour, when there was no possibility of his having gained any direct knowledge of his antagonist's intentions. It was uttered many hours before General Stuart, the Confederate cavalry commander, had informed General Lee of the movement of Union wagon-trains southward, which movement served only to verify the accuracy with which he had divined General Grant's purposes and predicted his next manœuvre.

This notable prophecy of General Lee and its fulfilment by General Grant show that the brains of these two foemen had been working at the same problem. The known quantities in that problem were the aims of Grant to crush Lee and capture Richmond, to which had been added the results of the last two days' fighting. The unknown quantity which both were endeavoring to find was the next movement which the aggressor would probably make. Grant stood in his own place and calculated from his own standpoint; Lee put himself in Grant's place and calculated from the same standpoint: and both found the same answer—Spottsylvania.

Having reached the same conclusion, both acted upon it with characteristic promptness; and then there was a race between them. Leaving their respective pioneer corps to bury the dead, and the surgeons and nurses to care for the wounded, they pressed toward the goal which their own convictions had set before them.

CHAPTER XX

General Lee's prophecy fulfilled—Hancock's assault on May 12—One
of his greatest achievements—General Lee to the head of the column
—Turned back by his own men—Hancock repulsed—The most remarkable battle of the war—Heroism on both sides.

THE first battles in the Wilderness were the grim
heralds of those that were to follow, and both
armies knew it. These experienced soldiers were too
intelligent not to understand that a campaign was now
inaugurated which was to end in the practical destruction of one army or the other. The conditions around
them were not greatly changed by the change of locality.
They were still in the woods, but these were less dense
and were broken by fields and open spaces in which
there was room for manœuvre and the more effective
handling of artillery.

The meeting of the advance-guards at Spottsylvania
was the fulfilment to the letter of Lee's remarkable
prophecy. As the heads of the columns collided, the
armies quickly spread into zigzag formation as each
brigade, division, or corps struck its counterpart in the
opposing lines. These haphazard collisions, however,
rapidly developed a more orderly alignment and systematic battle, which culminated in that unparalleled struggle for the possession of a short line of Lee's breastworks. I say unparalleled, because the character of the

271

fighting, its duration, and the individual heroism exhibited have no precedent, so far as my knowledge extends, in our Civil War, or in any other war.

During these preliminary and somewhat random engagements, General Lee, in order to secure the most advantageous locality offered by the peculiar topography of the country, had placed his battle line so that it should conform in large measure to the undulations of the field. Along the brow of these slopes earthworks were speedily constructed. On one portion of the line, which embraced what was afterward known as the " Bloody Angle," there was a long stretch of breastworks forming almost a complete semicircle. Its most advanced or outer salient was the point against which Hancock made his famous charge.

My command had been withdrawn from position in the regular line, and a rôle was assigned me which no officer could covet if he had the least conception of the responsibilities involved. I was ordered to take position in rear of that salient, and as nearly equidistant as practicable from every point of the wide and threatened semicircle, to watch every part of it, to move quickly, without waiting for orders, to the support of any point that might be assaulted, and to restore, if possible, any breach that might be made. We were reserves to no one command, but to all commands occupying that entire stretch of works. It will be seen that, with no possibility of knowing when or where General Grant would make his next effort to penetrate our lines, the task to be performed by my troops was not an easy one, and that the tension upon the brain and nerves of one upon whom rested the responsibility was not light nor conducive to sleep. No serious breach of the lines occurred until the 10th, when a heavy column of Federals swept over the Confederate breastworks and penetrated some distance in their rear.

Burnside was at this time operating on Lee's right wing, while Warren, Hancock, and Mott concentrated upon our centre and assaulted with immense vigor. Warren and Mott were both driven back with heavy loss, but the gallant Union commander, Upton, broke over the Confederate breastworks, capturing artillery and prisoners, and was sweeping in column to our rear. It was a critical moment, but my troops in reserve, being quickly joined by those of Daniel and Steuart, were thrown across Upton's front, and at the command "Fire!" the Confederates poured consuming volleys into the Union ranks, wounding General Upton, shattering his forces, retaking the captured artillery, and reëstablishing Lee's lines. General Daniel was killed while leading his men with characteristic impetuosity. The fighting on the 10th of May at Spottsylvania ended with this charge by the Federals and their bloody repulse, in which more than 5000 dead and wounded were left in front of the Confederate works. On the same day, but on a different field, the South sustained a great loss in the death of General J. E. B. Stuart, who was killed in a cavalry fight with Sheridan's command at Yellow Tavern, Virginia, within a few miles of the Confederate capital. Stuart had few equals as a commander of cavalry on either side or in any war, and his fall was a serious blow to that branch of Lee's army. Stuart's temperament, his exuberance of spirit, his relish for adventure, and his readiness of resource in extremity, added to a striking personality and charm of manner which greatly enhanced his influence over his men, combined to make him an ideal leader for that dashing arm of the service. General Lee and his whole army, as well as the authorities at Richmond, were profoundly grieved at his fall. As soon as his death was reported, General Lee at once withdrew to his tent, saying: "I can scarcely think of him without weeping."

Night and day my troops were on watch or moving. At one point or another, there was almost continuous fighting; but in comparison with what followed, this was only the muttering of a storm that was to break with almost inconceivable fury on the morning of the 12th of May.

During the night preceding May 12, 1864, the report brought by scouts of some unusual movements in General Grant's army left little doubt that a heavy blow was soon to fall on some portion of the Confederate lines; but it was impossible to obtain reliable information as to whether it was to descend upon some part of that wide and long crescent or upon one of the wings. It came at last where it was perhaps least expected—at a point on the salient from which a large portion of the artillery had been withdrawn for use elsewhere.

Before daylight on May 12th the assault was made by Hancock, who during the night had massed his corps close to that extreme point of the semicircle which was held by the command of General Edward Johnson of Virginia. For several hours after sunrise dense clouds obscured the sun, and a heavy mist, which almost amounted to a rain, intensified the gloom.

At about 4:30 or 5 A.M. a soldier, one of the vedettes stationed during the night at different points to listen for any unusual sounds, came hurriedly in from the front and said to me: "General, I think there's something wrong down in the woods near where General Edward Johnson's men are."

"Why do you think so? There's been no unusual amount of firing."

"No, sir; there's been very little firing. But I tell you, sir, there are some mighty strange sounds down there — something like officers giving commands, and a jumble of voices."

In the next few minutes, before saddles could be

strapped on the officers' horses and cartridge-boxes on the men, report after report in quick succession reached me, each adding its quota of information; and finally there came the positive statement that the enemy had carried the outer angle on General Edward Johnson's front and seemed to be moving in rear of our works. There had been, and still were, so few discharges of small arms (not a heavy gun had been fired) that it was difficult to believe the reports true. But they were accurate.

During the night Hancock had massed a large portion of General Grant's army in front of that salient, and so near to it that, with a quick rush, his column had gone over the breastworks, capturing General Edward Johnson and General George Steuart and the great body of their men before these alert officers or their trained soldiers were aware of the movement. The surprise was complete and the assault practically unresisted. In all its details—its planning, its execution, and its fearful import to Lee's army—this charge of Hancock was one of that great soldier's most brilliant achievements.

Meantime my command was rapidly moving by the flank through the woods and underbrush toward the captured salient. The mist and fog were so heavy that it was impossible to see farther than a few rods. Throwing out in front a small force to apprise us of our near approach to the enemy, I rode at the head of the main column, and by my side rode General Robert Johnson, who commanded a brigade of North Carolinians. So rapidly and silently had the enemy moved inside of our works—indeed, so much longer time had he been on the inside than the reports indicated—that before we had moved one half the distance to the salient the head of my column butted squarely against Hancock's line of battle. The men who had been placed in our front to give warning were against that battle line before they knew it. They were shot down or made prisoners. The sudden and unexpected blaze from Hancock's rifles made the dark woodland strangely lurid. General Johnson, who rode immediately at my side, was shot from his horse, severely but not, as I supposed, fatally wounded in the head. His brigade was thrown inevitably into great confusion, but did not break to the rear. As quickly as possible, I had the next ranking officer in that brigade notified of General Johnson's fall and directed him at once to assume command. He proved equal to the emergency. With great coolness and courage he promptly executed my orders. The Federals were still advancing, and every movement of the North Carolina brigade had to be made under heavy fire. The officer in charge was directed to hastily withdraw his brigade a short distance, to change front so as to face Hancock's lines, and to deploy his whole force in close order as skirmishers, so as to stretch, if possible, across the entire front of Hancock. This done, he was ordered to charge with his line of skirmishers the solid battle lines before him. His looks indicated some amazement at the purpose to make an attack which appeared so utterly hopeless, and which would have been the very essence of rashness but for the extremity of the situation. He was, however, full of the fire of battle and too good a soldier not to yield prompt and cheerful obedience. That order was given in the hope and belief that in the fog and mists which concealed our numbers the sheer audacity of the movement would confuse and check the Union advance long enough for me to change front and form line of battle with the other brigades. The result was not disappointing except in the fact that Johnson's brigade, even when so deployed, was still too short to reach across Hancock's entire front. This fact was soon developed: not by sight, but by the direction from which the Union bullets began to come.

When the daring charge of the North Carolina brigade had temporarily checked that portion of the Federal forces struck by it, and while my brigades in the rear were being placed in position, I rode with Thomas G. Jones, the youngest member of my staff, into the intervening woods, in order, if possible, to locate Hancock more definitely. Sitting on my horse near the line of the North Carolina brigade, I was endeavoring to get a view of the Union lines, through the woods and through the gradually lifting mists. It was impossible, however, to see those lines; but, as stated, the direction from which they sent their bullets soon informed us that they were still moving and had already gone beyond our right. One of those bullets passed through my coat from side to side, just grazing my back. Jones, who was close to me, and sitting on his horse in a not very erect posture, anxiously inquired: " General, did n't that ball hit you ? "

" No," I said; " but suppose my back had been in a bow like yours? Don't you see that the bullet would have gone straight through my spine? Sit up or you 'll be killed."

The sudden jerk with which he straightened himself, and the duration of the impression made, showed that this ocular demonstration of the necessity for a soldier to sit upright on his horse had been more effective than all the ordinary lessons that could have been given. It is but simple justice to say of this immature boy that even then his courage, his coolness in the presence of danger, and his strong moral and mental characteristics gave promise of his brilliant future.

The bullets from Hancock's rifles furnished the information which I was seeking as to the progress he had made within and along our earthworks. I then took advantage of this brief check given to the Union advance, and placed my troops in line for a countercharge, upon the success or failure of which the fate of the Confederate army seemed to hang. General Lee evidently thought so. His army had been cut in twain by Hancock's brilliant *coup de main*. Through that wide breach in the Confederate lines, which was becoming wider with every step, the Union forces were rushing like a swollen torrent through a broken mill-dam. General Lee knew, as did every one else who realized the momentous import of the situation, that the bulk of the Confederate army was in such imminent peril that nothing could rescue it except a counter-movement, quick, impetuous, and decisive. Lee resolved to save it, and, if need be, to save it at the sacrifice of his own life. With perfect self-poise, he rode to the margin of that breach, and appeared upon the scene just as I had completed the alignment of my troops and was in the act of moving in that crucial countercharge upon which so much depended. As he rode majestically in front of my line of battle, with uncovered head and mounted on Old Traveller, Lee looked a very god of war. Calmly and grandly, he rode to a point near the centre of my line and turned his horse's head to the front, evidently resolved to lead in person the desperate charge and drive Hancock back or perish in the effort. I knew what he meant; and although the passing moments were of priceless value, I resolved to arrest him in his effort, and thus save to the Confederacy the life of its great leader. I was at the centre of that line when General Lee rode to it. With uncovered head, he turned his face toward Hancock's advancing column. Instantly I spurred my horse across Old Traveller's front, and grasping his bridle in my hand, I checked him. Then, in a voice which I hoped might reach the ears of my men and command their attention, I called out, "General Lee, you shall not lead my men in a charge. No man can do that, sir. Another is here for that purpose. These men behind you are

Georgians, Virginians, and Carolinians. They have never failed you on any field. They will not fail you here. Will you, boys?" The response came like a mighty anthem that must have stirred his emotions as no other music could have done. Although the answer to those three words, "Will you, boys?" came in the monosyllables, "No, no, no; we'll not fail him," yet they were doubtless to him more eloquent because of their simplicity and momentous meaning. But his great heart was destined to be quickly cheered by a still sublimer testimony of their deathless devotion. As this first thrilling response died away, I uttered the words for which they were now fully prepared. I shouted to General Lee, "You must go to rear." The echo, "General Lee to the rear, General Lee to the rear!" rolled back with tremendous emphasis from the throats of my men; and they gathered around him, turned his horse in the opposite direction, some clutching his bridle, some his stirrups, while others pressed close to Old Traveller's hips, ready to shove him by main force to the rear. I verily believe that, had it been necessary or possible, they would have carried on their shoulders both horse and rider to a place of safety.

This entire scene, with all its details of wonderful pathos and deep meaning, had lasted but a few minutes, and yet it was a powerful factor in the rescue of Lee's army. It had lifted these soldiers to the very highest plane of martial enthusiasm. The presence of their idolized commander-in-chief, his purpose to lead them in person, his magnetic and majestic presence, and the spontaneous pledges which they had just made to him, all conspired to fill them with an ardor and intensity of emotion such as have rarely possessed a body of troops in any war. The most commonplace soldier was uplifted and transformed into a veritable Ajax. To say that every man in those brigades was prepared for the most heroic work or to meet a heroic death would be but a lame description of the impulse which seemed to bear them forward in wildest transport. Fully realizing the value of such inspiration for the accomplishment of the bloody task assigned them, I turned to my men as Lee was forced to the rear, and reminding them of their pledges to him, and of the fact that the eyes of their great leader were still upon them, I ordered, "Forward!" With the fury of a cyclone, and almost with its resistless power, they rushed upon Hancock's advancing column. With their first terrific onset, the impetuosity of which was indescribable, his leading lines were shivered and hurled back upon their stalwart supports. In the inextricable confusion that followed, and before Hancock's lines could be reformed, every officer on horseback in my division, the brigade and regimental commanders, and my own superb staff, were riding among the troops, shouting in unison: "Forward, men, forward!" But the brave line officers on foot and the enthused privates needed no additional spur to their already rapt spirits. Onward they swept, pouring their rapid volleys into Hancock's confused ranks, and swelling the deafening din of battle with their piercing shouts. Like the débris in the track of a storm, the dead and dying of both armies were left in the wake of this Confederate charge. In the meantime the magnificent troops of Ramseur and Rodes were rushing upon Hancock's dissolving corps from another point, and Long's artillery and other batteries were pouring a deadly fire into the broken Federal ranks. Hancock was repulsed and driven out. Every foot of the lost salient and earthworks was retaken, except that small stretch which the Confederate line was too short to cover.

These glorious troops had redeemed the pledge which they had sent ringing through the air, thrilling the spirit of Lee: "No, we will not fail him." Grandly had they redeemed it, and at fearful cost; but the living were happy, and I verily believe that if the dead could have spoken, they, too, would have assured him of their compensation in the rescue of his army   Among the gallant men who gave up their lives here was the accomplished and knightly Major Daniel Hale of Maryland, who served upon General Early's staff   He was so wrought up by the enthusiasm which fired the troops that he insisted on accompanying me through the battle.   Riding at my side, and joining in the exultant shouts of the men over the wild pursuit, he had passed unscathed through the heaviest fire; but at the very climax of the victory he fell dead upon the recaptured breastworks as we spurred our horses across them.[1]

If speculation be desired as to what would have been the result of failure in that fearful assault upon Hancock, some other pen must be invoked for the task.   It is enough for me to repeat in this connection that the two wings of Lee's army had been completely and widely severed; that Hancock, who was justly called "the Superb," and who was one of the boldest of fighters and most accomplished of soldiers, was in that breach and literally revelling in his victory, as evidenced by his

[1] General A. L. Long, who served for a time on General Lee's staff as military secretary, describes, in his "Memoirs of Lee," p. 338, the effort of the commander-in-chief to lead my troops in the desperate charge, and says: "During the hottest portion of this engagement, when the Federals were pouring through the broken Confederate lines and disaster seemed imminent, General Lee rode forward and took his position at the head of General Gordon's column, then preparing to charge. Perceiving that it was his intention to lead the charge, Gordon spurred hastily to his side, seized the reins of his horse, and excitedly cried: 'General Lee, this is no place for you. . . . These are Virginians and Georgians—men who have never failed, and they will not fail now. Will you, boys?'" Then, giving the thrilling reply of the men, and describing my order and appeal to them, General Long adds: "The charge that followed was fierce and telling, and the Federals, who had entered the lines, were hurled back before the resolute advance of Gordon's gallant men. The works were retaken, the Confederate line again established, and an impending disaster converted into a brilliant victory "

characteristic field despatch to General Grant: "I have used up Johnson and am going into Early"; that through this fearful breach Grant could quickly hurl the bulk of his army upon the right and left flanks of Lee's wings, which were now cleft asunder; and that Lee himself thought that the time had come, as such times do come in the experience of all truly great leaders, when the crisis demanded that the commander-in-chief should in person lead the "forlorn hope."

Long afterward, when the last bitter trial at Appomattox came, Lee's overburdened spirit recurred to that momentous hour at Spottsylvania, and he lamented that he had not been permitted to fall in that furious charge or in some subsequent battle.

As above stated, there was a short stretch of the Confederate works still left in dispute. All that portion to the right of the salient, the salient itself over which Hancock had charged, and where General Edward Johnson and his troops were captured, and a portion of our works to the left of the salient, had been retaken. There was not one Union soldier left with arms in his hands inside of that great crescent. All had been repulsed and driven out; but these daring men in blue still stood against the outer slope of the short line of intrenchment which had not been struck by the Confederate hurricane.

There on that short stretch of breastworks occurred the unparalleled fighting of which I have made brief mention. The questions have often been asked: Why did the commanders of the two armies put forth such herculean efforts over so short a line? In what respect was this small space of earthworks so essential to either army as to justify the expenditure of tons of lead and barrels of blood? I will endeavor to make clear the answer to these very natural inquiries. That short reach of works was an integral part of Lee's battle line. The Confederates held the inside of it, the Federals the outside. These high-spirited American foemen were standing against the opposite slopes of the same works, and so close together that they could almost thrust their bayonets into one another's breasts. If Lee could drive Grant's men from the outer slope his entire line would be completely reëstablished. If Grant could drive the Confederates from the inner slope he would hold a breach in their lines, narrow it is true, but still a breach, through which he might again force his way, riving Lee's army a second time, as the rail-splitter's wedge rives the timber as it is driven into the narrow crack. Therefore, the complete possession by the Federals of that disputed section meant to Grant a coveted opportunity. To Lee it meant a serious menace. Neither could afford to surrender so important a point without a desperate struggle; and the followers of both seemed intuitively to comprehend the situation, and to be prepared for any exaction of blood or life which it might make upon them.

Of that struggle at Spottsylvania I write as an eye-witness and not from hearsay. It was a drama of three great acts. The first act was Hancock's charge. The second was the Confederate countercharge. The third and last was the night-and-day wrestle of the giants on the same breastworks. The whole of that long and gory drama upon which the curtain rose in the morning mists of the 12th, and did not fall for more than twenty hours, is as vivid and real to me now as it was the day after it was enacted. Each act of it differed from the preceding act in no respect except in shifting the scene from one bloody phase to another still more bloody, from its beginning with Hancock's charge in the darkness to its ending twenty hours later in the succeeding night, amidst the incessant flashes of the battle-storm. Its second act had been played under Lee's eye, and largely by that splendid soldiery whom it was my fortune and pride to command; but even that did not end their share of the performance. As soon as it was ascertained that the Confederate lines had been too short to stretch across the whole of the wide-spreading crescent, and that the outer slope of a portion of Lee's works was still held by Grant's stalwart fighters, the third and last act of that memorable performance was opened. Under my orders, and under cover of the intrenchment, my men began to slip to the left a few feet at a time, in order to occupy, unobserved if possible, that still open space. The ditch along which they slowly glided, and from which the earth had been thrown to form the embankment, favored them; but immediately opposite to them and within a few feet of them on the outer side stood their keen-eyed, alert foemen, holding to their positions with a relentless grip. This noiseless sliding process had not proceeded far before it was discovered by the watchful men in blue. The discovery was made at the moment when Lee and Grant began to hurl their columns against that portion of the works held by both. Thus was inaugurated that roll of musketry which is likely to remain without a parallel, at least in the length of time it lasted.

Mounting to the crest of the embankment, the Union men poured upon the Confederates a galling fire. To the support of the latter other Confederate commands quickly came, crowding into the ditches, clambering up the embankment's side, and returning volley for volley. Then followed the mighty rush from both armies, filling the entire disputed space. Firing into one another's faces, beating one another down with clubbed muskets, the front ranks fought across the embankment's crest almost within an arm's reach, the men behind passing up to them freshly loaded rifles as their own were emptied. As those in front fell, others quickly sprang forward to take their places. On both sides the dead were piled in heaps. As Confederates fell their bodies rolled into the ditch, and upon their bleeding forms their living comrades stood, beating back Grant's furiously charging columns. The bullets seemed to fly in sheets. Before the pelting hail and withering blast the standing timber fell. The breastworks were literally drenched in blood. The coming of the darkness failed to check the raging battle. It only served to increase the awful terror of the scene.

As I now recall that scene, looking back to it over the intervening years and with the calmer thought and clearer perceptions that come in more advanced age, I am still more deeply impressed with the conviction that, considered in all its phases, this battle between Americans on the 12th of May and the succeeding night at Spottsylvania has no parallel in the annals of war. Considered merely in their sanguinary character,—the number of lives lost, the area over which they extended, and the panorama presented by vast armies manœuvring, charging, repelling, retreating, and reforming,— many of the battles of our Civil War surpassed it. Among these were Chickamauga, Gettysburg, Chancellorsville, Cold Harbor, the battles around Atlanta, Fredericksburg, Sharpsburg, or Antietam, and perhaps Shiloh and Franklin, Tennessee. But to Spottsylvania history will accord the palm, I am sure, for having furnished an unexampled muzzle-to-muzzle fire; the longest roll of incessant, unbroken musketry; the most splendid exhibition of individual heroism and personal daring by large numbers, who, standing in the freshly spilt blood of their fellows, faced for so long a period and at so short a range the flaming rifles as they heralded the decrees of death.

This heroism was confined to neither side. It was exhibited by both armies, and in that hand-to-hand struggle for the possession of the breastworks it seemed almost universal. It would be a commonplace truism to say that such examples will not be lost to the Republic. The thought has found its expression in a thousand memorial addresses in every section of the Union; but in the spectacle then, as in the contemplation now, there was much that was harrowing as well as inspiring. The gifted Father Ryan, Southern patriot and poet, writing of the South's sacrifices in war, of her sufferings in final defeat, and of the record made by her sons, said:

> There's a glory in gloom,
> And a grandeur in graves.

And he wrote truly. The pathos of this wail, like that of the Roman adage, "Dulce et decorum est pro patria mori," or of those still nobler words, "The blood of the martyrs is the seed of the church," will impress every one who reads it and who appreciates the grandeur of a man who is ready to die for his convictions.[1]

[1] As proof that the description I have given of the horrible scenes of the 12th of May is not overdrawn, and that no language could exaggerate either the heroism or the horrors of that battle, I give two extracts from Northern writers. Swinton, in his "History of the Army of the Potomac," says: "Of all the struggles of the war, this was perhaps the fiercest and most deadly." He then describes the charges, and states that the fearful slaughter continued "till the ground was literally covered with piles of the dead and the woods in front of the salient were one hideous Golgotha."

General Horace Porter, of General Grant's staff, says: "The battle near the 'Angle' was probably the most desperate engagement in modern warfare. . . . Rank after rank was riddled by shot and shell and bayonet thrusts, and finally sank, a mass of torn and mutilated corpses. . . . Trees over a foot and a half in diameter were cut completely in two by the incessant musketry fire. . . . We had not only shot down an army, but also a forest. . . . Skulls were crushed with clubbed muskets, and men were stabbed to death with swords and bayonets thrust between the logs of the parapet which separated the combatants. . . . Even the darkness . . . failed to stop the fierce contest, and the deadly strife did not cease till after midnight." General Porter then describes the scene which met him on his visit to that Angle the next day, and says that the dead "were piled upon each other in some places four layers deep. . . . Below the mass of fast-decaying corpses, the convulsive twitching of limbs and the writhing of bodies showed that there were wounded men still alive and struggling to extricate themselves from their horrid entombment."

CHAPTER XXI

MOVEMENTS AFTER SPOTTSYLVANIA

A surprising capture—Kind treatment received by prisoners—Five rainy days of inaction—Fighting resumed on May 18—Hancock's corps ordered to the assault—General Grant's order to Meade: "Where Lee goes, there you will go also"—How Lee turned the tables—Fightng it out on this line all summer—Lee's men still resolute after the Wilderness.

AS Hancock's troops were driven out of our lines on the morning of the 12th, the commander of one of my regiments, Colonel Davant of the Thirty-eighth Georgia, became so enthused that he ran in pursuit ahead of his men, and passed some distance beyond the breastworks. A squad of Hancock's retreating men at once halted, and, in the quaint phraseology of the army, "quietly took him in." Davant, surprised to find himself in the hands of Hancock's bluecoats instead of in the company of his Confederate comrades, attempted to give notice to his men in the rear that he was captured. His adjutant, John Gordon Law, my first cousin, heard the colonel's call, and sprang forward through the thicket to aid him. Law was likewise captured, and was kept in prison to the end of the war. He is now a prominent minister of the Presbyterian Church, and delights to tell of the great kindness shown him by the guard to whose care he was assigned. The soldier in blue who guarded Law was a private, and had no possible use for a sword-belt; but he wanted it, nevertheless. Instead of taking it forcibly, he paid for it, in greenbacks, the full price named by Law. In answer to Law's lament that he was going to prison without a change of clothing or any blankets, this generous Union boy offered to sell him his own blankets. Law replied to the suggestion:

"I have no money to pay you for your blankets, except Confederate bills and the greenbacks which you have just paid me for the sword-belt."

"Oh, well," said the Federal private, "you can pay me for the blankets in Confederate money, and if I should be captured it will answer my purpose. If I should not be captured I will not need the money. Give me your 'graybacks' and you keep my 'greenbacks' to help you along during your stay in Fort Warren."

The gallant General Edward Johnson of Virginia, who was captured at the salient in Hancock's charge, heartily reciprocated the cordial greetings of his West Point comrades into whose hands he came as prisoner of war, and received from them great consideration and soldierly courtesy. Such courtesy and kind treatment were frequently shown by the Confederates to captured Union officers and men, and it is a special pleasure, therefore, to record these instances of the same kindly spirit among the Federals.

The appalling night scenes of the 12th did not mark the end of bloodshed at Spottsylvania, but only compelled a pause in the sickening slaughter long enough to give the armies time to take breath.

General Lee had failed to drive the Federals from the outer slope of that short and disputed section of breastworks. General Grant had failed to drive the Confederates from the inner slope or to extend his possession of the works either to the right or to the left. Another test, therefore, of the mettle of the two armies was to be made on the same field. Five days passed, however, before the Union chief clearly indicated to his antagonist his next move.

The weather was doubtless largely responsible for the delay. The continued rain had soaked the ground as well as the jackets and blankets of the men. It was impracticable to move artillery or wagon-trains; and while infantry could march and fight without bogging in the soft earth, there was naturally less of the fighting tendency under such conditions. Soldiers, in a certain sense, are machines; but they are impressible, sentient machines. With clothing drenched, gun-barrels wet, fingers benumbed, and bodies cold, the flaming enthusiasm requisite for the charge was somewhat dormant.

May 17th was a brighter day. The rain had ceased and the sun and brisk winds had dried the clothing of the men, and their spirits responded to the aspect of the bright spring morning.

General Grant decided to make another desperate attempt to drive Lee from his position at Spottsylvania. On the morning of the 18th he sent Hancock's corps, reënforced by fully 8000 fresh troops, with Wright's corps to aid him, back to the point where the assault of May 12th had been made. Hancock had already twice passed over this " Bloody Angle," once in his successful advance and again upon his repulse by the Confederate countercharge. He was now to pass the third time over "Hell's Half Acre," another name by which this gory angle was known. In this last effort he was, however, to have the coöperation of that excellent corps commander, General Wright. The attack was to be made by daylight, and not in the darkness or under cloudy cover, as on the morning of the 12th, and not upon the same breastworks, but upon new Confederate intrenchments which had been constructed behind them. General Grant was to superintend the daring movement in person.

In superb style and evidently with high hopes, the Union army moved to the assault. The Confederates, although their numbers had been materially decreased by the casualties of battle and withdrawals from this left wing to strengthen our right, were ready for them; and as Hancock's and Wright's brave men climbed over the old abandoned works and debouched from the intervening bushes, a consuming fire of grape, canister, and Minié balls was poured in incessant volleys upon them. Such a fire was too much for any troops. They first halted before it, and staggered. Then they rallied, moved forward, halted again, wavered, bent into irregular zigzag lines, and at last broke in confusion and precipitate retreat. Again and again they renewed the charge, but each assault ended, as the first, in repulse and heavy slaughter.

Thus ended the second series of battles in which the Union commander had failed to drive the Confederate forces from the field. In both Lee had successfully repelled Grant's assaults—first in the Wilderness and now at Spottsylvania—and compelled him to seek other points at which to repeat his efforts.

In speaking of the plans marked out by his chief before the opening of the campaign of 1864, General Porter says: " It was the understanding that Lee's army was to be the objective point of the Army of the Potomac, and it was to move against Richmond only in case Lee went there." General Porter further adds that General Grant's own words to Meade were, " Where Lee goes, there you will go also." And yet on the failure of these last desperate assaults upon Lee at Spottsylvania, General Porter represents his chief as writing " an order providing for a general movement by the left flank toward Richmond, to begin the next night."

With a soldier's admiration for General Grant, I submit that this order of May 18th is hardly consistent with his previously announced plans of looking for Lee's army, and for nothing else, nor with his instructions to Meade: " Where Lee goes, there you will go also."   Lee was not going toward Richmond except as Grant went toward Richmond.   He was not going in any direction.   He was standing still at Spottsylvania and awaiting the pleasure of General Grant.   He had been there for about ten days, and was showing no disposition whatever to run away.   There was no difficulty in finding him, and it was not necessary for General Meade to go to the North Anna or toward Richmond to find Lee in order to obey intelligently the instructions, " there you will go also."

General Lee first went into the Wilderness because General Grant had gone there, and Lee did not " get out of the Wilderness " until his antagonist had gone out and moved to another place.   Lee moved to Spottsylvania because the Union commander was moving there; and any movement of General Meade away from Spottsylvania would be going where Lee was not.   He was not on the Rappahannock, where the Union commander proposed to make his base; he was not retreating, he was not hiding.   He was close by on the field which had been selected by his able antagonist, and was ready for a renewal of the struggle.

Verily it would seem that Grant's martial shibboleth, " Where Lee goes, there you will go also," had been reversed; for, in literal truth, Meade was not going where Lee went, but Lee was going where Meade went. It was General Grant's intention that General Lee should learn from every Union cannon's brazen throat, from every hot muzzle of every Union rifle, that nothing could prevent the Army of the Potomac from following him until the Confederate hosts were swept from the overland highways to Richmond.   The impartial verdict of history, however, and the testimony of every bloody field on which these great American armies met in this overland campaign, from the Wilderness to the water route and to the south side of the James, must necessarily be that the going where the other goes was more literally the work of Lee than of Grant.

On May 11, 1864, at Spottsylvania, that remarkable letter was written to General Halleck by General Grant in which he used those words which became at once famous: "I propose to fight it out on this line if it takes all summer." This declaration by the illustrious commander of the Union army evidenced that wonderful tenacity of purpose upon which General Lee had commented previously on the morning of the 7th in the Wilderness.

General Grant was not quite explicit as to what he meant by "this line." If he meant the overland route to Richmond which McDowell and Pope and Burnside and Hooker had each essayed and on which each had failed, as distinguished from the water route by the James River, which McClellan had attempted, General Grant found reasons to change his mind before the summer was ended. He did not "fight it out on this line"; for, long before the "all summer" limit which he had set was reached, the Union army found itself on an entirely different line—the James River or McClellan line. It will be noted that this celebrated letter of General Grant was written prior to the twenty hours of death-struggle on the 12th of May. Had he waited forty-eight hours, that letter probably never would have been penned.

Martin Luther once said: "Great soldiers make not many words, but when they speak the deed is done." General Grant measured up to Martin Luther's standard. He was a soldier of prompt and resolute action and of few words; but the few words he did speak in

that letter to General Halleck would now seem to indicate that he overestimated the value of numbers and
underestimated the steadfastness of the small army that
opposed him.   He was led to say to General Halleck in
that same letter: "I am satisfied that the enemy are
very shaky, and are only kept up to the mark by the
greatest exertion on the part of their officers." This
opinion of the morale of Lee's army General Grant had
abundant reasons to change, as he did to change his
determination to "fight it out on this line if it takes
all summer." The simple truth is, as General Grant
afterward must have learned, there was no period of the
war, since the day on which Lee assumed the command,
when his army as a whole was less "shaky," more steadfast, more self-reliant, more devoted to its great leader
and to the Southern cause.   There was no period when
that army more constantly exhibited "a spirit yet un-
quelled and high" than during the fearful experiences
of 1864.

Fragments of broken iron are welded closest and
strongest in the hottest fires.   So the shattered corps
of Lee's army seemed to be welded together by Grant's
hammering—by the blood and the sweat and the fury
of the flames that swept over and around them.   In the
tangled jungles of the Wilderness; through the incessant uproar by day and night at Spottsylvania; on the
reddened banks of the North Anna; amidst the sickening slaughter of Cold Harbor,—everywhere, and on every
field where the American armies met in deadly grapple,
whether behind breastworks or in the open, whether
assaulting or repelling, whether broken by the resistless
impact or beating back with clubbed muskets the headlong charges of Grant,—these worn and battered soldiers
of Lee seemed determined to compensate him for his
paucity of numbers by a self-immolation and a steadfast
valor never surpassed, if ever equalled.

This estimate of the marvellous courage displayed by Lee's men will not be regarded as too partial when the salient facts of this campaign are recalled.

I might safely rest the overwhelming vindication of these Southern soldiers against the statement of General Grant that they were "shaky" on the single and signal fact that, from the Wilderness to Cold Harbor inclusive, in the brief space of twenty-eight days, they had placed *hors du combat* about as many men as Lee commanded, killing, wounding, or capturing one of Grant's men for every Confederate in Lee's army. Or, to state the fact in different form, had General Grant inflicted equal damage upon Lee's troops, the last Confederate of that army would have been killed, wounded, or captured, still leaving General Grant with an army very much larger than any force that had been under Lee's command at any period of the campaign.

Of course this wonderful disparity of relative losses is due in a measure to the fact that the Confederate army acted generally upon the defensive, on shorter lines, and behind intrenchments. This, however, was not always true. In the two days of terrific combat in the Wilderness, neither side was protected by breastworks, except those hastily constructed by both sides as the men were halted in line of battle. Both sides were engaged in assaulting and repelling. The lines of both were repeatedly broken by furious charges and countercharges. But Lee's army remained upon the field until its great antagonist had selected another field of conflict.

At Spottsylvania also the armies at first met and wrestled upon exactly equal footing, as far as breastworks were concerned; and when, finally, Lee's rude intrenchments were hastily thrown up, they were thrice carried by Grant's determined assault, by the resistless momentum of his concentrated columns, and carried under such conditions as would have imperilled the safety, if not the very existence, of an ordinary army—conditions which would assuredly have filled Lee's soldiers with panic, had they been in any sense "shaky," as General Grant supposed them to be.

At the very moment when the Union commander was penning that letter to General Halleck, there must have been sounding in his ears the ominous notes of Hancock's preparations for the momentous movement to occur the next morning, before the dawn of the 12th of May. I repeat that had General Grant waited a few hours he would have found a word of exactly opposite import to convey to General Halleck his impression as to the morale of Lee's army. He would have found the attenuated line of my troops thrown quickly and defiantly across Hancock's formidable front. He would have found these Confederates standing calmly in the open field, waiting the command to rush upon Hancock's advancing legions, and filled with more anxiety for Lee's safety than for their own, thus exhibiting that true intrepidity which is begotten only in bravest breasts amid greatest perils. He would have seen these Confederates in the next moment, uplifted and inspired by Lee's presence, rushing upon Hancock's advancing column, and hurling it back in the wildest confusion. General Grant was too thoughtful, too great a soldier, to misinterpret this sudden transition of his army from exultant victory to depressing defeat. He was too experienced a warrior to call an army "shaky" when one of its thin lines of battle with no supports could hurl itself without hesitation, without a tremor, in a whirlwind of enthusiasm, against tenfold its number. Had that letter to General Halleck been delayed until he decided to withdraw from Spottsylvania, from the Pamunkey, from the North Anna, and from Cold Harbor, where many thousands of his brave men lay breathless and cold, he would more probably have told General Halleck that he would not "fight it out on this line," because the enemy seemed to gather additional hope and confidence and courage on every field of conflict.

Bourrienne, who served with Napoleon as private secretary, represents the Austrian general, who had been hammered and baffled at every turn by the great Frenchman, as supremely disgusted with the Napoleonic style of fighting. He regarded the little Corsican as an untrained boy, a mere tyro in the art of war, violating all its recognized rules, turning up with his army at the oddest places, now on the Austrian flank, now in the rear and then in front, observing none of the established laws of tactics or strategy, but unceremoniously knocking the Austrians to pieces in a manner that was truly shocking to all scientific ideas of campaigning.

I do not pretend to give Bourrienne's words, but the above is a fair though somewhat liberal interpretation of his statement. It is not possible to rely upon any representations made by Bourrienne, for his character did not command the confidence and respect of honorable men. If he had lived in the Southern States of America after the war and during the period of reconstruction, he would have been designated, in the picturesque slang of the period, as a "scalawag"; for he not only deserted Napoleon in his final defeat and deepest woe, but joined his enemies, took office from the victors, perverted his public trust to private gain, and ended his career dishonored in the estimation of all true men. But, whatever may be said of Bourrienne's statement, it is certain that Napoleon's methods furnished frequent surprises to the commanders of opposing armies. And the unbiassed historian, in reviewing and analyzing the moves made by Grant on the vast chess-board reaching from the Wilderness to Petersburg, and the partial checkmates made by Lee in every game, will be forced to the conclusion that Lee's ubiquity must have been as great a marvel to Grant as Napoleon's was to the astounded Austrian. On May 5th Grant hurried his magnificent army, unmolested by even a picket shot, across the Rapidan to turn Lee's right; but the great leader of the Union forces found his wily antagonist not only checking him in the Wilderness, but on the next day (the 6th) turning the Union right flank and sweeping with the destructive energy of a whirlwind to the Union rear.

Protected from observation by the density of the forest, Grant withdrew his bleeding army, and, under the cover of night, pressed with all possible speed to Spottsylvania; but there again he found Lee's vanguard across the line of his march, disputing his further advance. Again, after more than ten days of fighting and manœuvring, of alternate successes and reverses, of desperate charges and deadly repulses, capturing breastworks only to see them recaptured, General Grant inaugurated the third and fourth and subsequent swiftly recurring movements, seeking by forced marches to plant his army in advantageous fields on Lee's right, only to find the Southern leader in possession of the coveted stronghold and successfully resisting all efforts to dislodge him. As Lee divined Grant's movement to Spottsylvania almost at the very instant the movement was taking shape in Grant's brain, so on each succeeding field he read the mind of the Union commander, and developed his own plans accordingly. There was no mental telepathy in all this. Lee's native and tutored genius enabled him to place himself in Grant's position, to reason out his antagonist's mental processes, to trace with accuracy the lines of his marches, and to mark on the map the points of future conflict which were to become the blood-lettered mile-posts marking Grant's compulsory halts and turnings in his zigzag route to Richmond. Finally, at Cold Harbor, where a supreme effort was made to rip open Lee's lines by driving through them the stiff and compact Union columns, and where the slaughtered Federals presented the ghastliest scene ever witnessed on any field of the war, General Grant decided promptly and wisely to abandon further efforts on the north side and cross to the south side of the James River.

After this sanguinary repulse of the Union forces at Cold Harbor, a report gained circulation, and was generally credited, that General Grant's troops refused to obey the orders of their officers to advance in another assault. This statement, which it was difficult for me to believe at the time, has found a place in several books, written by both Northern and Southern authors. I am glad to find this grave injustice to the brave men of the Union army corrected by General Porter in his "Campaigning with Grant." Shocking as had been the slaughter of Union troops in their last charges, costly and hopeless as succeeding assaults must have appeared to the practised eye and sharpened comprehension of Grant's veterans, they still seemed ready for the sacrifice if demanded by necessity or ordered by the commanding general. As a Confederate who had occasion to observe the conduct of these men on many fields, I am glad that General Porter has given to posterity his own witness of a pathetic scene which eloquently refutes the slander of these brave men in blue. With the "appalling revelry" of the last futile onsets still ringing in their ears, with the unburied bodies of their dead comrades lying in full view on the blood-stained stretch of wooded swamp and plain at Cold Harbor, these self-immolating men were calmly and courageously preparing for the next charge and sacrifice. According to General Porter, who was in a position to know whereof he affirms, there was not the slightest indication of rebellion or defiance of orders, not a trace of stubbornness or sullenness in the bearing of these battered Federals; but they were quietly sewing to their jackets strips of cloth marked with their names, in order that their dead bodies might be identified the next day amidst the prospective débris of the coming storm.   It gives me genuine pleasure to aid as far as I can in correcting the wrong which this ill-founded report has done to these high-spirited Americans.

CHAPTER XXII

HUNTER'S RAID AND EARLY'S CHASE

The movement upon Lynchburg—Hunter's sudden panic—Devastation in the Valley—Burning of private homes—Lee's orders against destruction of private property—Washington threatened—The battle of Monocacy—A brave charge—The defeat of General Lew Wallace.

AS the Union army prepared to cross the James, with the purpose of surprising the small Confederate force at Petersburg and capturing the city, my command under General Early began, on June 13, 1864, the movement to check Hunter's raid upon Lynchburg. By rapid marching, and by seizing all railroad trains, passenger and freight, and loading the men into box and stock cars, Early's little army reached Lynchburg very soon after General Hunter's Union forces occupied the adjacent hills. There was no fighting of consequence at Lynchburg; and it was then and still is incomprehensible to me that the small force under Early seemed to have filled Hunter with sudden panic. His hurried exit from Lynchburg was in marked contrast with his confident advance upon it, and suggests an improvement in the adage:

> He who fights and runs away
> Will live to fight another day;

for he ran away without any fight at all—at least, without any demonstration that could be called a fight. He not only fled without a test of relative strength, but fled precipitately, and did not stop until he had found a safe retreat beyond the mountains toward the Ohio.

If I were asked for an opinion as to this utterly cause-less fright and flight, I should be tempted to say that conscience, the inward monitor which "makes cowards of us all," was harrowing General Hunter, and causing him to see an avenger wrapped in every gray jacket before him. He was not a Virginian; but his Virginia kinsmen almost to a man were enlisted in the struggle for Southern independence. One of his relatives, Major Robert W. Hunter, was a member of my staff. Another, the Hon. R. M. T. Hunter, was Confederate Secretary of State. In the Valley of Virginia dwelt many of his kindred, who were often made to feel the sting of his military power. Had he been a Virginian, however, his support of the Union cause would have engendered no bitterness toward him if he had worn his uniform worthily, remembering that he was an American soldier, bearing a high commission from the foremost and freest Republic of earth. General Lee's own sister was a Union woman, the wife of a Union officer; but that fact did not deprive her of the affectionate interest of her family, nor of the chivalric regard of Southern soldiers. It did not obliterate or apparently lessen in any degree her devotion to her brother, Robert E. Lee, nor her appreciation of him as a great soldier. In expressing her loyalty to her husband and the Union cause, and her hope for the triumph of the Federal armies, she would usually add a doubt as to their ability to "whip Robert." General Thomas, one of the ablest commanders of the Union forces, was a Virginian, but he did not apply the torch to private homes or order the burning of his kindred's barns. Hence the esteem with which he will always be regarded by the Southern people.

General Hunter must have possessed some high qualities, or he would not have been intrusted with the grave responsibilities which attach to the commander of a department; but it is hard to trace any evidences of knighthood in the wreck and ravage which marked the lines of his marches. He ordered the destruction of the Virginia Military Institute, one of the most important educational institutions in the State. It will be difficult to find any rule of civilized warfare or any plea of necessity which could justify General Hunter in the burning of these buildings. He could scarcely plead as an excuse the fact that the boys of this school had marched down the Valley in a body, joined General Breckinridge, and aided materially in the brilliant victory at New Market over his predecessor, General Sigel. Upon any such ground the destruction of every university, college, and common school in the South could have been justified; for all of them were converting their pupils into soldiers. My youngest brother ran away from school before he was fifteen years old as captain of a company of schoolboys of his own age and younger, who reported in a body to General Joseph E. Johnston at Dalton for service. They were too young for soldiers, and General Johnston declined to accept them for any service except that of guarding a bridge across the Chattahoochee River, which they defended in gallant style. The Southern armies contained a very much larger proportion of boys under proper age than the Union armies, but there were notable instances of young Northern boys who demanded places in the fighting-line. General Grant's own son, now Brigadier-General Frederick D. Grant of the United States army, whose courtesy and consideration have won for him the esteem and friendship of the Southern people, wore a blue uniform and was under fire before he was fifteen.

General Hunter's campaign of destruction did not end with the burning of the Virginia Military Institute.

The homes of Governor Letcher, of the Hon. Andrew Hunter, of Charles James Faulkner, whose wife was Hunter's relative; of Edmund Lee (a first cousin of General Lee), and of Alexander B. Boteler, were burned, with their entire contents; and only time enough was given the women and children to escape with their lives. Many other peaceful homes were burned under orders. Had General Hunter been captured at this time it would doubtless have been difficult to save him from the vengeance of the troops.

General Edward Johnson, who was captured by Hancock in his brilliant charge at Spottsylvania (May 12th), and who knew General Hunter well in other days, described him as a noted duelist in early life, who had killed two of his brother officers in such combats. It was said that Jefferson Davis, who was at West Point with Hunter, consented to act as second in one of these duels. When the war was over, General Hunter made repeated but unavailing advances for reconciliation with his Southern relatives, among whom were some of the best families in Virginia.

There was so much that was commendable, so much that was truly chivalrous, in both Union and Confederate armies, that I would gladly fill this book only with incidents illustrative of that phase of the war. It is impossible, however, to write truthfully of the campaigns of 1864 in the Valley of Virginia without some allusion to those officers who left behind them the wide stretch of desolation through which we were called to pass.

The official announcement of General Philip Sheridan, who was regarded, I believe, as the ablest cavalry leader of the Union army, that he had "destroyed over two thousand barns filled with wheat and hay and farming implements; over seventy mills filled with flour and wheat," etc., and that "the destruction embraces Luray valley, Little Fort valley, as well as the main valley," will give some conception of the indescribable suffering which the women and children of that beautiful region were made to endure. General Sheridan, as far as could be ascertained, did not imitate the example of General Hunter in burning private homes; but homes without the means of support were no longer homes. With barns and mills and implements for tilling the soil all gone, with cattle, sheep, and every animal that furnished food to ·the helpless inmates carried off, they were dismal abodes of hunger, of hopelessness, and of almost measureless woe.

It is to be hoped that official records will show that this mode of warfare was not ordered by the authorities at Washington. It is impossible to believe that it could have been approved by President Lincoln, whose entire life, whose every characteristic, was a protest against needless oppression and cruelty.

If General Sheridan was acting at that time under the orders of the Union commander-in-chief, I am constrained to believe that he interpreted his instructions with great laxity. I recall no act of General Grant in the immediate conduct of his campaigns that would indicate his disposition to bring upon any people such sweeping desolation. Nor can I recall any speech of his that can fairly be interpreted as expressing sympathy with General Sherman in his declaration, " War is hell," or with Sherman's purpose to make it hell. General Grant's fame as a commander of armies in an enemy's country will, in the sober estimation of posterity, be the more lasting because of the fact that his blows fell upon armed soldiery, and not upon defenceless private citizens. Unless his instructions to Sheridan were specific, he cannot be held responsible for the torch that was applied to almost every kind of private property in the Virginia valleys. It would be almost as just to charge General Lee with responsibility for the burning of Chambersburg in the Cumberland Valley of Pennsylvania. This act of his subordinate was a great shock to General Lee's sensibilities. Although the destruction of Chambersburg was wholly in the nature of reprisal for the wholesale destruction of the Virginia valleys and the burning of Southern cities, yet it was so directly in contravention of General Lee's orders, and so abhorrent to the ideas and maxims with which he imbued his army, that a highspirited Virginia soldier flatly refused to obey the order when directed by his superior officer to apply the torch to the city. That soldier, whose disobedience was prompted by the highest dictates of humanity, deserves a place of honor in history. He was not only a man of iron resolution and imperturbable courage, who fought from April, 1861, to April, 1865, and was repeatedly wounded in battle, but he was a fit representative of that noblest type of soldier who will inflict every legitimate damage on the enemy in arms against his people, but who scorns, even as a retaliatory measure, to wage war upon defenceless citizens and upon women and children. This knightly Southern soldier was Colonel William E. Peters of the Twenty-first Virginia Cavalry, who has for fortysix years been a professor in the University of Virginia and at Emory and Henry College. He obeyed the order to move into Chambersburg with his troops and occupy the town, as he was not apprised of the purpose of its occupancy; but when the next order reached him to move his men to the court-house, arm them with torches, and fire the town, his spirit rose in righteous revolt. He calmly but resolutely refused obedience, preferring to risk any consequences that disobedience might involve, rather than be instrumental in devoting defenceless inhabitants to so dire a fate. If all the officers who commanded troops in that war, in which Americans fought one another so fiercely and yet so grandly, had possessed the chivalry of Colonel Peters, the history of the conflict would not have been blurred and blackened by such ugly records of widespread and pitiless desolation. Colonel Peters was promptly placed under arrest for disobedience to orders; but, prudently and wisely, he was never brought to trial.

A number of Federal generals led armies through different portions of the South without leaving behind them any lasting marks of reckless waste. In all of General Grant's triumphant marches I do not believe he ever directly ordered or willingly permitted the burning of a single home. And of his illustrious opponent, General Robert E. Lee, I am impelled to say in this connection that of the world's great chieftains who have led armies into an enemy's territory, not one has left a nobler example to posterity in his dealings with non-combatants and in the protection which he afforded to private property. When the Confederates crossed the Potomac into Maryland in 1862, he issued the most stringent orders against all plundering and all straggling through the country. On one of his rides in rear of his lines he chanced to find one of Jackson's men with a stolen pig. This evidence of disregard of the explicit orders against pilfering so enraged General Lee that he ordered the soldier to be delivered to General Jackson and executed; but as Jackson was at the moment advancing in an attack, he directed that the soldier be placed in the front rank of his column, in order that he might be despatched by a Union rather than a Confederate bullet. The culprit went through the fire, however, unscathed, and purchased redemption from the death penalty by his conspicuous courage. The representatives of foreign governments who visited General Lee and accompanied him for a time on his campaigns were impressed by the manifestations of his solicitude for the protection of private citizens and private property in the enemy's territory; and Colonel Freemantle of the English army, who accompanied General Lee in his invasion of Pennsylvania, has given to the world his testimony to the effect that there was no straggling into private homes, "nor were the inhabitants disturbed or annoyed by the soldiers." He adds that, in view of the ravages which he saw in the Valley of Virginia, "this forbearance was most commendable and surprising."

"This forbearance," which I think posterity will unite in pronouncing "most commendable," was also a worthy response by the Confederate army to the wishes and explicit orders of its idolized commander. No comment that can be made, no eulogy that can ever be pronounced upon General Lee, can equal the force and earnestness of his own words embodied in his general order, issued at Chambersburg as his hitherto victorious army was just beginning its invasion of Pennsylvania. The order is here given in full. It was a source of special and poignant pain to General Lee that the very town in which this order was penned and issued should become, at a later period, the scene of retaliatory action. In the interest of civilized and Christian warfare, and as an inspiration to American soldiers in all the future, these words of Lee ought to be printed and preserved in letters of gold:

HEADQUARTERS ARMY OF NORTHERN VIRGINIA.
CHAMBERSBURG, PA., June 27, 1863.

General Order No. 73.

The commanding general has observed with marked satisfaction the conduct of the troops on the march, and confidently anticipates results commensurate with the high spirit they have manifested. No troops could have displayed greater fortitude or better performed the arduous marches of the past ten days. Their conduct in other respects has, with few exceptions, been in keeping with their character as soldiers and entitles them to approbation and praise.

There have, however, been instances of forgetfulness on the

part of some that they have in keeping the yet unsullied reputation of the army, and that the duties exacted of us by civilization and Christianity are not less obligatory in the country of the enemy than in our own. The commanding general considers that no greater disgrace could befall the army, and through it our whole people, than the perpetration of the barbarous outrages upon the innocent and defenseless and the wanton destruction of private property that have marked the course of the enemy in our own country. Such proceedings not only disgrace the perpetrators and all connected with them, but are subversive of the discipline and efficiency of the army and destructive of the ends of our present movements. It must be remembered that we make war only on armed men, and that we cannot take vengeance for the wrongs our people have suffered without lowering ourselves in the eyes of all whose abhorrence has been excited by the atrocities of our enemy, and offending against Him to whom vengeance belongeth, without whose favor and support our efforts must all prove in vain.

The commanding general, therefore, earnestly exhorts the troops to abstain with most scrupulous care from unnecessary or wanton injury to private property, and he enjoins upon all officers to arrest and bring to summary punishment all who shall in any way offend against the orders on this subject.

R. E. LEE, General.

Among the great warriors who gave special lustre to Roman arms, no one of them left a reputation more to be coveted by the true soldier than Scipio Africanus. In native gifts and brilliancy of achievements, he was perhaps the equal of Julius Cæsar; while in the nobler attributes of manly courtesy to womanhood, of magnanimity to the defenceless who became subjects of his military power, in self-abnegation and faithful adherence to constitution and laws, he surpasses, I think, any warrior of his time.

Lee exhibited everywhere all those lofty characteristics which have made the name of Scipio immortal. He not only possessed true genius,— the " gift that

Heaven gives and which buys a place next to a king," —
but he had what was better than genius — a heart whose
every throb was in harmony with the teachings of the
Great Captain whom he served. He had a spirit naturally robust and aggressive, but he made it loyally
obedient to the precepts of the Divine Master. In the
combination of great qualities, he will be adjudged in
history as measuring up as few commanders have ever
done to Scipio's lofty conception of the noblest soldier:
the commander who could win victories, but who found
more pleasure in the protection afforded defenceless citizens than in the disasters inflicted upon armed enemies.

As the last of Hunter's men, who were worthy of a
nobler leader, filed through the mountain passes in their
westward flight, and the Southern troops in tattered
gray were seen coming down the valley pikes, the relief
felt by that suffering people was apparent on every
hand. From every home on the pike along which
Hunter had marched came a fervid welcome.

With the hope of creating some apprehension for the
safety of the national capital and thus inducing General
Grant to slacken his hold on the Confederacy's throat, it
was decided that we should again cross the Potomac
and threaten Washington. The Federal authorities sent
the dashing soldier, General Lew Wallace,— who afterward became famous as the author of " Ben Hur," —
to meet us with his army at Monocacy River, near
Frederick City, Maryland. His business was to check the
rash Southern invaders, and, if possible, to drive them
back across the Potomac.

The battle of Monocacy which ensued was short,
decisive, and bloody. While the two armies, under the
command respectively of Lew Wallace and Jubal Early,
were contemplating each other from the opposite banks,
my division was selected, not to prevent Wallace from

driving us out of Maryland, but to drive him from our front and thus reopen the highway for our march upon the capital. My movement was down the right bank of the Monocacy to a fording-place below, the object being to cross the river and then turn upon the Federal stronghold. My hope and effort were to conceal the movement from Wallace's watchful eye until my troops were over, and then apprise him of my presence on his side of the river by a sudden rush upon his left flank; but General McCausland's brigade of Confederate cavalry had already gallantly attacked a portion of his troops, and he discovered the manœuvre of my division before it could drag itself through the water and up the Monocacy's muddy and slippery banks. He at once changed front and drew up his lines in strong position to meet the assault.

This movement presented new difficulties. Instead of realizing my hope of finding the Union forces still facing Early's other divisions beyond the river, giving my isolated command the immense advantage of the proposed flank attack, I found myself separated from all other Confederate infantry, with the bristling front of Wallace's army before me. In addition to this trouble, I found difficulties before unknown which strongly militated against the probable success of my movement. Across the intervening fields through which we were to advance there were strong farm fences, which my men must climb while under fire. Worse still, those fields were thickly studded with huge grain-stacks which the harvesters had recently piled. They were so broad and high and close together that no line of battle could possibly be maintained while advancing through them. Every intelligent private in my command, as he looked over the field, must have known before we started that my battle-line would become tangled and confused in the attempt to charge through these obstructions.

With an able commander in my front, and his compact ranks so placed as to rake every foot of the field with their fire, with the certainty of having my lines broken and tangled by fences and grain-stacks at every rod of advance, it is not difficult to understand the responsibility of hazarding battle without supporting Confederate infantry in reach. The nerve of the best-trained and bravest troops is sorely taxed, even under most favorable conditions, when assaulting an enemy well posted, and pouring an incessant well-directed fire into their advancing ranks. To how much severer test of nerve were my troops to be subjected in this attempt to charge where the conditions forced them while under fire to break into column, halt and reform, and make another start, only to be broken again by the immovable stacks all over the field! I knew, however, that if any troops in the world could win victory against such adverse conditions, those high-mettled Southern boys would achieve it there.

En échelon by brigades from the right the movement began. As we reached the first line of strong and high fencing, and my men began to climb over it, they were met by a tempest of bullets, and many of the brave fellows fell at the first volley. But over they climbed or tumbled, and rushed forward, some of them halting to break down gaps in the fence, so that the mounted officers might ride through. Then came the grain-stacks. Around them and between them they pressed on, with no possibility of maintaining orderly alignment or of returning any effective fire. Deadly missiles from Wallace's ranks were cutting down the line and company officers with their words of cheer to the men but half spoken. It was one of those fights where success depends largely upon the prowess of the individual soldier. The men were deprived of that support and strength imparted by a compact line, where the elbow touch of

312 REMINISCENCES OF THE CIVIL WAR

comrade with comrade gives confidence to each and sends the electric thrill of enthusiasm through all. But nothing could deter them. Neither the obstructions nor the leaden blast in their front could check them. The supreme test of their marvellous nerve and self-control now came. They had passed the forest of malign wheat-stacks; they had climbed the second fence and were in close proximity to Wallace's first line of battle, which stood firmly and was little hurt. The remaining officers, on horseback and on foot, rapidly adjusted their commands, and I ordered "Forward!" and forward they went. I recall no charge of the war, except that of the 12th of May against Hancock, in which my brave fellows seemed so swayed by an enthusiasm which amounted almost to a martial delirium; and the swell of the Southern yell rose high above the din of battle as they rushed upon the resolute Federals and hurled them back upon the second line.

The Union lines stood firmly in this second position, bravely defending the railroad and the highway to Washington. Between the two hostile lines there was a narrow ravine down which ran a small stream of limpid water. In this ravine the fighting was desperate and at close quarters. To and fro the battle swayed across the little stream, the dead and wounded of both sides mingling their blood in its waters; and when the struggle was ended a crimsoned current ran toward the river. Nearly one half of my men and large numbers of the Federals fell there. Many of my officers went down, and General Clement A. Evans, the trusted leader of my largest brigade, was severely wounded. A Minié ball struck him in his left side, passing through a pocket of his coat, and carrying with it a number of pins, which were so deeply embedded that they were not all extracted for a number of years. But the execution of his orders was superintended by his staff officer,

Major Eugene C. Gordon, who was himself severely wounded.

In that vortex of fire my favorite battle-horse, presented to me by my generous comrades, which had never hitherto been wounded, was struck by a Minié ball, and plunged and fell in the midst of my men, carrying me down with him. Ordinarily the killing of a horse in battle, though ridden by the commander, would scarcely be worth noting; but in this case it was serious. By his death I had been unhorsed in the very crisis of the battle. Many of my leading officers were killed or disabled. The chances for victory or defeat were at the moment so evenly balanced that a temporary halt or slight blunder might turn the scales. My staff were bearing orders to different portions of the field. But some thoughtful officer sent me a horse and I was again mounted.

Wallace's army, after the most stubborn resistance and heavy loss, was driven from railroad and pike in the direction of Baltimore. The Confederate victory was won at fearful cost and by practically a single division, but it was complete, and the way to Washington was opened for General Early's march.

CHAPTER XXIII

The Confederate army within sight of Washington—The city could have been taken—Reasons for the retreat—Abandonment of plan to release Confederate prisoners—The Winchester campaign—Assault on Sheridan's front—Sudden rally—Retreat of Early's army—The battle of Fisher's Hill.

ON July 11, 1864, the second day after the battle of Monocacy, we were at the defences of Washington. We were nearer to the national capital than any armed Confederates had ever been, and nearer to it than any Federal army had ever approached to Richmond. It has been claimed that at the time we reached these outer works they were fully manned by troops. This is a mistake. I myself rode to a point on those breastworks at which there was no force whatever. The unprotected space was broad enough for the easy passage of Early's army without resistance. It is true that, as we approached, Rodes's division had driven in some skirmishers, and during the day (July 11th) another small affair had occurred on the Seventh Street road; but all the Federals encountered on this approach could not have manned any considerable portion of the defences. Undoubtedly we could have marched into Washington; but in the council of war called by General Early there was not a dissenting opinion as to the impolicy of entering the city. While General Early and his division commanders were considering in jocular vein the propriety

314

of putting General John C. Breckinridge at the head of
the column and of escorting him to the Senate chamber
and seating him again in the Vice-President's chair, the
sore-footed men in gray were lazily lounging about the
cool waters of Silver Spring, picking blackberries in
the orchards of Postmaster-General Blair, and merrily
estimating the amount of gold and greenbacks that
would come into our possession when we should seize
the vaults of the United States Treasury. The privates
also had opinions about the wisdom or unwisdom of
going into the city. One of them who supposed we
were going in asked another:

"I say, Mac, what do you suppose we are going to do
with the city of Washington when we take it?"

"That question reminds me," replied Mac, "of old
Simon's answer to Tony Towns when he asked Simon if
he were not afraid he would lose his dog that was running after every train that came by. The old darky
replied that he was not thinking about losing his dog,
but was just 'wonderin' what dat dorg was gwine do
wid dem kyars when he kotched 'em.'" It is evident
that neither of these soldiers believed in the wisdom of
any serious effort to capture Washington at that time.

While we debated, the Federal troops were arriving
from Grant's army and entering the city on the opposite side.

The two objects of our approach to the national
capital were, first and mainly, to compel General Grant
to detach a portion of his army from Lee's front at
Petersburg; and, second and incidentally, to release, if
possible, the Confederates held as prisoners of war at
Point Lookout. We had succeeded in accomplishing
only the first of these. We had, by the signal victory
over Lew Wallace's protecting army at Monocacy and
by the ring of our rifles in ear-shot of President Lincoln's cabinet, created enough consternation to induce

the Federal authorities to debate the contingencies of our entrance and to hurry Grant's troops across the Potomac.

The second object (the release of our prisoners confined at Point Lookout) had to be abandoned at a somewhat earlier date because of the inability to perfect needful antecedent arrangements. Some days prior to our crossing the Potomac into Maryland, General Lee wrote twice to President Davis (June 26th and 29th) touching the possibility of effecting this release. It was General Lee's opinion that it would not require a large force to accomplish this object. He said to the President: " I have understood that most of the garrison at Point Lookout is composed of negroes. . . . A stubborn resistance, therefore, may not reasonably be expected." He was ready to devote to the enterprise the courage and dash of all Marylanders in his army. The greatest difficulty, he thought, was to find a suitable leader, as success in such a venture depended largely on the brains and pluck of the man who guided it. He asked the President if such a leader could be found; his own opinion was that General Bradley T. Johnson of Maryland was the best man in his acquaintance for this special work. Our march, however, toward Washington was so rapid, and our retreat from it so necessary to avoid being captured ourselves by the heavy forces just arriving from Grant's army, coöperating with those forming in our rear, that the recruiting of our ranks by releasing our expectant boys at Point Lookout had to be abandoned. There was not time enough for the delicate and difficult task of communicating secretly with our prisoners so as to have them ready for prompt coöperation in overpowering the negro guards, nor time for procuring the flotillas necessary silently to transport across the Potomac the forces who were to assault the fortress.

General Bradley Johnson captured at this time Major General Franklin of the Union army, and the railroad train between Washington and Philadelphia on which this distinguished passenger was travelling. However, in the hurry of the Confederates to get away from that point, General Franklin made his escape.

Thenceforward to the end of July, through the entire month of August, and during more than half of September, 1864, Early's little army was marching and countermarching toward every point of the compass in the Shenandoah Valley, with scarcely a day of rest, skirmishing, fighting, rushing hither and thither to meet and drive back cavalry raids, while General Sheridan gathered his army of more than double our numbers for his general advance up the valley.

General Jubal A. Early, who commanded the Confederate forces in the Valley of Virginia in the autumn of 1864, was an able strategist and one of the coolest and most imperturbable of men under fire and in extremity. He had, however, certain characteristics which militated against his achieving the greatest successes. Like the brilliant George B. McClellan (whom I knew personally and greatly admired), and like many other noted soldiers who might be named in all armies, he lacked what I shall term official courage, or what is known as the courage of one's convictions — that courage which I think both Lee and Grant possessed in an eminent degree, and which in Stonewall Jackson was one of the prime sources of his marvellous achievements. This peculiar courage must not be confounded with rashness, although there is a certain similarity between them. They both strike boldly, fiercely, and with all possible energy. They are, however, as widely separated as the poles in other and essential qualities. The rash officer's boldness is blind. He strikes in the dark, madly, wildly, and often impotently. The possessor of the courage which I am trying to describe is equally bold, but sees with quick, clear, keen vision the weak and strong points in the adversary, measures with unerring judgment his own strength and resources, and then, with utmost faith in the result, devotes his all to its attainment — and wins. Thus thought and thus fought Jackson and many of the world's greatest leaders. Thus Lee's faultless eye saw at Gettysburg, and thus he intended to strike the last decisive blow on the morning of the third day; and if his orders had been obeyed—if, as he directed, every unemployed soldier of his army had been hurled at dawn against Meade's centre, and with the impetuosity which his assurance of victory should have imparted to General Longstreet—there is not a reasonable doubt that the whole Union centre would have been shattered, the two wings hopelessly separated, and the great army in blue, like a mill-dam broken by the rushing current, would have been swept away.

General Early possessed other characteristics peculiarly his own, which were the parents of more or less trouble to him and to those under him: namely, his indisposition to act upon suggestions submitted by subordinates and his distrust of the accuracy of reports by scouts, than whom there were no more intelligent, reliable, and trustworthy men in the army. Incidentally I alluded to this marked characteristic of General Early's mind in speaking of his refusal to permit me to assail General Grant's right flank on the 6th of May in the Wilderness until the day was nearly gone and until General Lee himself ordered the attack.

General Early was a bachelor, with a pungent style of commenting on things he did not like; but he had a kind heart and was always courteous to women. As might be expected, however, of a man who had passed the meridian of life without marrying, he had little or no patience with wives who insisted on following the army in order to be near their husbands. There were numbers of women — wives and mothers — who would gladly have accompanied their husbands and sons had it been possible for them to do so. Mrs. Gordon was one of the few who were able to consult their wishes in this regard. General Early, hearing of her constant presence, is said to have exclaimed, "I wish the Yankees would capture Mrs. Gordon and hold her till the war is over!" Near Winchester, as the wagon-trains were being parked at night, he discovered a conveyance unlike any of the others that were going into camp. He immediately called out to his quartermaster in excited tones: "What's that?" "That is Mrs. Gordon's carriage, sir," replied the officer. "Well, I'll be ——! If my men would keep up as she does, I'd never issue another order against straggling."

Mrs. Gordon was fully aware of the general's sentiments, and had heard of his wishing for her capture; and during a camp dinner given in honor of General Ewell, she sat near General Early and good-naturedly rallied him about it. He was momentarily embarrassed, but rose to the occasion and replied: "Mrs. Gordon, General Gordon is a better soldier when you are close by him than when you are away, and so hereafter, when I issue orders that officers' wives must go to the rear, you may know that you are excepted." This gallant reply called forth a round of applause from the officers at table.

Faithful and enterprising scouts, those keen-eyed, acute-eared, and nimble-footed heralds of an army who, "light-armed, scour each quarter to descry the distant foe," and who had been hovering around the Union army for some days after it crossed the Potomac, reported that General Sheridan was in command and was approaching Winchester with a force greatly superior to that commanded by General Early. The four divisions of Early's little army were commanded at this time respectively by General John C. Breckinridge, the "Kentucky Game-cock," by General Rodes of Alabama, who had few equals in either army, by General Ramseur of North Carolina, who was a most valiant and skillful leader of men, and by myself. These divisions were widely separated from one another. They had been posted by General Early in position for guarding the different approaches to Winchester, and for easy concentration when the exigencies of the campaign should require it. The reports of the Federal approach, however, did not seem to impress General Early, and he delayed the order for concentration until Sheridan was upon him, ready to devour him piecemeal, a division at a time. When at last the order came to me, on the Martinsburg pike, to move with utmost speed to Winchester, the far-off reverberant artillery was already giving painful notice that Ramseur was fighting practically alone, while the increasingly violent concussions were passionate appeals to the other divisions for help.

As the fighting was near Winchester, through which Mrs. Gordon was compelled to pass in going to the rear, she drove rapidly down the pike in that direction. Her light conveyance was drawn by two horses driven by a faithful negro boy, who was as anxious to escape capture as she. As she overtook the troops of General Rodes's division, marching to the aid of Ramseur, and drove into their midst, a cloud of dust loomed up in the rear, and a wild clatter of hoofs announced, "Cavalry in pursuit!" General Rodes halted a body of his men, and threw them in line across the pike, just behind Mrs. Gordon's carriage, as she hurried on, urged by the solicitude of the "boys in gray" around her. In crossing a wide stream, which they were compelled to ford, the tongue of the carriage broke loose from the axle. The horses went on, but Mrs. Gordon, the driver, and carriage were left in the middle of the stream. She barely escaped; for the detachment of Union cavalry were still in pursuit as a number of Confederate soldiers rushed into the stream, dragged the carriage out, and by some temporary makeshift attached the tongue and started her again on her flight.

Ramseur's division was nearly overwhelmed and Rodes was heavily pressed as the head of my column reached the crest from which we could dimly discern the steady advance of the blue lines through the murky clouds of mingled smoke and dust that rose above the contending hosts.

Breckinridge's troops were also furiously fighting on another part of the field, and they, too, were soon doubled up by charges in front and on the flank.

This left practically only Rodes's division and mine, with parts of Ramseur's bleeding brigades, not more than 6000 men in all, to contend with Sheridan's whole army of about 30,000 men, reaching in both directions far beyond our exposed right and left. In the absence of specific orders from the commander-in-chief, I rode up to Rodes for hasty conference. A moment's interchange of views brought both of us to the conclusion that the only chance to save our commands was to make an impetuous and simultaneous charge with both divisions, in the hope of creating confusion in Sheridan's lines, so that we might withdraw in good order. As the last words between us were spoken, Rodes fell, mortally wounded, near my horse's feet, and was borne bleeding and almost lifeless to the rear.

There are times in battle—and they come often—when the strain and the quick shifting of events compel the commander to stifle sensibilities and silence the natural promptings of his heart as cherished friends fall around him. This was one of those occasions. General Rodes was not only a comrade whom I greatly admired, but a friend whom I loved. To ride away without even expressing to him my deep grief was sorely trying to my feelings; but I had to go. His fall had left both divisions to my immediate control for the moment, and under the most perplexing and desperate conditions.

The proposed assault on Sheridan's front was made with an impetuosity that caused his advancing lines to halt, bend, and finally to break at different points; but his steadfast battalions, which my divisions could not reach and which overlapped me in both directions, quickly doubled around the unprotected right and left, throwing the Confederate ranks into inextricable confusion and making orderly retreat impossible. Meantime, that superb fighter, General Wharton of Virginia, had repelled from my rear and left flank a number of charges by Sheridan's cavalry; but finally the overpowered Confederate cavalry was broken and Wharton's infantry forced back, leaving the vast plain to our left open for the almost unobstructed sweep of the Federal horsemen.

General Breckinridge, who had scarcely a corporal's guard of his magnificent division around him, rode to my side. His Apollo-like face was begrimed with sweat and smoke. He was desperately reckless—the impersonation of despair. He literally seemed to court death. Indeed, to my protest against his unnecessary exposure by riding at my side, he said: "Well, general, there is little left for me if our cause is to fail." Later, when the cause had failed, he acted upon this belief and left the country, and only returned after long absence, to end his brilliant career in coveted privacy among his Kentucky friends.

To my horror, as I rode among my disorganized troops through Winchester I found Mrs. Gordon on the street, where shells from Sheridan's batteries were falling and Minié balls flying around her. She was apparently unconscious of the danger. I had supposed that, in accordance with instructions, she had gone to the rear at the opening of the battle, and was many miles away. But she was stopping at the house of her friend Mrs. Hugh Lee, and as the first Confederates began to pass to the rear, she stood upon the veranda, appealing to them to return to the front. Many yielded to her entreaties and turned back—one waggish fellow shouting aloud to his comrades: "Come, boys, let 's go back. We might not obey the general, but we can't resist Mrs. Gordon." The fact is, it was the first time in all her army experience that she had ever seen the Confederate lines broken. As the different squads passed, she inquired to what command they belonged. When, finally, to her question the answer came, "We are Gordon's men," she lost her self-control, and rushed into the street, urging them to go back and meet the enemy. She was thus engaged when I found her. I insisted that she go immediately into the house, where she would be at least partially protected. She obeyed; but she did not for a moment accept my statement that there was nothing left for her except capture by Sheridan's army. I learned afterward that her negro driver had been frightened by the shells bursting about the stable, and had not brought out her carriage and horses. She acquainted some of my men with these facts. With the assurance, "We 'll get it for you, Mrs. Gordon," they broke down the fences and brought the carriage to her a few moments after I had passed on. She sprang into it, and, taking her six-year-old son Frank and one or two wounded officers with her, she was driven rapidly away amidst the flying missiles from Sheridan's advancing troops and with the prayers of my brave men for her safety.

The pursuit was pressed far into the twilight, and only ended when night came and dropped her protecting curtains around us.

Drearily and silently, with burdened brains and aching hearts, leaving our dead and many of the wounded behind us, we rode hour after hour, with our sore-footed, suffering men doing their best to keep up, anxiously inquiring for their commands and eagerly listening for orders to halt and sleep.

Lucky was the Confederate private who on that mournful retreat knew his own captain, and most lucky was the commander who knew where to find the main body of his own troops. The only lamps to guide us were the benignant stars, dimly lighting the gray surface of the broad limestone turnpike. It was, however, a merciful darkness. It came too slowly for our comfort; but it came at last, and screened our weary and confused infantry from further annoyance by Sheridan's horsemen. Little was said by any officer. Each was left to his own thoughts and the contemplation of the shadows that were thickening around us. What was the morrow to bring, or the next month, or the next year? There was no limit to lofty courage, to loyal devotion, and the spirit of self-sacrifice; but where were the men to come from to take the places of the maimed and the dead? Where were the arsenals from which to replace the diminishing materials of war so essential to our future defence? It was evident that these thoughts were running through the brains of rank and file; for now and then there came a cheering flash of rustic wit or grim humor from the privates: "Cheer up, boys; don't be worried. We'll lick them Yankees the first fair chance, and get more grub and guns and things than our poor old quartermaster mules can pull." Distinct in my memory now (they will be there till I die) are those startling manifestations of a spirit which nothing could break, that strange commingling of deep-drawn sighs and merry songs, the marvellous blending of an hour of despair with an hour of bounding hope, inspired by the most resolute manhood ever exhibited in any age or country.

At a late hour of the night on that doleful retreat, the depressing silence was again broken by a characteristic shot at General Breckinridge from Early's battery of good-natured sarcasm, which was always surcharged and ready to go off at the slightest touch. These two soldiers became very good friends after the war began, but previously they had held antagonistic political views. Early was an uncompromising Unionist until Virginia passed the ordinance of secession. Breckinridge, on the other hand, had long been a distinguished champion of what was called " the rights of the South in the Territories," and in 1860 he was nominated for President by the " Southern Rights " wing of the Democratic party. The prospect of establishing Southern rights by arms was not encouraging on that dismal retreat from Winchester. General Early could not resist the temptation presented by the conditions around us; and, at a time when the oppressive stillness was disturbed only by the dull sound of tramping feet and tinkling canteens, his shrill tones rang out:

" General Breckinridge, what do you think of the 'rights of the South in the Territories' now ? "

Breckinridge made no reply. He was in no humor for badinage, or for reminiscences of the period of his political power when he was Kentucky's most eloquent representative in the halls of Congress, or pleaded for Southern rights on the floor of the Senate, or made parliamentary rulings as Vice-President of the United States, or carried the flag of a great party as its selected candidate for the still higher office of President.

When the night was far spent and a sufficient distance between the Confederate rear and Union front had been reached, there came the order to halt — more grateful than sweetest music to the weary soldiers' ears; and down they dropped upon their beds of grass or earth, their heads pillowed on dust-covered knapsacks, their rifles at their sides, and their often shoeless feet bruised and aching.

But they slept. Priceless boon—sleep and rest for tired frame and heart and brain!

General Sheridan graciously granted us two days and a part of the third to sleep and rest and pull ourselves together for the struggle of September 22. The battle, or, to speak more accurately, the bout at Fisher's Hill, was so quickly ended that it may be described in a few words. Indeed, to all experienced soldiers the whole story is told in one word — "flanked."

We had again halted and spread our banners on the ramparts which nature built along the Shenandoah's banks. Our stay was short, however, and our leaving was hurried, without ceremony or concert. It is the old story of failure to protect flanks. Although the Union forces more than doubled Early's army, our position was such that in our stronghold we could have whipped General Sheridan had the weak point on our left been sufficiently protected. Sheridan demonstrated in front while he slipped his infantry around our left and completely enveloped that flank. An effort was made to move Battle and Wharton to the enveloped flank in order to protect it, but the effort was made too late. The Federals saw their advantage, and seized and pressed it. The Confederates saw the hopelessness of their situation, and realized that they had only the option of retreat or capture. They were not long in deciding. The retreat (it is always so) was at first stubborn and slow, then rapid, then — a rout.

It is not just to blame the troops. There are conditions in war when courage, firmness, steadiness of nerve, and self-reliance are of small avail. Such were the conditions at Fisher's Hill.

CHAPTER XXIV

CEDAR CREEK—A VICTORY AND A DEFEAT

Sheridan's dallying for twenty-six days—Arrival of General Kershaw—
Position of Early's army with reference to Sheridan's—The outlook
from Massanutten Mountain—Weakness of Sheridan's left revealed—
The plan of battle—A midnight march—Complete surprise and rout
of Sheridan's army—Early's decision not to follow up the victory—
Why Sheridan's ride succeeded—Victory changed into defeat.

NEARLY a month—twenty-six days, to be exact—of
comparative rest and recuperation ensued after
Fisher's Hill. General Sheridan followed our retreat
very languidly. The record of one day did not differ
widely from the record of every other day of the twenty-
six. His cavalry manœuvred before ours, and ours
manœuvred before his. His artillery saluted, and ours
answered. His infantry made demonstrations, and ours
responded by forming lines. This was all very fine for
Early's battered little army; and it seemed that Sheridan's victories of the 19th and 22d had been so costly,
notwithstanding his great preponderance in numbers,
that he sympathized with our desire for a few weeks of
dallying. He appeared to be anxious to do just enough
to keep us reminded that he was still there. So he decided upon a season of burning, instead of battling; of
assaults with matches and torches upon barns and hay-
stacks, instead of upon armed men who were lined up in
front of him.

The province of uncomplimentary criticism is a most

distasteful one to me. It would be far more agreeable to applaud and eulogize every officer in both armies of whom it is necessary for me to speak. But if I write at all, I must write as I think. I must be honest with myself, and honest with those who may do me the honor to read what I write. In a former chapter I have already spoken of General Sheridan as probably the most brilliant cavalry officer who fought on the Union side. I shall not be misunderstood, therefore, when I say that his twenty-six days of apparent indecision, of feeble pursuit, of discursive and disjointed fighting after his two crushing victories, are to me a military mystery. Why did he halt or hesitate, why turn to the torch in the hope of starving his enemy, instead of beating him in resolute battle? Would Grant have thus hesitated for a month or a day under such conditions—with a broken army in his front, and his own greatly superior in numbers and inspired by victory? How long would it require any intelligent soldier who fought under Grant, or against him, to answer that question?

General Meade was criticised for the delay of a single day at Gettysburg—for not assailing the Confederate army the next morning after the last Southern assault— after the brilliant charge and bloody repulse of Pickett's command. From the standpoint of a Confederate who participated in the conflicts both at Gettysburg and in the Valley, I feel impelled to say, and with absolute impartiality, that the Union archers who from sheltered positions in Washington hurled their sharpened arrows at Union generals in the field for not gathering the fruits of victory must have emptied their quivers into Meade, or have broken their bows prior to that month of Sheridan's campaigning after the 19th and 22d of September.

From my point of view, it is easy to see why Meade halted after the Confederate repulse of the last day at

Gettysburg. In his front was Robert E. Lee, still resolute and defiant. The Confederate commander had not
been driven one foot from his original position. He was
supported by an army still complete in organization,
with faith in its great leader and its own prowess undiminished, eagerly waiting for the Union troops to leave
the trenches, and ready at Lee's command to retrieve in
open field and at any sacrifice the loss of the victory
which it had been impossible to wrench from Meade's
splendid army intrenched on the heights and flanked
by the Round Tops. It is not so easy, however, to
furnish an explanation for Sheridan's indecision after
Winchester and Fisher's Hill. There was no Robert E.
Lee in his front, inspiring unfaltering faith. The men
before whom Sheridan hesitated were not complete in
organization, as were the men at Gettysburg, who still
held their original lines and were still confident of victory in open field. On the contrary, the army before
him, although not demoralized, was vastly inferior to
his own in numbers and equipment—of which fact every
officer and private was cognizant. It had been shattered
and driven in precipitate flight from every portion of
both fields. Why did General Sheridan hesitate to hurl
his inspirited and overwhelming army upon us? Why
retreat and intrench and wait to be assaulted? Was it
because of commanding necessity, or from what George
Washington would have termed "untimely discretion"?

Taking advantage of Sheridan's tardiness, Early withdrew from the main pike to Brown's Gap in order to
refresh his little army. Brown's Gap was the same grand
amphitheatre in the Blue Ridge Mountains in which
General Jackson had rested two years before, during
that wonderful campaign so graphically described by
Colonel Henderson, of the British army, in his "Life of
Stonewall Jackson." In that campaign, Jackson had
baffled and beaten four Union armies, under Milroy,

Banks, Frémont, and Shields, each larger than his own; and having thus cleared the Valley of Federal troops, had promptly joined in the seven days' battles around Richmond, which drove McClellan to the protection of his gunboats, and prevented a long siege of the Confederate capital.

This reference to Early's encampment on the mountain-rimmed plateau, to which Jackson withdrew at intervals in his marvellous campaign, reminds me that unfair contrasts have been drawn between the results achieved by these two generals in the same Valley. It is only just to General Early to call attention to the fact that General Jackson was never, in any one of his great battles, there, so greatly outnumbered as was General Early at Winchester and Fisher's Hill. Early had in neither of these battles more than 10,000 men, including all arms of the service, while the Official Reports show that General Sheridan brought against him over 30,000 well-equipped troops. The marvel is that Early was not utterly routed and his army captured by the Union cavalry in the early morning at Winchester; for, at the opening of the battle, Early's divisions were separated by a greater distance than intervened between Sheridan and the Confederate command which he first struck. The magnificently mounted and equipped Union cavalry alone very nearly equalled in number Early's entire army. With an open country and fordable streams before him, with an immense preponderance in numbers, it seems incomprehensible that General Sheridan should have failed to destroy utterly General Early's army by promptly and vigorously following up the advantages resulting at Winchester and Fisher's Hill.

While we were resting on Jackson's "old campground," which kind nature seemed to have supplied as an inspiring and secure retreat for the defenders of the Valley, General Kershaw, who was one of the ablest division commanders in Lee's army, came with his dashing South Carolinians to reënforce and cheer Early's brave and weary men. The most seasoned American troops, and especially volunteer forces, composed largely of immature boys, are under such conditions as subject to capricious humors as are volatile Frenchmen. This was true at least of the warm-hearted, impetuous Southern boys who filled our ranks. But no change of conditions or sudden caprice ever involved the slightest diminution of devotion to the Southern cause. Whether victorious or defeated, they were always resolved to fight it out to the last extremity. The arrival of Kershaw's division awakened the latent enthusiasm with which they had pommelled Sheridan at the beginning of the battle of Winchester, but which had been made dormant by the subsequent disastrous defeats on that field and at Fisher's Hill. The news of Kershaw's approach ran along the sleeping ranks, and aroused them as if an electric battery had been sending its stimulating current through their weary bodies. Cheer after cheer came from their husky throats and rolled along the mountain cliffs, the harbinger of a coming victory. "Hurrah for the Palmetto boys!" "Glad to see you, South Ca'liny!" "Whar did you come from?" "Did you bring any more guns for Phil Sheridan?" We had delivered a number of guns to that officer without taking any receipts for them; but the Confederate authorities at Richmond were still straining every nerve to supply us with more. Among the pieces of artillery sent us by the War Department was a long black rifle-cannon, on which some wag had printed in white letters words to this effect: "Respectfully consigned to General Sheridan through General Early"; and Sheridan got it. Some days later at Cedar Creek, or on some other field, Sheridan's men captured the gun which had been consigned to him "through General Early."

On the morning of the surrender at Appomattox, just prior to the meeting of Lee and Grant, General Sheridan referred, in our conversation, to this incident.

The arrival of reënforcements under Kershaw not only revived the hopes of our high-mettled men, but enabled General Early and his division commanders to await with confidence General Sheridan's advance, which was daily expected. He did not come, however. Our rations were nearly exhausted, and after holding a council of war, General Early decided to advance upon the Union forces strongly intrenched on the left bank of Cedar Creek.

No battle of the entire war, with the single exception of Gettysburg, has provoked such varied and conflicting comments and such prolonged controversy as this remarkable engagement between Sheridan and Early at Cedar Creek. No battle has been so greatly misunderstood in important particulars, nor have the accounts of any battle been so productive of injustice to certain actors in it, nor so strangely effective in converting misapprehensions into so-called history. Some of these misapprehensions I shall endeavor to correct in this and succeeding chapters; and, so far as I am able, I shall do justice to the men to whom it has been denied for so many years. I do not underestimate the nature of the task I now undertake; but every statement made by me bearing on controverted points will be supported by the Official Records which the Government has published in recent years, and by other incontrovertible proofs. It is enough to say, in explanation of this long-deferred effort on my part, that I had no access to official reports until they were made public; and until very recently I did not doubt that my own official report of Cedar Creek would be published with others, and stand beside the others, and that the facts stated in my report would vindicate the brave men who fought that marvellous battle. It seems, however, that my report never reached General Lee, or was lost when his official papers were captured at the fall of the Confederate capital.

On the right of the Confederate line, as drawn up at Fisher's Hill, was Massanutten Mountain, rising to a great height, and so rugged and steep as to make our position practically unassailable on that flank. It was also the generally accepted belief that this mountain was an absolute barrier against any movement by our army in that direction. The plan of battle, therefore, which had been adopted was to move upon Sheridan in the other direction or by our left. I was not entirely satisfied with the general plan of attack, and decided to go to the top of the mountain, where a Confederate Signal Corps had been placed, and from that lofty peak to survey and study Sheridan's position and the topography of the intervening country. I undertook the ascent of the rugged steep, accompanied by that superb officer, General Clement A. Evans of Georgia, in whose conservatism and sound judgment I had the most implicit confidence, and by Captain Hotchkiss[1] of General Early's staff, and my chief of staff, Major Robert W. Hunter. Through tangled underbrush and over giant boulders and jutting cliffs we finally reached the summit, from which the entire landscape was plainly visible. It was an inspiring panorama. With strong field-glasses, every road and habitation and hill and stream could be seen and noted. The abruptly curved and precipitous highlands bordering Cedar Creek, on which the army of Sheridan was strongly posted; the historic Shenandoah, into which Cedar Creek emptied at the foot of the towering peak on which we stood, and, most important and intensely interesting of all, the entire Union army—all

[1] See Journal of Captain Jed Hotchkiss of General Early's staff, penned at the time, and published in War Records, First Series, Vol. XLIII, Part I, p. 580, Monday, October 17.

seemed but a stone's throw away from us as we stood contemplating the scene through the magnifying lenses of our field-glasses. Not only the general outlines of Sheridan's breastworks, but every parapet where his heavy guns were mounted, and every piece of artillery, every wagon and tent and supporting line of troops, were in easy range of our vision. I could count, and did count, the number of his guns. I could see distinctly the three colors of trimmings on the jackets respectively of infantry, artillery, and cavalry, and locate each, while the number of flags gave a basis for estimating approximately the forces with which we were to contend in the proposed attack. If, however, the plan of battle which at once suggested itself to my mind should be adopted, it mattered little how large a force General Sheridan had; for the movement which I intended to propose contemplated the turning of Sheridan's flank where he least expected it, a sudden irruption upon his left and rear, and the complete surprise of his entire army.

It was unmistakably evident that General Sheridan concurred in the universally accepted opinion that it was impracticable for the Confederates to pass or march along the rugged and almost perpendicular face of Massanutten Mountain and assail his left. This fact was made manifest at the first sweep of the eye from that mountain-top. For he had left that end of his line with no protection save the natural barriers, and a very small detachment of cavalry on the left bank of the river, with vedettes on their horses in the middle of the stream. His entire force of superb cavalry was massed on his right, where he supposed, as all others had supposed, that General Early must come, if he came with any hope of success. The disposition of his divisions and available resources were all for defence of his right flank and front, or for aggressive movement from one or both of these points. As to his left flank — well, that needed no defence ; the impassable Massanutten, with the Shenandoah River at its base, was the sufficient protecting fortress. Thus reasoned the commanders of each of the opposing armies. Both were of the same mind, and Early prepared to assail, and Sheridan to defend, his right and centre only. Captain Hotchkiss, who was an engineer, made a rough map of the positions in our view.

It required, therefore, no transcendent military genius to decide quickly and unequivocally upon the movement which the conditions invited. I was so deeply impressed by the situation revealed to us, so sure that it afforded an opportunity for an overwhelming Confederate victory, that I expressed to those around me the conviction that if General Early would adopt the plan of battle which I would submit, and would press it to its legitimate results, the destruction of Sheridan's army was inevitable. Indeed, there are those still living who remember my statement that if General Early would acquiesce, and the plan failed, I would assume the responsibility of failure.[1] Briefly, the plan was to abandon serious attack of Sheridan's forces where all things were in readiness, making only a demonstration upon that right flank by Rosser's cavalry dismounted, and upon the centre by a movement of infantry and artillery along the pike, while the heavy and decisive blow should be given upon the Union left, where no preparation was made to resist us. This movement on the left I myself proposed to make with the Second Army Corps, led by General Clement A. Evans's division, followed by Ramseur's and Pegram's.

"But how are you going to pass the precipice of Massanutten Mountain?"

That was the one obstacle in the way of the successful

---

[1] See statements of General Evans, General Rosser, General Wharton, Major R. W. Hunter, and of Thomas G. Jones, ex-governor of Alabama and now United States judge.

execution of the plan I intended to submit, and I felt sure that this could be overcome. A dim and narrow pathway was found, along which but one man could pass at a time; but by beginning the movement at nightfall the entire corps could be passed before daylight.

This plan was finally adopted by General Early, and the movement was begun with the coming of the darkness. The men were stripped of canteens and of everything calculated to make noise and arouse Sheridan's pickets below us, and our watches were set so that at the same moment the right, the centre, and the left of Sheridan should be assaulted. With every man, from the commanders of divisions to the brave privates under them, impressed with the gravity of our enterprise, speaking only when necessary and then in whispers, and striving to suppress every sound, the long gray line like a great serpent glided noiselessly along the dim pathway above the precipice. Before the hour agreed upon for the simultaneous attack, my entire command had slowly and safely passed the narrow and difficult defile.

Some watchful and keen-eyed Confederate thought he discovered ahead of us two of the enemy's pickets. If they should fire their rifles it would give to Sheridan's vedettes the alarm and possibly seriously interfere with our success. I sent Jones of my staff, with a well-trained scout and one or two others, noiselessly to capture them. Concealing their movements behind a fence until near the point where the pickets stood, my men crawled on hands and knees, and were in the act of demanding surrender when they discovered that the two hostile figures were cedar-bushes in the corner of the rail fence.

Late in the afternoon I had directed that one of my couriers be stationed at every fork of the dim pathway after it left the mountain, to avoid the possibility of missing the way which I had selected to the ford of the river. At one fork, however, a small tree across the right-hand road was sufficient to guide us into the road on the left, which was the proper one. Late that afternoon, a farmer passed with his wagon and threw this sapling across the other road. But small things impress themselves very vividly at such momentous times, and when we reached that point in our night march I thought at once that the tree had been moved. To leave no doubt on so vital a point, a member of my staff inquired at a near-by cabin, and we had our impressions confirmed by the old man who had come so near being the innocent cause of our taking the road away from the ford. On such small things sometimes hangs the fate of great battles.

For nearly an hour we waited for the appointed time, resting near the bank of the river in the middle of which the Union vedettes sat upon their horses, wholly unconscious of the presence of the gray-jacketed foe, who from the ambush of night, like crouching lions from the jungle, were ready to spring upon them. The whole situation was unspeakably impressive. Everything conspired to make the conditions both thrilling and weird. The men were resting, lying in long lines on the thickly matted grass or reclining in groups, their hearts thumping, their ears eagerly listening for the orders: "Attention, men!" "Fall in!" "Forward!" At brief intervals members of the staff withdrew to a point where they could safely strike a match and examine watches in order to keep me advised of the time. In the still starlit night, the only sounds heard were the gentle rustle of leaves by the October wind, the low murmur of the Shenandoah flowing swiftly along its rocky bed and dashing against the limestone cliffs that bordered it, the churning of the water by the feet of horses on which sat Sheridan's faithful pickets, and the subdued tones or half-whispers of my men as they thoughtfully communed with each other as to the fate which might befall each in the next hour.

It was during this weird time of waiting that my comrade and friend, General Ramseur, had that wonderful presentiment of his coming fate. Before the battle ended, his premonition had been proved a literal prophecy, and his voice was silenced forever.

His mantle fell upon one worthy to wear it. General Bryan Grimes of North Carolina had already distinguished himself among the illustrious sons of a State prolific in a soldiery unsurpassed in any war, and his record as chief of this stalwart command added to his high reputation.

The minute-hand of the watch admonished us that it was time to move in order to reach Sheridan's flank at the hour agreed upon. General Payne of Virginia, one of the ablest and most knightly soldiers in the Confederate army, plunged with his intrepid cavalry into the river, and firing as they went upon Sheridan's mounted pickets and supporting squadrons, the Virginians dashed in pursuit as if in steeplechase with the Union riders, the coveted goal for both being the rear of Sheridan's army. The Federals sought it for safety. Payne was seeking it to spread confusion and panic in the Federal ranks and camps; and magnificently did he accomplish his purpose.

In my survey of the field from the mountain-top I had located Sheridan's headquarters; and this daring Virginian enthusiastically agreed to ride into the Union camps on the heels of the flying body of Federal cavalry, and, by sudden dash at headquarters, attempt to capture the commander-in-chief and bring him back as a cavalry trophy.

As soon as Payne had cleared the ford for the infantry, Evans, with his Virginians, North Carolinians, and Georgians, the old Stonewall Brigade leading, rushed into the cold current of the Shenandoah, chilled as it was by

the October nights and frosts. The brave fellows did
not hesitate for a moment. Reaching the eastern bank
drenched and cold, they were ready for the "double
quick," which warmed them up and brought them
speedily to the left flank of Sheridan's sleeping army.
From that eyry on the mountain-top I had selected a
country road which led to the flank, and had located a
white farm-house which stood on this road at a point
precisely opposite the end of Sheridan's intrenchments.
I knew, therefore, that when the head of my column
reached that house we would be on the Union flank and
slightly in the rear. No time, therefore, was lost in
scouting or in locating lines. There was no need for
either. There was not a moment's delay. Nothing was
needed except to close up, front face, and forward. This
was accomplished by Evans with remarkable celerity.
His splendid division, with Ramseur's farther to the
right and Pegram's in support, rushed upon the unpre-
pared and unsuspecting Federals, great numbers of whom
were still asleep in their tents. Even those who had
been aroused by Payne's sudden irruption in the rear,
and had sprung to the defence of the breastworks, were
thrown into the wildest confusion and terror by Kershaw's simultaneous assault in front. That admirable
officer had more than filled his part in this game of battle.
He had not only demonstrated against the centre while
Evans was assailing flank and rear, but his high-spirited
South Carolinians, like a resistless sea driven by the
tempest, poured a steady stream of gray-jackets over
the works and into the Union camp. The intrepid
Wharton was soon across with his superb division,
adding momentum to the jubilant Confederate host.

The surprise was complete. The victory was won in
a space of time inconceivably short, and with a loss to
the Confederates incredibly small. Sheridan's brave
men had lain down in their tents on the preceding night

feeling absolutely protected by his intrenchments and his faithful riflemen who stood on guard. They were startled in their dreams and aroused from their slumbers by the rolls of musketry in nearly every direction around them, and terrified by the whizzing of Minié balls through their tents and the yelling of exultant foemen in their very midst. They sprang from their beds to find Confederate bayonets at their breasts. Large numbers were captured. Many hundreds were shot down as they attempted to escape. Two entire corps, the Eighth and Nineteenth, constituting more than two thirds of Sheridan's army, broke and fled, leaving the ground covered with arms, accoutrements, knapsacks, and the dead bodies of their comrades. Across the open fields they swarmed in utter disorganization, heedless of their officers' commands—heedless of all things save getting to the rear. There was nothing else for them to do; for Sheridan's magnificent cavalry was in full retreat before Rosser's bold troopers, who were in position to sweep down upon the other Union flank and rear.

At little after sunrise we had captured nearly all of the Union artillery; we had scattered in veriest rout two thirds of the Union army; while less than one third of the Confederate forces had been under fire, and that third intact and jubilant. Only the Sixth Corps of Sheridan's entire force held its ground. It was on the right rear and had been held in reserve. It stood like a granite breakwater, built to beat back the oncoming flood; but it was also doomed unless some marvellous intervention should check the Confederate concentration which was forming against it. That intervention did occur, as will be seen; and it was a truly marvellous intervention, because it came from the Confederate commander himself. Sheridan's Sixth Corps was so situated after the other corps were dispersed that nothing could have saved it if the arrangement for its destruction had been carried out. It was at that hour largely outnumbered, and I had directed every Confederate command then subject to my orders to assail it in front and upon both flanks simultaneously. At the same time I had directed the brilliant chief of artillery, Colonel Thomas H. Carter of Virginia, who had no superior in ability and fighting qualities in that arm of the service in either army, to gallop along the broad highway with all his batteries and with every piece of captured artillery available, and to pour an incessant stream of shot and shell upon this solitary remaining corps, explaining to him at the same time the movements I had ordered the infantry to make. As Colonel Carter surveyed the position of Sheridan's Sixth Corps (it could not have been better placed for our purposes), he exclaimed: "General, you will need no infantry. With enfilade fire from my batteries I will destroy that corps in twenty minutes."

At this moment General Early came upon the field, and said:

"Well, Gordon, this is glory enough for one day. This is the 19th. Precisely one month ago to-day we were going in the opposite direction."

His allusion was to our flight from Winchester on the 19th of September. I replied: "It is very well so far, general; but we have one more blow to strike, and then there will not be left an organized company of infantry in Sheridan's army."

I pointed to the Sixth Corps and explained the movements I had ordered, which I felt sure would compass the capture of that corps—certainly its destruction. When I had finished, he said: "No use in that; they will all go directly."

"That is the Sixth Corps, general. It will not go unless we drive it from the field."

"Yes, it will go too, directly."

My heart went into my boots. Visions of the fatal

halt on the first day at Gettysburg, and of the whole day's hesitation to permit an assault on Grant's exposed flank on the 6th of May in the Wilderness, rose before me. And so it came to pass that the fatal halting, the hesitation, the spasmodic firing, and the isolated movements in the face of the sullen, slow, and orderly retreat of this superb Federal corps, lost us the great opportunity, and converted the brilliant victory of the morning into disastrous defeat in the evening.

Congress thanked General Sheridan and his men for having "averted a great disaster." By order of the President, he was made a major-general, because, as stated in the order, "under the blessing of Providence his routed army was reorganized and a great national disaster averted," etc. Medical Director Ghiselin, in his official report, says: "At dawn on the 19th of October the enemy attacked and turned the left flank of the army. Their attack was so sudden and unexpected that our troops were thrown into confusion, and it was not until we had fallen back four miles that another line of battle was established and confidence restored." In the itinerary of the Second Brigade (p. 74), dated October 19, are these words: "For a time the foe was held in check, but soon they had completely routed the Eighth and Nineteenth corps, and the Sixth Corps fell back." General Sheridan says in his report that he met these flying troops at nine o'clock in the morning within half a mile of Winchester. "Until the middle of the day the game was completely in the enemy's hands," is the Federal record of another itinerary (p. 82, Vol. XLIII). Impartial history must declare that, under these conditions, if one more heavy blow had been delivered with unhesitating energy, with Jacksonian confidence and vigor, and with the combined power of every heavy gun and every exultant soldier of Early's army, the battle would have ended in one of the most complete and inexpensive victories ever won in war. The now established facts warrant this assertion. Although Sheridan's army at the beginning of the battle outnumbered Early's, according to official reports, nearly or quite three to one,[1] yet the complete surprise of our sudden attack at dawn upon flank and rear had placed the brave men in blue at such disadvantage that more than two thirds of them were compelled to fly or be captured. Thus before eight o'clock in the morning the Confederate infantry outnumbered the organized Federal forces in our front. At this hour the one army was aroused and electrified by victory, while all that remained of the other was necessarily dismayed by the most adverse conditions, especially by the panic that had seized and shaken to pieces the Eighth and Nineteenth corps.

The brave and steady Sixth Corps could not possibly have escaped had the proposed concentration upon it

---

[1] General Early's army was scarcely 12,000 strong. On October 25 General Sheridan telegraphed General Grant from Cedar Creek: "We are now reduced to effective force of not over 22,000 infantry." Add to this his heavy force of cavalry, his artillery, his killed and wounded at Cedar Creek, and the 1300 prisoners, and it becomes evident that his army at the beginning of the battle of the 19th was not less than 35,000.

The official returns regarding the Valley campaign are very meagre, and the computation of the strength of the respective armies made by writers on the war are indefinite and unsatisfactory.

Sheridan's official return of September 10, 1864, shows his effective force as 45,487 (Official Records, XLIII, Part I, p. 61); "Battles and Leaders of the Civil War" states that of these about 43,000 were available for active field duty.

Estimates of Early's army at Winchester:

"Battles and Leaders" states that monthly returns for August 31 (exclusive of Kershaw's troops, who were not engaged) show an effective force of infantry and artillery of 10,646. To this are added 1200 cavalry under Fitz Lee and 1700 under Lomax, making a total of 13,288. The figures given for cavalry under Lee and Lomax were given the editors by General Early in a letter, so they may not be disputed. Early claims, however, that the figures for infantry and artillery are placed too high — that between August 31 and September 19 his losses were considerable, and that at Winchester he had only 8500 muskets.

and around it been permitted. Within twenty minutes that isolated command would have had Carter's thirty or forty guns hurling their whizzing shells and solid shot, like so many shivering lightning-bolts, through its entire lines. Within thirty minutes the yelling Confederate infantry would have been rushing resistlessly upon its flanks and front and rear. No troops on earth could have withstood such unprecedented disadvantages, such a combination of death-dealing agencies.

But the concentration was stopped; the blow was not delivered. We halted, we hesitated, we dallied, firing a few shots here, attacking with a brigade or a division there, and before such feeble assaults the superb Union corps retired at intervals and by short stages. We waited—for what? It is claimed by the Confederate commander that we were threatened with cavalry on our right, whereas General L. L. Lomax of the Confederate cavalry, who combined the high qualities of great courage and wise caution, was on that flank and had already advanced to a point within a few miles of Winchester. It is also true that the Federal reports show that Union cavalry was sent to that flank to prevent our turning Sheridan's left, and was sent back to Sheridan's right when it was discovered that there was no danger of serious assault by Early's army. We waited — waited for weary hours; waited till those stirring, driving, and able Federal leaders, Wright, Crook, and Getty, could gather again their shattered fragments; waited till the routed men in blue found that no foe was pursuing them and until they had time to recover their normal composure and courage; waited till Confederate officers lost hope and the fires had gone out in the hearts of the privates, who for hours had been asking, "What is the matter? Why don't we go forward?"— waited for Sheridan to make his ride, rally and bring back his routed army, mass it upon our left flank in broad daylight and assail us, and thus rout our whole army just as, eight hours before, we had under cover of darkness massed upon and assailed his left flank and routed two thirds of his army.

General Sheridan had not slept on the field the preceding night. He was absent — had gone, I believe, to Washington; and if Payne had succeeded in capturing the commanding Union general, as he came near doing, he would have discovered that he had not secured the man he wanted. Sheridan, however, was on his way back to the front. At Winchester he heard the distant thunder as it rolled down the Valley from Cedar Creek. The western wind brought to his ears what Patrick Henry called "the clash of resounding arms"; and he started in the direction from which came the roar of the storm. As he rode up the historic pike he met his broken and scattered corps, flying in dismay from an army which was not pursuing them, running pell-mell to the rear from the same foe which, just one month before, they had pursued in the opposite direction and over the same ground.

The Federal General Wright, to whom tardy justice —if justice at all—has been done (and who suffered the same defeat from our flank movement which would have overtaken General Sheridan had he been there), had done all that any officer could do to stem the resistless Confederate rush in the early morning. This gallant Union officer had already begun to rally his scattered forces to the support of the Sixth Corps, before whose front we had strangely dallied for six precious hours. In paying this altogether insufficient tribute to General Wright, whose valor and skill had been manifested in many battles, in no sense do I disparage the achievement of Philip Sheridan. He deserved much, and richly did his grateful countrymen reward him. His energy and dash were equal to the demands upon them. His was a clear case of *veni, vidi, vici.* He halted and rallied and enthused his panic-stricken men. While we waited he reorganized his dismembered regiments, brigades, and divisions, and turned them back toward the lines from which they had fled in veriest panic.

His movements were seen by the clear eyes of the vigilant Confederate Signal Corps from their lofty perch on Massanutten Mountain. Their flags at once waved left and right and front, signalling to us the news, " The Yankees are halting and reforming." Next, " They are moving back, some on the main pike and some on other roads." Next, " The enemy's cavalry has checked Rosser's pursuit and assumed the offensive."

Rosser was greatly outnumbered by Sheridan's cavalry, which, supported as it now was by two corps of rallied infantry, drove, in turn, these sturdy Confederate horsemen to the rear. They contested, however, every foot of advance, and joined our Signal Corps in sending information of the heavy column approaching.

The flag signals from the mountain and the messages from Rosser became more intense in their warning and more frequent as the hours passed. Sheridan's marchers were coming closer and massing in heavy column on the left, while his cavalry were gathering on our flank and rear; but the commander of the Confederate forces evidently did not share in the apprehension manifested by the warning signals as to the danger which immediately threatened us.

When the battle began in the morning my command was on the Confederate right; but at the end of the morning's fight, when the fatal halt was called, my immediate division was on the Confederate left. General Early in his report, now published, states that I had gotten on the left with my division. He did not seem to understand how we reached the left, when we were on the right at the opening of the morning fight. Had

General Early been there when our ringing rifles were sounding a reveille to Sheridan's sleeping braves, had he seen Evans and Kershaw as I saw them, sweeping with the scattering fury of a whirlwind down the Union intrenchments, and following the flying Federals far beyond our extreme left, he would have known exactly how we got there. From the Confederate right to the Confederate left we had passed in swift pursuit of the routed enemy. Across the whole length of the Confederate front these divisions had swept, trying to catch Sheridan's panic-stricken men, and they did catch a great many of them.

When the long hours of dallying with the Sixth [Union] Corps had passed, and our afternoon alignment was made, there was a long gap, with scarcely a vedette to guard it between my right and the main Confederate line. The flapping flags from the mountain and the messages from Rosser were burdened with warnings that the rallied Union infantry and heavy bodies of cavalry were already in front of the gap and threatening both flank and rear. With that fearful gap in the line, and the appalling conditions which our long delay had invited, every Confederate commander of our left wing foresaw the crash which speedily came. One after another of my staff was directed to ride with all speed to General Early and apprise him of the hazardous situation. Receiving no satisfactory answer, I myself finally rode to headquarters to urge that he reënforce the left and fill the gap, which would prove a veritable death-trap if left open many minutes longer; or else that he concentrate his entire force for desperate defence or immediate withdrawal. He instructed me to stretch out the already weak lines and take a battery of guns to the left. I rode back at a furious gallop to execute these most unpromising movements. It was too late. The last chance had passed of saving the army from the doom which had been threatened for hours. Major Kirkpatrick had started with his guns, rushing across the plain to the crumbling Confederate lines like fire-engines tearing through streets in the vain effort to save a building already wrapped in flames and tumbling to the ground. I reached my command only in time to find the unresisted columns of Sheridan rushing through this gap, and, worse still, to find Clement A. Evans, whom I left in command, almost completely surrounded by literally overwhelming numbers; but he was handling the men with great skill, and fighting in almost every direction with characteristic coolness. It required counter-charges of the most daring character to prevent the utter destruction of the command and effect its withdrawal. At the same instant additional Union forces, which had penetrated through the vacant space, were assailing our main line on the flank and rolling it up like a scroll. Regiment after regiment, brigade after brigade, in rapid succession was crushed, and, like hard clods of clay under a pelting rain, the superb commands crumbled to pieces. The sun was sinking, but the spasmodic battle still raged. Wrapped in clouds of smoke and gathering darkness, the overpowered Confederates stubbornly yielded before the advancing Federals.

There was no yelling on the one side, nor huzzahs on the other. The gleaming blazes from hot muzzles made the murky twilight lurid. The line of light from Confederate guns grew shorter and resistance fainter. The steady roll of musketry, punctuated now and then by peals of thunder from retreating or advancing batteries, suddenly ceased; and resistance ended as the last organized regiment of Early's literally overwhelmed army broke and fled in the darkness. As the tumult of battle died away, there came from the north side of the plain a dull, heavy swelling sound like the roaring of a distant cyclone, the omen of additional disaster. It was unmistakable. Sheridan's horsemen were riding furiously across the open fields of grass to intercept the Confederates before they crossed Cedar Creek. Many were cut off and captured. As the sullen roar from horses' hoofs beating the soft turf of the plain told of the near approach of the cavalry, all effort at orderly retreat was abandoned. The only possibility of saving the rear regiments was in unrestrained flight—every man for himself. Mounted officers gathered here and there squads of brave men who poured volleys into the advancing lines of blue; but it was too late to make effective resistance.

In the dim starlight, after crossing the creek, I gathered around me a small force representing nearly every command in Early's army, intending to check, if possible, the further pursuit, or at least to delay it long enough to enable the shattered and rapidly retreating fragments to escape. The brave fellows responded to my call and formed a line across the pike. The effort was utterly fruitless, however, and resulted only in hair-breadth escapes and unexampled experiences.

It has never been settled whether, in escaping from the British dragoons under Tryon, General Israel Putnam rode or rolled or slid down the precipice at Horse Neck in 1779; but whichever method of escape he adopted, I can "go him two better," as the sportsmen say, for I did all three at Cedar Creek, eighty-five years later, in escaping from American dragoons under Philip Sheridan. At the point where I attempted to make a stand at night, the pike ran immediately on the edge of one of those abrupt and rugged limestone cliffs down which it was supposed not even a rabbit could plunge without breaking his neck; and I proved it to be nearly true. One end of my short line of gray-jackets rested on the pike at this forbidding precipice. I had scarcely gotten my men in position when I discovered that Sheridan's dragoons had crossed the creek higher up, and that I was surrounded by them on three sides, while on the other was this breakneck escarpment. These enterprising horsemen in search of their game had located my little band, and at the sound of the bugle they came in headlong charge. Only one volley from my men and the Federal cavalry were upon them. Realizing that our capture was imminent, I shouted to my men to escape, if possible, in the darkness. One minute more and I should have had a Yankee carbine at my head, inviting my surrender. The alternatives were the precipice or Yankee prison. There was no time to debate the question, not a moment. Wheeling my horse to the dismal brink, I drove my spurs into his flanks, and he plunged downward and tumbled headlong in one direction, sending me in another. How I reached the bottom of that abyss I shall never know; for I was rendered temporarily unconscious. Strangely enough, I was only stunned, and in no way seriously hurt. My horse, too, though bruised, was not disabled. For a moment I thought he was dead, for he lay motionless and prone at full length. However, he promptly responded to my call and rose to his feet; and although the bare places on his head and hips showed that he had been hurt, he was ready without a groan to bear me again in any direction I might wish to go. The question was, which way to go. I was alone in that dark wooded glen—that is, my faithful horse was the only comrade and friend near enough to aid me. I was safe enough from discovery, although so near the pike that the rumble of wheels and even the orders of the Union officers were at times quite audible. It was, perhaps, an hour or more after nightfall, and yet the vanguard of Sheridan's army had not halted. Considerable numbers of them were now between me and the retreating Confederates. The greater part of the country on each side of the pike, however, was open, and I was

fairly familiar with it all. There was no serious difficulty, therefore, in passing around the Union forces, who
soon went into camp for the night. Lonely, thoughtful,
and sad,—sadder and more thoughtful, if possible, on this
nineteenth night of October than on the corresponding
night of the previous month at Winchester,—I rode
through open fields, now and then finding squads of
Confederates avoiding the pike to escape capture, and
occasionally a solitary soldier as lonely, if not as sad and
thoughtful, as I.

Thus ended the day which had witnessed a most brilliant victory converted into one of the most complete
and ruinous routs of the entire war. It makes one dizzy
to think of such a headlong descent from the Elysium of
triumph to the Erebus of complete collapse.

CHAPTER XXV

THE FATAL HALT AT CEDAR CREEK

Analysis of the great mistake—Marshalling of testimony—Documentary proof of the error—Early's "glory enough for one day" theory —What eye-witnesses say—The defence of the Confederate soldier— A complete vindication.

THE sun in his circuit shines on few lovelier landscapes than that of Cedar Creek in the Valley of Virginia, which was the wrestling-ground of the two armies on October 19, 1864; and no day in the great war's calendar, nor in the chronicles of any other war, so far as my knowledge extends, was filled with such great surprises — so much of the unexpected to both armies. Other days during our war witnessed a brilliant triumph or a crushing defeat for the one army or the other; but no other single day saw each of the contending armies victorious and vanquished on the same field and between the rising and setting of the same sun. This nineteenth day of October, therefore, is, I believe, the most unique day in the annals of war. It was Derby day for fleet-footed racers on both sides; and the combined experiences of the two combatants during this single day constitute the very climax of battle-born antitheses.

Thomas G. Jones, since governor of Alabama and now judge of the United States Court, was then an aide on my staff, and sat on his horse at my side when General

Early announced that we had had "glory enough for one day." Boy soldier as he was then, he felt and expressed serious forebodings of the disaster which was to follow in the wake of our great victory.

It was the anniversary of Yorktown and of the surrender of Cornwallis to Washington, which virtually ended the struggle of our fathers for liberty. After General Early consented to adopt the plan which had been submitted and urged, members of my staff and others, reposing implicit faith in the fulfilment of my predictions of a crushing defeat to Sheridan's army, confidently anticipated that the next morning — October 19, 1864 — would witness for the Confederates, who were fighting for Southern independence, a victory almost as signal as that won October 19, 1781, by the Rebels of the Revolution, who were fighting for American independence. It is true that the conditions surrounding the Confederate cause in the autumn of 1864 were far more desperate than those around the American Revolutionists in the autumn of 1781. There were, however, in our calculations, elements which still inspired hope. If General Sheridan's army could be crushed and large numbers captured, if it could be even disorganized and dispersed, new life and vigor would be given to the still defiant Confederacy. If the victory of the coming morning, which seemed assured, should be followed by incessant blows and pressing pursuit, it would open the way to Washington, expose Northern States to immediate invasion, magnify to Northern apprehension the numbers and effectiveness of Early's army, compel General Grant to send a larger force than Sheridan's to meet us, enable General Lee at Petersburg to assume the offensive and possibly arouse a strong peace sentiment among the Northern masses. The complete surprise of the Union army, and the resistless Confederate charges at dawn in flank, front, and rear, vindicated the confident predictions of victory. The disastrous Confederate defeat in the evening made clear the mistake of hesitating and halting which were a fatal abandonment of an essential part of the plan.

The story is short and simple, but sombre to the last degree. To briefly recapitulate, orders from headquarters put an end in the early morning to concentration and energetic pursuit, and, therefore, to all hope of completing the great victory by capturing or crushing the last intervening line in blue between us and the Potomac. General Cullen A. Battle of Alabama was severely wounded while leading his men with characteristic dash and enthusiasm; but his brigade, one of the smallest, and also one of the pluckiest, charged a battery supported by the Sixth Corps,— the only one left,— and captured in open field six additional pieces of artillery.[1] What would have been the inevitable result of the concentrated enfilade fire from all of Carter's guns tearing through the whole length of that line, while the entire army of Confederate infantry assailed it in front, flank, and rear?

History (so called) does not always give a true diagnosis of the cases it deals with and attempts to analyze. It will be a long time, I fear, before all the records of the great fight between the States will tell, like sworn witnesses in the courts, "the truth, the whole truth, and nothing but the truth."

I am writing reminiscences; but if they are to be of any value they must also stand the test applied to witnesses in courts of justice. The unexpected and unexplained absence of my official report of Cedar Creek from the list of those published with General Early's in the War Records makes clear my duty to record in these

[1] An old memorandum written by General Battle after he was carried to hospital states that the number of guns captured by his brigade was twelve instead of six.

reminiscences some statements which appear to me essential to the truth of history.

Captain Jed Hotchkiss, of General Early's staff, has fortunately left a Journal in which he recorded events as they occurred day by day. In that Journal, which has been published by the Government among official papers in the records of the "War of the Rebellion" (First Series, Vol. XLIII, Part I, pp. 567–588), Captain Hotchkiss made at the time this memomrandum: "Saturday, October 29th. . . . A contention between Generals Gordon and Early about the battle of Cedar Creek," etc.

There were a number of strongly controverted points between us; but the only one in which the whole country is concerned, involving as it does the character of Southern soldiery, the only one which I feel compelled to notice in this book, is the question as to the responsibility for the disaster at Cedar Creek after the signal victory had been won. Two reasons have been given for this revulsion, and both have evoked no little discussion. If General Sheridan and his friends had been consulted, they doubtless would have added a third, namely, his arrival on the field. This, however, was not considered by General Early and myself, and it did not disturb the harmony of our counsels. We had widely differing explanations for the disaster, but neither of us suggested General Sheridan's arrival as the cause. General Early insisted, and so stated in his now published report, that the "bad conduct" of his own men caused the astounding disaster; while I was convinced that it was due solely to the unfortunate halting and delay after the morning victory. I insisted then, and still insist, that our men deserved only unstinted praise. I believed then, and I believe now, that neither General Sheridan nor any other commander could have prevented the complete destruction of his infantry if in the early hours of the morning we had concentrated our fire and assaults upon his only remaining corps. The situation was this: two thirds of Sheridan's army had been shivered by blows delivered in flank and rear. If, therefore, Early's entire army, triumphant, unhurt, and exhilarated, had been instantly hurled against that solitary corps in accordance with the general plan of the battle, it is certain that there would not have been left in it an organized company; and many hours before General Sheridan made his ride, the last nucleus around which he could possibly have rallied his shattered and flying forces would have been destroyed.

If my official report of the battle of Cedar Creek had been published with General Early's, it would perhaps not be necessary for me to speak of the "contention" mentioned by Captain Hotchkiss in his Journal, which I have recently seen for the first time. Justice to others, however, to the living and the dead, demands that I now make record in this book of some facts connected with that "contention," and that I send to posterity this record in connection with his report.

Thousands of living men and hundreds of thousands of their descendants, and of the descendants of those who fell heroically fighting under the Southern flag, have a profound, a measureless interest in the final settlement of that controverted point of which I am now to speak from personal knowledge, and from the testimony of scores of witnesses who participated in the battle and whose military acumen and experience give special weight to their words.

It is due to General Early to say that his physical strength was not sufficient to enable him to ascend Massanutten Mountain and survey the field from that lofty peak. He had not, therefore, the opportunity to take in the tremendous possibilities which that view revealed. He had not been permitted to stand upon that summit and trace with his own eye the inviting lines for the Confederate night march; to see for himself, in the conditions immediately before him, the sure prophecy of Confederate victory, and to have his brain set on fire by clearly perceiving that the movement, if adopted and executed with vigor and pressed to the end, must inevitably result in bringing to Sheridan's army, in quick succession, complete surprise, universal dismay, boundless panic, and finally rout, capture, or annihilation. Again, General Early was not on that portion of the field which was struck by the Confederate cyclone at dawn; nor did he witness its destructive sweep through Sheridan's camps and along his breastworks, leaving in its wide track not a Federal soldier with arms in his hands. Major Hunter, my chief of staff, rode back to meet General Early, with instructions to give him my compliments and inform him that two thirds of Sheridan's army were routed and nearly all his artillery captured, while our troops had suffered no serious loss. The Confederate commander was naturally elated, and felt that we had had " glory enough for one day." He, therefore, halted. The pressing question is, Was that halt fatal? Was it responsible for the afternoon disaster, or was the " bad conduct " of the men responsible? This question was the cause of the "contention" of which Captain Hotchkiss made record, and which, in view of the absence of my report from the published records, and under the inexorable demands of duty to living and dead comrades, I am bound to answer in perfect fairness but also with truth and candor.

General Sheridan, in his official report of Cedar Creek,[1] speaking of the "heavy turning column" (my command) which crossed the river at Bowman's Ford, describes the assault as "striking Crook, who held the left of our line in flank and rear, so unexpectedly and forcibly as

[1] "War of the Rebellion," First Series, Vol. XLIII, Part I, p. 52.

to drive in his outposts, invade his camp, and turn his position. . . . This was followed by a direct attack upon our front [this was Kershaw's assault], and the result was that the whole army was driven back in confusion to a point about one mile and a half north of Middletown, a very large portion of the infantry not even preserving a company organization." He adds that about nine o'clock, "on reaching Mill Creek, half a mile south of Winchester, the head of the fugitives appeared in sight, trains and men coming to the rear with appalling rapidity." He left officers to do what they could "in stemming the torrent of fugitives." This frank statement of General Sheridan makes plain the truth that the exultant Confederates were halted at the time when the "whole army [Union] had been driven back in confusion," when there was not left in a large portion of Union infantry "a company organization," and when "the torrent of fugitives" had gone to the rear with such "appalling rapidity" as to have reached Mill Creek, eight or ten miles away, by nine o'clock in the morning. I submit that I might rest the whole of my "contention" on these remarkable admissions of General Sheridan as to the condition of his army when the fatal Confederate halt was ordered.

General Sheridan also states that the attack in flank and rear, which was made by my troops, was followed by one in front. This latter was promptly and superbly made by Kershaw. General Sheridan's statement clearly shows that the assault of my command preceded, but was promptly followed by, Kershaw's. Captain Hotchkiss of General Early's staff records in his Journal, penned at the time, precisely the same facts (Vol. XLIII, p. 581). These Official Records from both sides render it unnecessary for me to make any reply whatever to General Early's intimation in his report that I was a little late in making my attack at Cedar Creek. A vast array of testimony (Federal and Confederate) is at hand showing conclusively that General Early was mistaken in supposing that my command was late on that October morning.

Colonel Thomas H. Carter, General Early's chief of artillery on this field, and now the honored proctor of the University of Virginia, writes me from the university: "I confirm with emphasis your opinion that General Early made a fatal mistake in stopping the pursuit of the enemy, with the Sixth Corps retiring before artillery alone and the other two corps in full and disorganized flight at nine o'clock in the morning. Captain Southall's letter will show plainly my views as expressed to General Early in his presence."

Captain S. V. Southall, now of Charlottesville, Virginia, in the letter to which Colonel Carter refers, in speaking of General Early at the moment he received the news of the morning victory, says: "His face became radiant with joy, and in his gladness he exclaimed, 'The sun of Middletown! The sun of Middletown!'" The last of Sheridan's army in its retreat had then reached the borders of Middletown. Captain Southall then reminds Colonel Carter of his suggesting to General Early the propriety of advancing, and says: "Your suggestion looking to the completion of our victory was ignored. Things remained in this way for hours, during which time Sheridan returned." Colonel Carter, in his own letter on that point, says: "At a later interview with General Early, I explained that the troops were eager to go ahead, and I had been questioned all along the line to know the cause of the delay. . . . Of course, Sheridan, finding his cavalry corps intact and equal in number to our army, and the Sixth Corps unbroken, though demoralized, was right to assume the offensive, and his ride on the black horse will go down in history and romance as a tribute to his military fame. Nevertheless, if we had done our proper part in pursuit, his arrival would have accomplished nothing. Every practical fighting man in our war knows that troops scattered and panic-stricken cannot be rallied in the face of hot and vigorous pursuit."

Major R. W. Hunter, who was all day actively participating in the battle, speaking of the destruction of two thirds of the Union army by that flank and rear attack, says in his written statement of facts: "Neither the famous Macedonian phalanx, nor Cæsar's Tenth Legion, nor the Old Guard of Napoleon, nor Wellington's hollow squares, which saved him at Waterloo, nor any possible organization of troops, could have withstood the combined assault of infantry, artillery, and cavalry that it was in our power to have made upon the Sixth Corps on that eventful morning after the complete rout of the Eighth and Nineteenth Corps. Why was not that concentrated assault made?"

Shortly after the battle of Cedar Creek the newspapers were filled with descriptions of the morning victory and evening rout. That "contention" between General Early and myself was inaugurated by his intimation, in the presence of other officers, that I had inspired some of those accounts. Notwithstanding my appreciation of General Early's high qualities, and in spite of the official courtesy due him as my superior officer (which, I believe, was never ignored), I could not do less than indignantly resent the injustice of such an intimation. At the same time, my sense of duty to the army and regard for truth compelled me candidly to say, and I did say, that the facts had been truly stated as to our unfortunate halt and fatal delay.

General Clement A. Evans, whose superb record as a soldier and exalted character as a man and minister of the gospel entitle any statement from him to unquestioning belief, was a division commander in the moving attack which swept away Sheridan's two corps. General Evans is now at the head of the Board of Pardons of the State of Georgia, and, learning that I was writing of Cedar Creek, sent me a strong letter, from which I make a brief quotation. His statements fully corroborate those made at the time in the newspaper reports. For reasons which will be readily understood, I omit from the quotation the words used by General Evans as to the credit for the morning victory and the responsibility for the evening disaster, and give only this concluding clause: " And the Cedar Creek disaster was caused by the halt which you did not order and which I know you opposed."

General Thomas L. Rosser, who commanded the Confederate cavalry on the field, says: " The sun never rose on a more glorious victory and never set on a more inglorious defeat. Had . . . the fight continued . . . as it was so gloriously begun, Sheridan's ride of twenty miles away would never have been sung," etc.

General Gabriel C. Wharton, now of Radford, Virginia, who commanded a division of General Early's army at Cedar Creek, speaking of some movements by our troops just after the rout of Sheridan's two corps, says: " I supposed we were arranging for a general movement to the front, and expected every minute orders to advance; but no orders came, and there we stood — no enemy in our front for hours, except some troops moving about in the woodland on a hill nearly a mile in our front." He adds: " I have never been able to understand why General Early did not advance, or why he remained in line for four or five hours after the brilliant victory of the morning."

Captain Hotchkiss, in his contribution to the recently published " Confederate Military History " (Vol. III, p. 509), after paying to his old chief, General Early, the compliments which he richly deserved as an " able strategist, most skilful commander, and one of the bravest of the brave," nevertheless characterizes the fatal halt at Cedar Creek as " this inexcusable delay."

I also present another item of testimony, which was given under most interesting circumstances. During the winter which followed this battle there occurred, in connection with this Valley campaign, one of the most thrilling incidents of the entire war. It exhibited as much daring and dash as the famous scouting expedition of the brave Federal squad who came into Georgia and scouted in rear of our army, and then, seizing an engine on the Western and Atlantic Railroad, fled upon it back toward Chattanooga and the Union lines. The daring adventure of which I now speak was, however, far more successful than this bold scouting in Georgia. While northern Virginia and Maryland were in the icy embrace of midwinter, a small squad of plucky Confederates from Captain McNeill's Partisan Rangers rode at night into Cumberland, Maryland, where 5000 armed men of the Union army were stationed. These audacious young Confederates eluded the Union guards, located the headquarters of Major-Generals Crook and Kelley, captured them in their beds, and brought them, as prisoners of war mounted on their own horses, safely into Confederate lines. General Crook was the distinguished commander of the Union troops whose flank and rear my command had struck at dawn on Cedar Creek. When he was brought to headquarters as prisoner, General Early interviewed him in reference to that battle. Captain Hotchkiss states that in the interview General Crook represented the Sixth Corps, on the morning of the 19th of October at Cedar Creek, as almost as "badly damaged" as the other corps, and in no condition to resist attack.[1]

It will not surprise the thoughtful student of this

[1] "Confederate Military History," Vol. III, p. 538.

marvellous battle to know that General Early himself
realized later the fatal mistake of the halt at Cedar
Creek, and gave an indicative caution to his faithful
staff officer, who was leaving with a sketch of Cedar
Creek for General Lee. Captain Hotchkiss says: "General Early told me not to tell General Lee that we ought
to have advanced in the morning at Middletown, for,
said he, 'we ought to have done so.'"[1]

Anything more on this point would be superfluous.
I should not have felt it necessary to produce these
proofs as to the responsibility of the halting and delay
but for the fact that they bear directly and cogently
upon the other infinitely more important inquiry, "Was
the 'bad conduct' of the troops wholly or partially, directly
or remotely, responsible for that evening disaster?"
Posterity may not trouble itself much about the halting
and hesitation at Cedar Creek; but posterity—undoubtedly Confederate posterity—will be profoundly interested
in this inquiry: "Did Confederate officers and men
abandon their posts of duty and danger to plunder the
captured camps and thus convert one of the most brilliant of victories into a most disastrous defeat and utter
rout?"

This charge so directly, so vitally concerns the reputation, the honor, the character of Southern soldiers (it
concerns all American soldiers, for these men were
Americans of purest blood) as to demand the most
exhaustive examination. Let the fiercest search-light
of historical scrutiny be turned upon those men. Let
the truth, the whole truth, and nothing but the truth go
to posterity. With the purpose of contributing to this
end, I shall incorporate, not in foot-notes but in the
body of this chapter, all the important and trustworthy
evidence at my command bearing upon this question,

[1] Hotchkiss's Journal, "War Records," First Series, Part I,
Vol. XLIII, p. 582.

which is the gravest that has ever been asked or could be asked concerning Confederate soldiers. I shall give proofs which cannot be called in question, in extracts from the official reports and written statements of all the prominent Confederate actors in that battle, so far as I can possibly procure them.

To begin with, I quote fully and carefully from General Early's reports to General Lee, which I did not see until they were published by the Government in the records of the "War of the Rebellion." In his despatch, dated October 20, 1864, speaking of his troops, General Early says: "But for their bad conduct I should have defeated Sheridan's whole force." [1] In his more formal report of October 21st, speaking of an order said to have been sent to Kershaw and Gordon to advance, he says: "They stated in reply that . . . their ranks were so depleted by the number of men who had stopped in the camps to plunder that they could not advance." [2] In the same report on the same page, he says: "So many of our men had stopped in camp to plunder (in which I am sorry to say that officers participated)," etc. Again, in another connection, he says: "We had within our grasp a glorious victory, and lost it by the uncontrollable propensity to plunder, in the first place, and the subsequent panic, . . . which was without sufficient cause," etc. In another connection, speaking of the efforts to guard against plundering, he says: "The truth is, we have few field and company officers worth anything," etc. Before closing his report he again says: "But the victory already gained was lost by the subsequent bad conduct of the troops."

Before introducing the array of witnesses and the incontrovertible facts which overwhelmingly vindicate these chivalrous and self-sacrificing men, I wish to say,

---

[1] War Records, First Series, Vol. XLIII, Part I, p. 560.
[2] Ibid., pp. 562 and 563.

as a matter of simple justice to General Early, that he was misled. His place was at the front, and after he came upon the field he was there — as he always was, when duty called him. No soldier or citizen was braver or more loyally devoted to our cause than Jubal A. Early; but, as General Lee once said of another, he was "very pertinacious of his opinions," and when once formed he rarely abandoned them. He fought against secession and for the Union until it was broken. He tied his faith to the Confederacy and fought for that while it lived, and he did not abandon its cause until both the Confederacy and himself were dead. He had been led to believe that his men at Cedar Creek had left their places in line to gather the tempting débris from the Federal wreck, and he steadfastly stood by this statement. Little wonder, then, that there should be the "contention" which Captain Hotchkiss has noted.

General Kershaw is dead, but were he living he would unite with me, as shown by the reports of his officers, in the statement that no such order ever reached us as the one which General Early sent. No reply was ever returned by General Kershaw or myself to the effect that we could not advance. The truth is we were not only urgently anxious to advance, but were astounded at any halt whatever. Our troops were not absent. They were there in line, eager to advance, as will appear from the unanswerable proofs submitted. General Evans, who commanded my division while I commanded the Second Corps in the morning victory, says: "When you congratulated me on the field immediately after our great victory . . . I was so impressed by your remarks as to be convinced that we would at once pursue our advantage. . . . I had small details sent over the ground we had traversed in order to bring up every man who had fallen out for any cause except for wounds. . . . When the attack [afternoon] came from the enemy my command was not straggling and plundering. . . . I wish I could see my men fully vindicated as to their conduct in this battle."

General Cullen A. Battle says: "I saw no plundering at Cedar Creek, not even a straggler. My troops were in the best possible condition." In another statement he says: "I never saw troops behave better than ours did at Cedar Creek."

Major-General Wharton, who was in the best possible position to know if there was any straggling or plundering, uses these words: "The report of the soldiers straggling and pillaging the enemy's camps is not correct. . . . I had a pretty fair view of a large part of the field over which you had driven the enemy. It is true that there were parties passing over the field and perhaps pillaging, but most of them were citizens, teamsters and persons attached to the quartermaster's and other departments, and perhaps a few soldiers who had taken the wounded to the rear. No, general; the disaster was not due to the soldiers leaving their commands and pillaging."

Of all the reports of Cedar Creek which have been published in the War Records, not one except General Early's alone remotely hints at plundering as the cause of that unprecedented revulsion after the morning victory. Only two of those reports refer to the matter in any way whatever, and in both the language completely exonerates these devoted men. General Bryan Grimes, who was promoted to command of Ramseur's division, says: "Up to the hour of 4 P.M. the troops of this division, both officers and men, with a few exceptions, behaved most admirably and were kept well in hand, but little plundering and only a few shirking duty." He adds: "Major Whiting, inspector, rendered signal service by preventing all straggling and plundering."[1]

---

[1] War Records, First Series, Vol. XLIII, Part I, p. 600.

John R. Winston, in his report (same vol., p. 608), says:

"The men went through a camp just as it was deserted, with hats, boots, blankets, tents, and such things as tempt our soldiers scattered over it, and after diligent inquiry I heard of but one man who even stopped to pick up a thing. He got a hat, and has charges preferred against him." He refers with pride to the "splendid conduct of these troops," etc.

That gallant soldier J. M. Goggin, who commanded Conner's brigade of Kershaw's division, in his official report, says: "Up to this time" [the afternoon assault by Sheridan] "both men and officers had obeyed with commendable cheerfulness and alacrity all orders given them. . . . I cannot forbear giving both officers and men that praise which is so justly their due for the noble display of all the admirable and true qualities of the soldier up to the time the retreat was ordered; and no one who witnessed the advance of the brigade that day against different positions of the enemy will hesitate to bestow upon it their [his] unqualified admiration" (p. 594).

While almost any one of these pointed and just testimonials would be a sufficient vindication of these self-immolating veterans, yet I must introduce here the most comprehensive statement of all. It was written by the Rev. A. C. Hopkins, now pastor of the Presbyterian Church of Charlestown, West Virginia. He was, during the war, one of the leading Confederate chaplains. In the different battles he was present, mingling with the soldiers, caring for the wounded, and doing admirable service in encouraging the men who were on the fighting-line. No dangers deterred him; no sacrifices were too great for him to make. Dr. Hopkins was one of those sterling characters who esteemed honor and truth as of far greater value than life itself. In the carefully prepared statement which he wrote of Cedar

Creek, he says: "The writer was a 'free-lance' that day, and all over the field from rear to front, from the time Gordon struck Crook's lines at daybreak till the afternoon. He was sometimes with our lines and sometimes with the wounded, over the field and through the Yankee camps. . . . It is true that many men straggled and plundered; but they were men who in large numbers had been wounded in the summer's campaign, who had come up to the army for medical examination, and who came like a division down the pike behind Wharton, and soon scattered over the field and camps and helped themselves. They were soldiers more or less disabled, and not on duty. This body I myself saw as they came on the battle-field and scattered. They were not men with guns. But there can be no doubt that General Early mistook them for men who had fallen out of ranks." In speaking of that "contention" between General Early and myself which was evoked by this serious misapprehension as to the "bad conduct" of our brave men, Dr. Hopkins says: "Nearly all the inspectors who sent reports for 19th October to General Gordon either gave the numbers of men carried up to the lines during the day or vindicated their commands from General Early's imputation. And these inspectors' reports were consolidated at General Gordon's headquarters and the substance forwarded in his report to General Early. Unfortunately, no inspectors' reports appear among the published records, and they [the records] contain not one word from General Gordon on this battle."

It seems to me unnecessary to lengthen this chapter by additional evidence or by any argument. The proofs already adduced compass the irrefutable vindication of the winners of the morning victory at Cedar Creek. Many of the dead commanders left on record their testimony; and it is true, I think, that every living Confederate officer who commanded at Cedar Creek a corps, or division, or brigade, or regiment, or company, would testify that his men fought with unabated ardor, and did not abandon their places in line to plunder the captured camps. It is truly marvellous, therefore, that the statement that their "bad conduct" caused the disastrous reverse has gone into books and is treated as history in all sections of the country. Even ex-President Jefferson Davis, the last man on earth who would knowingly do Confederate soldiers an injustice, was totally misled by General Early's statement.

If my official report of the battle of Cedar Creek had been forwarded to General Lee and published in the War Records, I might be pardoned by my comrades and their children if I did not write as I am now writing in vindication of the men who fought so superbly and exhibited such marked self-denial in that most unique of battles. Not for my sake, but for theirs, I deeply regret the absence of my report from those records. It is only since this book was begun that my attention was called to this fact. It would seem that my report never reached General Lee. Otherwise it would have been among his papers, and assuredly have found its place in the volumes issued by the Government. General Lee, however, did not agree with his lieutenant commanding in the Valley as to the kind of metal these men were made of. On September 27th he wrote General Early: "I have such confidence in the men and officers that I am sure all will unite in defence of the country." [1] These men were not strangers to General Lee. He knew them. He had seen them in the past years of the war, performing deeds of valor and exercising a self-denial the simple record of which would rival the legends of the romantic era of chivalry. They had not changed, except to grow, if possible, into a more self-sacrificing manhood as the de-

[1] War Records, First Series, Vol. XLIII, Part I, p. 558.

mands upon them became more exacting. Whatever they had been in the battles around Richmond, at Fredericksburg, at Chancellorsville, at Gettysburg, at Cold Harbor, in the Wilderness, and in the great counter-charge at Spottsylvania, they were the same at Cedar Creek. The men who were in the captured camps were not the soldiers who fought the morning battle and won the morning victory. The "plunderers," if such they may be called, were not the fiery South Carolinians who, under Kershaw, had so fearlessly and fiercely stormed and carried the Union breastworks at dawn. They were not the steadfast Virginians who, under Wharton, had rushed into the combat, adding fresh momentum to the resistless Confederate charge. They were not the men under my command, the Second Corps, which Jackson had immortalized and which had helped to immortalize him. They were not the men who, under Evans, and Ramseur, and Grimes, and Battle, and Pegram, had before daybreak plunged into the cold water to their waists or armpits, and with drenched bodies and water-soaked uniforms had warmed themselves in the hot furnace of battle. These men at Cedar Creek were heroes, descended from heroic sires, inspired by heroic women, trained to self-denial and self-sacrifice through four years of the most heroic of wars, and battling through cold and heat and hunger against heroic Americans. Were these the men to abandon their places in front to plunder in the rear? Who, then, were the men in the captured camps who were reported to General Early? They were men without arms, the partially disabled, whom the army surgeons had pronounced scarcely strong enough for the long and rough night march and the strenuous work of the battle. These half-sick and disabled men had come along the smooth, open pike at their leisure, when they learned of the great victory. They came thinking it no robbery to supply themselves with shoes and trousers

and overcoats and blankets and "grub" from the vast
accumulations purchased that morning by the toil and
blood of their able-bodied comrades—from the stores
which the richly provided Federals, in their unceremon-
ious departure, had neglected to take away.

Many years have passed since the Confederate commander at Cedar Creek was misled and induced to place
on record his belief as to the bad conduct of his men —
a belief, I repeat, fixed in his mind by misinformation
and grounded on total misapprehension. But many
years had also passed after the battle of Cold Harbor
before the exculpation of the brave men of the Union
army was effected by General Horace Porter in his book,
"Campaigning with Grant." The refutation of that
wrong, although long delayed, will be none the less appreciated by Union veterans and by all their descendants. It is not too late, I trust, for the truth, as now
revealed, to vindicate these Confederates. Appeals,
pathetic and earnest, have been made to me for years,
the burden of which has been: "I want you, before you
die, to do justice to the men who fought at Cedar
Creek." The stoniest heart would be moved by such
appeals. They would stir the sensibilities of any man
who saw those dauntless veterans on that field or who
fought and suffered with them in the Confederate army.
I had a right, however, to suppose that the great War
Records would include my report and the inspectors'
reports, every one of which, I believe, without an exception, was a vindication of that little army whose valor
and scrupulous, soldierly bearing has never been surpassed. I protested at the time against the injustice
done them. Hence the "contention" recorded by Captain Hotchkiss. I left the substance of that protest in
permanent form, but that is lost; and now I esteem it
one of the most imperative duties devolving upon me to
do all in my power to guide the future historian to a

clear apprehension of the truth in regard to the chivalrous character and conduct of these loyal men. Although the unparalleled wrong which, through misapprehension, was done them may have already crystallized in war records and so-called histories, yet I shall live and die in the confident hope that the irrefutable proofs herein adduced, which have never before been grouped and marshalled, will stand as their complete though tardy vindication.

No man, I think, has a higher or more just appreciation than myself of our Confederate leaders; but the brilliant victories won by our arms will be found, in their last analyses, to be in a large measure due to the strong individuality, the deep-seated convictions, the moral stamina, the martial instinct, and the personal prowess of our private soldiers; and in no divisions of Lee's army were these characteristics more completely developed than in those which fought at Cedar Creek.

CHAPTER XXVI

THE LAST WINTER OF THE WAR

Frequent skirmishes follow Cedar Creek—Neither commander anxious for a general engagement—Desolation in the Valley—A fated family —Transferred to Petersburg—A gloomy Christmas—All troops on reduced rations—Summoned to Lee's headquarters—Consideration of the dire straits of the army—Three possible courses.

THE Cedar Creek catastrophe did not wholly dispirit Early's army nor greatly increase the aggressive energy of Sheridan's. It was the last of the great conflicts in the historic Valley which for four years had been torn and blood-stained by almost incessant battle. Following on Cedar Creek were frequent skirmishes, some sharp tilts with Sheridan's cavalry, a number of captures and losses of guns and wagons by both sides, and an amount of marching—often twenty to twenty-five miles a day—that sorely taxed the bruised and poorly shod feet of the still cheerful Confederates. On November 16th Captain Hotchkiss made this memorandum in his Journal: " Sent a document to Colonel Boteler showing that to this date we had marched, since the opening of the campaign, sixteen hundred and seventy miles, and had seventy-five battles and skirmishes." All of the encounters which followed Cedar Creek, however, would not have equalled in casualties a second-rate battle; but they served to emphasize the fact that neither commander was disposed to bring the other to a general engagement. Evidently the grievous castigation which each received at Cedar Creek had left him in the sad plight of the Irishman who, recovering from an attack of grip, declared that it was the worst disease he ever had, for it kept him sick four months after he got well.

During this period of Union and Confederate convalescence I was transferred, by General Lee's orders, to the lines of defence around the beleagured Confederate capital and its sympathizing sister city, Petersburg. My command, the Second Corps, consisted of the divisions of Evans, Grimes, and Pegram. Before dawn on December 8th the long trains were bearing two divisions of my command up the western slope of the Blue Ridge range which separated that hitherto enchanting Valley from the undulating Piedmont region, which Thomas Jefferson thought was some day to become the most populous portion of our country because so richly endowed by nature. As I stood on the back platform of the last car in the train and looked back upon that stricken Valley, I could but contrast the aspect of devastation and woe which it then presented, with the bounty and peace in all its homes at the beginning of the war. Prior to 1862 it was, if possible, more beautiful and prosperous than the famed blue-grass region of Kentucky. Before the blasting breath of war swept over its rich meadows and fields of clover, they had been filled with high-mettled horses, herds of fine cattle, and flocks of sheep that rivalled England's best. These were all gone. The great water-wheels which four years before had driven the busy machinery of the mills were motionless— standing and rotting, the silent vouchers of wholesale destruction. Heaps of ashes, of half-melted iron axles and bent tires, were the melancholy remains of burnt barns and farm-wagons and implements of husbandry. Stone and brick chimneys, standing alone in the midst of charred trees which once shaded the porches of luxurious and happy homes, told of hostile torches which had left these grim sentinels the only guards of those sacred spots. At the close of this campaign of General Sheridan there was in that entire fertile valley—the former American Arcadia—scarcely a family that was not struggling for subsistence.

Among the excellent soldiers who participated in all that Valley campaign was a Virginian, who is now Dr. Charles H. Harris of Cedartown, Georgia. Dr. Harris's high character as a man and his familiarity with the facts justify me in giving his written account of the marvellous fatality which attended the representatives of a Virginia family which contributed perhaps a larger number of soldiers to the Confederate army than any other in the Southern States. Two companies of the Sixtieth Virginia Regiment were enlisted in and around Christiansburg, which seems to have received its name from the family which contributed eighteen of its members — brothers and cousins — to those two Confederate companies. These eighteen kinsmen had inherited their love of liberty from Revolutionary ancestors, and had imbibed from the history and traditions of the Old Dominion those lofty ideals of manhood of which her great people are so justly proud. When, therefore, Virginia passed the solemn ordinance of secession and cast her lot with that of her sister States, these high-spirited young men enlisted in the Confederate army. I recall nothing in history or even in romance which equals in uniqueness and pathos the fate that befell them. The decrees of that fate were uniform and inexorable. One by one, these kinsmen fell in succeeding engagements. In every fight in which the regiment was engaged one of this brave family was numbered among the dead. As battle succeeded battle, and each, with appalling regularity, claimed its victim, there ran through company and regiment the unvarying question,

"Which one of the Christians was killed to-day, and which one will go next?" Yet among the survivors there was no wavering, no effort to escape the doom which seemed surely awaiting each in his turn. With a consecration truly sublime, each took his place in line, ready for the sacrifice which duty demanded. For seventeen successive engagements the gruesome record of death had not varied. Then came Cedar Creek. Only one of the gallant eighteen was left. His record for courage was unsurpassed. A number of times he had been wounded, and in the deadly hand-to-hand struggle at Cold Harbor he had been pierced by a bayonet. Faithful to every duty, he had never missed a fight. When the orders were issued for the night march and the assault at dawn upon Sheridan's army, a deep fraternal concern for this last survivor of the Christians was manifested by all of his comrades. He was privately importuned to stay out of the fight; or, if unwilling to remain in camp while his comrades fought, he was urged to go home. Whether he yielded to these warnings and entreaties will probably never be known. He was seen by his comrades no more after that night march to Cedar Creek. Many believe that he was loyal " even unto death," and that he lies with the heroic and " unknown dead " who fell upon that eventful field.

On reaching Petersburg it fell to my lot to hold the extreme right of Lee's infantry. In front of this exposed wing was a dense second growth of pines in which the daring scouts of both armies often passed each other at night and found hiding-places during their adventures. This forest also served to conceal the movements of troops and made artillery practically useless.

Behind my position was the South Side Railroad—the last of the long commercial arteries that had not been cut. General Grant saw that to cut it was to starve Lee's army, and this meant the death of the

Confederacy. His constant aim, therefore, was to seize and sever it. My instructions were to prevent this at any cost. The winter rains and snows and boggy roads were my helpers, and no great battles ensued. There were, however, occasional demonstrations of Grant's purpose, and he managed to keep us alert night and day. It was a very lame railroad, even when left without Federal interference. The iron rails were nearly worn out, and there were no new ones to replace them. If the old and badly maimed locomotives broke down, there were few or no facilities for repairing them. So that if the supplies had been in the far South this crippled road could not have brought them to us; but, like the woman who said that she had "but one tooth above and one below, but, thank God, they hit," we felicitated ourselves that the shackling engines did fit the old track and could help us somewhat. The commissary informed me, soon after my troops were in their new position, that it was impossible for the Government to supply us with more than half-rations, and that even these were by no means certain. My different commands, therefore, were at once instructed to send wagons into the back country and remote settlements and purchase everything obtainable that would sustain life.

"But suppose the teams and wagons are attacked and captured by raiding-parties?"

"That chance must not deter you. Men are worth more than mules and wagons, and we shall have no men unless we can feed them," I replied.

This haphazard method of feeding the corps proved to be the best then available; and later I had the satisfaction of receiving General Lee's congratulations.

In one of General Grant's efforts to break through my lines, General John Pegram, one of my most accomplished commanders, fell, his blood reddening the white snow that carpeted the field. He had just married Miss

Carey of Baltimore, one of the South's most beautiful and accomplished women. Thus, within a few months, ravenous war had claimed as victims two distinguished officers of my command, almost immediately after their marriages. One of these was Pegram of Virginia; the other was Lamar of Georgia.

Christmas (December 25, 1864) came while we were fighting famine within and Grant without our lines. To meet either was a serious problem. The Southern people from their earliest history had observed Christmas as the great holiday season of the year. It was the time of times, the longed-for period of universal and innocent but almost boundless jollification among young and old. In towns and on the plantations, purse-strings were loosened and restraints relaxed—so relaxed that even the fun-loving negro slaves were permitted to take some liberties with their masters, to perpetrate practical jokes upon them, and before daylight to storm "de white folks" houses with their merry calls: "Christmas gift, master!" "Christmas gift, everybody!" The holiday, however, on Hatcher's Run, near Petersburg, was joyless enough for the most misanthropic. The one worn-out railroad running to the far South could not bring to us half enough necessary supplies; and even if it could have transported Christmas boxes of good things, the people at home were too depleted to send them. They had already impoverished themselves to help their struggling Government, and large areas of our territory had been made desolate by the ravages of marching armies. The brave fellows at the front, however, knew that their friends at home would gladly send them the last pound of sugar in the pantry, and the last turkey or chicken from the barnyard. So they facetiously wished each other "Merry Christmas!" as they dined on their wretched fare. There was no complaining, no repining, for they knew their exhausted country was doing all it could for them.

At my headquarters on that Christmas day there was unusual merrymaking. Mrs. Gordon, on leaving home four years before, had placed in her little army-trunk a small package of excellent coffee, and had used it only on very special occasions—"to celebrate," as she said, "our victories in the first years, and to sustain us in defeat at the last." When I asked her, on the morning of December 25, 1864, what we could do for a Christmas celebration, she replied, "I can give you some of that coffee which I brought from home." She could scarcely have made an announcement more grateful to a hungry Confederate. Coffee—genuine coffee! The aroma of it filled my official family with epicurean enthusiasm before a cup was passed from the boiling pot. If every man of us was not intoxicated by that indulgence after long and enforced abstinence, the hilarity of the party was misleading.

The left of my line rested on the west bank of Hatcher's Run. A. P. Hill's corps was on the east side, with its right flank upon the same stream. The commanding general directed that I build a fort at the left of my line, and that A. P. Hill construct a similar one near it on the opposite side of the run. General Hill became ill after the order was received, and the construction of his fort was not pressed. Indeed, the weather was so severe and the roads so nearly impassable that there was no urgent necessity for haste. General Lee, however, who habitually interested himself in the smaller as well as the larger matters connected with his army, did not forget these forts. Riding up to my headquarters on a cold morning in January, 1865, he requested me to ride with him to see the forts. As I mounted he said: "We will go by General ——'s quarters and ask him to accompany us, and we will examine both forts." When this officer joined us (he was temporarily in command of Hill's corps during the latter's absence on sick-leave), General Lee at once asked: "General Gordon, how are you getting along with your fort?"

"Very well, sir. It is nearly finished."

Turning to the other officer, he asked: "Well, General ——, how is the work upon your fort progressing?"

This officer, who had felt no special responsibility for the fort, as he was only temporarily in charge, was considerably embarrassed by the general's pointed inquiry. He really had little or no knowledge of the amount of work done upon it, but ventured, after some hesitation, the reply: "I think the fort on my side of the run is also about finished, sir."

Passing by my work after a short halt, we rode to the point at which the A. P. Hill fort was to be located. No fort was there; the work was scarcely begun. General Lee reined up his horse, and looking first at the place where the fort was to be, and then at the officer, he said: "General, you say the fort is about finished?"

"I must have misunderstood my engineers, sir."

"But you did not speak of your engineers. You spoke of the fort as nearly completed."

This officer was riding a superb animal which General Lee knew had been presented to his wife. His extreme embarrassment made him unusually nervous, and his agitation was imparted to the high-mettled animal, which became restless and was not easily controlled. General Lee in the blandest manner asked: "General, does n't Mrs. —— ride that horse occasionally?"

"Yes, sir," he replied.

"Well, general, you know that I am very much interested in Mrs. ——'s safety. I fear that horse is too nervous for her to ride without danger, and I suggest that, in order to make him more quiet, you ride him at least once every day to this fort."

This was his only reprimand; but no amount of severity on the part of the commander-in-chief could have been more trying to the sensibilities of the officer, who was an admirable soldier, commanding General Lee's entire confidence. The officer's mortification was so overwhelming that, on our return, he rode considerably in the rear. General Lee observed this, and could not resist the impulse to mitigate, as far as possible, the pang caused by the rebuke that he had felt compelled to administer. Halting his horse for a moment and looking back at the officer in the rear, he called to him: "Ride up and join us, general. I want to ask you and General Gordon how long this war is to last." As we rode three abreast, he continued: "I am led to ask this question because it has been propounded to me. I received a letter this morning from my brother, Captain Lee of the Confederate navy"—and he stressed with peculiar emphasis the words "Confederate navy." We had no navy except our marvellously destructive ironclads and some wild rovers of the sea. He continued: "You know these sailors are great people for signs, and my brother says that the signs are conflicting: that the girls are all getting married, and that is a sure sign of war; but nearly all of the babies are girls, and that is a sign of peace. I want you gentlemen to tell me what reply I shall make to Captain Lee of the Confederate navy." I do not recall our answer; but the fort was speedily built.

The condition of our army was daily becoming more desperate. Starvation, literal starvation, was doing its deadly work. So depleted and poisoned was the blood of many of Lee's men from insufficient and unsound food that a slight wound which would probably not have been reported at the beginning of the war would often cause blood-poison, gangrene, and death. Yet the spirits of these brave men seemed to rise as their condition grew more desperate. The grim humor of the camp was waging incessant warfare against despondency. They would not permit one another to be disheartened at any trial, or to complain at the burden or the chafing of any yoke which duty imposed. It was a harrowing but not uncommon sight to see those hungry men gather the wasted corn from under the feet of half-fed horses, and wash and parch and eat it to satisfy in some measure their craving for food. It was marvellous that their spirits were not crushed, and still more marvellous that they would extract fun from every phase of destitution. If one was made sick at night by his supper of parched corn, his salutation the next morning would be: "Hello, general; I am all right this morning. I ate a lot of corn last night, and if you will have the commissary issue me a good mess of hay for my breakfast, I'll be ready for the next fight."

Another would advise his hungry companion to spend his month's pay of Confederate money for a bottle of strong astringent and draw in his stomach to the size of his ration.

It was during this doleful period that the suggestion to give freedom to Southern slaves and arm them for Southern defence became the pressing, vital problem at Richmond. It had been seriously considered for a long period by the civil authorities, and the opinions of certain officers in the field were at this time formally solicited. General Lee strongly favored it, and so did many members of Congress; but the bill as finally passed was absurdly deficient in the most important provisions. It did not make plain the fact that the slave's enlistment would at once secure his freedom. Public sentiment was widely divided as to the policy of such a step. In its favor was the stern fact, universally recognized, that it was no longer possible to fill our ranks except by converting slaves into soldiers; while the great Government at Washington could enlist men not only from the populous States of the Union, but from the teeming populations of foreign countries.

Again, it was argued in favor of the proposition that the loyalty and proven devotion of the Southern negroes to their owners would make them serviceable and reliable as fighters, while their inherited habits of obedience would make it easy to drill and discipline them. The fidelity of the race during the past years of the war, their refusal to strike for their freedom in any organized movement that would involve the peace and safety of the communities where they largely outnumbered the whites, and the innumerable instances of individual devotion to masters and their families, which have never been equalled in any servile race, were all considered as arguments for the enlistment of slaves as Confederate soldiers. Indeed, many of them who were with the army as body-servants repeatedly risked their lives in following their young masters and bringing them off the battle-field when wounded or dead. These faithful servants at that time boasted of being Confederates, and many of them meet now with the veterans in their reunions, and, pointing to their Confederate badges, relate with great satisfaction and pride their experiences and services during the war. One of them, who attends nearly all the reunions, can, after a lapse of nearly forty years, repeat from memory the roll-call of the company to which his master belonged. General Lee used to tell with decided relish of the old negro (a cook of one of his officers) who called to see him at his headquarters. He was shown into the general's presence, and, pulling off his hat, he said, "General Lee, I been wanting to see you a long time. I'm a soldier."

"Ah? To what army do you belong—to the Union army or to the Southern army?"

"Oh, general, I belong to your army."

"Well, have you been shot?"

"No, sir; I ain't been shot yet."

"How is that? Nearly all of our men get shot."

"Why, general, I ain't been shot 'cause I stays back whar de generals stay."

Against the enlistment of negroes were urged the facts that they were needed—were absolutely essential—on the plantations to produce supplies for the armies and the people; that even with their labor the country was exhausted, and without it neither the armies nor the people at home could survive; that the sentiment of the army itself was not prepared for it, and that our condition was too critical for radical experiments.

The meeting of the Southern commissioners—Mr. Stephens, Mr. Hunter, and Judge Campbell, with Mr. Lincoln, at Hampton Roads—had brought the warring sections no nearer to peace. All things seemed now prophetic of the Confederacy's certain and speedy death. And yet I must record in this connection a truth of which I had constant evidence—that our great commander, in the midst of all these depressing and overwhelming trials, never lost for an hour his faith in the devotion and unconquerable spirit of his army. And grandly did that army vindicate the justice of his confidence. Although the thought of speedy surrender or ultimate failure must have occurred to officers and men, it did not find expression even in the most confidential interviews. At least, not the remotest suggestion of such possibility reached my ears from any source. An intense loyalty to the cause seemed to imbue every man with the conviction that nothing should be done or said which could discourage his comrades or in any degree impair their wonderful enthusiasm. The orders were necessarily stringent as to granting furloughs, but desertions were astonishingly rare, although there were no restrictions upon correspondence, and the mails were loaded with letters telling the soldiers of the sufferings of those at home whom they loved and who needed their support and care. No one, however gifted with the power of vigorous statement, could do justice to the manhood displayed under such conditions. The commander appreciated this exhibition of patience and endurance, and never lost an opportunity to let his men know it.

In addition to the inspiration of devotion to him, every man of them was supported by that extraordinary consecration resulting from the conviction that he was fighting in defence of home and the rights of his State. Hence their unfaltering faith in the justice of the cause, their fortitude in extremest privations, their readiness to stand shoeless and shivering in the trenches at night, and to face any danger at their leader's call, while their astounding cheerfulness and never-failing humor were gilding with an ineffable radiance the darkness gathering around them in these last days.

The months of December, January, and February had passed, and only March was to intervene before the last desperate struggle of the two armies would be inaugurated. Intelligent scouts kept us advised of the immense preparations progressing in the Union lines for assaults upon our breastworks at an early date.

During the first week in March, 1865, General Lee sent a messenger, about two o'clock in the morning, to summon me to his headquarters. It was one of the bitterest nights of that trying winter, and it required a ride of several miles to reach the house on the outskirts of Petersburg where the commanding-general made his headquarters. As I entered, General Lee, who was entirely alone, was standing at the fireplace, his arm on the mantel and his head resting on his arm as he gazed into the coal fire burning in the grate. He had evidently been up all the previous part of the night. For the first time in all my intercourse with him, I saw a look of painful depression on his face. Of course he had experienced many hours of depression, but he had concealed from those around him all evidence of discouragement. He had carried the burden in his own soul—wrapping his doubts and apprehensions in an exterior of cheerfulness and apparent confidence. The hour had come, however, when he could no longer carry alone the burden, or entirely conceal his forebodings of impending disaster. General Longstreet and General Ewell were both twenty miles away on their lines in front of Richmond; A. P. Hill, who for weeks had been in delicate health, was absent on furlough; and I found myself alone with the evidently depressed commander. To me he had the appearance of one suffering from physical illness. In answer to my inquiry as to his health, he stated that he was well enough bodily, and had sent for me in order to counsel with me as to our prospects, etc. In his room was a long table covered with recent reports from every portion of his army. Some of these reports had just reached him. He motioned me to a chair on one side of the table, and seated himself opposite me. I had known before I came that our army was in desperate straits; but when I entered that room I realized at once, from the gravity of the commander's bearing, that I was to learn of a situation worse than I had anticipated. The interview was a long one, intensely absorbing, and in many respects harrowing. It led, as will be seen, to the last desperate assault upon Grant's lines at Petersburg which was made by my troops. The interview also produced in me a keen sense of responsibility; for I was then less than thirty-three years of age, much the youngest corps-commander in Lee's army, and I expected to be called upon to express opinions upon matters involving the fate of the army and of the Southern people.

I shall not attempt to quote General Lee literally, except where his words were so engraved on my mind that

I cannot forget them while I remember anything. He opened the conference by directing me to read the reports from the different commands as he should hand them to me, and to carefully note every important fact contained in them.

The revelation was startling. Each report was bad enough, and all the distressing facts combined were sufficient, it seemed to me, to destroy all cohesive power and lead to the inevitable disintegration of any other army that was ever marshalled. Of the great disparity of numbers between the two hostile forces I was already apprised. I had also learned much of the general suffering among the troops; but the condition of my own command, due to the special efforts of which I have spoken, was not a fair measure of the suffering in the army. I was not prepared for the picture presented by these reports of extreme destitution—of the lack of shoes, of hats, of overcoats, and of blankets, as well as of food. Some of the officers had gone outside the formal official statement as to numbers of the sick, to tell in plain, terse, and forceful words of depleted strength, emaciation, and decreased power of endurance among those who appeared on the rolls as fit for duty. Cases were given, and not a few, where good men, faithful, tried, and devoted, gave evidence of temporary insanity and indifference to orders or to the consequences of disobedience—the natural and inevitable effect of their mental and bodily sufferings. My recollection is that General Lee stated that, since the reports from A. P. Hill's corps had been sent in, he had learned that those men had just been rationed on one sixth of a pound of beef, whereas the army ration was a pound of beef per man per day, with the addition of other supplies; that is to say, 600 of A. P. Hill's men were compelled to subsist on less food than was issued to 100 men in General Grant's army.

When I had finished the inspection of this array of serious facts, and contemplated the bewildering woe which they presented, General Lee began his own analysis of the situation. He first considered the relative strength of his army and that of General Grant. The exact number of his own men was given in the reports before him—about 50,000, or 35,000 fit for duty. Against them he estimated that General Grant had in front of Richmond and Petersburg, or within his reach, about 150,000. Coming up from Knoxville was Thomas with an estimated force of 30,000 superb troops, to whose progress General Lee said we could offer practically no resistance—only a very small force of poorly equipped cavalry and detached bodies of infantry being available for that purpose.

"From the Valley," he said, "General Grant can and will bring upon us nearly 20,000, against whom I can oppose scarcely a vedette." This made an army of 200,000 well-fed, well-equipped men which General Grant could soon concentrate upon our force of 50,000, whose efficiency was greatly impaired by suffering. Sherman was approaching from North Carolina, and his force, when united with Schofield's, would reach 80,000. What force had we to confront that army? General Beauregard had telegraphed a few days before that, with the aid of Governor Vance's Home Guards, he could muster probably 20,000 to 25,000. But General Joseph E. Johnston had just sent a despatch saying in substance that General Beauregard had overestimated his strength, and that it would be nearer the truth to place the available Confederate force at from 13,000 to 15,000. So that the final summing up gave Grant the available crushing power of 280,000 men, while to resist this overwhelming force Lee had in round numbers only 65,000.

This estimate ended, the commander rose, and with one hand resting upon the depressing reports, he stood contemplating them for a moment, and then gravely walked to and fro across the room, leaving me to my thoughts. My emotions were stirred to their depths; and as I now recall him standing at the table at four o'clock on that March morning, silently contemplating those reports,—the irrefutable demonstration of his inability to satisfy the longings of the Southern people for independence,—it seems to me that no commander could ever have felt a greater burden than did Robert E. Lee at that hour.

My sense of responsibility reached its climax when he again took his seat facing me at the table, and asked me to state frankly what I thought under those conditions it was best to do—or what duty to the army and our people required of us. Looking at me intently, he awaited my answer. I had opinions, and by this time they were fixed; but I hesitated to express them, not only because of the tremendous importance of the question he had propounded, but because I was uncertain of General Lee's views, and it is never agreeable to a junior officer to maintain opinions in conflict with those of the commander-in-chief, especially a commander whom he regards, as I did Lee, as almost infallible in such a crisis. But I replied:

"General, it seems to me there are but three courses, and I name them in the order in which I think they should be tried:

" First, make terms with the enemy, the best we can get.

" Second, if that is not practicable, the best thing to do is to retreat—abandon Richmond and Petersburg, unite by rapid marches with General Johnston in North Carolina, and strike Sherman before Grant can join him; or,

" Lastly, we must fight, and without delay."

Then again there was a period of silence, lasting, it is true, but a few moments; but they were moments of extreme anxiety to me. The question which he then asked only intensified my anxiety. "Is that your opinion?"

It may have been due to the tension of my nerves, but I thought there was a slight coloring of satire in his words and manner; and this wounded and nettled me. I mildly resented it by reminding him that I was there at his bidding, that I had answered his question thoughtfully and frankly, that no man was more concerned than I for the safety of the army and the welfare of our people, and that I felt, under the circumstances, that I also had the right to ask *his* opinion. I then discovered that General Lee's manner was a method of testing the strength of my convictions; for he replied in the kindest and most reassuring manner:

"Certainly, general, you have the right to ask my opinion. I agree with you fully."

I then asked him if he had made his views known to President Davis or to the Congress. He replied that he had not; that he scarcely felt authorized to suggest to the civil authorities the advisability of making terms with the Government of the United States. He said that he was a soldier, that it was his province to obey the orders of the Government, and to advise or counsel with the civil authorities only upon questions directly affecting his army and its defence of the capital and the country.

These remarks applied to the first course that had been suggested. He then came to the second, namely, the retreat and the uniting of his forces with those of Johnston in North Carolina. He said that while he felt sure that this was the next best thing to do, it would be attended with the gravest difficulties; that, in the first place, he doubted whether the authorities in Richmond would consent to the movement, and, in the next place, it would probably be still more difficult to get General Grant's consent; but that if both President Davis and

General Grant should notify him that he could go, there would still be in his way the deplorable plight of his army. He dwelt at length upon it. Among other things, he mentioned the fact that, in addition to the starving condition of his men, his horses were dying from starvation, and that he could not move one half of his artillery and ammunition and supply trains. He added that the cavalry horses were in horrid condition, and that he could not supply their places, as the country was exhausted; that when a cavalry horse died or was shot, it was equivalent to the loss of both horse and rider, so far as that arm of the service was concerned; whereas General Grant could mount ten thousand additional horsemen in a few days if he wished to do so, and could retard our retreat, vex our flanks, and cut off our supplies.

General Lee, like his private soldiers, had a vein of humor in him which was rarely exhibited except when it served some good purpose. It often appeared when least expected, but was always most opportune. While speaking of the vast superiority of Grant's numbers and resources and his own rapidly accumulating embarrassments, he relaxed the tension for a moment by saying:

" By the way, I received a verbal message from General Grant to-day."

" What was it ? " I asked.

He explained that General Grant had sent, under flag of truce, a request to cease firing long enough for him to bury his dead between the picket-lines. The officer who bore the flag of truce asked to be conducted to army headquarters, as he had a message to deliver to General Lee in person. Arriving at headquarters, he received General Lee's courteous salutations, and, having explained the nature of his mission, said: " General, as I left General Grant's tent this morning he gave me these instructions: ' Give General Lee my personal compliments, and say to him that I keep in such close touch with him that I know what he eats for breakfast every morning.'" I asked General Lee what reply he made. He said: "I told the officer to tell General Grant that I thought there must be some mistake about the latter part of his message; for unless he [General Grant] had fallen from grace since I saw him last, he would not permit me to eat such breakfasts as mine without dividing his with me." He then added: "I also requested the officer to present my compliments to General Grant, and say to him that I knew perhaps as much about his dinners as he knew about my breakfasts."

This, of course, meant that each of the commanders, through scouts and spies, and through such statements as they could extract from prisoners or deserters, kept fairly well posted as to what was transpiring in the opponent's camp.

This little diversion ended, the commander returned to the discussion of the three courses which the serious situation presented. Without an explicit expression to that effect, the entire trend of his words led me to the conclusion that he thought immediate steps should be taken to secure peace, and I ventured to suggest that it was not only legitimate for him to see President Davis on the subject, but that the Southern people had placed their hopes largely in their commanding general. With characteristic modesty, he thought that the people expected of him only the best services he could give them at the head of the army. As nearly as I can recall my words, I said to him at this point: " General, if the newspapers correctly represent the thought and sentiment of the people, there can be no doubt that they are looking to you for deliverance more than to President Davis or the Congress, or both combined; and it seems to me that your responsibility is such as to entitle you to the aid of the civil authorities in finding the shortest way, consistent with honor, out of our troubles." I urged, with as much earnestness as my position would permit, the probability of securing more favorable terms while our army was still organized and resisting than would be accorded us after that army was scattered or captured. His long training as a soldier and his extreme delicacy were still in his way — a barrier against even apparent interference in any department not his own and against any step not in accord with the strictest military and official ethics. He said as much, but then added: "I will go, and will send for you again on my return from Richmond."

It was near sunrise when I left him and rode back to my quarters. Although he had not slept during the night, he took the first train to Richmond, and spent two days, I believe, in conferences over the tremendous issue. Promptly on his return he again summoned me. He proceeded at once to state, concisely and clearly, the result of his interviews. He said nothing could be done at Richmond. The Congress did not seem to appreciate the situation. Of President Davis he spoke in terms of strong eulogy: of the strength of his convictions, of his devotedness, of his remarkable faith in the possibility of still winning our independence, and of his unconquerable will power. The nearest approach to complaint or criticism were the words which I can never forget: "You know that the President is very pertinacious in opinion and purpose." President Davis did not believe we could secure such terms as we could afford to accept, and was indisposed to make further effort after the failure of the Hampton Roads conference. Neither were the authorities ready to evacuate the capital and abandon our lines of defence, although every railroad except the South Side was already broken.

Paganini, the unrivalled violinist of Genoa, in one of

his great exhibitions is said to have had the strings of his violin break, one after another, until he had but one left. Undismayed by these serious mishaps, and pointing to his dismantled instrument, he proudly exclaimed to the audience that he still had left, "*One string and Paganini!*" Jefferson Davis, holding to the Confederate capital, notwithstanding every line of railroad except one had been broken by the enemy, was yet confident, and felt in his heart that he still had enough left in the "one string and Lee's army."

Having heard the commander's report of his interviews in Richmond, I asked:

"What, then, is to be done, general?"

He replied that there seemed to be but one thing that we could do — fight. To stand still was death. It could only be death if we fought and failed.

This was the prelude to my assault upon Fort Stedman on March 25, 1865 — the last Confederate attack on Grant's lines at Petersburg.

CHAPTER XXVII

CAPTURE OF FORT STEDMAN

In the trenches at Petersburg—General Lee's instructions—A daring plan formed—Preparations for a night assault—An ingenious war ruse—The fort captured with small loss—Failure of reënforcements to arrive—Loss of guides—Necessary withdrawal from the fort—The last effort to break Grant's hold.

LIKE fires that consume the dross and make pure the metal, Confederate distress and extremity seemed to strengthen and ennoble rather than weaken Confederate manhood. My hungry and debilitated men welcomed with a readiness intensely pathetic the order to break camp and move into the trenches at Petersburg. Their buoyancy of spirit was in no degree due to a lack of appreciation of the meaning of that night march. They were not mere machine soldiers, moved by a superior intelligence to which they blindly yielded obedience. They were thoughtful men, with naturally keen perceptions sharpened by long experience in actual war. They well knew that the order meant more suffering, more fighting, more slaughter; yet, if their conduct and assurances are trustworthy witnesses, these men were prepared for any additional sacrifices. There was no shouting or yelling; but silently, quickly, and cheerfully they folded their little sheet tents, packed their frying-pans and tin cups, and were promptly in line, with their knapsacks on their backs, their lean and empty haversacks on one side and

395

full cartridge-boxes on the other, ready for the rapid night march to Petersburg, where every bloody ditch and frowning fort was to them a herald of another deadly conflict.

As I now look back to that scene of busy preparation by the dim light of the camp-fires, and recall the fact that not only the officers but the intelligent privates in the ranks knew that this hasty preparation was the prelude to perhaps the last desperate effort of Lee's little army to break Grant's grip on the Confederate capital, the question presses itself upon me: How can we account for such self-command and steadfast fidelity in the presence of apparently inevitable and overwhelming disaster? An English nobleman, while placing his head upon the block, is said to have indulged in jest at the executioner's axe; but there was no such vainglory in the wonderful serenity of these thoughtful men. To one who has experienced it, there is no difficulty in understanding what the Romans called the glory of battle; but that stimulant was entirely wanting in this case. It is easy enough to explain the mental intoxication of the young Earl of Essex, who, as he sailed in to a naval fight, threw his hat into the sea in a transport of martial ecstasy. This boundless joy of Essex was the presentiment of a coming triumph, and is no more mysterious than the instinct of the eagle bending to catch the roar of the rising tempest, conscious that its wildest blasts will bear him to higher and prouder flights. It is easy enough to comprehend the enthusiasm of these same Confederates during the long period when recurring battles meant recurring victories. Now, however, in the last days of the Confederacy, and especially during the dreary winter of 1864–65, these conditions were all changed. Practically every available man in the South was already at the front, and the inability to secure an exchange of prisoners made it impossible to fill the thinning ranks of our armies.   The supplies were exhausted, and it was impracticable to give the men sufficient food. Everything was exhausted except devotion and valor. The very air we breathed was changed.   There was no longer in it the exhilaration of victory with which it had been so constantly surcharged in past years.   Yet in the light of their camp-fires I could see in the faces of these men an expression of manly resolve almost equal to that which they had worn in the days of their brightest hopes. It is impossible to explain this unswerving purpose to fight to the last, except upon this one hypothesis.   They felt that their struggle was a defence of State, of home, and of liberty; and for these they were ready to die. The world's most consecrated martyrs can lay no higher claim to immortality.

General Lee's instructions to me were substantially as follows: "Move your troops into the works around the city as I withdraw one of the other commands from them. Make your headquarters in the city.   Study General Grant's works at all points, consider carefully all plans and possibilities, and then tell me what you can do, if anything, to help us in our dilemma."

The very narrow space between Lee's and Grant's lines, the vigilance of the pickets who stood within speaking range of each other, and the heavily loaded guns which commanded every foot of intrenchments, made the removal of one body of troops and the installing of another impracticable by daylight and quite hazardous even at night.   We moved, however, cautiously through the city to the breastworks, and, as the other corps was secretly withdrawn, my command glided into the vacated trenches as softly and noiselessly as the smooth flow of a river.

More than a month prior to this change, General Lee wrote to the authorities at Richmond, after these men had stood in line for three days and nights in extremely cold weather: "Some of the men have been without meat for three days, and all of them are suffering from reduced rations and scant clothing while exposed to battle, cold, hail, and sleet." He also stated that the chief commissary reported that he had not a pound of meat at his disposal. General Lee added: "The physical strength of the men, if their courage survives, must fail under this treatment." These were the men with whom I was soon to make a most daring assault, and these the conditions under which it must be made.

The breastworks behind which stood the brave army in blue appeared to be as impenetrable by any force which Lee could send against them as is a modern iron-clad to the missiles from an ordinary field battery: but if there was a weak point in those defences, I was expected to find it. If such a point could be found, I was expected to submit to General Lee some plan by which it would be feasible, or at least possible, for his depleted army to assail it successfully.

Giving but few hours in the twenty-four to rest and sleep, I labored day and night at this exceedingly grave and discouraging problem, on the proper solution of which depended the commander's decision as to when and where he would deliver his last blow for the life of the Confederacy. My efficient staff — Majors Moore, Hunter, Dabney, and Pace, and Captains Markoe, Wilmer, and Jones—were constantly engaged gathering information from every possible source. The prisoners captured were closely questioned, and their answers noted and weighed. Deserters from the Federal army added valuable material to the information I was acquiring.

The fact that there were desertions from the Union to the Confederate army at this late period of the war is difficult to understand. Indeed, such desertions were among those mysterious occurrences which are inexplicable on any ordinary hypothesis. It was to be expected

that some of the newly enlisted Confederates, some of
those reluctant recruits who were induced to join our
ranks under the persuasive influence of the Confederate
Conscript Law, should abandon us in our extremity;
but when all the conditions pointed to certain and speedy
Union success, where can we find impelling motives
strong enough to induce General Grant's men to desert
his overwhelming forces and seek shelter with the
maimed and starving Confederate army? The bravest
and most loyal sailors will abandon a sinking battle-ship
and accept safety on the deck of the triumphant vessel
of the enemy. In the case of General Grant's men, however, this natural impulse seemed to be reversed. They
were not leaving a disabled ship. They were deserting
a mighty and increasing fleet for a place on the deck of
an isolated and badly crippled man-of-war—one that
was fighting grandly, it is true, but fighting single-handed,
almost hopelessly, with its ammunition and supplies
nearly exhausted, its engines disabled, and its hull heavily
leaking.

It required a week of laborious examination and intense thought to enable me to reach any definite conclusion. Every rod of the Federal intrenchments, every
fort and parapet on the opposing line of breastworks
and on the commanding hills in rear of them, every
sunken path of the pickets and every supporting division
of infantry behind the works, had to be noted and carefully scrutinized. The character of the obstructions in
front of each portion of the Union works had to be crit-
ically examined and an estimate made as to the time it
would require to cut them away so that my men could
mount the breastworks or rush into the fort selected for
our attack. The distance between the opposing works
and the number of seconds or minutes it would require
for my troops to rush across were important factors in
estimating the chances of success or failure, and required

the closest calculation. The decision as to the most vulnerable point for attack involved two additional questions of vital importance. The first was: From what point on my own intrenchments could my assaulting column rush forth on its desperate night sally, with the least probability of arousing the sleeping foe? The second was: How many intervening ditches were there, and of what width and depth, over which my men were to leap or into which they might fall in the perilous passage? All these points considered, I decided that Fort Stedman on Grant's lines was the most inviting point for attack and Colquitt's Salient on Lee's lines the proper place from which to sally. This point in our lines took its name from my lifelong friend, General Alfred Holt Colquitt of Georgia, whose memory will live in Southern hearts, as fresh and green as the fadeless verdure of the pines which now grow upon the salient's embankment, striking their roots deep into the earth which was reddened by the blood of his stalwart Georgians. These men stood and fought and suffered there, commanded by this superb officer, who won by his brilliant victory in Florida the proud title, "Hero of Olustee." General Colquitt lived long after the war closed, giving conservative counsel to his people, recognized as the friend of both races, and serving with distinction as governor of his State and as United States senator. He died at his post of duty in Washington in 1893.

The plan of the attack on Fort Stedman was fully developed in my own mind; and whether it was good or bad, the responsibility for it was upon me, not because there was any indisposition on General Lee's part to make a plan of his own and order its execution, but because he had called me from the extreme right to his centre at Petersburg for this purpose. With him was the final decision—approval or rejection.

As soon as he was notified that I was ready to report, he summoned me to his quarters. After such a lapse of time I cannot give General Lee's exact words in so prolonged a conference, but the following questions and answers faithfully represent the substance of the interview.

"What can you do?" he asked.

"I can take Fort Stedman, sir."

"How, and from what point?"

"By a night assault from Colquitt's Salient, and a sudden, quick rush across ditches, where the enemy's pickets are on watch, running over the pickets and capturing them, or, if they resist, using the bayonet."

"But the chevaux-de-frise protecting your front is, I believe, fastened together at Colquitt's Salient with chains and spikes. This obstruction will have to be removed before your column of attack can pass out of our works. Do you think you can remove these obstructions without attracting the attention of Union pickets which are only a few rods away? You are aware that they are especially vigilant at night, and that any unusual noise on your lines would cause them to give the alarm, arousing their men in the fort, who would quickly turn loose upon you their heavy guns loaded with grape and canister."

"This is a serious difficulty; but I feel confident that it can be overcome. I propose to intrust the delicate task of getting our obstructions removed to a few select men, who will begin the work after dark, and, with the least possible noise, make a passageway for my troops by 4 A.M., at which hour the sally is to be made."

"But suppose you succeed in removing the obstructions in front of your own lines without attracting the attention of General Grant's pickets and get your column under full headway and succeed in capturing or killing the pickets before they can give the alarm; you will have a still more serious difficulty to overcome when you reach the strong and closely built obstructions in front of Fort Stedman and along the enemy's works. Have you ascertained how these obstructions are made and thought of any way to get over them or through them? You know that a delay of even a few minutes would insure a consuming fire upon your men, who, while halting, would be immediately in front of the heavy guns in the fort."

"I recognize fully, general, the force of all you say; but let me explain. Through prisoners and deserters I have learned during the past week all about the obstructions in front of General Grant's lines. They are exceedingly formidable. They are made of rails, with the lower ends deeply buried in the ground. The upper ends are sharpened and rest upon poles, to which they are fastened by strong wires. These sharp points are about breast-high, and my men could not possibly get over them. They are about six or eight inches apart; and we could not get through them. They are so securely fastened together and to the horizontal poles by the telegraph wires that we could not possibly shove them apart so as to pass them. There is but one thing to do. They must be chopped to pieces by heavy, quick blows with sharp axes. I propose to select fifty brave and especially robust and active men, who will be armed only with axes. These axemen will rush across, closely followed by my troops, and will slash down a passage for my men almost at a single blow. This stalwart force will rush into the fort with the head of my column, and, if necessary, use their axes instead of bayonets in any hand-to-hand conflict inside the fort. I think I can promise you, general, that we will go into that fort; but what we are going to do when we get in is the most serious problem of all."

At this point General Lee discussed and carefully

considered every phase of the hazardous programme. He expressed neither approval nor disapproval ; but he directed me to explain fully the further details of the plan on the supposition that by possibility we could take Fort Stedman and the lines on each side of it.

The purpose of the movement was not simply the capture of Fort Stedman and the breastworks flanking it. The prisoners and guns we might thus capture would not justify the peril of the undertaking. The tremendous possibility was the disintegration of the whole left wing of the Federal army, or at least the dealing of such a staggering blow upon it as would disable it temporarily, enabling us to withdraw from Petersburg in safety and join Johnston in North Carolina. The capture of the fort was only the breasting of the first wave in the ocean of difficulties to be encountered. It was simply the opening of a road through the wilderness of hostile works nearest to us in order that my corps and the additional forces to be sent me could pass toward the rear of Grant's lines and then turn upon his flanks.

General Lee resumed his questions, saying in substance :

" Well, suppose you capture the fort, what are you going to do with the strong line of infantry in the ravine behind the fort and the three other forts in the rear which command Fort Stedman ? Do you think you can carry those three forts by assault after General Grant's army has been aroused by your movement ?"

" Those forts, general, cannot be taken by direct assault when fully manned, except at great sacrifice to our troops. In front of them is a network of abatis which makes a direct advance upon them extremely difficult. There is, however, an open space in the rear of them, and if I can reach that space in the darkness with a sufficient number of men to overpower the guards, I can take those three forts also, without heavy loss. I suggest that we attempt their capture by a legitimate stratagem; if that fails, then at dawn to rush with all the troops available toward Grant's left, meeting emergencies as best we can. To accomplish much by such a movement, you would have to send me nearly or quite one half of your army. I greatly prefer to try the stratagem, the success of which depends on a number of contingencies."

He asked me to state fully each step in the programme, and I continued:

"During the week of investigation I have learned the name of every officer of rank in my front. I propose to select three officers from my corps, who are to command each a body of 100 men. These officers are to assume the names of three Union officers who are in and near Fort Stedman. When I have carried Fort Stedman, each of these selected officers is to rush in the darkness to the rear with his 100 men, shouting: 'The Rebels have carried Fort Stedman and our front lines!' They are to maintain no regular order, but each body of 100 is to keep close to its leader. As these three officers strike the line of infantry in rear of the fort and at different points, they will be halted; but each of them will at once represent himself as the Union officer whose name he bears, and is to repeat: 'The Rebels have captured our works, and I am ordered by General McLaughlin to rush back to the fort in rear and hold it at all hazards.'

"Each body of 100 men will thus pass the supporting line of Union infantry and go to the rear of the fort to which I will direct the leader. They are to enter, overpower the Union guards, and take possession of the fort. Thus the three forts will be captured."

General Lee asked if I thought my officers would each be able in the darkness to find the fort which he was seeking. I replied:

"That depends, general, upon my ability to get proper

guides. The trees have been cut down, the houses have been burned, and the whole topography of that portion of the field so changed that it will require men who are thoroughly familiar with the locality to act as guides. I have no such men in my corps; and without proper guides my three detachments will be sacrificed after taking Fort Stedman and passing the rear line of infantry."

Again there was a long discussion of the chances and the serious difficulties in this desperate adventure. These were fully recognized by General Lee, as they had been by myself when the successive steps in the undertaking were formulated in my own mind. He said in substance: "If you think, after careful consideration, that you can probably carry Fort Stedman, and then get your three companies of 100 through the line of supporting infantry, I will endeavor to find among the Virginia volunteers three men whose homes were on that part of the field where the rear forts stand, to act as guides to your three officers. I do not know of such men now, but will at once make search for them."

He directed me to proceed with the selection of my men for the different parts of the programme, but not to notify them until he had made search for the guides and had thought the whole plan over. Twenty-four hours later occurred the final conference before the attack. With the exception of the last council of war on the night before the surrender, I believe this conference on the night of March 23, 1865, was the most serious and impressive in my experience. General Lee had thought of all the chances: he had found three men, whom he did not know in person, but who were recommended for the three guides; he had selected different troops to send me from other corps, making, with mine, nearly one half of his army, and had decided that we should make one supreme effort to break the cordon tightening around us. These troops were to come from Longstreet's and

A. P. Hill's corps. A body of cavalry was to be sent me, which, in case we succeeded in getting into the three rear forts, was to ride across the broken gap at Fort Stedman, and then gallop to the rear, destroy Grant's railroad and telegraph lines, and cut away his pontoons across the river, while the infantry swept down the rear of the Union intrenchments.

With full recognition by both the commander and myself of the hopelessness of our cause if we waited longer on General Grant's advance, and also of the great hazard in moving against him, the tremendous undertaking was ordered.

All night my troops were moving and concentrating behind Colquitt's Salient. For hours Mrs. Gordon sat in her room in Petersburg, tearing strips of white cloth to tie across the breasts of the leading detachments, that they might recognize each other in the darkness and in the hand-to-hand battle expected at the Federal breastworks and inside the fort.

The fifty heavy keen-edged axes were placed in the hands of the fifty brave and stalwart fellows who were to lead the column and hew down Grant's obstructions. The strips of white cloth were tied upon them, and they were ready for the desperate plunge.

The chosen 300, in three companies, under the three officers bearing names of Union officers, were also bedecked with the white cotton Confederate scarfs. To each of these companies was assigned one of the three selected guides. I explained to the 300 men the nature of their duties, and told them that, in addition to the joy it would give them to aid in giving victory to the army, I would see to it, if the three forts were captured, that each of them should have a thirty days' furlough and a silver medal. Although the rear forts were not captured, the failure was not the fault of the 300; and even to this day, nearly forty years afterward, I occasionally receive applications for the medal, accompanied by the statement that I need not trouble myself to get the furlough, as they received that some days later at Appomattox.

The hour for the assault (4 A.M.) arrived. The column of attack was arranged in the following order: the 50 axemen in front, and immediately behind and close to them the selected 300. Next came the different commands of infantry who were to move in compact column close behind the 300, the cavalry being held in reserve until the way for them was cleared.

While my preparations were progressing I received from General Lee the following note, which is here given because it was written with his own hand, and because it expresses the earnest prayer for our success which came from his burdened heart, and which he could not suppress even in this short semi-official communication:

4:30 P.M. Hd Qr (24) March '65.

Genl: I have received yours of 2:30 P.M. and telegraphed for Pickett's Division, but I do not think it will reach here in time. Still we will try. If you need more troops one or both of Heth's brigades can be called to Colquitt's Salient and Wilcox's to the Baxter road. Dispose of the troops as needed. I pray that a merciful God may grant us success and deliver us from our enemies.   Yours truly,

R. E. LEE,

Genl.

Genl. J. B. GORDON, etc.

P. S. The Cavalry is ordered to report to you at Halifax road and Norfolk R.R. Iron Bridge at 3 A.M. tomorrow. W. F. Lee to be in vicinity of Monk's corner Road at 6 A.M.

All things ready, at 4 A.M. I stood on the top of the breastworks, with no one at my side except a single private soldier with rifle in hand, who was to fire the signal shot for the headlong rush. This night charge on the fort was to be across the intervening space covered with ditches, in one of which stood the watchful Federal pickets. There still remained near my works some of the débris of our obstructions, which had not been completely removed and which I feared might retard the rapid exit of my men; and I ordered it cleared away. The noise made by this removal, though slight, attracted the attention of a Union picket who stood on guard only a few rods from me, and he called out:

"What are you doing over there, Johnny? What is that noise? Answer quick or I'll shoot."

The pickets of the two armies were so close together at this point that there was an understanding between them, either expressed or implied, that they would not shoot each other down except when necessary. The call of this Union picket filled me with apprehension. I expected him to fire and start the entire picket-line to firing, thus giving the alarm to the fort, the capture of which depended largely upon the secrecy of my movement. The quick mother-wit of the private soldier at my side came to my relief. In an instant he replied:

"Never mind, Yank. Lie down and go to sleep. We are just gathering a little corn. You know rations are mighty short over here."

There was a narrow strip of corn which the bullets had not shot away still standing between the lines. The Union picket promptly answered: "All right, Johnny; go ahead and get your corn. I'll not shoot at you while you are drawing your rations."

Such soldierly courtesy was constantly illustrated between these generous foes, who stood so close to one another in the hostile lines. The Rev. J. William Jones, D.D., now chaplain-general of the United Confederate Veterans, when standing near this same point had his hat carried away by a gust of wind, and it fell near the

Union lines. The loss of a hat meant the loss to the chaplain of nearly a month's pay. He turned away sorrowfully, not knowing how he could get another. A heroic young private, George Haner of Virginia, said to him: " Chaplain, I will get your hat." Taking a pole in his hand, he crawled along the ditch which led to our picket-line, and began to drag the hat in with his pole. At this moment a Yankee bullet went through the sleeve of his jacket. He at once shouted to the Union picket: "Hello, Yank; quit your foolishness. I am doing no harm. I am just trying to get the chaplain's hat." Immediately the reply came: " All right, Johnny; I 'll not shoot at you any more. But you 'd better hurry up and get it before the next relief comes."

My troops stood in close column, ready for the hazardous rush upon Fort Stedman. While the fraternal dialogue in reference to drawing rations from the cornfield was progressing between the Union picket and the resourceful private at my side, the last of the obstructions in my front were removed, and I ordered the private to fire the signal for the assault. He pointed his rifle upward, with his finger on the trigger, but hesitated. His conscience seemed to get hold of him. He was going into the fearful charge, and he evidently did not feel disposed to go into eternity with the lie on his lips, although it might be a permissible war lie, by which he had thrown the Union picket off his guard. He evidently felt that it was hardly fair to take advantage of the generosity and soldierly sympathy of his foe, who had so magnanimously assured him that he would not be shot while drawing his rations from the little field of corn. His hesitation surprised me, and I again ordered: "Fire your gun, sir." He at once called to his kindhearted foe and said: "Hello, Yank! Wake up; we are going to shell the woods. Look out; we are coming." And with this effort to satisfy his conscience and even up accounts with the Yankee picket, he fired the shot and rushed forward in the darkness.

As the solitary signal shot rang out in the stillness, my alert pickets, who had crept close to the Union sentinels, sprang like sinewy Ajaxes upon them and prevented the discharge of a single alarm shot. Had these faithful Union sentinels been permitted to fire alarm guns, my dense columns, while rushing upon the fort, would have been torn into fragments by the heavy guns. Simultaneously with the seizing and silencing of the Federal sentinels, my stalwart axemen leaped over our breastworks, closely followed by the selected 300 and the packed column of infantry. Although it required but a few minutes to reach the Union works, those minutes were to me like hours of suspense and breathless anxiety; but soon was heard the thud of the heavy axes as my brave fellows slashed down the Federal obstructions. The next moment the infantry sprang upon the Union breastworks and into the fort, overpowering the gunners before their destructive charges could be emptied into the mass of Confederates. They turned this captured artillery upon the flanking lines on each side of the fort, clearing the Union breastworks of their defenders for some distance in both directions. Up to this point, the success had exceeded my most sanguine expectations. We had taken Fort Stedman and a long line of breastworks on either side. We had captured nine heavy cannon, eleven mortars, nearly 1000 prisoners, including General McLaughlin, with the loss of less than half a dozen men. One of these fell upon the works, pierced through the body by a Federal bayonet, one of the few men thus killed in the four years of war. I was in the fort myself, and relieved General McLaughlin by assuming command of Fort Stedman.

From the fort I sent word to General Lee, who was on a hill in the rear, that we were in the works and that the 300 were on their way to the lines in the rear. Soon I received a message from one of these three officers, I believe General Lewis of North Carolina, that he had passed the line of Federal infantry without trouble by representing himself as Colonel —— of the Hundredth Pennsylvania, but that he could not find his fort, as the guide had been lost in the rush upon Stedman. I soon received a similar message from the other two, and so notified General Lee.

Daylight was coming. Through the failure of the three guides, we had failed to occupy the three forts in the rear, and they were now filled with Federals. Our wretched railroad trains had broken down, and the troops who were coming to my aid did not reach me. The full light of the morning revealed the gathering forces of Grant and the great preponderance of his numbers. It was impossible for me to make further headway with my isolated corps, and General Lee directed me to withdraw. This was not easily accomplished. Foiled by the failure of the guides, deprived of the great bodies of infantry which Lee ordered to my support, I had necessarily stretched out my corps to occupy the intrenchments which we had captured. The other troops were expected to arrive and join in the general advance. The breaking down of the trains and the non-arrival of these heavy supports left me to battle alone with Grant's gathering and overwhelming forces, and at the same time to draw in my own lines toward Fort Stedman. A consuming fire on both flanks and front during this withdrawal caused a heavy loss to my command. I myself was wounded, but not seriously, in recrossing the space over which we had charged in the darkness. Among the disabled was the gallant Brigadier-General Philip Cook of Georgia, who after the war represented his people in the United States Congress.

When the retreat to our own works had ended, a

report reached me that an entire Confederate regiment had not received the order to withdraw, and was still standing in the Union breastworks, bravely fighting. It was necessary to send them orders or leave them to their fate. I called my staff around me, and explained the situation and the extreme danger the officer would encounter in carrying that order. I stated to them that the pain I experienced in sending one of them on so perilous a mission was greater than I could express. Every one of them quickly volunteered to go; but Thomas G. Jones of Alabama insisted that as he was the youngest and had no special responsibilities, it should fall to his lot to incur the danger. I bade him good-by with earnest prayers that God would protect him, and without an apparent tremor he rode away. A portion of the trip was through a literal furnace of fire, but he passed through it, both going and returning, without a scratch.

This last supreme effort to break the hold of General Grant upon Petersburg and Richmond was the expiring struggle of the Confederate giant, whose strength was nearly exhausted and whose limbs were heavily shackled by the most onerous conditions. Lee knew, as we all did, that the chances against us were as a hundred is to one; but we remembered how George Washington, with his band of ragged rebels, had won American independence through trials and sufferings and difficulties, and although they were far less discouraging and insurmountable than those around us, they were nevertheless many and great. It seemed better, therefore, to take the one chance, though it might be one in a thousand, rather than to stand still while the little army was being depleted, its vitality lessening with each setting sun, and its life gradually ebbing, while the great army in its front was growing and strengthening day by day. To wait was certain destruction: it could not be worse if we tried and failed. The accidents and mishaps which checked the brilliant assault made by my brave men, and which rendered their further advance impossible, could not have been anticipated. But for those adverse happenings, it would seem that we might have won on that single chance.

This spasm of Confederate aggressive vigor inaugurated the period of more than two weeks of almost incessant battle, beginning on the morning of March 25th with the charge of my troops at Petersburg, and ending with the last charge of Lee's army, made by these same men on the morning of April 9th at Appomattox.

CHAPTER XXVIII

EVACUATION OF PETERSBURG

Religious spirit of the soldiers in extremity—Some amusing anecdotes
—Fall of Five Forks—Death of General A. P. Hill—The line of defence stretched to breaking—General Lee's order to withdraw from
Petersburg—Continuous fighting during the retreat—Stirring adventure of a Confederate scout—His retaliation—Lee directs the
movement toward Appomattox.

PETERSBURG—the Cockade City—was scarcely less
noted than Richmond itself for its high military
spirit, its devotion to the Confederacy, and the extent
of its sacrifices for the Southern cause. There was
scarcely a home within its corporate limits that was
not open to the sick and wounded of Lee's army. Its
patriotic citizens denied themselves all luxuries and
almost actual necessaries in order to feed and strengthen
the hungry fighters in the trenches. Its women, who
were noted for culture and refinement, became nurses,
as consecrated as Florence Nightingale, as they soothed
the sufferings and strengthened the hopes of the dying
soldiers. Now and then, in the experiences of the young
people, the subtle radiance of romance lighted up the
gloom of the hospitals.

A beautiful Southern girl, on her daily mission of
love and mercy, asked a badly wounded soldier boy what
she could do for him. He replied: " I 'm greatly obliged
to you, but it is too late for you to do anything for me.
I am so badly shot that I can't live long."

"Will you not let me pray for you? I hope that I am one of the Lord's daughters, and I would like to ask Him to help you."

Looking intently into her bewitching face, he replied: "Yes, pray at once, and ask the Lord to let me be His son-in-law."

The susceptible young soldier had evidently received, at this interview, another wound, which served to convert his apprehensions of death into a longing for domestic life.

During the two weeks following the sudden seizure of Fort Stedman and its equally sudden release, my legs were rarely out of my long boots. For eight days the shifting scenes and threatening demonstrations on my front, and in front of A. P. Hill on my right, kept me on horseback until my tired limbs and aching joints made a constant appeal for rest. The coming of night brought little or no cessation of the perplexing and fatiguing activities. Night after night troops were marching, heavy guns were roaring, picket-lines were driven in and had to be reëstablished; and the great mortars from both Union and Confederate works were hurling high in the air their ponderous shells, which crossed each other's paths and, with burning fuses, like tails of flying comets, descended in meteoric showers on the opposing intrenchments. The breastworks protecting the battle-lines were so high and broad that the ordinary cannon-balls and shells could not penetrate them and reach the soldiers who stood behind them. In order, therefore, to throw shells into the ranks of the opposing army, these mortars were introduced. They were short, big-mouthed cannon, and were pointed upward, but leaning slightly toward the enemy's lines, and their great shells were hurled skyward, and then came whirling down, exploding with terrific force among the men who stood or slept behind the breastworks.

At a point near where the left of A. P. Hill's corps touched the right of mine, a threatened attack brought together for counsel a number of officers from each of these commands. After this conference as to the proper disposition of troops for resisting the expected assault, we withdrew into a small log hut standing near, and united in prayer to Almighty God for His guidance. As we assembled, one of our generals was riding within hailing distance, and General Harry Heth of Hill's corps stepped to the door of the log cabin and called to him to come in and unite with us in prayer. The officer did not understand the nature of General Heth's invitation, and replied: "No, thank you, general; no more at present; I 've just had some."

This amusing incident, while it convulsed the small assemblage with laughter, did not delay many moments the earnest petitions for deliverance. From the commander-in-chief to the privates in the ranks, there was a deep and sincere religious feeling in Lee's army. Whenever it was convenient or practicable, these hungry but unyielding men were holding prayer-meetings. Their supplications were fervent and often inspiring, but now and then there were irresistibly amusing touches. At one of these gatherings for prayer was a private who had lost one leg. Unable to kneel, he sat with bowed head, while one of his comrades, whom we shall call Brother Jones, led in prayer. Brother Jones was earnestly praying for more manhood, more strength, and more courage. The brave old one-legged Confederate did not like Brother Jones's prayer. At that period of the war, he felt that it was almost absurd to be asking God to give the Confederates more courage, of which virtue they already had an abundant supply. So he called out from his seat: "Hold on there, Brother Jones. Don't you know you are praying all wrong? Why don't you pray for more provisions? We 've got more courage now than we have any use for!"

This did not occur in my immediate camp, but a similar incident did. In a meeting for prayer near my headquarters, there was more than the usual impressiveness — more of that peculiar sadness which is significant of a brave despair. As in all the religious gatherings in the army, all denominations of Christians were represented. The chaplain who conducted the solemn services asked a number of officers and others to lead in prayer. Among them, he called upon a private who belonged to my sharpshooters, and who had not had the advantages of an early education. This consecrated soldier knelt close by my side, and with his heart all aglow with the spirit of the meeting, and his mind filled with strong convictions as to the justice of our cause, he said in a clear, ringing voice: "Oh, Lord, we are having a mighty big fight down here, and a sight of trouble; and we do hope, Lord, that you will take a proper view of this subject, and give us the victory."

As for himself, he had no doubt as to what a "proper view" of the great conflict was. None of them had. While they fully comprehended the situation from an earthly or purely military point of view, they hoped to the last that by some miraculous intervention the "proper view of the subject" would ultimately prevail.

The general-in-chief and his corps commanders were kept fairly well advised by our scouts as to General Grant's preparations and movements; but, independent of this direct intelligence, there were other indications which could not be misunderstood. The roads were wet, and hence no clouds of dust rose above the the tree-tops to tell us during the day of Grant's progress; but at night his camp-fires in the pines painted a light on the horizon near us which admonished us that he was marching around our right to seize the South Side Railroad and force us out of our trenches. Sheridan's large bodies of cavalry, supported by infantry, soon appeared in the neighborhood of Five Forks—a point from which roads led in five directions. It was a strategic point of such importance to Lee, for either the continued defence of Petersburg or the withdrawal of his army, that he determined to hold it until surrender was inevitable. He, therefore, adopted the same bold, aggressive policy which had so repeatedly thwarted the flank movements of his great antagonist on every battle-field from the Wilderness to Petersburg. Withdrawing all the troops that could be spared from the trenches, Lee hurled his depleted but still resolute little army against Grant's heavy lines of infantry on the march to Five Forks, and drove back in confusion that portion of the Federal army; but the small Confederate force there employed was utterly inadequate either to press the temporary advantage or to hold the position it had won. It was quickly swept from the front of the overpowering Federals, and the concentration upon Five Forks was accomplished. The small force of Confederates which defended it fought with characteristic courage. In the first encounter General Sheridan's forces were repelled from the breastworks. But soon the devoted little band of gray was torn by artillery, harried by cavalry, and assaulted by infantry on every side; and the Confederate flags went down, while their brave defenders were surrounded by a cordon of fire. Five Forks fell, with the loss of large numbers of Confederates in killed, wounded, and prisoners. Turning from Five Forks in the direction of Petersburg, the victorious Federals came upon the flank and rear of the defensive works around the city. Longstreet's corps had been ordered from the lines around Richmond, but came too late to prevent the disaster at Five Forks. It was not too late, however, to check the flanking force of Federals marching upon the city from that direction. A part of A. P. Hill's corps was formed at right angles to the trenches and shared in the furious fighting. That brilliant corps-commander and devoted patriot, whose name was the synonym of chivalry, gave his life to the cause he loved in these last dark hours of the expiring Confederacy.

As General Lee rode back toward Petersburg from Five Forks, near which he had led in person a brilliant and successful charge, he said to one of his aides: "This is a sad business, colonel." In a few minutes he added: "It has happened as I told them in Richmond it would happen. The line has been stretched until it is broken." On this melancholy ride the shattered and ragged remnants of his army, still proud, hopeful, and defiant, saluted him at every point with shouts of welcome, indicating their undiminished admiration and confidence.

This was the first day of April. Not one day of rest had been given these starving men to recover from the winter's trials and sufferings, which have been so truthfully described by the graphic pen of Dr. Henry Alexander White:

Winter poured down its snows and its sleets upon Lee's shelterless men in the trenches. Some of them burrowed into the earth. Most of them shivered over the feeble fires, kept burning along the lines. Scanty and thin were the garments of these heroes. Most of them were clad in mere rags. Gaunt famine oppressed them every hour. One quarter of a pound of rancid bacon and a little meal was the daily portion assigned to each man by the rules of the War Department. But even this allowance failed when the railroads broke down and left the bacon and the flour and the meal piled up beside the tracks in Georgia and the Carolinas. One sixth of this daily ration was the allotment for a considerable time, and very often the supply of bacon failed entirely. . . . With dauntless hearts these gaunt-faced men endured the almost ceaseless fire of Grant's mortar-batteries. The frozen fingers of Lee's army of sharpshooters clutched the musket barrel with an aim so steady that Grant's men scarcely ever lifted their heads from their bomb-proofs.

These men—less than 40,000 in number—had held for many months a battle-line forty miles long, stretching from the Chickahominy to Hatcher's Run. My own corps was stretched until the men stood like a row of vedettes, fifteen feet apart, in the trenches. Portions of my line—it was not a line; it was the mere skeleton of a line—had been broken by assaults at daybreak on April 2. There were no troops—not a man—in reserve to help us; but no extremity appalled my grim and gaunt-visaged fighters. At the command they assembled at double quick in more compact lines around those points which had been seized and were still held by the Federals, densely packed in the captured intrenchments. By desperate charges, one after another of these breaches in my line was restored, until but one remained in possession of the enemy. I was in the act of concentrating for a supreme effort to restore this last breach, when Colonel Charles Marshall of General Lee's staff reached me with a message from the commander-in-chief. It was to admonish me of the dire disaster at Five Forks on the extreme right flank of our army, of the approach of the triumphant and overwhelming Union forces in rear of our defences, of the forced abandonment by A. P. Hill of his works, and of the death of that superb officer. In the face of this almost complete crushing of every command defending the entire length of our lines on my right, the restoration of the remaining breach in my front could contribute nothing toward the rescue of Lee's army. He, therefore, directed that I sacrifice no more men in the effort to recover entire control of my works, but that I maintain my compact line around this last breach, prevent, if possible, Grant's effort to send through it his forces into the city, and at any sacrifice hold my position until night, and until all the other commands could be withdrawn. When this withdrawal had been accomplished, my command was to silently evacuate

Petersburg, and cover the retreat of Lee's brave but shattered little army.

The indomitable spirit of my men was never more strikingly shown than in their cheerful response to this command.   I feel constrained at this point to place upon record the fact that these were the same men who scarcely one week before had made the daring plunge in the darkness which resulted in the capture of Fort Stedman and its flanking lines; the same men who on the first day at Gettysburg had turned the tide of battle; who at sunset on the 6th of May, in the Wilderness, had carried dismay to the right flank of the Federal army; who at Spottsylvania had made the furious counter-charge under the eye of Lee; who at Cedar Creek had rushed upon Sheridan's left with resistless momentum, and to whom I have endeavored to do but simple justice in my account of the oscillating fortunes of the two armies on that field.   They were the men whose record will brighten for all time every page of the history of that immortal army which a knightly and able Federal soldier has pronounced "the best which has existed on this continent."   In a paper read before the Military Historical Society of Massachusetts, General Charles A. Whittier of the Union army says:

The Army of Northern Virginia will deservedly rank as the best which has existed on this continent.   Suffering privations unknown to its opponents, it fought well from the early Peninsula days to the surrender of that small remnant at Appomattox. It seemed always ready, active, mobile.   Without doubt, it was composed of the best men of the South, rushing to what they considered the defence of their country against a bitter invader; and they took the places assigned them, officer or private, and fought until beaten by superiority of numbers.   The North sent no such army to the field, and its patriotism was of easier character, etc.

In the same historical paper General Whittier says:

As a matter of comparison, we have lately read that from William and Mary College, Virginia, thirty-two out of thirty-five professors and instructors abandoned the college work and joined the army in the field. Harvard College sent one professor from its large corps of professors and instructors.

In every Southern State the universities and colleges sent to the front their students and the flower of their alumni as volunteers. It is stated that nine tenths of the students of the University of Virginia enlisted for the war. In the Rockbridge battery there were seven masters of arts of the university, twenty-eight college graduates, and twenty-five theological students. Among these privates was R. E. Lee, Jr., son of the great commander.

On my staff as volunteer aide was Professor Basil A. Gildersleeve of the University of Virginia, now of Johns Hopkins University. Dr. Gildersleeve has no superior in the country as a Greek scholar, and is one of the most distinguished of our classical writers. He was a most efficient officer, and exhibited in extreme peril a high order of courage and composure. While bearing an order in battle he was desperately wounded and maimed for life.

These and many similar facts which could be given demonstrate the justice of General Whittier's estimate.

General Grant, in this last movement upon our lines at Petersburg, hurled against us his army of 124,000[1] brave and superbly equipped soldiers. To resist them General Lee could then bring into line about 35,000 worn and wan but consecrated fighters. Possibly one half of these had been, on the 1st and 2d of April, killed, wounded, and captured, or the commands to which they belonged had been so broken to pieces as to eliminate them from the effective forces. There was no hope for us except in retreat.

[1] These figures are taken from the "Confederate Military History," Vol. III, p. 531.

Under orders from the general-in-chief, the old corps of Stonewall Jackson, which it was my privilege to command, was the last of his army to abandon forever those mortar-battered lines of defence around Petersburg. After the hour of midnight, when all other troops were safely on the march to the rear, the Second Army Corps silently and sadly withdrew from the blood-stained trenches in which Lee's peerless army had exhibited for nine weary months a patience in suffering, a steadfastness under discouraging conditions, and a strength in resistance unexampled in war.

As the last broken file of that matchless army stepped from the bridge and my pioneer corps lighted the flames that consumed it, there came to me a vivid and depressing realization of the meaning of the appalling tragedy of the last two days. The breaking of Lee's power had shattered the last hope of Southern independence. But another burden—a personal woe—was weighing upon me. I had left behind me in that city of gloom the wife who had followed me during the entire war. She was ill. But as I rode away from Petersburg during the dismal hours of that night, I found comfort in the hope that some chivalric soldier of the Union army would learn of her presence and guard her home against all intruders. My confidence in American manhood was not misplaced.

To bring up the rear and adequately protect the retreating army was an impossible task. With characteristic vigor General Grant pressed the pursuit. Soon began the continuous and final battle. Fighting all day, marching all night, with exhaustion and hunger claiming their victims at every mile of the march, with charges of infantry in rear and of cavalry on the flanks, it seemed the war god had turned loose all his furies to revel in havoc. On and on, hour after hour, from hilltop to hilltop, the lines were alternately forming, fighting, and retreating, making one almost continuous shifting battle.

Here, in one direction, a battery of artillery became involved; there, in another, a blocked ammunition train required rescue: and thus came short but sharp little battles which made up the side shows of the main performance, while the different divisions of Lee's lionhearted army were being broken and scattered or captured. Out of one of these whirlwinds there came running at the top of his speed a boy soldier whose wit flashed out even in that dire extremity. When asked why he was running, he shouted back:

"Golly, captain, I 'm running 'cause I can't fly!"

On the night of the 6th of April, three days before the final surrender, my superb scout, young George of Virginia, who recently died in Danville, greatly honored and loved by his people, brought to me under guard two soldiers dressed in full Confederate uniform, whom he had arrested on suspicion, believing that they belonged to the enemy. About two months prior to this arrest I had sent George out of Petersburg on a most perilous mission. All of his scouting was full of peril. I directed him to go in the rear of General Grant's lines, to get as close as he could to the general's headquarters, and, if possible, catch some one with despatches, or in some way bring me reliable information as to what was being done by the Union commander. George was remarkably conscientious, intelligent, and accurate in his reports. He always wore his Confederate gray jacket, which would protect him from the penalty of death as a spy if he should be captured. But he also wore, when on his scouting expeditions, a pale blue overcoat captured from the Union army. A great many of our soldiers wore these overcoats because they had no others.

On this particular expedition George was hiding in the woods not far from General Grant's headquarters, when he saw passing near him two men in Confederate uniform. It was late in the evening, nearly dark. He at once made himself known to them, supposing that they were scouting for some other corps in Lee's army. But they were Sheridan's men, belonging to his "Jessie scouts," and they instantly drew their revolvers upon George and marched him to General Grant's headquarters. He was closely questioned by the Union commander; but he was too intelligent to make any mistakes in his answers. He showed his gray jacket, which saved him from execution as a spy, and he was placed in the guard-house. His opportunity for escape came late one night, when he found a new recruit on guard at his prison door. This newly enlisted soldier was a foreigner, and had very little knowledge of the English language; but he knew what a twenty-dollar gold piece was. The Confederacy did not have much gold, but our scouts were kept supplied with it. George pulled out of the lining of his jacket the gold piece, placed it in the foreigner's hand, turned the fellow's back to the door, and walked quickly out of the guard-house. George would not have dared to attempt such a programme with an American on guard.

He reached our lines, and reported these details only a few days before our last retreat was begun. During that retreat on the night of April 6, 1865, as I rode among my men, he brought two soldiers under guard to me, and said: "General, here are two men who are wearing our uniforms and say they belong to Fitzhugh Lee's cavalry; but I believe they are Yankees. I had them placed under guard for you to examine."

I questioned the men closely, and could find no sufficient ground for George's suspicions. They seemed entirely self-possessed and at ease under my rigid examination. They gave me the names of Fitzhugh Lee's regimental and company commanders, said they belonged to a certain mess, and gave the names of the members, and, without a moment's hesitation, gave prompt answer to every question I asked. I said to George that they seemed to me all right; but he protested, saying: "No, general, they are not all right. I saw them by the starlight counting your files." One of them at once said: "Yes; we were trying to get some idea of your force. We have been at home on sick-leave for a long time, and wanted to know if we had any army left." This struck me as a little suspicious, and I pounded them again with questions. "You say that you have been home on sick-leave?"

"Yes, sir; we have been at home several weeks, and fell in with your command to-night, hoping that you could tell us how to get to General Fitzhugh Lee's cavalry."

"If you have been at home sick, you ought to have your furloughs with you."

"We have, sir. We have our furlough papers here in our pockets, signed by our own officers, and approved by General R. E. Lee. If we had a light you could examine them and see that they are all right."

George, who was listening to this conversation, which occurred while we were riding, again insisted that it did not matter what these men said or what they had; they were Yankees. I directed that they be brought on under guard until I could examine their papers.

We soon came to a burning log heap on the roadside, which had been kindled by some of the troops who had passed at an earlier hour of the night. The moment the full light fell upon their faces, George exclaimed: "General, these are the two men who captured me nearly two months ago behind General Grant's headquarters."

They ridiculed the suggestion, and at once drew from their pockets the furloughs. These papers seemed to be correct, and the signatures of the officers, including that of General Lee, seemed to be genuine. This evidence did not yet satisfy George nor shake his convictions.

He said that the signatures of our officers were forged, or these men had captured some of our men who had furloughs, and had taken the papers from them, and were now personating the real owners. He asked me to make them dismount, that he might " go through them," as he described his proposed search. He fingered every seam in their coats, took off their cavalry sabres, and searched their garments, but found nothing. At last he asked me to make them sit down and let him pull off their boots. One personated a Confederate private; the other wore the uniform of a lieutenant of cavalry. George drew the boots from the lieutenant's feet, and under the lining of one he found an order from General Grant to General Ord, directing the latter to move rapidly by certain roads and cut off Lee's retreat at Appomattox. As soon as this order was found, the young soldier admitted the truth of George's statement—that they were the two men who captured him behind Grant's lines. I said to them: "Well, you know your fate. Under the laws of war you have forfeited your lives by wearing this uniform, and I shall have you shot at sunrise to-morrow morning."

They received this announcement without the slightest appearance of nervousness. The elder could not have been more than nineteen or twenty years of age, while his companion was a beardless youth. One of them said with perfect composure: " General, we understand it all. We knew when we entered this kind of service, and put on these uniforms, that we were taking our lives in our hands, and that we should be executed if we were captured. You have the right to have us shot; but the war can't last much longer, and it would do you no good to have us killed."

I had no thought of having them executed, but I did not tell them so. I sent the captured order to General Lee, and at four o'clock on the morning of the 7th he wrote me in pencil a note which was preserved by my chief of staff, Major R. W. Hunter, now of Alexandria, Virginia. It was sent, a few years ago, to Mrs. Gordon, to be kept by her as a memento of this most remarkable incident. Unhappily, it was lost in the fire which, in 1899, consumed my home. In that brief note, General Lee directed me to march by certain roads toward Appomattox as rapidly as the physical condition of my men would permit. Thus, by General Lee's direction, my command was thrown to the front, that we might thwart, if possible, the purpose of the Union commander to check at Appomattox our retrograde movement.

General Lee approved my suggestion to spare the lives of Sheridan's captured "Jessie scouts," and directed me to bring them along with my command. This incident closed with my delivery of the young soldiers to General Sheridan on the morning of Lee's surrender.

CHAPTER XXIX

THE SURRENDER

The Army of Northern Virginia reduced to a skeleton—General Lee's calm bearing—The last Confederate council of war—Decision upon a final attempt to break Grant's lines—The last charge of the war—Union breastworks carried—A fruitless victory—Flag of truce sent to General Ord—Conference with General Sheridan—An armistice.

BEFORE reaching the end of our journey, which terminated abruptly at the little village of Appomattox, the Army of Northern Virginia had become the mere skeleton of its former self. At Sailor's Creek, Anderson's corps was broken and destroyed, and General Ewell, with almost his entire command, was captured, as was General Kershaw, General Custis Lee, son of the general-in-chief, and other prominent officers. I had discovered the movement threatening Ewell, and had sought to apprise him of his danger and to aid in his escape; but my own command was assailed at almost the same instant, and was precipitated into a short but strenuous battle for its own safety. The advance of Grant's army struck Ewell upon one road and my command upon another almost simultaneously. Rushing through the broad gap between Ewell and myself, the heavy Federal force soon surrounded the command of that brave old one-legged hero, and forced him to surrender. Another Union column struck my command while we were endeavoring to push the ponderous wagon-trains through the bog, out of which the starved teams were unable to

429

drag them. Many of these wagons, loaded with ammunition, mired so deep in the mud that they had to be abandoned. It was necessary to charge and force back the Union lines in order to rescue my men from this perilous position. Indeed, not only was my command in almost incessant battle as we covered the retreat, but every portion of our marching column was being assailed by Grant's cavalry and infantry. The roads and fields and woods swarmed with eager pursuers, and Lee now and then was forced to halt his whole army, reduced to less than 10,000 fighters, in order to meet these simultaneous attacks. Various divisions along the line of march turned upon the Federals, and in each case checked them long enough for some other Confederate commands to move on. Mahone's infantry and Fitzhugh Lee's cavalry were engaged far in advance. The latter command captured General Gregg, who, with other prisoners, joined our retreat. I observed General Gregg marching on foot, and asked him to accept a mount, as he was not accustomed to travelling as an infantry soldier. He expressed appreciation of the offer, but declined, preferring to share the fate of his men.

General Lee was riding everywhere and watching everything, encouraging his brave men by his calm and cheerful bearing. He was often exposed to great danger from shells and bullets; but, in answer to protests, his reply was that he was obliged to see for himself what was going on. As he sat on his horse near Farmville during a sharp engagement, watching the effect of the fire from one of our batteries which was playing upon the enemy, a staff officer rode up to him with a message. The general noticed that this officer had exposed himself unnecessarily in approaching him, and he reprimanded the young soldier for not riding on the side of the hill where he would be protected from the enemy's fire. The young officer replied that he would be ashamed to seek protection while the commanding general was so exposing himself. General Lee sharply replied: "It is my duty to be here. Go back the way I told you, sir."

Thus the great chieftain was teaching by example the lesson of devotion to duty at any risk, and teaching by precept that noblest of lessons, unselfish consideration for others.

This was no new phase of his soldier life. It was not an exhibition of attributes developed by the trying conditions around him. It was simply a natural expression of the spirit that made him great and good. Many incidents in his army career illustrate the same elements of character. At some point below Richmond, he was standing near a battery, when the men crowded around him, evidencing their admiration and affection. The group grew so large as to attract the enemy's attention, and drew a heavy fire; whereupon the general said to the privates around him: "Men, you had better go back to your places. They are firing at this point, and you are exposing yourselves to unnecessary danger." He remained there himself for some minutes, and then, as he walked quietly away, he picked up a small object and placed it on the limb of a tree. It was afterward ascertained that it was an unfledged sparrow that had fallen from its nest.

In the Wilderness, at Spottsylvania, and along the lines at Petersburg, he exposed himself whenever and wherever his presence seemed needful. The protests of his officers and soldiers against this habit were so frequent that he said on one occasion, half humorously, half complainingly: "I do wish somebody would tell me where my place is on the field of battle; wherever I go to look after the fight, I am told, 'This is no place for you; you must go away.'"

General Benjamin Butterworth of Ohio ("Honest

Ben," as he was familarly called during his service as member of Congress from the Buckeye State) gave me, after the war, an account of an incident occurring on this final retreat which was both pathetic and amusing. It illustrates that remarkable and unique phase of the great struggle, the feeling of genuine comradeship, which existed between the soldiers of the hostile armies. On that doleful retreat of Lee's army, it was impossible for us to bury our dead or carry with us the disabled wounded. There was no longer any room in the crowded ambulances which had escaped capture and still accompanied our trains. We could do nothing for the unfortunate sufferers who were too severely wounded to march, except leave them on the roadside with canteens of water. A big-hearted soldier-boy in blue came across a desperately wounded Confederate shot through legs and body, lying in his bloody bed of leaves, groaning with pain and sighing for relief in death. The generous Federal was so moved by the harrowing spectacle that he stopped at the side of the Confederate and asked: "What can I do for you, Johnny? I want to help you if I can."

"Thank you for your sympathy," the sufferer replied, "but no one can help me now. It will not be long till death relieves me."

The Union soldier bade him good-by, and was in the act of leaving, when the wounded Southerner called to him: "Yes, Yank; there is something you might do for me. You might pray for me before you go."

This Union boy had probably never uttered aloud a word of prayer in all his life. But his emotions were deeply stirred, and through his tears he looked around for some one more accustomed to lead in prayer. Discovering some of his comrades passing, he called to them: "Come here, boys, and come quick. Here is a poor Johnny shot all to pieces, and he 's dying. One of you must come and pray for him. He wants me to pray for him; but you know I can't pray worth a ——."

Two days before the surrender, a number of officers held a council as to what was best to be done. I was not present, but I learned through others that three propositions were discussed:

1. To disband and allow the troops to get away as best they could, and reform at some designated point.

This was abandoned because a dispersion over the country would be a dreadful infliction upon our impoverished people, and because it was most improbable that all the men would reach the rallying-point.

2. To abandon all trains, and concentrate the entire Confederate army in a compact body, and cut through Grant's lines.

This proposition was in turn discarded, because without ammunition trains we could not hope to continue the struggle many days.

3. To surrender at once.

It was decided that this last course would be wisest, and these devoted officers felt that they should do all in their power to relieve General Lee by giving him their moral support in taking the step. General Grant had not then written his first note to Lee, asking surrender. General Pendleton, who was the Confederate chief of artillery, and a close personal friend of the commander, was selected by the council to acquaint him with the result of its deliberations. General Pendleton gave a most graphic description of his interview with General Lee. He said that the general-in-chief instantly replied:

" Oh, no. I trust it has not come to that. We have too many bold men to think of laying down our arms."

General Pendleton related that the general referred to the beginning of the Southern struggle for independence, and said, in substance, that he had never believed that, with the vast power against us, we could win our independence unless we were aided by foreign powers. "But," added General Lee, "such considerations really made no difference with me." And then he uttered those memorable words: "We had, I was satisfied, sacred principles to maintain and rights to defend, for which we were in duty bound to do our best, even if wo perished in the endeavor."

This great soldier understood the spirit which led the officers in that conference to recommend his surrender. He knew their devotion to the cause and their devotion to him, but he was not ready to consider the necessity for surrender. He doubtless had this conference in mind later, when he perpetrated upon General Wise the joke which General Long has recorded. General Wise, in the absence of either basin or towel, had washed his face in a pool of water impregnated with red clay. The water dried, leaving the red stains on his countenance. General Lee was much amused at the grotesque appearance of Wise, and saluted him as he approached:

"Good morning, General Wise. I perceive that you, at any rate, have not given up the contest, as you are in your war-paint this morning."

In his report written three days after the surrender, and addressed to "His Excellency, Jefferson Davis," General Lee states that when we reached Appomattox his army had been "reduced to two corps under Longstreet and Gordon." He also says in that report: "On the morning of the 9th, according to the reports of the ordnance officers, there were 7892 organized infantry with arms."

On the evening of April 8th, this little army, with its ammunition nearly exhausted, was confronted by the forces of General Grant, which had been thrown across our line of retreat at Appomattox. Then came the last sad Confederate council of war. It was called by Lee to meet at night. It met in the woods at his headquarters

and by a low-burning bivouac-fire. There was no tent
there, no table, no chairs, and no camp-stools. On
blankets spread upon the ground or on saddles at the
roots of the trees, we sat around the great commander.
A painter's brush might transfer to canvas the physical
features of that scene, but no tongue or pen will ever be
able to describe the unutterable anguish of Lee's commanders as they looked into the clouded face of their
beloved leader and sought to draw from it some ray of
hope.

There were present at this final council the general-
in-chief, the commander of his artillery, General Pendleton; General Fitzhugh Lee, who in the absence of Wade
Hampton commanded the cavalry, and General Longstreet and myself, commanding all that was left of his
immortal infantry. These fragments of each arm of
the service still represented the consecration and courage
that had made Lee's army, at the meridian of its power,
almost invincible.

The numbers and names of the staff officers who were
present I cannot now recall; and it would be as impossible to give the words that were spoken or the suggestions that were made as it would to photograph the
thoughts and emotions of that soldier group gathered at
Lee's last bivouac. The letters of General Grant asking
surrender, and the replies thereto, evoked a discussion as
to the fate of the Southern people and the condition in
which the failure of our cause would leave them. There
was also some discussion as to the possibility of forcing
a passage through Grant's lines and saving a small portion of the army, and continuing a desultory warfare
until the government at Washington should grow weary
and grant to our people peace, and the safeguards of
local self-government. If all that was said and felt at
that meeting could be given it would make a volume of
measureless pathos. In no hour of the great war did

General Lee's masterful characteristics appear to me so conspicuous as they did in that last council. We knew by our own aching hearts that his was breaking. Yet he commanded himself, and stood calmly facing and discussing the long-dreaded inevitable.

It was finally determined that with Fitz Lee's cavalry, my infantry, and Long's artillery, under Colonel Thomas H. Carter, we should attempt at daylight the next morning to cut through Grant's lines. Longstreet was to follow in support of the movement.

The utmost that could be hoped for was that we might reach the mountains of Virginia and Tennessee with a remnant of the army, and ultimately join General Johnston. As we rode away from the meeting I directed a staff officer to return to General Lee and ask him if he had any specific directions as to where I should halt and camp for the night. He said: "Yes; tell General Gordon that I should be glad for him to halt just beyond the Tennessee line." That line was about two hundred miles away, and Grant's battle-lines and breastworks were in our immediate front, ready to check any movement in that direction; but General Lee knew that I would interpret his facetious message exactly as he intended it. His purpose was to let me infer that there was little hope of our escape and that it did not matter where I camped for the night; but if we should succeed in cutting our way out, he expected me to press toward the goal in the mountains.

The Federals had constructed a line of breastworks across our front during the night. The audacious movement of our troops was begun at dawn. The dashing cavalry leader, Fitzhugh Lee, swept around the Union left flank, while the infantry and artillery attacked the front. I take especial pride in recording the fact that this last charge of the war was made by the footsore and starving men of my command with a spirit worthy the best days of Lee's army. The Union breastworks were carried. Two pieces of artillery were captured. The Federals were driven from all that portion of the field, and the brave boys in tattered gray cheered as their battle-flags waved in triumph on that last morning.

The Confederate battle-lines were still advancing when I discovered a heavy column of Union infantry coming from the right and upon my rear. I gathered around me my sharpshooters, who were now held for such emergencies, and directed Colonel Thomas H. Carter of the artillery to turn all his guns upon the advancing column. It was held at bay by his shrapnel, grape, and canister. While the Confederate infantry and cavalry were thus fighting at the front, and the artillery was checking the development of Federal forces around my right and rear, Longstreet was assailed by other portions of the Federal army. He was so hardly pressed that he could not join, as contemplated, in the effort to break the cordon of men and metal around us. At this critical juncture a column of Union cavalry appeared on the hills to my left, headed for the broad space between Longstreet's command and mine. In a few minutes that body of Federal cavalry would not only have seized the trains but cut off all communication between the two wings of Lee's army and rendered its capture inevitable. I therefore detached a brigade to double-quick and intercept this Federal force.

Such was the situation, its phases rapidly shifting and growing more intensely thrilling at each moment, when I received a significant inquiry from General Lee. It was borne by Colonel Charles S. Venable of his staff, afterward the chairman of the faculty of the University of Virginia. The commander wished me to report at once as to the conditions on my portion of the field, what progress I was making, and what encouragement I could give. I said: "Tell General Lee that my command has been fought to a frazzle, and unless Longstreet can unite in the movement, or prevent these forces from coming upon my rear, I cannot long go forward." Colonel Venable has left on record this statement:

"At three o'clock on the morning of that fatal day, General Lee rode forward, still hoping that we might break through the countless hordes of the enemy who hemmed us in. Halting a short distance in rear of our vanguard, he sent me on to General Gordon to ask him if he could cut through the enemy. I found General Gordon and General Fitz Lee on their front line in the light of the morning, arranging an attack. Gordon's reply to the message (I give the expressive phrase of the Georgian) was this: 'Tell General Lee I have fought my corps to a frazzle, and I fear I can do nothing unless I am heavily supported by Longstreet's corps.'"

Colonel Venable adds that when General Lee received my message, he said: "There is nothing left me but to go and see General Grant, and I had rather die a thousand deaths."

My troops were still fighting, furiously fighting in nearly every direction, when the final note from General Lee reached me. It notified me that there was a flag of truce between General Grant and himself, stopping hostilities, and that I could communicate that fact to the commander of the Union forces in my front. There was no unnecessary delay in sending that message. I called Colonel Green Peyton of my staff, and directed him to take a flag of truce and bear the message to General Ord, who commanded, as I supposed, the Union infantry in my front. I ordered him to say to the Union commander this, and nothing more: "General Gordon has received notice from General Lee of a flag of truce, stopping the battle." Colonel Peyton soon informed me that we had no flag of truce. I said: "Well, take your handkerchief and tie that on a stick, and go."

He felt in his pockets and said: "General, I have no handkerchief."

"Then tear your shirt, sir, and tie that to a stick."

He looked at his shirt, and then at mine, and said:

"General, I have on a flannel shirt, and I see you have. I don't believe there is a white shirt in the army."

"Get something, sir," I ordered. "Get something and go!"

He secured a rag of some sort, and rode rapidly away in search of General Ord. He did not find Ord, but he found Sheridan, and returned to me accompanied by an officer of strikingly picturesque appearance. This Union officer was slender and graceful, and a superb rider. He wore his hair very long, falling almost to his shoulders. Guided by my staff officer, he galloped to where I was sitting on my horse, and, with faultless grace and courtesy, saluted me with his sabre and said:

"I am General Custer, and bear a message to you from General Sheridan. The general desires me to present to you his compliments, and to demand the immediate and unconditional surrender of all the troops under your command. I replied: "You will please, general, return my compliments to General Sheridan, and say to him that I shall not surrender my command."

"He directs me to say to you, general, if there is any hesitation about your surrender, that he has you surrounded and can annihilate your command in an hour."

To this I answered that I was probably as well aware of my situation as was General Sheridan; that I had nothing to add to my message informing him of the contents of the note from General Lee; that if General Sheridan decided to continue the fighting in the face of the flag of truce, the responsibility for the blood shed would be his and not mine.

In a short time thereafter a white flag was seen approaching. Under it was Philip Sheridan, accompanied by a mounted escort almost as large as one of Fitz Lee's regiments. Sheridan was mounted on an enormous horse, a very handsome animal. He rode in front of the escort, and an orderly carrying the flag rode beside him. Around me at the time were my faithful sharpshooters, and as General Sheridan and his escort came within easy range of the rifles, a half-witted fellow raised his gun as if to fire. I ordered him to lower his gun, and explained that he must not fire on a flag of truce. He did not obey my order cheerfully, but held his rifle in position to be quickly thrown to his shoulder. In fact, he was again in the act of raising his gun to fire at Sheridan, when I caught the gun and said to him, with emphasis, that he must not shoot men under flag of truce. He at once protested: "Well, general, let him stay on his own side."

I did not tell General Sheridan of his narrow escape. Had he known the facts,—that this weak-minded but strong-hearted Confederate private was one of the deadliest of marksmen,—he probably would have realized that I had saved his life.

Meantime another member of my staff, Major R. W. Hunter of Virginia, had ridden off with General Custer, who asked to be guided to Longstreet's position. As General Sheridan, with the flag of truce, came nearer, I rode out to meet him. Between General Sheridan and myself occurred another controversy very similar to the one I had had previously with General Custer. No message from General Grant in reference to the truce between the commanders-in-chief had reached General Sheridan. It had miscarried. But upon my exhibiting to him the note from Lee, he at once proposed that the firing cease and that our respective lines be withdrawn to certain positions, while we waited further intelligence from the commanders of the two armies. Our respective staff officers were despatched to inaugurate this temporary armistice, and Sheridan and I dismounted and sat together on the ground.

Quickly the firing was stopped and silence reigned on the field. But I had forgotten the brigade which I had sent far off to my left to check the movement of Union cavalry, and as General Sheridan and I sat and conversed, a sudden roll of musketry was heard from that quarter. General Sheridan sprang to his feet and fiercely asked: "What does that mean, sir?" I replied: "It is my fault, general. I had forgotten that brigade. But let me stop the firing first, and then I will explain."

I called for a member of my staff to ride with all speed to that brigade. None of my staff was there. They had not returned from executing my previous orders. General Sheridan proposed to lend me one of his staff. I accepted the offer; and it so happened that a Union officer, Captain Vanderbilt Allen, bore the last order to my troops, directing them to cease firing, thus practically ending the four years of battle for Southern independence. It was necessary, however, to protect Captain Allen from the fire of my men or from their demand for his surrender. For this purpose I sent with him as guide and protector one of my ragged privates. That private had belonged to the old Stonewall Brigade.

I had never seen General Sheridan before, nor received from those who knew him any definite impressions of him as man or soldier. I had seen something of his work in the latter capacity during the campaigns in the Valley of Virginia. His destruction of barns and mills and farming implements impressed me as in conflict with the laws of war and inconsistent with the enlightened, Christian sentiment of the age, and had prepared me in a measure for his somewhat brusque manners. Truth demands that I say of General Sheridan that his style of conversation and general bearing, while never discourteous, were far less agreeable and pleasing than those of any other officer of the Union army whom it was my fortune to meet. I do not recall a word he said which I could regard as in any degree offensive, but there was an absence of that delicacy and consideration which was exhibited by other Union officers.

General Sheridan began the conversation after we had dismounted by saying, in substance: "We have met before, I believe, at Winchester and Cedar Creek in the Valley."

I replied that I was there, and he continued: "I had the pleasure of receiving some artillery from your Government, consigned to me through your commander, General Early."

He referred, of course, to the piece on which the Confederate wag had painted in white letters the words given in a former chapter. There was nothing offensive in that; but I thought there was in his manner a slight tinge of exultation which was not altogether pleasing, and I replied:

"That is true; and I have this morning received from your government artillery consigned to me through General Sheridan."

He evidently did not know that within the previous hour we had captured some of his artillery, and he was reluctant to believe it.

The meeting of Lee and Grant, and the impressive formalities which followed, put an end to the interview, and we parted without the slightest breach of strict military courtesy.

CHAPTER XXX

THE END OF THE WAR

Appomattox—25,000 men surrender—Only 8000 able to bear arms—Uniform courtesy of the victorious Federals—A salute for the vanquished—What Lincoln might have done—General Sherman's liberal terms to Johnston—An estimate of General Lee and General Grant—The war and the reunited country.

GENERAL LONGSTREET'S forces and mine at Appomattox, numbered, together, less than 8000 men; but every man able to bear arms was still resolute and ready for battle. There were present three times that many enrolled Confederates; but two thirds of them were so enfeebled by hunger, so wasted by sickness, and so foot-sore from constant marching that it was difficult for them to keep up with the army. They were wholly unfit for duty. It is important to note this fact as explaining the great difference in the number of those who fought and those who were to be fed. At the final meeting between General Lee and General Grant rations were ordered by General Grant for 25,000 Confederates.

Marked consideration and courtesy were exhibited at Appomattox by the victorious Federals, from the commanding generals to the privates in the ranks. General Meade, who had known General Lee in the old army, paid, after the surrender, an unofficial visit to the Confederate chieftain. After cordial salutations, General Lee said playfully to his former comrade in arms that years were telling upon him. General Meade, who had

443

fought Lee at Gettysburg and in many subsequent battles, made the strikingly gracious and magnanimous answer: "Not years, but General Lee himself has made me gray."

Some of the scenes on the field, immediately after the cessation of hostilities and prior to the formal surrender, illustrate the same magnanimous spirit, and were peculiarly impressive and thrilling. As my command, in worn-out shoes and ragged uniforms, but with proud mien, moved to the designated point to stack their arms and surrender their cherished battle-flags, they challenged the admiration of the brave victors. One of the knightliest soldiers of the Federal army, General Joshua L. Chamberlain of Maine, who afterward served with distinction as governor of his State, called his troops into line, and as my men marched in front of them, the veterans in blue gave a soldierly salute to those vanquished heroes — a token of respect from Americans to Americans, a final and fitting tribute from Northern to Southern chivalry.

General Chamberlain describes this incident in the following words:

At the sound of that machine-like snap of arms, General Gordon started, caught in a moment its significance, and instantly assumed the finest attitude of a soldier. He wheeled his horse, facing me, touching him gently with the spur, so that the animal slightly reared, and, as he wheeled, horse and rider made one motion, the horse's head swung down with a graceful bow, and General Gordon dropped his sword-point to his toe in salutation.

By word of mouth the general sent back orders to the rear that his own troops take the same position of the manual in the march past as did our line. That was done, and a truly imposing sight was the mutual salutation and farewell.

Bayonets were affixed to muskets, arms stacked, and cartridge-boxes unslung and hung upon the stacks. Then, slowly and with a reluctance that was appealingly pathetic, the torn and tattered battle-flags were either leaned against the stacks or laid upon the ground. The emotion of the conquered soldiery was really sad to witness. Some of the men who had carried and followed those ragged standards through the four long years of strife rushed, regardless of all discipline, from the ranks, bent about their old flags, and pressed them to their lips.

And it can well be imagined, too, that there was no lack of emotion on our side, but the Union men were held steady in their lines, without the least show of demonstration by word or by motion. There was, though, a twitching of the muscles of their faces, and, be it said, their battle-bronzed cheeks were not altogether dry. Our men felt the import of the occasion, and realized fully how they would have been affected if defeat and surrender had been their lot after such a fearful struggle. [1]

When the proud and sensitive sons of Dixie came to a full realization of the truth that the Confederacy was overthrown and their leader had been compelled to surrender his once invincible army, they could no longer control their emotions, and tears ran like water down their shrunken faces. The flags which they still carried were objects of undisguised affection. These Southern banners had gone down before overwhelming numbers; and torn by shells, riddled by bullets, and laden with the powder and smoke of battle, they aroused intense emotion in the men who had so often followed them to victory. Yielding to overpowering sentiment, these high-mettled men began to tear the flags from the staffs and hide them in their bosoms, as they wet them with burning tears.

The Confederate officers faithfully endeavored to check this exhibition of loyalty and love for the old flags. A great majority of them were duly surrendered; but many were secretly carried by devoted veterans to their

---

[1] New York "Times," May 4, 1901.

homes, and will be cherished forever as honored heir-looms.

There was nothing unnatural or censurable in all this. The Confederates who clung to those pieces of battered bunting knew they would never again wave as martial ensigns above embattled hosts; but they wanted to keep them, just as they wanted to keep the old canteen with a bullet-hole through it, or the rusty gray jacket that had been torn by canister. They loved those flags, and will love them forever, as mementoes of the unparalleled struggle. They cherish them because they represent the consecration and courage not only of Lee's army but of all the Southern armies, because they symbolize the bloodshed and the glory of nearly a thousand battles.

Some narrow but very good and patriotic people object to this expression of Southern sentiment. It was not so, however, with William McKinley, that typical American, who, while living and while dying, exhibited in their fulness and strength the virtues of a true and lofty manhood. That chivalric Union soldier, far-seeing statesman, and truly great President saw in this Southern fidelity to past memories the surest pledge of loyalty to future duties. William McKinley fought as bravely as the bravest on the Union side; but he was broad enough to recognize in his Southern countrymen a loyal adherence to the great fundamental truths to which both sides were devoted. He was too wise and too just to doubt the South's fealty to the Constitution or to the doctrines of the Declaration of Independence; for Madison was father of the one and Jefferson of the other. He was great enough to trust implicitly the South's renewed allegiance to the Union and its flag; for hers was the most liberal hand in studding its field with stars. He did not hesitate to trust Southern pluck and patriotism to uphold the honor of the country and give liberty to Cuba; for he remembered Washington and his rebels in the Revolution, Jackson and his Southern volunteers at New Orleans; Zachary Taylor and his Louisianians, Clay and his Kentuckians, Butler and his South Carolinians, and Davis and his Mississippians in Mexico.

The heartstrings of the mother, woven around the grave of her lost child, will never be severed while she lives; but does that hinder the continued flow of maternal devotion to those who are left her? The South's affections are bound, with links that cannot be broken, around the graves of her sons who fell in her defence, and to the mementoes and memories of the great struggle; but does that fact lessen her loyalty to the proud emblem of a reunited country? Does her unparalleled defence of the now dead Confederacy argue less readiness to battle for this ever-living Republic, in the making and the administering of which she bore so conspicuous a part?

If those unhappy patriots who find a scarecrow in every faded, riddled Confederate flag would delve deeper into the philosophy of human nature, or rise higher,—say to the plane on which McKinley stood,—they would be better satisfied with their Southern countrymen, with Southern sentiment, with the breadth and strength of the unobtrusive but sincere Southern patriotism. They would see that man is so constituted—the immutable laws of our being are such—that to stifle the sentiment and extinguish the hallowed memories of a people is to destroy their manhood.

During these last scenes at Appomattox some of the Confederates were so depressed in spirit, so filled with apprehensions as to the policy to be adopted by the civil authorities at Washington, that the future seemed to them shrouded in gloom. They knew that burnt homes and fenceless farms, poverty and ashes, would greet them on their return from the war. Even if the administration at Washington should be friendly, they did not believe that the Southern States could recover in half a century from the chaotic condition in which the war had left them. The situation was enough to daunt the most hopeful and appall the stoutest hearts. "What are we to do? How are we to begin life again?" they asked. "Every dollar of our circulating medium has been rendered worthless. Our banks and rich men have no money. The commodities and personal property which formerly gave us credit have been destroyed. The Northern banks and money-lenders will not take as security our lands, denuded of houses and without animals and implements for their cultivation. The railroads are torn up or the tracks are worn out. The negroes are freed and may refuse to work. Besides, what assurance can we have of law and order and the safety of our families with four million slaves suddenly emancipated in the midst of us and the restraints to which they have been accustomed entirely removed?"

To many intelligent soldiers and some of the officers the conditions were so discouraging, the gloom so impenetrable, that they seriously discussed the advisability of leaving the country and beginning life anew in some other land.

While recognizing the dire extremity which confronted us, I was inclined to take a more hopeful view of the future. I therefore spoke to the Southern soldiers on the field at Appomattox, in order to check as best I could their disposition to leave the country, and to counteract, if possible, the paralyzing effect of the overwhelming discouragements which met them on every side.

As we reached the designated point, the arms were stacked and the battle-flags were folded. Those sad and suffering men, many of them weeping as they saw the old banners laid upon the stacked guns like trappings on

the coffin of their dead hopes, at once gathered in compact mass around me. Sitting on my horse in the midst
of them, I spoke to them for the last time as their commander. In all my past life I had never undertaken to
speak where my own emotions were so literally overwhelming. I counselled such course of action as I
believed most conducive to the welfare of the South
and of the whole country. I told them of my own grief,
which almost stifled utterance, and that I realized most
keenly the sorrow that was breaking their hearts, and
appreciated fully the countless and stupendous barriers
across the paths they were to tread.

Reminding them of the benign Southern climate, of
the fertility of their lands, of the vastly increased demand for the South's great staple and the high prices
paid for it, I offered these facts as legitimate bases of
hope and encouragement. I said to them that through
the rifts in the clouds then above us I could see the hand
of Almighty God stretched out to help us in the impending battle with adversity; that He would guide us in
the gloom, and bless every manly effort to bring back to
desolated homes the sunshine and comforts of former
years. I told them the principles for which they had so
grandly fought and uncomplainingly suffered were not
lost,—could not be lost,—for they were the principles on
which the Fathers had built the Republic, and that the
very throne of Jehovah was pledged that truth should
triumph and liberty live. As to the thought of their
leaving the country, that must be abandoned. It was
their duty as patriots to remain and work for the recuperation of our stricken section with the same courage,
energy, and devotion with which they had fought for her
in war. I urged them to enter cheerfully and hopefully
upon the tasks imposed by the fortunes of war, obeying
the laws, and giving, as I knew they would, the same
loyal support to the general Government which they had

yielded to the Confederacy. I closed with a prophecy that passion would speedily die, and that the brave and magnanimous soldiers of the Union army, when disbanded and scattered among the people, would become promoters of sectional peace and fraternity.

That prophecy would have been speedily fulfilled but for the calamitous fate that befell the country in the death of President Lincoln; and even in spite of that great misfortune, we should have much sooner reached the era of good-will and sectional concord if the spirit of the soldiers who did the fighting had animated the civilians who did the talking.

As I began to speak from my horse, large numbers of Union soldiers came near to hear what I had to say, giving me a rather queerly mixed audience. The Hon. Elihu Washburne, afterward United States Minister to France, the close friend of both President Lincoln and General Grant, was present at the surrender, as the guest of the Union commander. He either heard this parting speech or else its substance was reported to him. As soon as the formalities were ended, he made himself known to me, and in a most gracious manner expressed his pleasure at the general trend of my remarks. He assured me that the South would receive generous treatment at the hands of the general Government. My special object in referring to Mr. Washburne in this connection is to leave on record an emphatic statement made by him which greatly encouraged me. I can never forget his laconic answer to my inquiry: "Why do you think, Mr. Washburne, that the South will be generously dealt with by the Government?" "Because Abraham Lincoln is at its head," was his reply.

I knew something of Mr. Lincoln's past history, of his lifelong hostility to slavery, of his Emancipation Proclamation and vigorous prosecution of the war; but I had no knowledge whatever of any kindly sentiment entertained by him toward the Southern people. The emphatic words of Mr. Washburne, his intimate friend and counsellor, greatly interested me. I was with Mr. Washburne for several succeeding days—we rode on horseback together from Appomattox back toward Petersburg; and his description of Mr. Lincoln's character, of his genial and philanthropic nature, accompanied with illustrative anecdotes, was not only extremely entertaining, but was to me a revelation. He supported his declaration as to Mr. Lincoln's kindly sentiments by giving an elaborate and detailed account of his meeting with our commissioners at Hampton Roads. He expressed the opinion that the President went to that meeting with the fixed purpose of ending the war by granting the most liberal terms, provided the Southern commissioners acquiesced in the *sine qua non*—the restoration of the Union.

We parted at Petersburg, and among the last things he enjoined was faith in the kindly purposes of Abraham Lincoln in reference to the Southern people. Mr. Washburne said that the President would recommend to Congress such legislation as in his opinion would promote the prosperity of the South. He was emphatic in his declaration that Mr. Lincoln desired only the restoration of the Union—that even the abolition of slavery was secondary to this prime object. He stated that the President had declared that if he could restore the Union without abolition, he would gladly do it; if he could save the Union by partial abolition of slavery, he would do it that way; but that if it became necessary to abolish slavery entirely in order to save the Union, then slavery would be abolished: that as his great object had been achieved by the surrender of Lee's army, it would speedily be known to the Southern people that the President was deeply concerned for their welfare, that there would be no prosecutions and no discriminations, but that the State governments would be promptly recognized, and every effort made to help the Southern people. These impressive assurances were adding strength to my hopes when the whole country was shocked by the assassination of the President.

General Gibbon, General Griffin, and General Merritt were appointed by General Grant to meet Generals Pendleton, Longstreet, and myself, appointed by General Lee. The special duty which devolved on these six officers was the discussion and drafting of all details to carry out the formal surrender, according to the general terms agreed upon by the commanders-in-chief. In all our intercourse with those three Union officers I can recall no expression or word that could possibly wound the sensibility of a Confederate. Rejoiced as they naturally were at the termination of the long and costly struggle, and at the ultimate triumph of the Union cause, they scrupulously avoided allusions to battles in which the Federal armies had been victors, and endeavored rather to direct conversation to engagements in which the Union forces had been vanquished. Indeed, Confederate officers generally observed and commented upon this spirit, which at that time seemed to actuate the privates as well as the officers of the victorious army.

As the Confederates were taking leave of Appomattox, and about to begin their long and dreary tramp homeward, many of the Union men bade them cordial farewell. One of Grant's men said good-naturedly to one of Lee's veterans:

"Well, Johnny, I guess you fellows will go home now to stay."

The tired and tried Confederate, who did not clearly understand the spirit in which these playful words were spoken, and who was not at the moment in the best mood for badinage, replied:

"Look here, Yank; you *guess*, do you, that we fellows

are going home to stay? Maybe we are. But don't be giving us any of your impudence. If you do, we'll come back and lick you again."

Probably in no military organization that ever existed were there such cordial relations between officers and private soldiers as in the Confederate army. This was due, doubtless, to the fact that in our ranks there were lawyers, teachers, bankers, merchants, planters, college professors, and students who afterward became chief justices, governors, and occupants of the highest public stations. Since the war some of these privates have told with great relish of the old farmer near Appomattox who decided to give employment, after the surrender, to any of Lee's veterans who might wish to work a few days for food and small wages. He divided the Confederate employés into squads according to the respective ranks held by them in the army. He was uneducated, but entirely loyal to the Southern cause. A neighbor inquired of him as to the different squads:

"Who are those men working over there?"

"Them is privates, sir, of Lee's army."

"Well, how do they work?"

"Very fine, sir; first-rate workers."

"Who are those in the second group?"

"Them is lieutenants and captains, and they works fairly well, but not as good workers as the privates."

"I see you have a third squad: who are they?"

"Them is colonels."

"Well, what about the colonels? How do they work?"

"Now, neighbor, you'll never hear me say one word ag'in' any man who fit in the Southern army; but I ain't a-gwine to hire no generals."

The paroles issued to the Confederates were carefully examined by the possessors, and elicited a great variety of comment. Each man's parole bore his name and the name of his company and regiment, and recorded his pledge to fight no more until he was regularly exchanged. A few hoped for an early exchange and release from this pledge, that they might continue the struggle with some organized force, operating in a different section of the Confederacy. They were looking hopefully to the Trans-Mississippi, where, even after the surrender of Lee and Joe Johnston and Richard Taylor east of the Mississippi, Generals Kirby Smith, Magruder, and Forney, with Simon Bolivar Buckner as chief of staff, were still appealing to Confederates to "stand to their colors." That gallant little army of the Trans-Mississippi had fought many desperate battles under such leaders as McCulloch, McIntosh, Ross, Green, Maxey, Waul, Price, Van Dorn, Pike, Walker, Shelby, and W. L. Cabell, of whom General Marmaduke wrote: "The élan and chivalrous bearing of Cabell inspired all who looked upon him"; and these few unyielding spirits at Appomattox were still panting for continued combat in the ranks of those unsurrendered forces beyond the great Father of Waters. The more thoughtful, however, knew that the war was over. They carefully preserved their paroles, and were as proud of them as a young graduate is of his diploma, because these strips of paper furnished official proof of the fact that they were in the fight to the last. This fact they transmit as a priceless legacy to their children.

When I returned to Petersburg from Appomattox, I found Mrs. Gordon rapidly recovering, and as soon as she was able to travel, in company with Captain James M. Pace of my staff and his little family, who had joined him, we began our arduous trip homeward, over broken railroads and in such dilapidated conveyances as had been left in the track of the armies. In Petersburg it was impossible to secure among the recently emancipated negroes any one willing to accompany us as nurse for our child. This fact imposed upon me the necessity of continuing for a time my command of infantry in arms — a situation more trying to me in some respects than the one from which I had just been relieved by General Grant at Appomattox.

The generous terms of surrender given to Lee by Grant were exceeded in liberality by those which W. T. Sherman offered to Joseph E. Johnston in North Carolina. In the memorandum of agreement between Generals Sherman and Johnston (April 18, 1865) occur the following items:

"The Confederate armies now in existence to be disbanded and conducted to their State capitals, there to deposit their arms and public property in the State arsenals," etc. The President of the United States was to recognize the "several State governments on their officers and legislatures taking the oaths prescribed by the Constitution of the United States." The Federal courts were to be reëstablished in the Southern States, the people of the South were to be guaranteed their political rights, and rights of person and property, with a general amnesty. Briefly analyzed, these liberal terms meant that, with the exception of slavery (nothing was said on that subject), the Southern States and people were instantly to resume the relations to the general Government which they had occupied before the war began, and, instead of surrendering their arms, were to deposit them in State arsenals for ready use in suppressing riots, enforcing law, and protecting homes and property.

These terms of surrender proposed by General Sherman reveal a spirit in extreme contrast to that which he showed toward the Southern people in his unobstructed march to the sea. In his agreement with General Johnston his magnanimity is scarcely paralleled by that of any victorious commander, whereas in his long general orders for the conduct of his troops on their travel from demolished Atlanta to his goal by the sea, fully one half of his words are directions for systematic "foraging," destruction of "mills, houses, cotton-gins," etc., and for spreading "a devastation more or less relentless" according to the hostility shown by different localities on the line of his march. It is due to General Sherman to say that he had his peculiar ideas of waging war and making it "hell," but when it was over he declared, "It is our solemn duty to protect and not to plunder."

The terms proposed by him to General Johnston were so liberal that they were promptly rejected by the civil authorities at Washington. Mr. Lincoln was dead and Andrew Johnson was President; Mr. Stanton was Secretary of War, and General Halleck ranked General Sherman in the field. This vindictive trio—Johnson, Stanton, and Halleck—rejected General Sherman's agreement with General Johnston; and Stanton and Halleck sought to humiliate Sherman and, as he declared, to insult him. In his "Memoirs" General Sherman writes: "To say that I was angry at the tone and substance of these bulletins of the War Department would hardly express my feelings. I was outraged beyond measure, and was resolved to resent the insult, cost what it might"; and he did resent it in the most emphatic manner. In regard to the absurd report that Mr. Davis had carried out of Richmond vast sums of money, General Sherman writes: "The thirteen millions of treasure with which Jeff Davis was to corrupt our armies and buy his escape dwindled down to the contents of a hand-valise."

A great Frenchman pronounced the French Revolution an "about-face of the universe." The meeting of Lee and Grant at Appomattox was the momentous epoch of the century. It marked greater changes, uprooted a grander and nobler civilization, and, in the emancipation of one race and the impoverishment of another, it involved vaster consequences than had ever followed the fall of a dynasty or the wreck of an empire. It will stand in history as the Brook Kedron over which the Southern people passed to their Gethsemane; where every landscape was marred by ruins; where every breath of air was a lament and every home a house of mourning.

The magnanimity exhibited at Appomattox justifies me in recording here my conviction that, had it been possible for General Grant and his soldiers to foresee the bloody sweat which through ten successive years was wrung from Southern brows, the whole Union army would then and there have resolved to combat all unfriendly legislation. Or, later, if Booth's bullet had not terminated the life filled with "charity to all and malice toward none," President Lincoln's benign purposes, seconded by the great-hearted among our Northern countrymen, would have saved the South from those caricatures of government which cursed and crushed her.

In looking back now over that valley of death—the period of reconstruction,—its waste and its woe, it is hard to realize that the worn and impoverished Confederates were able to go through it. The risen South of to-day is a memorial of the same patience, endurance, and valor which immortalized the four years' struggle for Southern independence.

All accounts agree that when the two great commanders met in the little brick house at Appomattox, they presented a contrast that was unique and strikingly picturesque. A stranger, unacquainted with the situation, would have selected Lee for the conqueror and Grant for the vanquished hero. Prompted by a sincere respect for the illustrious Federal chieftain, General Lee was dressed in his best uniform, and appeared at the place of conference in faultless military attire. General

Grant, on the other hand, had received, while on his lines among his soldiers, General Lee's reply to his last note. Without returning to headquarters for his dress uniform, the Union commander rode at once to the point of meeting, wearing his fatigue suit, his cavalry boots begrimed with Virginia mud, and his plain blue overcoat concealing all insignia of rank. I never heard General Grant say so, but his characteristic modesty and magnanimity, with which I became familiar in after years, lead me to believe that consideration for General Lee prompted this absence of ostentation.

Probably nothing I can say of these illustrious soldiers will add to the fame of either. I am conscious of my inability to give a clear conception of their distinguishing and dissimilar but altogether admirable characteristics. Nevertheless, as the follower and friend of Lee and the sincere admirer of Grant, I desire to place on record in this concluding chapter my estimate of both these representative Americans.

Unless it be Washington, there is no military chieftain of the past to whom Lee can be justly likened, either in attributes of character or in the impress for good made upon the age in which he lived. Those who knew him best and studied him most have agreed that he was unlike any of the great captains of history. In his entire public career there was a singular absence of self-seeking. Otherwise he would have listened to the wooings of ambition when debating the course he should take at the beginning of our sectional conflict. He knew that he could hold any position he might wish in the armies of the Union. Not only by General Scott, the commander-in-chief, but by his brother officers and the civil authorities, Lee was recognized as the foremost soldier in the United States army. He knew, for he so declared, that the South's chances for success, except through foreign intervention, were far from encouraging.

What would Cæsar or Frederick or Napoleon have done? Deaf to every suggestion of a duty whose only promised reward was an approving conscience in ultimate defeat, allured by the prospect of leading armies with overwhelming numbers and backed by limitless resources, any one of these great captains would have eagerly grasped the tendered power. It was not so with Lee. Trained soldier that he was, he stood on the mountain-top of temptation, while before his imagination there passed the splendid pageant of conquering armies swayed by his word of command; and he was unmoved by it. Graduated at West Point, where he subsequently served as perhaps its most honored superintendent; proud of his profession, near the head of which he stood; devoted to the Union and its emblematic flag, which he long had followed; revered by the army, to the command of which he would have been invited—he calmly abandoned them all to lead the forlorn hope of his people, impelled by his conviction that their cause was just. Turning his back upon ambition, putting selfish considerations behind him, like George Washington in the old Revolution, he threw himself and all his interests into an unequal struggle for separate government. When John Adams of Massachusetts declared that, sink or swim, survive or perish, he gave his heart and hand to the Declaration of Independence, he stood on precisely the same moral plane on which Robert E. Lee stood from the beginning to the end of the war. As the north star to the sailor, so was duty to this self-denying soldier. Having decided that in the impending and to him unwelcome conflict his place was with his people, he did not stop to consider the cost. He resolved to do his best; and in estimating now the relative resources and numbers, it cannot be denied that he did more than any leader has ever accomplished under similar conditions. And when the end came and he realized that Appomattox was the grave of his people's hopes, he regretted that Providence had not willed that his own life should end there also. He not only said in substance, to Colonel Venable of his staff and to others, that he would rather die than surrender the cause, but he said to me on that fatal morning that he was sorry he had not fallen in one of the last battles. Yet no man who saw him at Appomattox could detect the slightest wavering in his marvellous self-poise or any lowering of his lofty bearing. Only for a fleeting moment did he lose complete self-control. As he rode back from the McLean house to his bivouac, his weeping men crowded around him; and as they assured him in broken voices of their confidence and love, his emotions momentarily overmastered him, and his wet cheeks told of the sorrow which his words could not express. Throughout that crucial test at Appomattox he was the impersonation of every manly virtue, of all that is great and true and brave—the fittest representative of his own sublimely beautiful adage that human virtue should always equal human calamity.

The ancient Romans and Greeks deified after death their heroes who possessed any one of the great virtues, all of which were harmoniously blended in this great Southerner. It required, however, neither his removal by death nor the hallowing influences of distance or time to consign him to the Pantheon of Immortals. It was more literally true of him than of any man I ever knew, among those whom the world honors, that distance was not needed to enhance his greatness.

A distinguished Georgian, the Hon. Benjamin H. Hill, truthfully declared that Lee was Cæsar without his crimes, Bonaparte without his ambition, and George Washington without his crown of success; and it is my firm conviction that when his campaigns and his character are both understood, such will be the verdict of Christendom.

General Grant's bearing at Appomattox, his acts and

his words, did much to alleviate the anguish inseparable from such an ordeal. The tenor of his formal notes, the terms granted at the appointed meeting, the prompt and cordial manner in which he acquiesced in each and every suggestion made by the Southern commander, left upon the minds of Confederates an ineffaceable impression. In looking back now over the intervening years, I am glad that I have never been tempted, in the heat of political contests, even while the South was enduring the agony of the carpet-baggers' rule, to utter one word of bitterness against that great and magnanimous Union soldier. Before the meeting at Appomattox the Confederates were decidedly prejudiced against General Grant, chiefly because of his refusal to exchange prisoners and thus relieve from unspeakable suffering the thousands of incarcerated men of both armies. On this account Southern men expected from him cold austerity rather than soldierly sympathy. Their previous conceptions of him, however, were totally changed when they learned that our officers were to retain their side-arms; that both officers and privates were to keep their horses; that their paroles protected them from molestation on their homeward trip and in their peaceful pursuits, so long as they obeyed the laws; and that in the prolonged official interview there was no trace of exultation at his triumph, but that he was in word and act the embodiment of manly modesty and soldierly magnanimity, and that from first to last he was evidently intent upon mitigating the bitterness of defeat and soothing to the utmost of his ability the lacerated sensibilities of his great antagonist.

General Grant's own declaration, made many years after the war, that he felt " sad and depressed " as he rode to meet General Lee in the little village of Appomattox, is entirely consistent with every account given of his bearing at the surrender.

It was reported at the time, and has since been confirmed by Union officers who were present, that he positively refused to permit Union artillery to fire a salute in celebration of the victory over his own countrymen. The exhibitions of General Grant's magnanimity which I observed during my personal intercourse with him immediately after the war, later while he was President, and when he became a private citizen, are all consistent with the spirit manifested by him at the surrender of Lee's army. In his " Memoirs" he has given a quietus to that widely circulated romance that he returned to Lee his proffered sword. I do not doubt that he would have done so; but there was no occasion for Lee's offering it, because in the terms agreed upon it was stipulated that the Confederate officers should retain their side-arms.

During the imprisonment and vicarious punishment of the inflexible and stainless ex-President of the Confederacy, both General Richard Taylor of Louisiana and I had repeated conferences with the general-in-chief of the United States army, in the hope of securing the release of the distinguished prisoner. After one of the visits of the gallant Louisianian to General Grant, Taylor told me of a conversation in reference to the probability of General Grant's becoming President. Taylor said that General Grant assured him, with evident sincerity, that he had no desire to be President, — that his tastes and training were those of a soldier, and that he was better fitted for the station he then held than for any civil office, — but that Taylor could rest assured, if the office of President ever came to him, he would endeavor to know no difference between the people of the different sections. The Southern people felt that they had cause to complain of President Grant for a lack of sympathy during those years when imported rulers misled credulous negroes and piled taxes to the point of confiscation in order to raise revenues which failed to find their way into State treasuries; but it must be remembered that General Grant was not a politician, and as the first civil office that came to him was the Presidency, he was naturally influenced by those whom he regarded as statesmen and whose long training in civil affairs seemed peculiarly to fit them for counsellors.

General Grant was not endowed by nature with the impressive personality and soldierly bearing of Winfield Scott Hancock, nor with the peculiarly winning and magnetic presence of William McKinley—few men are; but under a less attractive exterior he combined the strong qualities of both. There can be no doubt that Andrew Johnson, the infatuated zealot who came to the Presidency on the ill-fated martyrdom of Abraham Lincoln, would have followed his threat to "make treason odious" by an order for the arrest and imprisonment of Lee and other Confederate leaders but for the stern mandate of Grant that, in spite of Johnson's vindictive purposes, the Southern soldier who held a parole should be protected to the last extremity.

The strong and salutary characteristics of both Lee and Grant should live in history as an inspiration to coming generations. Posterity will find nobler and more wholesome incentives in their high attributes as men than in their brilliant careers as warriors. The lustre of a stainless life is more lasting than the fame of any soldier; and if General Lee's self-abnegation, his unblemished purity, his triumph over alluring temptations, and his unwavering consecration to all life's duties do not lift him to the morally sublime and make him a fit ideal for young men to follow, then no human conduct can achieve such position.

And the repeated manifestations of General Grant's truly great qualities—his innate modesty, his freedom from every trace of vain-glory or ostentation, his magnanimity in victory, his genuine sympathy for his brave and sensitive foemen, and his inflexible resolve to protect paroled Confederates against any assault, and vindicate, at whatever cost, the sanctity of his pledge to the vanquished—will give him a place in history no less renowned and more to be envied than that secured by his triumphs as a soldier or his honors as a civilian. The Christian invocation which came from his dying lips, on Mount McGregor, summoning the spirit of peace and unity and equality for all of his countrymen, made a fitting close to the life of this illustrious American.

Scarcely less prominent in American annals than the record of these two lives, should stand a catalogue of the thrilling incidents which illustrate the nobler phase of soldier life so inadequately described in these reminiscences. The unseemly things which occurred in the great conflict between the States should be forgotten, or at least forgiven, and no longer permitted to disturb complete harmony between North and South. American youth in all sections should be taught to hold in perpetual remembrance all that was great and good on both sides; to comprehend the inherited convictions for which saintly women suffered and patriotic men died; to recognize the unparalleled carnage as proof of unrivalled courage; to appreciate the singular absence of personal animosity and the frequent manifestation between those brave antagonists of a good-fellowship such as had never before been witnessed between hostile armies. It will be a glorious day for our country when all the children within its borders shall learn that the four years of fratricidal war between the North and the South was waged by neither with criminal or unworthy intent, but by both to protect what they conceived to be threatened rights and imperilled liberty; that the issues which divided the sections were born when the Republic was born, and were forever buried in an ocean of fraternal blood. We shall then see that, under God's providence, every sheet of flame from the blazing rifles of the contending armies, every whizzing shell that tore through the forests at Shiloh and Chancellorsville, every cannon-shot that shook Chickamauga's hills or thundered around the heights of Gettysburg, and all the blood and the tears that were shed are yet to become contributions for the upbuilding of American manhood and for the future defence of American freedom. The Christian Church received its baptism of pentecostal power as it emerged from the shadows of Calvary, and went forth to its world-wide work with greater unity and a diviner purpose. So the Republic, rising from its baptism of blood with a national life more robust, a national union more complete, and a national influence ever widening, shall go forever forward in its benign mission to humanity.

INDEX